# The Politics of Betrayal

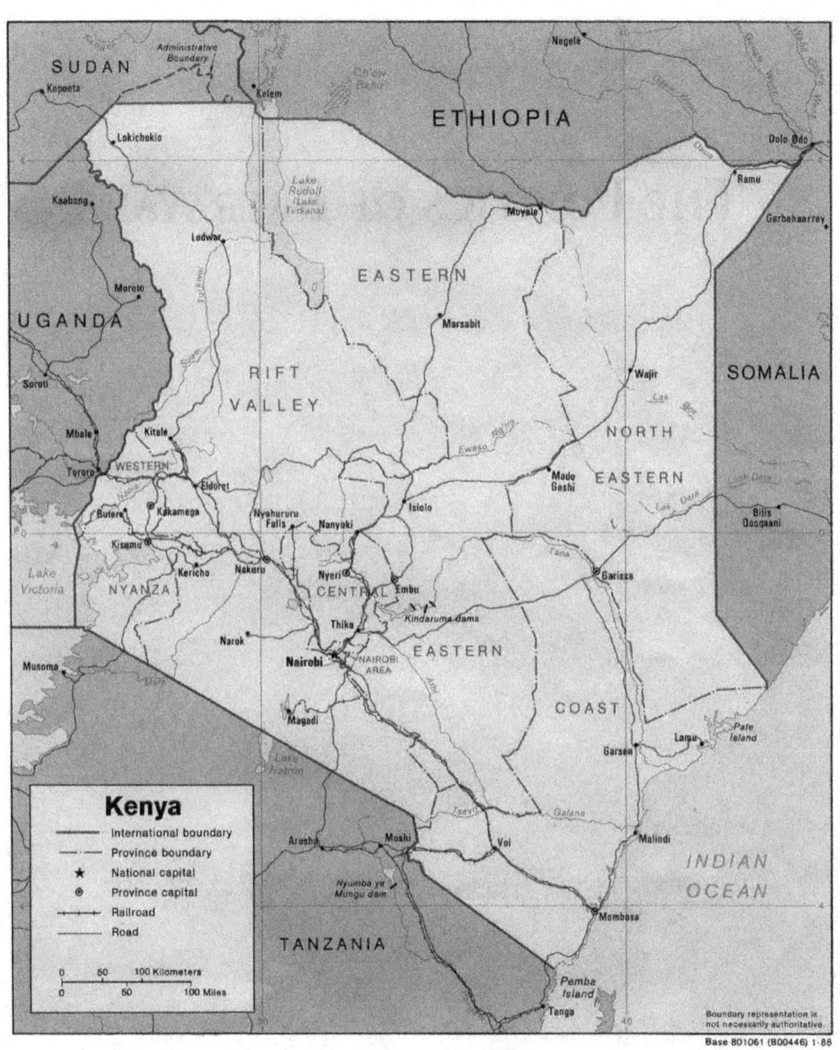


**Provinces of Kenya**

# The Politics of Betrayal

## Diary of a Kenyan Legislator

Joe Khamisi

Order this book online at www.trafford.com
or email orders@trafford.com

Most Trafford titles are also available at major online book retailers.



Printed in the United States of America.

ISBN: 978-1-4269-5445-0 (sc)
ISBN: 978-1-4269-8676-5 (e)

*Trafford rev. 09/29/2011*

www.trafford.com

**North America & international**
toll-free: 1 888 232 4444 (USA & Canada)
phone: 250 383 6864 • fax: 812 355 4082

**To Francis Joseph Khamisi & Maria Faida Khamisi**

**"As stomachs across the nation either protruded or rumbled with hunger, the divide between the rich and poor, the establishment, ever the wolf in a new sheepskin, grew further and further apart..." - Judy Kibinge, No Laughing Matter, February 16, 2008**

# Contents

**SECTION THREE**

# Preface

In writing these political memoirs, I drew my inspiration from those Kenyans who laid down their lives for the liberation of our beloved country: the men, women, and children who lived and died in bondage; those who suffered in detention camps like Jomo Kenyatta, Achieng Oneko, Paul Ngei, Fred Kubai, Kungu Karumba, and Bildad Kaggia; those who fought and perished in forests, ridges, and valleys like Dedan Kimathi and many of the Mau Mau freedom fighters; those who suffered while in exile or in banishment in faraway lands like Mekatilili wa Menza; those like Tom Mboya, Pio Gama Pinto, J.M. Kariuki and Robert Ouko, who died in defence of the truth and the right of every Kenyan to live peacefully and prosperously; and those like Ronald Ngala and Masinde Muliro who died under mysterious circumstances. They made the ultimate sacrifice: they did not die in vain. Through their sacrifices and selflessness, Kenyans are today enjoying many freedoms. But the journey for complete economic and political emancipation is yet to run its course. There will be more sacrifices, more martyrs, and many more challenges. It is for this reason, that I bequeath these memoirs to all Kenyans, of yesterday, today, and tomorrow.

This book traces the people and events during one of Kenya's most historic periods, from 2001 when President Daniel Arap Moi and Raila Amolo Odinga ventured into a tricky alliance, to when opposition against Moi peaked following the declaration of the youthful Uhuru Kenyatta as Moi's successor, to when the National Rainbow Alliance Government took over, to when President Emilio Mwai Kibaki's first term ended in violence, to when the Grand Coalition Government was formed in 2008.

Stephen Kalonzo Musyoka, a zealous born-again lawyer who spent most of his political life defending the unpopular Moi regime, also features in a substantial way. Raila and Kalonzo were Moi's allies at different times, but became bitter foes in the run-up to the 2007 general elections. The book narrates in detail how I helped Kalonzo, a third-place loser, wriggle his way to the number two most important position in the Kenyan leadership hierarchy, the Vice Presidency.

Why the *Politics of Betrayal*? Since Kenyan politics is about personalities not people; about individual interests not mass concerns; about the haves not the have-nots, the let down has been massive. The politics of Kenya has been dominated by the moneyed, not by ordinary folk. The hoity toity set the agenda; the hoi polloi comply. *The Politics of Betrayal*, therefore, is about festering inequalities in the distribution of resources; bad governance; arrogance, selfishness, shamelessness, and political myopia. It is about impunity and disrespect for the rule of law and it is about *wananchi* getting a raw deal. Prior to independence, politicians lied to the people that *uhuru* would bring better housing, more jobs, more food, and economic freedom. "You see that big house there," they would animatedly tell hapless Kenyans, "that will be yours when we get independence."

And gullible Kenyans believed them. Jaramogi Oginga Odinga was among the few in leadership who cautioned people against being too optimistic about the future: "Some people thought that independence meant the end of the struggle and all would be in order in a new Kenya," he wrote in his 1967 autobiography, *Not Yet Uhuru*. "Some people in the villages thought that there was lots of money in the bank and Kenya would give it all to us, that money could be printed easily enough. I told them how we had to work to accumulate wealth; that much of the wealth our work had amassed in the past had been taken out of the country." He added. "I told countless meetings of KANU[1] and the ordinary people: 'We must be busy now with reconstruction. It is your country now, don't shake it. It will take time for the Government to fulfill its duty to the people. We will do our best to put Kenya on its feet.'"[2]

---

1 Kenya African National Union

2 Oginga Odinga, Not Yet Uhuru, East African Publishers Ltd., p. 242

More than four decades later, Kenya is not yet on its feet. The three enemies Kenyatta declared and wanted tackled ferociously at the dawn of independence; poverty, illiteracy and ignorance, are still unconquered. The economy is struggling; more than half of Kenyans can't read or write; only a third of its population is in gainful employment; tens of thousands of people still go hungry every day; clean drinking water is a rare commodity; and people still die of preventable diseases. Kenyans are politically free, but they remain in economic bondage.

Therefore, if this book contributes—even in a small way—in helping to improve some of our governance and political structures, right political leadership, I will feel honoured to know that my humble contribution has not been in vain.

# Acknowledgements

I completed this book over a period of more than two years, working from my homes in Nairobi and Kilifi, on the Kenya coast, as well as from the homes of my two daughters and their families: Maria and her husband, Sydney, and my two grand-children, Bryan and Pauline, in Indianapolis, US; and Josephine, and her husband, Chiza, and their children, Noa and Luka, in New York. I thank my daughters and my son-in-laws for their critical advice and support. My gratitude also goes to my dear wife, Doretha, who helped with the technical aspects of the manuscript and encouraged me to continue even when I was about to despair.

I thank relatives and political friends for volunteering some of the information that made it possible for me to complete this book. I am indebted to all. I cannot forget the people of Bahari for giving me an opportunity to serve as their Member of Parliament from 2003 to 2007. My tenure was most enjoyable and fruitful. Together, we built water projects, improved health facilities, constructed schools, and provided thousands of scholarships to needy pupils, among many other achievements. Had they not given me the opportunity to serve, I would not have been able to make a contribution, and also to gather enough material for this book. I am especially indebted to Sylvanus Mathews Nasibu, my childhood friend, campaign manager, and office administrator, who spent days and nights strategising, and who after victory, worked assiduously to ensure that the needs of Bahari people were promptly and efficiently addressed. To the men and women in my campaign and development teams, I say thank you.

My profound appreciation also goes to Action Aid International for providing a grant of one million Kenya shillings[3] to help in the preparation of Bahari's 2003 to 2007 Strategic Plan. Special thanks go to the organisation's Coast Director, Carol Angir, for her unwavering support and professional encouragement throughout the plan development period. The Action Aid's local affiliate, the Kilifi-based Community Development Services Centre (CDSC), and its team leader, Oscar Nyapela, made it possible for the strategic plan to be finalised on time and for it to be launched formally by Vice President Moody Awori. To Uncle Moody, I say thank you for finding time to honour us in Kilifi.

I also thank the women and youth of Bahari who attended my many activities—come rain or sunshine—and who were always ready and willing to entertain us with songs of hope and support. For the love of these people, I dedicate all the development projects in Bahari to them—some funded through public finance and others through my own personal initiative. I was encouraged by their perseverance, and together, we comforted each other during difficult times.

For those who encouraged me to enter politics, and for the one man who inspired me most, my father, the late Francis Joseph Khamisi, I salute them. Had I not joined the youth wing of the MADU, of which he was the founder in the late 1950s, I possibly would not have developed interest in politics. Unfortunately, he died in 2000 before he could see the seed he planted germinate.

I sharpened my political skills in party politics, and for that, I especially thank David Musila and Joseph Kamotho, who showed me the ropes in political party management while in the Liberal Democratic Party LDP. My association with Raila Amolo Odinga was professionally profound, and his commitment for the good of Kenyans encouraged me to do the same for my people of Bahari. I still consider him a great leader who means well for the country. As for Stephen Kalonzo Musyoka, I hope he will one day realise his miracle dreams. And to Kibaki, *uji injoi baada ya siasa*, enjoy yourself after you retire.

---

3 1USD=approximately Kshs 74

Writing about politics in Kenya without mentioning Daniel Arap Moi is an exercise in futility. In these memoirs, Moi plays a leading role not only as the second President of the Republic of Kenya, but as a man who changed the course of history by allowing Kenya to move from a rigid single-party dictatorship to a more tolerable multi-partism, albeit grudgingly. His grip on power was monstrously brutal, but Kenyans enjoyed relative stability throughout his twenty-four-year rule, allowing citizens to go about their business with peace of mind. And when time was ripe for him to retire, he relinquished power gracefully, unlike many other African leaders, who stayed infinitely against their people's wishes. Many called him a dictator. He denied it. As a respected regional heavyweight, he worked tirelessly to sustain a semblance of hope and stability in the neighbouring volatile states of Somalia and Sudan and maintained good neighbourliness with Tanzania and Uganda. Even the most cynical critics of his policies agree that Moi was truly a patriot and a nationalist.

Last but not least, Kenyans will always memorise Jomo Kenyatta, the founding father, for his great sacrifice to the Kenyan nation. He was a lion, a great African giant.

Finally, I deliberately omitted some names for legal reasons, while I consigned others to the footnotes to aid the flow of thought. Overall, I made every effort to represent all players fairly, and to portray the events as accurately and truthfully as possible. Enjoy!

# SECTION ONE

# CHAPTER 1
## Wanjiku's dilemma

Giant-sized floats decked in different shades of hue slowly snaked their way into the capital city of Nairobi, turning the grey skyline and the green shrubbery along the usually busy Uhuru highway into a kaleidoscopic pattern of chromatic beauty. There were floats of different sizes and shapes: one displayed a huge multi-toned cell-phone mounted on top of a pompous truck; another paraded eager overall-covered construction workers complete with helmets and shovels in a consummate show of industrial zeal; and yet another showcased the ostentatious pride of the hospitality sector. There were dozens of them, representing almost every major sector of the economy in a carnival-style pageantry seen in the East African nation only every twelve months.

At Uhuru Park—a leafy recreational facility with flowered indigenous trees and manicured bushes, overlooking the Central Business District—thousands of workers had already assembled, and many more were trekking there through paths and roadways linking the city to the densely populated, outlying neighbourhoods. Uhuru Park is not just a choice venue where leaders go to shout themselves hoarse over this or that during meetings, or where families retreat for boat rides on an artificial lake, it's also an open-air pulpit where street preachers clutching worn-out Bibles attend to the lunch-time spiritual needs of people too broke to afford a simple meal. In Kenya, that aimless encounter with the environment, the nourishment of free limitless consumption of cool, highland breeze, is called the "airburger," and millions of Kenyans feed on it every day.

Even on this celebrated Labour Day—an occasion set aside to honour employees—ubiquitous preachers dressed in black suits and snow-white shirts lurked in the periphery, so did dazed and bedraggled urchins, *chokora*, glue-filled plastic bottles dangling precariously like giant cigars from their pimpled lips. These are the orphans, the petty thieves, and the cursed lot—some as young as five—that society has chosen to ignore.

Usually this day is marked with parades and fervent speeches delivered by leaders at rallies throughout the country. It is also a day when the government announces minimum wage increases for the lowest-paid workers. On this particular Labour Day, hopes were high that Mwai Kibaki—the third President after Jomo Kenyatta and Daniel Arap Moi—would declare new wage guidelines to cushion menial employees from the country's stiff, high cost of living. There were dances and street performers. Among the thousands of people at the open field was a dark, middle-aged woman in a flowery dress and mismatched headgear, her face dotted in small dark spots. Red, thick mud pasted her now colourless plastic shoes, her palms rough as sandpaper, her slim body a reflection of under-nourishment. She blended well in the mainly proletariat crowd. She had arrived early and had perched herself at the top far end of the uneven grounds. The sun was pounding relentlessly, and the wind, which would normally fan crowds in fall, was awfully still. Suddenly her eyes rolled, her knees buckled, her lifeless hands went up in a morbid display of lifelessness, and down she went! Luckily, hawk-eyed industrial workers caught her just before she hit the ground. There was a moment of panic as *wananchi*, the ordinary folk, frantically carried her out of the sweltering heat and placed her under a shaded tree. She was delirious but coherent. That morning, the downhearted woman had left her shack in a slum colony on an empty stomach and had trekked five kilometres to the park, hoping for the good news, the kind of news associated with Labour Day, a salary boost, but she was to return home disappointed.

For fifteen minutes, during the 2008 Labour Day celebrations, President Kibaki rumbled through his speech—boasting about the country's modest achievements and his government's bland commitment towards a better Kenya—but offered nothing in monetary terms to actualise the workers' financial expectations. "*Shida tuliyo nayo ni kubwa*," he said, offering the nation's dire economic straits as the reason for not proffering new wage guidelines. The last increase two years earlier had propelled the lowest paid industrial worker from 4,817 shillings to 5,395 shillings per month, even then barely enough to sustain life in one of Africa's most expensive cities. To rub salt in the wound, only a few months earlier, MPs had refused to pay taxes on their fat emoluments, stifling revenue that would have helped fund the wage increase for workers. They had argued that their allowances were already heavily committed to meeting their electorates' insatiable quest for handouts and they could sacrifice no more. Unconvinced by Kibaki's specious reasoning, hundreds of grumbling workers left the grounds in protest, some pelting the podium with pebbles of sand, while others merely walked away in silence. They didn't wait for the National Anthem.

The case of that woman, whom we will call Wanjiku, the name popularised by Moi to describe the downtrodden, symbolises the dilemma of the Kenyan nation. With all its human and natural resources—sandy beaches and popular national parks, rich cultural traditions and awe-inspiring topography, a fertile agricultural sector, and a vibrant middle class—Kenya remains a third world nation crippled by corruption, bad governance, and an increasingly widening social and economic gap. At independence, Kenya had a flourishing economy with an annual growth rate of six-point-six per cent, inflation was in the lower single digits, and both the agricultural and manufacturing sectors were active and profitable. Kenya's infrastructure was the envy of its common market neighbours, Tanzania and Uganda, and economically and politically, it was by far the most advanced of the three.

In the early years of independence, the Kenya government service was dominated by British civil servants. But as the bulk of the expatriates left and Kenyans took over, things began to change. Discipline and altruism in the service of the nation vanished. The newly installed political class began an orgy of looting, turning government-run institutions into cash cows through illegal tendering and outright theft of funds. The privileged lot turned from being national models of virtue, to being megalomaniac with a rapacious appetite for gluttony.

Land, the one big factor underlying Kenya's struggle for independence, was arbitrarily snatched from helpless Kenyans and dished out to politically compliant individuals, most of them friends and relatives of Kenyatta. Pheroze Nowrojee, an eminent Kenyan lawyer, human rights crusader, and a bitter critic of both Kenyatta and Moi regimes, blames Kenyatta for bad choices: "He chose to let his Government move resources from the poor to the rich. His followers moved from legitimate sources to illegitimate sources. They took public land, trust land, Government money, donor money and parastatal money, always actively disregarding the fact that the land and money were the land and money of the poor."[4] The thieving class had no boundaries. Crooked politicians even engaged in notorious criminal activities, employing gangs to rob banks at will, as security officers looked the other way, making Nairobi, at one time, one of the most dangerous cities in the world.

Kenyan leaders used the civil service to reward friends with plum jobs, and coerced private institutions into hiring close relatives. An example is when Kenyatta successfully convinced the Lonro Group of Companies to appoint his son-in-law, Udi Gecaga, as Chairman of the Board, and unsuccessfully tried to get H.E. Prince Karim Aga Khan, to employ Ngengi Muigai, his nephew, to a similar position in the Nation Group of Newspapers. Njenga Karume, a close friend of Kenyatta and himself an eminent Kikuyu, agrees in his autobiography, *Beyond Expectations: From Charcoal to Gold*, that Kenyatta did, in fact, lean more towards Kikuyus in government appointments and that "every place one went was either headed by a Kikuyu or was manned by a majority from that tribe…From the Civil Service to private business to the diplomatic corps and other institutions, the Kikuyu, were, in most cases, the top administrators."[5]

That conclusion appears to tally with one advanced by a British author who said that, "in extreme competition for jobs caused by unemployment, the Kikuyus looked after their fellow tribesmen, and would not give jobs readily to people from other tribes."[6] But Karume, a demure individual who loves to lick his lower lip, defends Kenyatta against charges of corruption, saying contrary to common belief, "Kenyatta did not make allowances for corruption…corruption was not condoned. People did not pay bribes to be served in Government offices." He, however, admitted that a few people in government were dishonest, but "not as outright or as blatant as it became

4 The Star, November 4, 2009.

5 Njenga Karume, Beyond Expectations: From Charcoal to Gold, p. 156.

6 Andrew Morton, The Making of an African Statesman, Michael O'Mara Books Ltd.

during the second regime."[7] True, Kenyatta may not personally have been corrupt (a highly arguable position), but he allowed his compatriots to take advantage of his advanced age and inattentiveness to shamelessly raid the nation of its resources.

As impunity took root, middle-level officials in government jumped into the fray, followed by messengers and cleaners. Official files in government registries would mysteriously disappear only for them magically to re-appear on payment of "something small." Fake receipt books were printed to replace official documents at entrances to national reserves, while at city parking lots and at heavy vehicle weighbridges, greedy government officials defalcated huge amounts of money by colluding with equally avaricious individuals. The immigration, the police, and customs offices, among others, emerged as the new frontier for sleaze in government.

The Judiciary, which would normally be relied upon to dispense justice was, itself, heavily compromised. Frivolous rulings would be made to recklessly throw out cases, some of a capital nature, on payment of bribes.

When Kenyatta died in his sleep in 1978—fifteen years after independence—a country that had started with the same economic indicators as South Korea, had lagged far behind. While the latter's economy grew "forty times larger than Kenya's"[8] transforming it into an economic giant in Asia within two decades, Kenya's economy floundered. During the first decade, the Gross Domestic Product (GDP) declined to less than four percent. By late 1990s, it had tumbled to one-point-five percent, well below the population growth of two-point-five percent per annum, thus leading to a decline in per capita incomes.[9] Inflation had reached a record one hundred percent by August 1993, and agricultural production had stagnated at three-point-nine percent.[10] The number of Kenyans classified as poor had doubled to more than fifty percent during the same period.

---

7 Njenga Karume, Beyond Expectations: From Charcoal to Gold, p. 156

8 Senator Barack Obama, From a speech delivered at the University of Nairobi, August 28, 2006.

9 Achieving Millennium Development Goals in Kenya, A Needs Assessment and Costing Report, Kenya Government/UNDP, p. 27.

10 The Travel Document Systems, Report on the Kenyan economy, undated.

As corruption flourished, the prodigious elite went further in their evil designs. They began to destroy the country's most treasured assets: wildlife and forests. Poaching of wild game escalated, endangering not only the future of the country's eco-system but also tourism, a key foreign exchange earner. Those entrusted to care for the nation's wildlife heritage became poachers and smugglers.

At heavily guarded warehouses, which I personally visited while on the staff of the Ministry of Tourism and Wildlife in the 1970s, elephant tusks, rhino horns, and cat skins were clearly marked as belonging to individuals high up in government. Those individuals opened foreign bank accounts and laundered their ill-gotten money irrepressibly. If that was not enough, amoral officers colluded with corrupt merchants to destroy indigenous trees in major forest areas around the country, selling them for timber. Instead of huge swathes of trees, flora and fauna flourishing in unperturbed eco-system, housing estates, farms, and office buildings emerged. For example, by 1996 "…a vast swathe of the Karura forest which had previously been protected, or gazetted, had been allocated to private developers…"[11]

Other pristine catchment areas, among them Mount Kenya and the Aberdares in Central Kenya, and the Mau forest complex and Cherangani Hills in the Rift Valley also fell into the hands of swinish merchants. Since "70 per cent of the country's electric power is hydro-generated and therefore relies on the existence of well protected forests which house water catchments…(and since forests) conserve water and soil and are reservoirs of biological diversity,"[12] the rampant destruction of the water towers threatened long-lasting implications. The massive damage of that destruction did not manifest itself until the late 1990s, when effects of climate change became clear; rivers dried, perennial drought set in and wildlife dwindled. In 1997, the International Monetary Fund (IMF) suspended the much-hyped Economic Structural Adjustment Programme because of high-level corruption and the government's failure to embrace

---

11 Wangari Maathai, Unbowed, First Anchor Books, p. 262. Karura Forest, just outside Nairobi, covers 2,500 acres (1,000 hectares).

12 Kenya National Commission of Human Rights/Kenya Land Alliance; Unjust Enrichment: The Making of Land Grabbing Millionaires, Living Large Series vol. 2, p. 5.

economic and political reforms, a move that deprived the country of essential development loans.

It wasn't long before the port of Mombasa—one of the largest in Africa—and other strategic institutions had been invaded. With the assistance of over-indulging politicians and customs officials, unscrupulous businessmen illegally imported essential products, such as sugar and grains, without paying duty. The products were sold on the local market at reduced prices, killing local industries. Other goods were illegally transported to land-locked neighbouring countries, enriching a few. Then, one financial scandal followed another. Billions of shillings of public funds were lost through questionable transactions spearheaded by a cabal of venal officials. When Kibaki took over in 2002, he inherited a government debt of 630 billion shillings in a country whose annual budget was only 117 billion shillings. Corruption was present during Kenyatta's time, but over the period of more than two decades that Moi was at the helm of government, it skyrocketed to shameful levels.

The plunder throughout the Kenyatta and Moi regimes was faintly similar to what happened in the 1950s and 1960s in Saudi Arabia when the royal family, taking advantage of the oil boom, went into a looting orgy. The only difference was that instead of raping the oil fields, Kenyan leaders expropriated land at will, leaving most of its citizens landless and displaced. And, what was Moi's response to repeated accusations of corruption? "I was merely a driver who cannot be blamed whenever some passengers at the back of the bus involve themselves in pick pocketing."[13] This was far from remorsefulness. It bordered on elitism and insolence.

Anyang' Nyong'o, the Minister for Planning and National Development, best captured the state of the country's economic decline in a write up: "During the past two decades, we have seen Kenya slide systematically into the abyss of underdevelopment and hopelessness. Poverty has increased, unemployment has become rampant, insecurity has visited almost every homestead, hunger is prevalent among the poor, the health condition of the people has declined significantly, while corruption and bad governance became entrenched as political oppression weighted heavily on the people. The oppression went on for long by dividing the people along ethnic lines,

[13] Africa Files, January 12, 2002.

nurturing hatred and suspicion among the people and creating a huge divide between the governors and the governed. Many Kenyans almost lost hope in their own nation."[14]

On the political front, dictatorship thrived. The 1982 attempted coup by the Kenya Air Force gave the irascible Moi a good excuse to torture and detain opponents. Many fled into exile. He corrupted the electoral system and rigged elections with impunity. And, instead of working to better the lives of people, politicians fought over positions and wealth.

In the meantime, Wanjiku was getting weaker each passing day: Her children could no longer go to school because she could not afford it; she was landless because her small plot had been grabbed; hungry because she could not sustain herself on the meagre, unregulated salary; dying young because she lacked health care.

Wanjiku is a victim of the *Politics of Betrayal.*

[14] The 2003–2007 Economic Recovery Strategy for Wealth and Employment Creation, prepared by the Government of Kenya, June 2003, p. xiii.

# CHAPTER 2
# The merger

The day's headline was as bold as it was assertive. "It's D-Day for Merger,"[15] one newspaper shouted. Ten kilometres north-east of Nairobi, six thousand delegates were converging at the Moi Sports Centre, Kasarani, for a landmark event to grace the merger between Raila's National Development Party (NDP) and Moi's Kenya African National Union (KANU). Negotiations had been going on for several years, and the previous December, Raila had announced readiness to disband his restless NDP for the ruling party. The whole process—from the start of the negotiations to full integration—took a rather circuitous journey for the two entities: from the platform of cooperation to collaboration, to partnership and eventually to merger.

Earlier in June that year, Moi had appointed Raila Minister for Energy and his close confidant Adhu Awiti Minister for Planning and Economic Development. Two other loyalists, Joshua Ojode and Peter Odoyo, had taken up positions as assistant ministers. A seventeen-member KANU/NDP joint committee had approved modalities for the merger, and had agreed that the name of the party would remain KANU even though Raila had proposed NEW KANU to signal a new beginning for the battered independence party. Moi, it was agreed, would retain the Chairmanship while Raila would become the new Secretary General.

15 Daily Nation, March 18, 2002.

At Kasarani—a striking multi-million shilling Chinese-built modern sports complex—buses packed with eager delegates were arriving from all directions. As the bus christened, *Peoples' Express,* came to a halt at the parking lot, an old man in a faded tweed coat, leaning heavily on his walking stick, hobbled out of the squeaky, dusty vehicle with worn-out tyres. Clutching a beaded flywhisk in one hand, and an old briefcase embossed with a faint map of Kenya on the other, the septuagenarian with thinning hair and speckled white beard, moved unsteadily to the gate reserved for delegates from the Rift Valley. He hesitated a bit, looked to the blue heavens as if in meditation, and then found his place in the long queue. At the main entrance to the building, a heavy-set woman in a red flowing gown and an over-sized wig, a salutary cockerel imprint—the KANU symbol—on her bosom, handed out small flags and conference programmes to new arrivals. A short distance away, a restless youth with shoulders as wide as the trunk of a mango tree, exhorted delegates to decongest the entrance and move quickly into the hall. The delegates were exuberant and the atmosphere fraternal. In the executive lounge, anxious KANU and NDP officials engaged in last minute consultations.

In the conference pavilion, the KANU colours of black, red, and green were omnipresent, while noisy conversations among delegates echoed through the huge, high-ceilinged structure. There were pastoralists from the far-flung Northern and Rift Valley regions, fishermen from Lake Victoria, burqa-covered Moslem women from the coast, and urbanites from Nairobi. It was a gathering of intellectuals and the unschooled, of different cultures and religious persuasions. Participants were united in one thing: their unwavering love for the independence party of *mama na baba*. Odinga, Raila's father, once described the party as the "guardian of our uhuru..."[16]

When Moi arrived, complete with his elaborate security arrangement, it was like a monarch had appeared; the mood changed into one of merriment and anxiety. Wearing a bright red shirt and a tie decked in party colours, his trademark silver-topped ivory stick *rungu* on his left hand, he exhibited signs of contentment and readiness to enter into a deal of a lifetime. The possibility of two of Kenya's political giants, albeit archenemies, coming

[16] Oginga Odinga, Not Yet Uhuru, East African Publishers Ltd., p. 270.

together to form a political alliance aroused a lot of excitement in Kenya and beyond.

A few weeks earlier, NDP had authored what it called: "NDP's Position on Cooperation among Political Parties and Reforms." The NDP, the document said, "was determined to chart a new path for Kenya's fledging multi-parties based on constructive dialogue with any political party, in the search for enduring solution to our national problems, especially problems faced by the impoverished masses including the perennial ethnic clashes."[17] From the very beginning of the NDP, Raila had been scouting for a strategic partner, and had identified the ruling party as that partner, admitting that the KANU was still the choice for millions of Kenyans. However, the document made it clear that the NDP's "disposition toward KANU was one of opening channels for dialogue, and identifying possible areas of cooperation, and not an endorsement of KANU's predatory policies of the past, present or the future."[18]

At the time, Moi was a pariah, isolated by the international community for abusing human rights and perpetuating corruption. He had arrested and tortured many of his opponents. He had barred them from travelling abroad without official permission, and had even restricted them from visiting foreign missions in Nairobi. Security agents were placed conspicuously outside most diplomatic missions, their job being to record the registration numbers of all cars passing in the vicinity. Surprised motorists would then be summoned to write statements with the police explaining reasons of their presence around such embassies.

Through the merger, Moi had a perfect opportunity to cleanse himself of his political evils.

The agenda at Kasarani was meant to be brief. Apart from the symbolic approval of the arrangement, the only other item was the adoption of the list of new officials that had been prepared in advance by the joint consultative committee. Since the universally accepted method of elections by secret ballot had been shelved by KANU, delegates were to shout their

---

17 Babafemi A. Badejo, Raila Odinga, An Enigma in Kenyan Politics, Yintab Books, p. 190.

18 Ibid.

concurrence or to raise their hands after every nominated name was called; an election by acclamation, which critics described as archaic. "The system is one where the free will of party members is subordinate to the wishes of the party broker," an editorial in one Kenyan newspaper thundered. "It is a backward, retrogressive system which, even though it sustains an appearance of order and unity, perpetuates mediocrity and sycophancy."[19] But it was KANU's *modus operandi* until it introduced *mlolongo*, the much abused queuing method of elections. From that time in 1988, it was commonly agreed that the two methods of elections—acclamation and queuing—would be used interchangeably.

There was nothing fundamentally orderly or unifying about the voting system used at that delegates' conference, the first in fourteen years. The delegates had been adequately primed and were ready and willing to play along, regardless of the election method. The expected entry of Raila and his team into the ruling party automatically meant that some of KANU's old guards would lose out in the process; and they did, resulting in a great sense of angst at the meeting.

Moi was a typical African dictator who thrived on the old British theory of divide and rule. Those who worked with him closely knew him as a man who had no particular friend or enemy. There were instances where he would summon officials to State House for purely routine matters, only to sack them immediately after they stepped out of the compound. He was a master of connivance, who was adept at playing one individual against another, even as he reserved a soft spot for buffoons. People like Mulu Mutisya, the Kamba kingpin, Kariuki Chotara, the illiterate Kikuyu smooth talker, and Sharif Nassir, his dependable mouth-piece, would be invited to offer comic relief to Moi in stressful times, entertaining him with corny jokes and crass anecdotes that left him with cracked ribs. Moi was most comfortable with these types of people. They offered no dissidence, instead kow-towed to Moi in all aspects.

But on that day at Kasarani, Moi was not in a jocular mood. He sat on the high table, his legs bobbing, and his palm resting on his chin. He had this stern look about him that conflated belligerence and trepidation. He was tense and leery. He had worked so hard to get the two parties

19 The Sunday Nation/Inter Press Service, March 18, 2002.

together and had wanted the day to be as uneventful as possible. Before the end of the day, he expected to bag the biggest political trophy of his career: Raila. At the same time, he was to consign some of his allies into a political dustbin, while elevating some of his erstwhile enemies to the highest ranks of the ruling party. One victim was to be Joseph Kamotho, the long serving KANU Secretary General and Moi's reliable trouble-shooter, whose position was now to go to Raila. The previous day, Kamotho had bought advertising space in newspapers to drum up support for his bid, unaware that a decision had already been made against voting by secret ballot. He had expected to canvass delegates for support to retain his position, but as it turned out, Moi had outsmarted him. Kamotho was one of the KANU's most influential officials, and for thirteen years, he was the party's most vociferous defender. He would be remembered for prophesying, rather thoughtlessly, that KANU would rule for one hundred years, a belief that did not come to pass.

The other loser was to be the Vice President and Minister for Home Affairs, George Saitoti, whose position of Vice Chairman was to be abolished and replaced by four slots that were to be distributed on a regional basis. The slots were reserved for Musalia Mudavadi (Western region); Kalonzo Musyoka (Eastern); Noah Katana Ngala (Coast); and Uhuru Kenyatta (Central). Broad-shouldered, necky, with a chiseled chin, and a relatively small head, Saitoti was plucked by Moi from the University of Nairobi's Mathematics Department where he was a lecturer in 1983, appointed to chair a publicly-owned bank, then nominated to Parliament and appointed Finance Minister. Intelligent but listless, Saitoti's first major clash with Moi occurred in 1997, when he was fired as Vice President for spurious reasons after serving in that position for eight years. He was re-appointed two years later following public pressure and served another five years, but the message from Moi was clear: I am the boss here! Surprisingly, on the very morning of the convention, Moi had hosted Saitoti and Kamotho to breakfast at State House and had told them clearly what was in store for them. That was how crude Moi was.

As the Kasarani meeting got underway, it became clear to the delegates and to Kenyans that the meeting was a *kichinjio*, a slaughterhouse. Moi was determined to ensnare Raila even if that meant losing his most cherished political friends. In Kenyan politics at the time, Raila was a big catch. He was an Odinga, had frenetic support from the Luo—one of Kenya's most politically sensitive tribes—and was gifted with exacting mobilisation skills. With him onboard, those on the chopping board had resigned to their fate. The only thing that could save them was a miracle, but no miracle was to take place on that cold day.

As the Managing Director of KBC, the state-owned broadcaster, my instructions were to broadcast the event live on television. Transmission began smoothly, but as the political theatrics unfolded on the floor of the convention hall, the screen suddenly went blank. We were told the orders to shut down transmission had come from "above." It was common during those days for overzealous technocrats to use that term to drive their own agenda and to scare away opponents. It could not be ascertained on that day though, whether the orders came from Moi or not, or from a touchy high ranking State House mandarin. After a while, permission to resume broadcast was given, but not long thereafter, fresh instructions came through, asking the broadcaster to shut down once again. Angry callers flooded the KBC switchboard, enquiring about the interruptions. Gideon Moi, the President's own son, called and angrily complained that the intermittent shutdowns were a nuisance and an embarrassment. I repeated my instructions and told him he should direct his anger elsewhere. The young Moi must have called someone, because from that moment, no more instructions were received from above, and transmission continued uninterrupted to the end.

The only time KANU had incorporated a partner into its ranks was in 1964 when KADU, the then opposition party, voluntarily disbanded after its leadership disintegrated. The Kasarani event was, therefore, historic. While Raila and his supporters were savouring the moments of the day, Saitoti and Kamotho were pitifully despondent and jaded. Minutes after entering the hall, they knew their game was over. Those who ordinarily would be advising them on strategy shunned them. Saitoti and Kamotho, diminutive with a balding head, felt betrayed, but the events of the day were moving too fast for any counter attack and, in any case, they didn't have the forces behind them.

The ancient dictum that "when you are weaker, never fight for honour's sake; choose surrender instead,"[20] must have been in their mind. In the vicissitudes of politics, it is suicidal to take on an enemy without a back

---

[20] Robert Greene, 48 Laws of Power, A Joost Elffers Production, p. 163.

up of a crude force. They studied the mood in the conference room and found it hostile for any form of defiance. It dawned on them that they had been dumped and consigned to the same pit as many others before them. Clearly, the delegates had been coached on what to say and do, and were behaving in a manner that displayed hostility towards the two. Having been transported, accommodated, and provided with a handsome stipend, the delegates, all trying to outdo each other in their monotonously red party colours, did not disappoint Moi. They chanted his praises and ferociously waived their party banners.

The only time the auditorium went silent was when Saitoti stood up to make a formal withdrawal. "There comes a time," he announced to a hushed hall, "when the interests of the nation are more important than those of an individual. I have, therefore, decided not to offer myself for any position." For a moment, one could hear a pin drop; then the room exploded into ululation. The delegates from his Kajiado North constituency gasped in shock and disbelief, but showed no open hostility towards anyone. A downtrodden Saitoti then moved to his seat, as Moi stoically slouched in his chair with a look that showed no remorse: a steely look of malevolence.

The now submissive Kamotho his shoulders drooping and his thinning gray hair sticking out soon followed suit, and bowed out spiritlessly. "I have worked for you as the party Secretary General for 13 years..." he said differentially, directing his comments to Moi. "I have made up my mind not to defend my seat, but I will continue to serve this nation, the President and the party that believes in peace and unity."[21] Once again, the hall exploded in a thunderous applause, as Kamotho mechanically went back to his seat. The tone and content of the surrender statements were classic textbook narrations, rehearsed studiously before delivery. They were not meant to embarrass Moi or to show disrespect for the ruling party. The statements smelt of reverence and idolatry. The two were like fallen soldiers, dishonoured, but unbowed. Expectedly, they behaved with utmost aplomb and equanimity despite the shrillness of sycophantic huffing and puffing all around them. What was clear was that far from surrendering, Saitoti and Kamotho had only temporarily retreated to await a fight another day.

---

21 Daily Nation, March 19, 2002.

With the ignominious departure of the two, the dauntless Moi exhaled deep breaths of satisfaction, and the elections proceeded smoothly and uneventfully up until when Kipgeny arap Ng'eny was called for the position of Deputy National Treasurer. The delegates rejected him, and when Moi intervened, he was heckled. The delegates alleged that Ng'eny had been implicated in the disappearance of millions of shillings during his tenure as head of the Kenya Posts and Telecommunications Corporation in the 1990s. After consultations, Ng'eny was allowed to keep his seat. He was subsequently arrested and taken to court on charges of corruption but the charges were dropped for lack of evidence, and he was set free.

Amidst chants of *Nyayo* and *Tinga*, NDP's flag was ceremoniously lowered and a single KANU flag hoisted to the jubilation of the delegates. The NDP "which had taken five years to build, was disbanded in nine minutes...."[22] said a commentator. The programme listed only one Speaker, Moi, for KANU did not want to take the risk of allowing uncensored speeches to ruffle the new dispensation. Moi sounded and looked like a suitor who had won the most beautiful girl in the village. Invariably, an African marriage ceremony calls for abundant joy and merry-making but also allows the spilling of blood: the slaughtering of animals as an offering to gods. On that day, Moi was the proud suitor and the butcher. He had sacrificed his able assistants to the gods. While consigning some of them to what could be termed political Siberia, he had also ushered in youthful leaders, some of whom were not even born when he entered politics in 1955 through the Colonial Legislative Council (LegCo). For him and his ilk, it was a day of joy.

## Toddlers in the midst

One commentator described the events of that day as "a fundamental shift in power to a cluster of politicians whom President Moi saw as toddlers when he interacted with their fathers earlier on in his political career."[23] Moi had worked with Mudavadi's father, Moses; Ngala's father, Ronald; Raila's father, Odinga; and Uhuru's father, Kenyatta. However, others had a dim view of the new top party defector: "Raila is now just a KANU official like so many others. He is no longer a leader of his own party, standing eyeball to eyeball with KANU's

[22] Ibid.

[23] IRIN April 2, 2002

President Moi."[24] Theoretically, Raila had surrendered his power and influence. He was a mere cabinet official, one of the many, who had to dance to Moi's tune. While he retained the unstinting support of his Luo people, his national clout was gone. Sounding optimistic about the future, Moi told the delegates that the merger had brought forth a new generation of leaders. "I have said, and I will say it again now that I would like to see younger people take over the running of the affairs in this country." Moi had made a similar point many times before, but not as strongly and as categorically as he did at Kasarani on that day. In the past, he had only referred to young people as leaders of tomorrow, even as he continued to reserve coveted positions in his government to over fifties and beyond, some of them with limited education.

Then, as if to prepare the delegates for the momentous decision about to be made, he added: "We will be called to make hard and difficult decisions which will have a lasting effect on our political future." The people cheered and the flags went up. Moi called the event a milestone while Raila likened the merger to two rivers "having combined into a new, fast, broad and powerful force on its way to the ocean..."[25]

Both Moi and Raila had reasons to be optimistic about the future. While the former looked forward to expanding his influence into the once closed Nyanza ambit dominated by the Odinga family, the latter had his eyes firmly on the presidency. He saw the merger as a chance for him to ascend the heights his father had failed to reach. However, Raila had a difficult time explaining his decision to plunge head on into KANU, a party he had chastised for years. But first, he had to empty his mind before the delegates, a third of whom belonged to NDP. Although he was not listed to speak, he could not resist the temptation of stealing the limelight of the day. As the newly installed Secretary General, he was only expected to read the resolutions adopted by the delegates, but he cleverly took advantage of the opportunity to deliver a well-prepared speech, much to the discomfort of officials present. He said he had merged to open up the ruling party, which he said, had "very much been a closed party. We are trying to democratise this party by giving it the influence of our own values," he said.

---

24 Daily Nation, March 19, 2002.

25 Ibid.

To Raila, those values included changes in the way KANU operated; the despotism, leadership obsoluteness, and so on, that had dominated the party over the years. But also, Raila had a much, much bigger agenda. In the preceding weeks, reports had circulated that Moi had "promised Luo elders that Raila would succeed him…."[26] If those reports were true, Raila was not confirming them even though they must have lingered in his mind. Could that have been the reason why he teamed up with Moi against all advice? Political commentators were dumb-founded by his move and felt Moi was luring his nemesis to the road to political destruction. "…While Raila and Co thought they were using Kasarani as a stepping stone to higher office, Moi, the political magician, had another rabbit in his cap,"[27] said a commentator, suggesting that the former NDP leader had been ensnared.

Many of his colleagues in the opposition, such as Kibaki of the DP, James Orengo of the SDP, and Wamalwa of the FORD-Kenya, had upbraided Raila for "sleeping with the enemy"[28] and had told him to be careful with Moi. Both Kibaki and Orengo knew what they were talking about. Kibaki had served under Moi as Vice President for eight years until his rushed resignation in 1991, when he could take no more of Moi's fastidious tendencies. He went ahead to found the DP, eventually becoming one of Moi's thorniest critics.

Orengo, on the other hand, had been a victim of Moi's over-bearance in the early eighties. As a lawyer, he was arrested allegedly for stealing a client's money. He allegedly jumped bail, escaped to neighbouring Tanzania but was extradited to Kenya before being exonerated of the charges. His short stint at the Kamiti Maximum Security Prison outside Nairobi, from where he emerged with cerebral malaria that almost killed him, endeared the former university student leader to Kenyans, who saw him as a gallant fighter for people's rights. Even Raila's own family did not approve of his association with Moi. "Both Ida (Raila's wife) and Rosemary Odinga (his daughter) remember that the entire family was against it."[29]

---

26 Babafemi A. Badejo, Raila Odinga, An Enigma in Kenyan Politics, Yintab Books, p. 207.

27 Kwendo Opanga, East African Standard, March 18, 2004.

28 ANB-BIA Supplement, Issue/Edition No. 436, June 15, 2002.

29 Babafemi A. Badejo, Raila Odinga, An Enigma in Kenyan Politics, Yintab Books, p. 194.

Despite pleas, Raila was adamant. "I am not out to compromise my political principles at any price," he defiantly told critics. "Nothing has been dangled at me. I have not been promised anything." Adding, "It is time for goodwill and a spirit of "give and take" on both sides of the political divide (in order) to help institutionalise democracy. It's neither a weakness nor a compromise as long as it is done without compromising the fundamental principles and objectives of the struggle for democratisation."[30] Raila saw nothing wrong in his new found liaison with Moi, seeing it instead as a quantum leap towards State House, and the realisation of his dream of transforming the country from an autocracy into a democratic, modern nation.

## KANU and purges

The changes at Kasarani marked the first time in thirty-six years that a major overhaul of the party's top echelon had taken place. In March 1966, at the party's delegates' conference at Limuru in Central Kenya, Odinga, then the party's Vice Chairman was purged and his position split into units to represent the eight provinces. Kenyatta's intention was "to reduce "Odinga's stature and influence."[31] Tom Mboya, KANU's competent Secretary General, was credited with crafting the evil intentions of leading a "disaffection campaign against the radicals and in particular against Vice President Odinga."[32]

The West-leaning Mboya was Kenyatta's blue-eyed boy, an attack dog let lose to disorganise Odinga, who was seen to be closely linked to China and Russia. An industrial management alumnus of Ruskin College, Oxford, in England, Mboya was intelligent and fiercely anti-Odinga. He started as leader of the Kenya Federation of Registered Trade Unions—later renamed the Kenya Federation of Labour—where he was Secretary General. However, according to Odinga, the union "lost the support of many nationalists when it chose to affiliate to the American-dominated International Confederation of Free Trade Unions, and also because it was suspect as a trade union federation as it was heavily promoted and financed

---

30 ANB-BIA Supplement, Issue/Edition No. 436, June 15, 2002.

31 A Kenya Human Rights Commission Report; Independence Without Freedom: The Legitimisation of Repressive Laws and Practices in Kenya, February, 1994, p. 16.

32 Ibid.

from outside Kenya, and because it was never a rank and file movement built and supported from below."[33] The rivalry between the two was, therefore, basically ideological, since "Tom Mboya supported the western countries from which Kenya received large development aid, while Odinga supported the communist countries. Kenyatta who liked the way England was run, tended to side with Mboya..."[34]

Born in the Kikuyu-dominated Kilimambogo area in Central Province, where his father worked as a sisal plantation overseer, Mboya's Luo parents originated from Rusinga Island, an idyllic spot on Lake Victoria. He later graduated to active politics. However, the evil machinations and Kenyatta's explicitly hostile treatment of him at Limuru forced Odinga to leave KANU to form his own party, the Kenya Peoples' Union (KPU). What Kenyatta did to Odinga was a betrayal of the highest order because, as we'll see later, it was Odinga who got Kenyatta from jail and harsh conditions of northern Kenya, to freedom and comfort of State House.

Even though KPU was banned barely three years later, it emboldened the opposition and heralded the beginning of a mass movement that was eventually to lead to major reforms in the country. To deal with the emerging rebellion from KPU, the Kenyatta Government rushed through a constitutional amendment barring any MP elected by one party from defecting to another. That law locked out the government politicians who wanted to follow Odinga to the opposition, and introduced a new dimension in party politics whose ramifications were to be felt many years later. Out of the twenty-nine MPs who had originally supported KPU, thirteen consequently changed their mind about defecting from KANU to KPU, fearing defeat at by-elections.[35]

## Raila faces questions

The KANU/NDP merger and the events at Kasarani raised many pertinent questions. Why would Moi sacrifice his most loyal supporters

---

33 Oginga Odinga, Not Yet Uhuru, East African Publishers, Ltd., p. 109.

34 Julian Friedmann, Jomo Kenyatta, Wayward History Makers, p. 80

35 A Kenya Human Rights Commission Report; Independence Without Freedom: The Legitimization of Repressive Laws and Practices in Kenya, February 1994, p. 19.

for Raila, a man he wanted politically destroyed? Was he setting him up for extinction, or was he truly committed to preparing him for the presidency, as per the alleged promise to Luo elders? And, was Raila's move to KANU a political blunder or a strategic manoeuvre? Baffled analysts questioned the motive behind Raila's decision to disband NDP—a party that though centred in Nyanza at the time, had great potential as a national movement—in favour of KANU. They wondered why a person of impeccable democratic credentials, such as Raila, would want to co-habit with an internationally discredited leader such as Moi, whose regime had caused so much misery in the country.

Did Raila believe that Moi had changed his incongruous ways and was now a reformed democrat? It became even more poignant when one considered that Moi detained Raila, not once, not twice but three times during his long reign of terror. Was Raila that forgiving? And most importantly, did Moi really think his political foe had forgotten the physical torture and mental suffering, the humiliation and separation from family, the loss of personal and political liberties and opportunities? One commentator described Moi as "the Machiavellian power broker who never gave anything for free and with Raila, there was no exception."[36]

From a pedestrian point of view, both Moi and Raila saw opportunities to explore. Raila dreamt of converting Moi from within hoping eventually to succeed him, while Moi wanted to capitalise on the massive support Raila had in Luo Nyanza where Moi's popularity was almost zero. To make his magic trick look real, he even included Raila in his delegation to Libya for the 2001 Summit of the Organisation of African Unity (OAU),[37] a gesture some in the Raila camp wrongly interpreted as a sign of unqualified endorsement. Again, was the self-proclaimed professor of politics just playing politics? That Moi wanted NDP's support in parliament to deal with the recalcitrant forces of DP and FORD-Kenya was not in doubt. The two parties had made it known that the battle for reforms would henceforth move from boardrooms and streets to the floor of the National Assembly, and had threatened to introduce a no-confidence motion against the President. Before, when Kenyans were aggrieved by Moi's wayward ways, they took to the streets, but Moi was always unmoved and hit them

36 The Nairobi Chronicle, June 28, 2008.
37 OAU later became AU, the African Union.

hard using brutal police force. The battle had now moved to Parliament. With the combined NDP/KANU forces and a fresh majority of one hundred and thirty-nine MPs in the two-hundred-and-twenty-two-member parliament, Moi was still confident he could beat the opposition on the floor of the House, even if it meant bribing MPs.

Having lost to Moi in 1997 elections, and cognisant of Moi's harsh and unpredictable behaviour, Raila was convinced that the only way to get even with the President was to work from within; that is, to display no outward ambition and to play the subservience card. To do anything else would be counter-productive and disastrous for him and his community. Moi, on the other hand, relished challenges and never countenanced defeat, saying at one time that the word defeat didn't exist in his vocabulary. He, therefore, went into the merger arrangement knowing it was a win-win situation for him. Moi was a shrewd and stealth politician. Odinga once compared him to a "giraffe with a long neck that saw far."[38] Moi was also mean and cunning. Since the 1992 multi-party elections, Moi had not "lost" a single election, even as it was commonly known that the 1992 and 1997 elections were highly compromised. Raila must have remembered those events, as well as the attendant issues that underlined Odinga's detention by Kenyatta in October 1969 and his incarceration by Moi in 1982.

After each of those purges, the elderly Odinga was rendered a pariah and his community ostracised. It was shut out of development and the civil service. Raila must then have concluded that enough was enough; that there was no reason to continue wasting his life in dark prison cells while his ambition lay elsewhere. He must have recollected Moi's ruthlessness in dealing with his opponents: the frightening night raids, the notorious *Nyayo House* torture chambers, the political assassinations, the banning of anti-government individuals from travelling overseas, the muzzling of the critical media; and saw no hope outside KANU. Opponents believed Moi was technically unbeatable given his acumen in poll manipulation.

A news columnist viewed the union between the two "as an authentication of the long-held belief that Moi was unbeatable, therefore, Mr. Odinga had decided if you can't beat them join them".[39] Another commentator was even more succinct: "The message the Moi regime was

---

[38] Oginga Odinga, Not Yet Uhuru, East African Educational Publishers, p. 145.

[39] The Daily Nation, December 26, 2009.

transmitting was clear: it would use all means at its disposal, including the law, to ensure that no one could challenge it politically, legally or otherwise."[40]

The situation got to a point where some Kenyans viewed Moi as politically immortal. They feared he was heading towards anointing himself Life President just as Kamuzu Banda had done in Malawi in 1970 and Macias Nguema in Equitorial Guinea in 1972. Oddly enough, Moi never displayed any physical demeanour of a dictator. He was particularly fond of children, and humbled himself to the rest of the people, as long as they didn't cross his political path. He went to church regularly and was present during baptism of children; he had a special place for orphans and the disabled, and came out as a truly caring individual. At one time, he even allowed a villager to take a ride in his official chopper! But that was just one side of Moi. In the course of duty, Moi never took chances with anyone. He ran his government like a military camp. He called the orders; you obeyed.

He never accepted the tag of dictator even after leaving office. He insisted he was a nationalist, and the decisions he made were for the good of the country. "I was not a dictator," he once told the National Pastors' Conference in Nairobi. "I was only instilling discipline among my Ministers."[41] Discipline! Maybe, for Moi, instilling discipline on stubborn officials meant little. After all, he had been a schoolteacher and Kenyan schoolteachers routinely imposed corporal punishment on their pupils. Nothing, however, exposed Moi as the crude leader that he was, than when he made the following remarks to his officials: "I would like Ministers, Assistant Ministers and others to sing like a parrot after me....During Kenyatta's time, I sang only 'Kenyatta'....I didn't have ideas of my own. Who was I to have my own ideas? ...So you play my tune. Where I put a full stop, you put a full stop."[42] Sycophants clapped and cheered, without thinking they were aiding further the entrenchment of autocracy.

---

40 A Kenya Human Rights Commission Report, Independence Without Freedom: The Legitimisation of Repressive Laws and Practices in Kenya, February 1994, p 28.

41 The Daily Nation, May 13, 2009.

42 Macharia Munene, United States International University, July 19, 2001.

Moi was also characteristically intolerant of criticisms, and refused to accept external meddling in the affairs of Kenya. In the 1990s, for example, he broke ranks with the international community and told off Western envoys for criticising his government's human rights record. He turned down their string-attached financial aid even when he knew the agricultural sector had collapsed and his citizens were starving. His plan to provide free milk to schoolchildren became unsustainable due to a huge budget deficit, leaving many children exposed to kwashiorkor and other deadly diseases. As the prices of basic commodities skyrocketed, Kenyans went into a state of despondency and hopelessness. There was a massive capital flight, causing the decline of the Kenya shilling to unprecedented levels. Worried about insecurity, tourists stayed away.

Nairobi, known as the green city in the sun, was now being referred to by foreign correspondents as Nairobbery because of increased criminal activities. Politically, the country was becoming ungovernable given the intense pressure for democratic reforms. The clarion call in the opposition was "no reforms no elections." For the first time, Moi was being likened to Zaire's Mobutu Sesse Seko, the implacable dictator, and was cynically being referred to as "Moibutu."

Amazingly, it took years for Moi to comment publicly on his government's torture chambers, located less than two kilometres from State House. In March 2004, he denied sanctioning torture of his critics, saying he was not aware of people being tortured at Nyayo House. If people were tortured, he added, they should have reported to authorities. Yet the "authorities" Moi was referring to was Moi himself. He was the absolute leader. For him, to suggest that he knew nothing about the extra judicial arrests, disappearances, and killings that took place throughout the country at the time, exposes him as either out of touch with his people, or economical with the truth. It was implausible that he could have been unaware of the atrocities taking place under his watch. At least, he was brave enough, much later on, to defend his decision to incarcerate opponents. In June 2010, he told Kenyans—in the presence of a former inmate, Koigi wa Wamwere—that he detained people to protect the country's security. However, that admission of guilt did not exonerate him from taking full responsibility for his actions. That the government finally agreed to compensate former detainees for their suffering following years of battles in court came as a sweet revenge to the afflicted.

One agency that Moi used or misused to keep him in power was the provincial administration, which briefed him almost hourly on what was happening in the rest of the country. Spread to the villages, the provincial administration was a useful tool for monitoring activities on the ground. The Special Branch, which later became the NSIS, on the other hand, kept a close tab on suspected critics at the national level. It trailed them and tapped their telephones. Moi was known to call officials in the dead of the night to enquire over this or that matter, and his tentacles spread beyond the Kenyan borders. Intelligence officers posted to Kenyan Missions abroad not only spied on Kenyans in the Diaspora but also on the Embassy officials. The officers did not report to the Head of Mission but to a specific office in Nairobi, from where the information received from across the globe was sifted and summarised for the Head of State. Where he saw danger, Moi acted quickly and harshly. Even his closest advisors feared confronting him on anything, leaving him to make decisions that were sometimes dangerous to the well-being of the nation. The fact that ministers did not protest or complain publicly about the grotesque abuse of power in government during all of Moi's long tenure was enough evidence of his intractable grip on Kenya's political system.

## A changed Moi

Moi's transformation from a quaint, humble born-again member of the AIC, to an unforgiving ruler, only became clear after the bloody events of August 1, 1982. The failed coup by some elements of the Kenya Air Force on that chilly dawn in Nairobi heightened his resolve to vanquish the opposition. He had seen bloody military coups in neighbouring countries, and he was not about to tolerate any such scenes in Kenya. Idi Amin overthrew Uganda's President, Milton Obote, in 1971, and three years later, Mengistu Haile Mariam deposed Emperor Haille Selassie of Ethiopia. Like a wounded buffalo, Moi trampled on his opponents without mercy. He ordered the arrest of oppositionists, academics, and anyone else the intelligence organisation suspected of involvement in the rebellion. Those who ran for safety abroad were followed by secret agents and brought back home. A good example was that of Koigi wa Wamwere who was captured in Uganda by Kenya security agents in 1990, hauled back to Kenya, and detained for three years. He later fled to Norway, but on his return in 1995, he was framed on a violent robbery charge and sentenced to four years in prison with six lashes. He was only released in 1996 following international pressure.

Torture chambers were quickly built in the basement of Nyayo House in downtown Nairobi—two thousand suspects were said to have passed through them during Moi's rule—and special magistrates were appointed to deal with the increased work load. Suspects would be taken before magistrates well after office hours, and within minutes, they would be heading to Kamiti Maximum Prison to serve long jail sentences, having been convicted on tramped up charges.

The horrors of Nyayo House were later captured in a book, entitled," *We Live To Tell: The Nyayo House Story,*"[43] in which former detainees narrated their ordeals of being immersed in water, of beatings, of starvation and of threats of forceful circumcision. Stories of two of them were among the most moving. "In total, there were seven torturers who were armed with machine guns, batons and whips. Two would work on me until they got tired. A woman torturer would mainly be interested in working on my sex organs which she would pierce with a sharp needle, burn the tip and testicles with a smouldering cigarette while a man would hold my legs apart. This would continue for several hours every day until I passed out."[44] Another torture victim talked about how he was stripped naked. "…my hands were chained to the chair and I could not move at all. From the moment the brutal interrogation started, everything in the room changed and the language of coercion and violence was introduced."[45]

Moi should read that book to understand the pain and suffering some of his citizens went through.

## Odingas' role in the coup

---

43 Friedrich Ebert Stiftung (FES), Citizens of Justice, 2009.

44 Kamau Munene, a former Kenyan detainee, FES/Citizens of Justice.

45 Maina wa Kinyatti, Ibid.

As for Raila and his father, Odinga, the attempted coup—if it had succeeded—would have been a major turning point in their political careers. After all, the attempted uprising was not just the work of drunken and mischievous young, non-commissioned officers at the Embakasi Air Force base; Odinga's hand and that of his favourite son, Raila, were firmly and solidly evident in it. Raila was the "central civilian accomplice of the coup plotters,"[46] even though Babafemi Badejo, author of Raila's unofficial biography: *Raila Odinga: an Enigma in Kenyan Politics*, says throughout the interview for the book, the young revolutionary "neither admitted nor confirmed his role in the planning of the coup attempt." [47] Several coup plotters, however, "admitted that they had received Luo traditional blessings and encouragement from Oginga Odinga to carry out the coup attempt…and that Raila was mentioned by the privates as having given assistance towards the execution of the failed coup." [48] The assistance, according to Badejo's account, included providing a command post in Nairobi for the plotters.

Events of that day would forever be etched in the minds of Kenyans of the time. For years, people had been used to seeing their seemingly harmless soldiers parading at national events, using fake armaments to simulate combat situations, but this was real. Young, trigger-happy servicemen were everywhere terrorising *wananchi*. Many shops in downtown Nairobi were broken into and looted. Women were raped. Never before had Kenyans seen so many soldiers with guns and so many dead bodies on the streets of the city. Dressed in their blue and white Air Force uniforms, the soldiers surrounded key installations, including the state-owned radio and television station, VOK—in 1989 renamed KBC—at dawn. They seized the station and announced the take-over. Others stormed military bases and forced fighter pilots to take to the air in a futile attempt to bomb State House and other key installations, while coup leaders, seeing the failure of their actions, hijacked a plane and flew to neighbouring Tanzania.

---

46 The Sunday Standard, March 14, 2004.

47 Babafemi A. Badejo, Raila Odinga: An Enigma in Kenyan Politics, Yintab Books, p. 94.

48 Ibid., p 106.

Moi, in his rural home at Kabarak in the Rift Valley at the time, was only saved by loyal forces that beat off the rebellion and within hours restored him to power. He was so infuriated by those events that he sent Raila to the slammer and his father into house arrest, accusing them of associating with the coup makers, many of whom were, like Raila, Luo. Raila was arrested on August 11, 1982 and placed under house arrest for seven months before being detained for six years. The coup leader, Senior Private Hezekiah Ochuka, was repatriated from Tanzania, where he was seized and sentenced to hang.

Even after his release in February 1988, freedom for Raila was short-lived. He was re-arrested seven months later, again, for alleged subversive activities. He was not set free until June 1989, only to be incarcerated once more in July 1990, together with two other prominent businessmen and politicians, Kenneth Matiba and Charles Rubia, under the draconian Public Security Act. Raila finally breathed the air of freedom on June 21, 1991. That same October he fled to Norway and did not return until the following year, ending an entire decade as a political detainee and a fugitive. On his arrival, he found that pluralism was flourishing, and he immediately joined FORD as Vice Chairman of the party's General Purposes Committee.

Raila's skills as a political tactician were evident early in his political career, as he moved from the General Purposes Committee, to become Director of Elections. His incisive understanding of the local political scene endeared him to his colleagues, even though he often came out as provocative and hostile. FORD was then the most popular opposition party with a horde of charismatic leaders, but that same year, 1992, an ethnic split occurred between Odinga, a Luo, and Matiba, a Kikuyu, leading the former to register a faction called FORD-Kenya and the latter to legalise a splinter group called FORD-Asili. Two years later, Odinga died, leaving Vice Chairman Wamalwa at the helm of the party. That is when serious internal problems began. Raila wanted to take over his late father's party post, but Wamalwa would have nothing of it. Although the latter was confirmed as interim Chairman, the post of Vice Chairman became a two-pronged duel between Raila and James Orengo, a Wamalwa ally. In the contest of votes, Raila lost. Finding no hope of leading FORD-Kenya, he left and acquired NDP, a small party, then owned by a flamboyant, but little-known politician from Raila's home region by the name, Stephen Omondi Oludhe. Raila also resigned as MP for Nairobi's Langata constituency to seek fresh mandate, as per the 1966

Constitutional amendment mentioned earlier. He easily won re-election on the NDP ticket, and in the general election that followed, NDP became the largest opposition political party in the country.

By the time of the merger, Raila had considerably toned down his radical rhetoric and was determined to democratise the KANU, even though he knew Moi was for the status quo. It can be said that Moi's alliance with Raila was partly intended to portray the President as a leader willing to change, but was that really true? As Moi's presidential mandate neared its end in December 2002, however, it dawned on Raila that the Kenyan leader had no intention of passing on the mantle to him. Moi viewed him as an intruder bent on mischief, and therefore, kept him on a round-the-clock check. The logic was simple: If Moi didn't trust Odinga, why would he want to trust his son, Raila? The Kiswahili proverb, *mtoto wa nyoka ni nyoka*, a baby snake is as dangerous as its mother, best explained Moi's perception of Raila at the time.

Instead, Moi had his eyes on Uhuru Kenyatta, the forty-one-year old American-educated son of the founding President. In July 2002, the Kenyan leader officially chose Uhuru as his successor, explaining that he favoured him because he was a young man who could be guided, a faint hint that the incumbent wanted someone to control, someone easy to manipulate, so as to be able to "perpetuate his legacy of looting the economy and ensure his cronies continue holding key positions in the Government to fleece the country's resources."[49]

"I have analysed the qualities of all the people around me," Moi said, "and I have seen the potential in this young man. I am not running again for office, but when you vote for Uhuru, you will be voting for me."[50] With that statement, the die had been cast of who was to succeed Moi. Raila was shattered. It meant his dream of ascending to the presidency after Moi had been crushed. His tryst with Moi, as many people expected was, after all, a blunder. He expressed his displeasure, saying the selection method was not democratic, that Uhuru's leadership credentials had not been tested, and his national support was opaque. He was right! Uhuru was elected a local KANU Chairman in 1996, but the following year, he failed to win

49 The People Daily, August 19, 2002.

50 Daily Nation, December 26, 2009.

his home's parliamentary seat. His only experience was as Chairman of the Government-funded Kenya Tourist Board, and as MP for Gatundu, the seat originally held by his father.

Having been born two years before independence, Uhuru (literally meaning freedom or independence) did not have any work experience either in government or in the private sector outside his family business. He was a political novice with no regional or international experience to his credit. Compared to everyone else at the top hierarchy of the ruling party at that time, he was the least suitable for the job of Commander-in-Chief. I first met Uhuru in 1988 when he made a brief business trip to Namibia, where I was serving as Head of the Kenya Mission there. Meeting him at the small Windhoek airport used by rich jet setters, I found him an affable individual despite his elevated status as son of a former president. He had a firm, confident handshake, an easy smile, and a welcoming attitude, starkly different from some of the Kenyattas who were haughty and unsociable

Now years later in Nairobi, Uhuru was playing on a different league. He was no longer the callow, wispy young man with skinny legs who liked to frequent beer joints in the city. His middle section had put on some fibre, and his facial features had strikingly turned out to resemble those of his father. He even talked and laughed like Jomo, but his choice as Moi's successor was ill advised, and infuriated not only Raila and Vice President Saitoti, but also all those others who were harbouring presidential ambitions. Following that decision, the possibility of KANU imploding was for everyone to see. Barely eight months later, the merger arrangement collapsed.

## Opposition emerges

By July 2002, rumours of an emerging opposition alliance against Moi had begun to circulate in Nairobi. Politicians and civil society groups were meeting clandestinely to plot an opposition movement against the Kenyan leader. Politicians were meeting in private homes, moving from one location to another, in an attempt to shake off intelligence officers who were on their trail. The following month, Raila, Saitoti, and Kamotho unexpectedly appeared together at the Norfolk Hotel for the first time since the Kasarani showdown. This time round, the three were meeting not as adversaries but as people with a common cause, "united to avenge their mistreatment by a party they had served with unflinching loyalty."[51]

At Kasarani, Moi had effectively driven a wedge between them by elevating a complete outsider to a position traditionally reserved for insiders, and had disrupted the careers of two of his most valuable allies. Now, the three were meeting to strategise on their collective political future. The wounds from the political shenanigan at Kasarani had not clearly healed, but fate had now brought them together: victims of Moi's cunning betrayal.

Media coverage of the surprise Norfolk Hotel talks sent shock waves across Moi's regime and got the nation talking. On leaving the hotel, Saitoti offered no details of the talks to the inquisitive media staking outside, but Raila met the press, with a reluctant Kamotho at his side, and revealed the coming of the "Rainbow Alliance." Saitoti and Kamotho were taken aback by the contents of the announcement, forcing them later to clarify that nothing tangible had been agreed upon. The clarification by Saitoti and Kamotho, notwithstanding, the nation's mood momentarily changed, as newspaper pages carried anonymous letters from Kenyans calling for change. Whether by releasing the supposedly much guarded "secret," Raila's intention was to grab headlines and project himself as the brain behind the idea was difficult to ascertain. But the cat had been let out of the bag. Surprisingly, Kalonzo, who had been expected to lend support at that very crucial moment, distanced himself, saying he knew nothing about plans to form an alliance.

On August 12, as internal rebellion spread across the ranks of the party, Moi relieved Kamotho of his Environment portfolio and sent home Fred Gumo, the burly, argumentative assistant minister in his own office, accusing them both of insubordination. Soon thereafter, he dropped Saitoti as Vice President and Minister for Home Affairs, offering the latter docket to an emerging young politician called William Ruto from his Rift Valley backyard. Saitoti was sacked because he had persisted in his opposition to Uhuru, and had angered Moi further by declaring his own presidential

---

51 Kwendo Opanga, East African Standard, March 18, 2004.

ambitions. After Saitoti departed, it was a free fall, as more top party officials and cabinet ministers either resigned or were fired.

The purge continued. Kalonzo, who had also denounced Uhuru's candidature, was relieved of his responsibilities as chairman of both the Somali and the Sudan peace talks, which had given him a high regional and international profile. Although his removal prompted short-term murmurs from a section of the international community over matters of continuity, Kalonzo chose to remain virtually silent, and at no time did he raise a protest over his replacement by John Koech, then Minister for the East African Community. His removal from the crucial regional talks notwithstanding, Kalonzo continued to serve loyally as a minister in the Moi regime even as he unexcitedly opposed Uhuru's selection. In September, cabinet ministers Ngala and Mudavadi, who had earlier left KANU, were enticed back into government. Mudavadi was rewarded with the position of Vice President. It is Mudavadi who has held the dubious distinction of having served the shortest stint as the personal assistant to the Head of State in the country's history—a period of less than three months.

Trouble for Moi escalated on October 12 when Raila and his top allies called a press conference at the Kenyatta International Conference Centre (KICC), and openly defied his choice of Uhuru. With the Rainbow Alliance no longer a secret, they declared they had lost confidence in their party chairman, accusing him of rigging names of representatives to a planned delegates' conference and refusing their request for secret ballot. In a statement, they explained that the objective of the proposed Rainbow Alliance was to fight for democracy, justice, and fairness, and declared they would boycott the Kasarani delegates' meeting scheduled two days later, instead holding their own rally at Uhuru Park on the same day.

Ruto, the then KANU Director of Elections, said the delegates' meeting would continue despite the announced boycott. And it did. At Kasarani, Uhuru accepted his nomination saying, if elected president, he would serve the nation with devotion, discipline, vigour, courage, and undivided loyalty. On those like Mudavadi and Ngala, who had made an about-turn after briefly defecting from KANU, Uhuru had a special tribute: "...Some would like to label them traitors to their communities... but it is men and women like them whom we need to build a new Kenya where ethnicity, religion, colour and race become irrelevant in the pursuit of national unity…" Partly as a result of their flip-flopping, both Mudavadi and Ngala lost their seats in the 2002 elections.

Moi's imperious action to impose a leader on Kenyans, in what came to be known as "Project Uhuru", was an unmitigated failure from the very beginning. While Moi was seen as a dictator, the fledgling Uhuru was viewed as his esoteric henchman. Moi wanted to use Uhuru as a pawn to preserve his own survival after retirement, but he failed to read the mood of Kenyans, who saw the election of Uhuru as a return to the Kenyatta era oligarchy. Some said it was a case of musical chairs, in which the Kikuyu had deferred to the Kalenjin; now the Kalenjin would, in turn, defer to Kikuyus through Uhuru; and, eventually Uhuru would defer to the Kalenjins through one of Moi's politically ambitious sons. The fury that met Uhuru's nomination was a clear indication that Kenyans were prepared and willing to break their long-standing association with KANU and Moi.

# CHAPTER 3
# Moi deserted

Overnight drizzles had led to a crispy dawn, and the grey sheet of menacing low clouds had threatened a full-blown downpour, but at day-break, the heavens had opened up, the frosty air had dissipated, and suddenly a blast of sunshine had engulfed the city, bringing with it a warm feeling of relief. At the Serena Hotel overlooking Uhuru Park, throngs had begun to gather. In no time, the hotel lobby, coffee shop, and the lavish grounds were full of noisy revellers, some carrying freshly cut tree branches as a sign of joy, while others hoisted faded posters of their political leaders. On the way there, they had extracted twigs from the flowerbeds at the round-about of Uhuru highway and had plucked boughs from the Freedom Corner, a section of Uhuru Park, which in 1992, was declared a peace monument after a group of women led by Prof. Wangari Maathai staged a sit-in to demand the release of political prisoners. They were singing freedom songs.

The situation was chaotic and the hotel management had to close down the entrance to stop marauding youths from over-running the facility. Guests, who were either arriving or departing, were caught up in the brouhaha. Outraged and frustrated, some protested loudly to the powerless staff who tried unsuccessfully to control the crowd. The hotel entrance had to be closed. From the coffee garden, I peeped through the flowering bougainvillea-decked fence and noticed that Uhuru Park—only a stone's throw away—was already fully packed. It was only mid-morning, hours before the start of the planned maiden Rainbow Alliance rally. On the grounds, some people were perched atop the few feeble trees, swinging and swaying to local hits;

the more daring ones dangled on flag posts, while others danced madly as if possessed. By holding the rally on the same day as the KANU delegates' conference, the brand new coalition was nose-thumbing Moi and his chosen successor. The country was clearly divided: reformists at Uhuru Park, and conservatives at Kasarani. Never in the country's post-independence period had KANU seen such a direct challenge to its authority.

That morning, the last of Moi's disillusioned ministers, Stephen Kalonzo Musyoka, appeared and announced his resignation from the government. Reports of his imminent departure had begun to circulate the previous day, and as expected, had attracted the attention of security officials, who tried desperately to stop him from reaching Nairobi from his rural home. His allies said he had to change routes and hop into different cars to avoid an ambush and possible de-routing. The version reportedly given by Kalonzo himself was that "KANU diehards planned to abduct and parade him during the endorsement of Uhuru Kenyatta."[52] If there was indeed such a plot, then it flopped miserably. Kalonzo did make it to the Serena Hotel, shaken and somewhat ruffled. The previous day, Raila and several other ministers had set the stage by resigning, sending an ominous message to their leader that there was no turning back in their protest against Uhuru's candidature. They had expected that Kalonzo would join them at the press conference, but the Minister for Information and Tourism was nowhere to be seen, prompting rumours that he had changed his mind.

Until then, Kalonzo appeared to be flip-flopping about whether to stick with Moi or to decamp. Although he had opposed Uhuru's choice, his statements were sometimes ambivalent and his wavering was unnerving. Even when he finally surfaced to announce his departure from the government, his hesitancy was evident. As he read his resignation statement, he appeared uncharacteristically subdued; his statement was meek and lacked sting, his body language shifty, and his reasoning unconvincing. "I have resigned," he said as a matter of fact. "The nomination process has been heavily manipulated in favour of one candidate." [53] With that done, Kalonzo sauntered away into the confines of the hotel for consultations with his colleagues.

52 Africa Press International, December 23, 2006.

53 Reuters, October 14, 2002.

## The real Kalonzo

Many know Kalonzo as a dapperly, born-again Christian; debonair and urbanite, but behind that clean-cut cosmopolitan disposition, is a background that places his early life far away from the flashing lights of downtown Nairobi. Several hours drive north-east of Nairobi is Tseikuru, a remote village off the tarmacked Mwingi-Garissa road, a key artery leading to northern Kenya. Leaving the relative luxury of that smooth highway, with an intermittent view of rocky hills and wild, scattered thorny vegetation, a visitor from Nairobi must veer off into a backbreaking section that requires a four-wheel drive vehicle and lots of endurance. For years, Mwingi District (then known as Kitui District) where Tseikuru is located, was rated as one of the poorest districts in the country with subliminal conditions of abject poverty affecting more than seventy percent of its population, while Tseikuru, which later became a district on its own, was rated as one of the driest areas in the country. Little has changed in those areas in the past few decades. People are still among the poorest in the country, the weather brutally unrelenting.

Traversing the open, expansive area, one could not fail to notice the daily struggles of women and children—trekking for miles, donkeys in tow—in search of water. As one moves away from the lush savannah of the Ukambani plains, ugly, giant cracks on riverbeds appear, standing out as evidence of long dry spells. Holes dug on the ground in desperate search for water remain abandoned for most of the year due to scanty rainfall, and emaciated goats and sheep wander the barren territory in search of hard-to-find foliage. When it rains, the rivers come alive in torrents, and the area is turned into a huge oasis of beauty, with maize and beans growing in abundance, but for most of the year, Tseikuru remains a forbidden territory. It is a desolate and unfriendly land, until one arrives at Kalonzo's opulent home. The stately mansion, complete with all the modern trappings of luxury is a far cry from the temporary, makeshift abodes of most of his constituents.

It is in this bucolic area that Kalonzo was born in 1953 to a struggling shopkeeper father and a peasant mother. Like most youths of those days, Kalonzo did not escape the drudgeries of rural life; he fetched water from the river, tended goats and cows, and worked on the farm. In the economy of those days, his father, Musyoka Mairu, was not entirely poor. Struggling yes, but he was relatively well-to-do by the standards of the area at the time. Every so often, he would travel to the capital, Nairobi, to buy goods for his store, and occasionally, Kalonzo would go along to offer help. From his earnings, and help from neighbours, Mairu was able to take his bright child from the run-down Tseikuru primary school, seven kilometres from their home, to Kitui High School and then to Meru Secondary School further afield, and later to the University of Nairobi.

The young, slim Kalonzo demonstrated his leadership potential early. While in high school, for example, he quelled a food riot, a feat that earned him a promotion to prefect. Invariably smart with an afro, Kalonzo was rather reserved but quite popular to his peers. He was an active member of the Christian Union and a disciplined and well-behaved student through his academic years. "Look at me," Kalonzo would boastfully say in later years. "I was born in a mud house in a far away village. I was a shoeless child who embraced education, which later gave me a profession."[54] After graduating from law school, Kalonzo proceeded to the Mediterranean Institute of Management in Nicosia, Cyprus, and on his return, he founded the Musyoka & Wambua Associates, serving as a consulting partner.

Although he had a virtuously fulfilling upbringing, thanks to his father's old-fashioned sense of honour, his political journey from a remote village in the backwaters of Ukambani to the epicentre of political power was mainly determined by chance and abstract miracles. He was never aggressive in the pursuance of anything, but exuded energy and eagerness to learn. True, his earlier actions and manner of speech exhibited a degree of ambition for higher office, but he was not spectacularly charismatic. "In politics," a lawyer friend of his says, "one needs to be combative and sometimes defiant, but Kalonzo was not that type. He was calm and very diplomatic."[55] In the same breath, he was an unflappable man who made his companions squeam, especially during a fit of anger.

From the moment Mulu Mutisya, the easy-going comic, introduced Kalonzo to his close friend Moi in the 1980s, the young lawyer lived and breathed KANU. He adored the powerful Mutisya as much as he revered Moi—two people who charted and moulded his political career. Pliable

54 Oscar Obonyo and Mutinda Mwanzia: The Standard Online, Undated.
55 Anonymous, December 2009.

but pertinacious, Kalonzo started off as the Kitui District KANU Branch Chairman, becoming an MP when the Kitui North seat became vacant in 1985 when he was only thirty-two years old. His entry into politics was made possible by a leading Mwingi businessman, Ahmed Talib (Kanavu), and Kitili Mwendwa, an MP who later became Chief Justice. The two did not only provide Kalonzo with his first campaign capital, but offered logistics to enable him cover the vast electoral area. After election to parliament, he rose quickly up the ladder to become a Deputy Speaker, Assistant Minister for Works, Housing, and Physical Planning, and the KANU Organizing Secretary. He showed a lot of promise, one of his childhood friends remembers of him. "He was then humble and a true servant of the people."[56]

In 1993, Kalonzo was appointed Foreign Minister for five years until 1998. As the KANU Organizing Secretary, he was responsible for mobilisation and recruitment, and ran the party with the aggressiveness needed of such an authoritarian apparatus. All-powerful and keen to crush its opponents for the flimsiest of reasons, KANU was not only intolerant of internal dissent but also brutal to peripheral opposition. Its youth wing operated like a militia. Its men and women were invariably dressed in party colours, complete with a necktie and a legionnaire's cap, were well drilled in military formations, and when the situation demanded, became monstrously barbaric.

Always ready to defend the party, the bumptious youths performed a variety of chores: they provided security at meetings; promoted the party through membership drives; and instilled discipline—sometimes physically—on wayward members. Some of the youths' actions were excessive, but nobody was there to offer restraint. There wasn't an overall commander to oversee the rudderless youths, most of them plucked from villages and slums by officials, on account of either tribal or political considerations. Kalonzo was nominally their head, but there is no evidence that he was, at all times, in full control of the brigade. There were always questions about who actually paid the youths who appeared to be everywhere, especially during KANU functions. Former KANU Secretary General Kamotho said the feckless youths did not belong to the party. "These were not party youths, but private militias," he said in an

56 Anonymous, Interview, June 15, 2010.

interview years later. "Several politicians used to have their own gangs of terror,"[57] he added.

The youths also took orders from the party's disciplinary committee established in 1986 to ensure members deemed to be "disloyal" were expelled or denied rights to conduct business or to join the civil service. Part of the committee's work was to enforce a coercive system of membership recruitment in which the youths played a pivotal role. By 1988, the number of members had risen to eight million,[58] approximately two thirds of the Kenyan population. "The mass recruitment drive was achieved largely by depriving non-KANU members of certain basic rights, including access to rural produce markets, trading licenses, education, administrative services, and land."[59] Apart from his State House responsibilities, Moi was also the supreme leader of KANU, which he used to purge opponents and to coerce civil servants into becoming life members. It was mandatory for government offices, homes of senior officials, and shops to display Moi's picture, and officials were compelled to wear badges with Moi's image. Anyone failing to do so was considered anti-Moi and subjected to harassment.

As a civil servant, I was a victim to that bizarre form of forced obedience. Although I did not apply to be a member of KANU, I was recruited without my consent while serving at the Kenya Mission in Namibia. The membership fee was deducted directly from my salary and a Life Membership Certificate No. 20068 was dispatched through the diplomatic pouch. For the next four years, I wore the badge and displayed Moi's portrait at both my office and in my sitting room. I had no one to complain to, since membership was compulsory.

KANU's disciplinary committee "had powers to expel party members, impose sanctions against those who committed acts which, in the opinion of KANU, were not in its interest, or undermined the party President, the headquarters or the KANU Government."[60] During his New Year

57 Standard Online, Undated.

58 Colin H. Kahl, From Chaos to Calm: States, Scarcity and Civil Strife in Developing World, p. 192.

59 Ibid.

60 Jennifer A. Widner, The Rise of a Party-State in Kenya; From Harambee to Nyayo, p. 166/167.

Speech in 1989, Moi further empowered the committee "to monitor public places such as bars, hotels, and restaurants, to identify those who opposed the office of the President."[61] The committee became so powerful and so intrusive that it had to be disbanded three years later.

As Organizing Secretary, Kalonzo was part of the inner team that shaped the party's ruthless conservative policies and was one of the party's most inexorable hardliners. For example, at the party's delegates' meeting at Kasarani on December 3, 1991, called to consider a recommendation to repeal Section 2A of the Constitution to allow for multi-parties, Kalonzo was among those who argued, "that the country would be torn apart by ethnic animosities if pluralism were introduced," saying the choice was "between KANU and violence. It is upon you to decide."[62] Had it not been for Moi's timely intervention, KANU's one-party rule would have continued for much longer. Moi proposed a third option, challenging participants "…to choose between the good eggs and the bad eggs…,"[63] (that is, pluralism and single party rule) urging the delegates to give multi partism a chance. That ruling paved the way for the introduction of more political parties, but it also tamed Kalonzo and got him to understand how unpredictable Moi was.

"This is a man," said Solomon Gakungu of Kalonzo, in a blog on October 22, 2007, "who defended the single party dictatorship with the tenacity of a religious zealot, supervised the injustice of queue voting and took it upon him to unleash regular tirades on those social justice crusaders like the great campaigner for a free Kenya, Jaramogi Oginga Odinga."

At a function in Nairobi also attended by Kalonzo many years later, Raila narrated an interesting story about how he and Kalonzo had been invited by a Committee of the US Congress to present views on the performance of the Moi Government in the 1990s. Raila, who was then in the opposition, told the Americans about the country's human rights abuses, corruption, and other evils committed by the KANU regime. Kalonzo, then Foreign Affairs Minister, went to great lengths to defend

---

61 Ibid.

62 B. A. Ogot and W.R. Ochieng, Decolonisation & Independence in Kenya, 1940–1993, p. 245.

63 Weekly Review, December 6, 1991.

Moi, saying the accusations against the government were exaggerated. It was clear from that story that Raila wanted to underline the significant differences between Kalonzo and him, projecting himself as a progressive, reform-minded leader and Kalonzo as ultra-conservative and non-reformist. That narration, made in jest, was punctuated by murmurs from the crowd present, and prompted facial looks of surprise from Kalonzo.

## He cannot escape blame

Kalonzo—like many in the leadership of KANU at the time—cannot, therefore, escape blame over some of the KANU's most notorious decisions, including those related to the muzzling of the media; the prolongation of the one-party dictatorship; violations of fundamental human rights; criminalization of opposition leading to detention without trial; the torture chambers; and a whole range of policies that Moi embraced and executed during his rule. No wonder Kenyans had difficulty accepting his declared reformist credentials during the presidential campaign in 2007. His heavily loaded manifesto, promising a myriad of reforms was, to many voters, a mere academic thesis sitting on quick sand.

Kalonzo was also a key player during the time when the media suffered their most brutal treatment. Way back in 1986, the Moi Government "arrested and detained several journalists…confiscated editions of foreign and domestic publications containing human rights stories…arrested several foreign reporters and announced that it would review the work permits of more than 100 domestic and foreign correspondents."[64] *Beyond*, a political magazine published by the Kenya National Council of Churches of Kenya, was banned and its editor, Bedan Mbugua, arrested and jailed for eight months for contravening the rarely used Books and Newspaper Act, while the *Financial Review* of Peter Kareithi was outlawed in 1988, forcing him to flee into exile. Local journalists were arrested and hauled to court on fictitious sedition charges, while foreign correspondents critical of the government, were threatened with de-registration and deportation.

64 Jennifer A. Wildner, The Rise of a Party-State in Kenya: From Harambee to Nyayo, p. 166.

At another time, four *Standard* journalists[65] were arrested for publishing stories of tribal fighting in the Rift Valley's farming area of Molo. The area was a hotbed of clashes between mainly Kikuyu and Kalenjin tribesmen over land, a sensitive issue the government did not want publicised. A few days later, a *Nation* journalist, Mutegi Njau, appeared in court accused of allowing the publication of a story that insinuated the involvement of a prominent politician in the clashes. Such activities were not the only ones that threatened the freedom of the press. Often, under-cover agents would buy all copies of newspapers and magazines with critical articles against the government from vendors. Consequently, the government spent a lot of money on such operations to ensure the public did not know the truth about what was actually happening in the country. With such raids in mind, crafty Kenyans would struggle to acquire only one copy of the publication, which they would then photocopy and clandestinely peddle on the back streets. The trick frustrated security forces and compelled them to review seizure methods. Instead of waiting for the publications to hit the streets, police went after them at printing shops.

The most horrifying incident happened in 1993 when police raided the Fotoform printing company and confiscated equipment, rendering the plant—used by mostly independent publishers—dysfunctional. Its owner Dominic Martin was charged with sedition. Although Martin was later released, the government refused to return the confiscated machine parts. The government also banned several other publications, including *Inooro*, a hard-hitting Kikuyu monthly newsletter and *Nuru*, a publication of the Mwangaza Trust, a non-governmental organisation. Similarly, a mysterious fire destroyed the offices of the *Finance Magazine*, another anti-government publication.

A high profile case sent to the court was one of sedition against Louise Nyamora and several journalists of the *Society Magazine*. The magazine was fiercely anti-government, exposed rot in Moi's regime, and gave a platform to oppositionists. Although the magazine was published in Nairobi, the government deliberately moved the case to Mombasa, five hundred kilometres away, making it difficult and expensive for the accused to meet costs of travel and accommodation during hearings. The publication was

---

65 Kamau Kanyanga, John Nyaosi, Ngumo wa Kuria, and correspondent Peter Makori.

crippled and could not continue publication, only for the government to terminate the case, according to a 1994 report by the *Independence without Freedom*, a publication of the Kenya Human Rights Commission. By 1994, the report said, "no sedition case…(had)…been pursued to completion… though about twenty prominent critics…(had)… been charged with the offence."[66] So, it was obvious the government was bent on harassing and intimidating journalists and publishers and running them out of business, rather than arresting and jailing them.

The government's blatant intolerance of the Fourth Estate and Kalonzo's charm and obsequiousness came to the fore on June 30 the following year when he introduced a motion in Parliament that sought to ban the *Nation* newspaper from covering parliamentary proceedings. Kalonzo accused the paper of being "anti-Government, subversive and tribalistic" for the simple reason that it had entered into a professional relationship with the American-based *St. Petersburg Times* for an exchange programme. In his remarks in Parliament, Kalonzo also charged that the *Nation* "had scandalized the reputation of Members of Parliament (by)…dismissing journalists and administrators who wanted to be loyal and active KANU Members."[67]

The *Nation* reacted to the ban by swiftly ending its liaison with the *Times*, and Mike Foley, its Managing Editor, shot back a response describing the allegations as "ridiculous." But that was as far as the *Nation* protest went. During debate, Kalonzo's motion and his anti-media sentiments were widely supported by the KANU-dominated August House led by the then Minister for Information and Broadcasting, Johnstone Makau, who was known for his disdain of the media. The motion was successful and the *Nation* was barred from covering Parliament for four months. That fatuous performance may have pleased the KANU, but it certainly exposed Kalonzo as a pliable and sycophantic individual. No wonder then that even as some of his colleagues made early decisions to resign from Moi's crumbling regime, Kalonzo waited until the very day when the Rainbow Alliance was officially launched to leap to the opposition.

---

66 Independence Without Freedom: The Legitimisation of Repressive Laws and Practices in Kenya, A Kenya Human Rights Commission Report, February, 1994.

67 Ibid., p. 166.

## Kalonzo tries to change

For several years after leaving KANU, Kalonzo appeared uncomfortable in the opposition. In KANU, Kalonzo was just a cog in a big wheel; not allowed to make independent decisions. Now out of KANU, he faced a crisis of confidence. He suddenly found himself at the national level facing a politically cunning strategist in Raila, who had his roadmap already charted. However, he lacked Raila's unique attributes: charisma, aggressiveness, courage. Kalonzo was often irresolute when circumstances called for his intervention, and shied away from direct political combat. "That is a complete contrast with Raila's approach,"[68] Mumbi Ng'aru, a one-time colleague said of him. While Raila was forthright and engaging, Kalonzo was aloof and impassive. Another writer says this of the politician: "...Kalonzo has proven himself to be a dawdler, a foot-dragger who can't make fundamental choices....(Kalonzo) is too mired in a cult of self-importance and is too cautious to champion a crucial national case."[69]

Despite the many shortcomings, Kalonzo possessed some positive attributes that came handy in his post-KANU political life, especially during the Presidential race in 2007. His humble background resonated well with many Kenyans. He was seen to be corruption free. He was deeply religious, and in a country where thieves are brave to steal from fellow thieves and daring enough to break into police stations, religion means a lot to many people. It occupies a special place in many peoples' lives. And for the deeply religious Kalonzo, that was a positive element.

Unfortunately, though, those are not the only characteristics voters look for in choosing leaders in Kenya. In 2007, when Kalonzo contested the presidency, Kenyans wanted a strong individual who could face up to the challenges rendered by years of neglect. They did not want a Kibaki, "the usually torpid President, a man often described as too lazy..."[70] nor a Moi, who "behaved like an emperor,"[71] but rather a leader who had grit and boldness, who was staid and reliable. Voters didn't think Kalonzo was up to

68 Denis Onyango, Africapress, August 11, 2007.

69 Sunday Standard, January 11, 2009.

70 Michela Wrong, It's Our Turn to Eat: The Story of a Kenyan Whistle-Blower, HarperCollins, p. 219.

71 Commentary, Uganda Rural Community Support USA.

kilter. "His fighting credentials are lacking and Kenyans are wary of a man who is not ready to break a sweat over an issue."[72] His blunder of waiting until the very last moment to defect to LDP, his miscalculated departure from LDP to the LPK, (that we will see later) all worked against him.

72 Edith Macharia, Sunday Nation Checklist.

# CHAPTER 4

# Scramble for positions

In the week before the Uhuru Park rally on October 14, the new opposition leaders met during several sessions to ponder who among them would be best suited to battle Uhuru. The Rainbow Alliance was only a few days old, but there was the urgency of putting structures in place and leadership in order in preparation for the polls in December. The Alliance was not short of qualified candidates. On the LDP side, there was the scholarly Saitoti; the diplomatic Kalonzo; the fatherly Moody Awori; and, the great mobiliser, Raila. On the side of the NAK—composed of the DP, the NPK, and the FORD-Kenya—there was the laid-back Kibaki; the erudite Wamalwa; and the strong-willed Charity Ngilu. The NAK had settled on Kibaki as its presidential candidate as early as September. Politically, Kibaki was the most experienced and, at seventy-one, the oldest of them all. Both Wamalwa and Ngilu had agreed to cede the position to Kibaki on condition that he would be a one-term president. They trusted that at his advanced age, Kibaki would not want to go through the vagaries of another election campaign five years down the line, and would be willing to leave the position to a younger person.

Apart from Kibaki, Wamalwa was the most promising. A NAK official said Wamalwa had agreed not to contest the presidency because Kibaki had promised to leave the position for him after the first term. "We agreed the leader of NAK was going to be Kibaki. We agreed because Wamalwa had said, 'Okay, I will let you go and I will run after five years.' Kibaki did agree to be a one-term president should the joint opposition pick him up as its candidate."[73] Musikari Kombo, the FORD-Kenya leader, who confirmed that Kibaki, in fact, did promise to vacate the seat after one term supported that position. "It was a clear Memorandum of Understanding and a gentleman's agreement. I was personally there and privy to the Memorandum of Understanding (MOU)," he said. "It is just a pity that the agreement was not written down."[74] Kibaki later denied entering into any such agreement. Was it another case of betrayal in the jungle of Kenyan politics?

The potential contenders in the Rainbow Coalition came from different ethnic, educational, and political backgrounds. Out of the eight, four—Kibaki, Raila, Wamalwa, and Ngilu—had contested the presidency before but had been unsuccessful. Four others—Saitoti, Nyachae, Awori, and Kalonzo—were eyeing the presidency for the first time. All of them, except Nyachae and Ngilu, were holders of either graduate or postgraduate degrees in fields as varied as economics, law, engineering, and mathematics. Nyachae, the FORD-People leader, compensated his shortfall in higher academic achievement with a long record of service in government administration and politics, while Ngilu, a former office secretary, possessed unique leadership skills that subsequently served her well as an MP and cabinet minister. Apart from Ngilu and Wamalwa, all had served in either the Kenyatta or Moi regimes, or in both. Regionally, Kibaki came from Central, Raila and Nyachae Nyanza, Wamalwa and Awori Western, Kalonzo Eastern, and Saitoti the Rift Valley.

A few days prior to the Uhuru Park rally, Raila had desperately sought Kibaki and Wamalwa of the NAK to get them to agree on a joint arrangement with the LDP but the two had been elusive. For some unexplained reasons, Kibaki had gone underground and Raila could not reach him for consultations. Fearing losing the key Gusiiland electorate in Nyanza Province, Raila went ahead and signed an MOU with Nyachae the same morning of October 14, giving Nyachae, the temperamental leader of FORD-People, an opportunity to contest the presidency, with

---

73 The East African Standard, January 28, 2007.

74 Charles Wachira, Africa Today, Voice of the Continent, March 7, 2007.

Raila as prime minister once the constitution was changed to provide for that position.

But minutes before the rally, Kibaki and his group showed up at the Serena Hotel and Raila immediately embraced them, completely sidestepping the MOU with Nyachae. It had been agreed between Awori, Saitoti, Kalonzo, and Raila that, in the absence of a consensus, no announcement would be made on the presidential candidate and that further consultations would follow after the rally. It was only agreed that Raila would launch his LDP and the Rainbow Alliance would be inaugurated, but once at Uhuru Park, Kibaki's endorsement appeared to be a fait accompli when speaker after speaker stood up and praised his leadership qualities.

Unbeknownst to others, Raila had already made up his mind that Kibaki would be the candidate. When his chance to speak came, he asked the ecstatic crowd a rhetorical question in Kiswahili as to why Kibaki was not fit enough to be president. "Isn't Kibaki fit enough (to be president)?" The crowd of over a hundred thousand went wild. That declaration, later known as *"Kibaki Tosha"*, sent a deafening crescendo of celebration throughout Uhuru Park and gave the reluctant economics professor a new lease of political life. Nyachae was bitter and described the endorsement as "an autocratic selection process."[75] Nyachae saw Raila's abstruse about-turn as the ultimate betrayal, and he was never to trust him again.

In fact, he did get his revenge a month later on December 19, when Raila, who was on his way to address a rally in Nyachae's stronghold, decided to land his privately rented chopper at a small town called Keroka. Thousands of locals flocked to where the chopper had landed, thinking Nyachae was on board. On seeing Raila, instead, the crowd menacingly surged forward and accosted him for allegedly disrespecting their leader. He was frisked and his pockets emptied by a section of the angry crowd. The police, who had to fire shots in the air to disperse the people, advised Raila to leave as he did not have a licence to address any meeting in the area. At a scheduled meeting venue later that day, angry crowds met him with placards that read: FORD-People *Juu*, Nyachae *Juu*, Only FORD-People, Only Nyachae, in praise of their leader.

---

[75] Election Watch, Kenya 2002 Elections, Issue, No. 4, October 30, 2002.

A defender of his peoples' rights, Nyachae was the tribal and political spokesman of the *Abagusii*. The FORD-People, which he chaired and personally funded, was hardly a national organisation. Its support was derived mainly from the *Abagusii* part of the Nyanza province, with pockets of followers scattered across the rest of the country. Even after being spat on at Uhuru Park, Nyachae tried to mend his ties with the coalition leaders until he realised that Raila no longer considered him of much political value. It was then that he declared his bid for the presidency, while knowing well that his chances of winning were remote. In fact, his presidential bid was more of an irritation than a serious ballot box challenge, his development and a corruption free record notwithstanding. He lost miserably in the race. The following year, a depressed Nyachae announced a coalition with Uhuru in readiness for the 2007 general elections, but the coalition failed to get off the ground and nothing more was ever heard of it again. But lady luck embraced him, and in 2005 he was appointed Minister for Energy when Kibaki sacked LDP-affiliated ministers after the defeat of the Constitutional referendum.

Nyachae was not completely done with Raila. He was still on a revenge mission in June 2010, when he sponsored a FORD-People candidate to battle it out with other party candidates, including one from Raila's ODM, in a by-election in Gusii's Bamachoge constituency. Nyachae's intention—though not publicly stated—was to humiliate Raila, who had boastfully ventured into his stronghold, to campaign for his candidate.

Sadly, instead of unifying the opposition, Raila's lone-ranger declaration also brought forth internal schisms. Leaders were surprised and shocked at the choice of Kibaki, and wondered how Raila could have made a decision of such a magnitude without consulting them. For weeks, therefore, confusion reigned, with some leaders condemning the LDP leader, and others saying he had violated an understanding agreed in advance. "When Raila said at Uhuru Park on October 14, "*Kibaki Tosha*", it just did not happen, we had agreed,"[76] said Dr. Noah Wekesa, then Chairman of NAK's Coordinating Committee, but Kalonzo and Saitoti of LDP disagreed. "That *Kibaki Tosha* declaration should not have been made at the time," said Kalonzo, "but when we got up to Uhuru Park, Mr. Odinga declared '*Kibaki Tosha*' thus going against the leaders'

---

76 East African Standard, January 28, 2007.

earlier agreement."[77] That notwithstanding, the jubilation that met the declaration was sufficient to convince even the most stubborn skeptic that the matter was a closed chapter, and that "Saitoti and Musyoka (Kalonzo) had little choice but to acquiesce to the fait accompli."[78]

Before that, Kibaki had been a lacklustre member of the opposition who had shunned confrontations and had failed to make a mark as the leader of the Opposition in Parliament. But today, lady luck had smiled at him, and he did not disappoint. "Today," he told the frenzied crowd, while accepting the nomination at Uhuru Park, "we have swallowed our pride and joined the National Rainbow Coalition (NARC) to remove Moi's autocratic rule."[79]

Kibaki had been reborn, his political career rekindled. He was not alone. Kenyans who had suffered through years of misrule finally saw hope for a brighter future.

## Wamalwa a threat

There were those who believed Raila's arbitrary decision to name Kibaki was a clever strategy to shut out Wamalwa from the presidential race for the reason that he was not yet ready himself for the big office. In addition, his LDP was too new in the political scene; it had no officials at the grassroots, and its popularity was difficult to predict. Despite their outward show of solidarity, Raila and Wamalwa were not friends. They had fallen out in 1994 following an acrimonious tussle over the control of FORD-Kenya after Odinga's death. The former had wanted to inherit the chairmanship from his father, but the latter had put up a spirited fight, using some of Raila's own tribesmen to block him. Eventually, Wamalwa succeeded in becoming Chairman, leaving Raila to bid for the deputy's position which he disappointingly lost to James Orengo. At a delegates' conference that followed, Raila once again offered himself for the top leadership position but tension and violence marred the meeting. Although Wamalwa's group showed up for the conference, it retreated after violence erupted, leaving Raila to proceed with the elections in which he was

77 Nation, December 23, 2006.

78 Centre for Strategic International Studies, Africa Notes, No. 12, December 2002. The two were the other leading contenders for the position.

79 New Vision, October 15, 2002.

elected Chairman. The raging leadership wrangles finally reached the courts and judgment given that Wamalwa would continue to hold the position until fresh elections were held.

That ruling deeply disappointed Raila and he decided to leave FORD-Kenya. As he grudgingly left, he poured vitriol on Wamalwa, saying Wamalwa cannot beat him in any political contest, and that he was not a coward to throw in the towel. He further said that he had decamped because bickering had taken a centre stage, and political solutions couldnot be found in unnecessary civil suits. It was perhaps the memories of that bruising altercation, observers surmised, that occupied Raila's mind during the tense negotiations to pick the Rainbow Alliance's presidential nominee. By picking Kibaki, Raila was convinced he had killed Wamalwa's presidential ambition and had somehow improved his own, with expectations that Kibaki's Kikuyu followers would back him when his time came.

At fifty-eight-years old, Wamalwa was rising fast in the country's murky political terrain. He was studious and mild-mannered while Raila was fastidious, hard-nosed, and provocative. After years of strong-arm leadership under Kenyatta and Moi, Kenyans wanted a moderate national icon capable of restoring hope and confidence. Kenya's relations with its key ally, Britain, were at its lowest ebb because of Moi's obstinacy, and London was anxious to improve them. The same could be said of the US and most of Europe.

To many, including the donor community, Wamalwa was the man. Urbane, intellectually stimulating, and free of corruption, he possessed all the fundamental leadership credentials. Unlike the East-Germany-educated Raila, who the West feared might have socialist connections; Wamalwa was known to be fiercely pro-West. He attended King's College at Cambridge and the London School of Economics, and was considered sufficiently safe as a reliable associate. He would have had no difficulty getting international support if NARC had chosen him to fight Moi's Uhuru. Wamalwa—who joined opposition politics in 1990, "after realising KANU was doing everything wrong…and a personality cult had developed around Moi to a point where he was being deified,"[80]—was a genuine threat to Raila.

80 International Republican Institute, Election Briefings, University of Pennsylvania, Africa Studies Centre, December 13, 1997.

Dr. Bonny Khalwale, the outspoken politician-cum-bull-fighter from Wamalwa's region was blunt in explaining his mentor's destiny. "If Wamalwa were alive today, (he)… would be President… and Raila leader of the official opposition."[81] Khalwale's thoughts, expressed in 2009 long after Wamalwa's death, underscored what would have been a potentially rancorous confrontation had the presidential field been left open for the two in 2002. But that was not to be. Wamalwa died of medical complications barely a year after NARC took office.

That aside, many Kenyans at the time were unsure Raila was the man they wanted for the top job. His alleged role in the August 1982 coup attempt had scared many, and those perceived links had portrayed him as power-hungry willing to go to any lengths to rule. They didn't see him as a democrat or a reformer, but as a socialist revolutionary with an ambiguous agenda. They felt "because of his zealotry to rule… (he was prepared to do) anything to reside at State House."[82] His inflated ambition could only be matched with that of his father, who spent years dreaming of an opportunity to serve as president. At one time, Odinga amused Kenyans when he pleaded with Kenyatta to allow him to serve as head of state even "for one day". But the high office eluded him, thanks to allegations that he was a Communist, a label he vehemently dismissed throughout his political life even as he admitted his admiration for China and Russia. "I am not a Communist," he said, "but I have been a constant target of anti-communist forces for all the years of my political history."[83]

It is possible also that in proposing Kibaki, Raila was baying for time to boost his credentials in preparation for 2007. And at only fifty-seven years old, he still had plenty of time on his side. Raila's choice of Kibaki was also baffling for another reason: Raila was not particularly known to hold Kibaki in high admiration. If he had any genuine respect for the man, that respect had vanished way back in June 1982 when Kibaki, as Vice President under Moi, successfully introduced legislation in Parliament to make Kenya a *de jure* single-party state through an amendment of section 2A of the Constitution. The Constitution of Kenya (Amendment) Bill, 1982, passed easily in the KANU-dominated National Assembly at a

---

81 Standard, August 23, 2009.

82 Professor Makau Mutua, Sunday Nation, July 9, 2007.

83 Oginga Odinga, Not Yet Uhuru, East African Publishers Ltd., p. 294.

time when leaders, among them Raila, were agitating for reforms in the country's electoral systems. However, that single action by Kibaki put to rest any further hopes for credible changes in governance and temporarily ended Raila's presidential ambitions. It could be surmised too that that Constitutional amendment played a role in triggering the attempted coup plan against Moi a month later, and contributed significantly to emboldening Raila against the abominable status quo.

But there were other reasons why Raila should not have supported Kibaki's candidature in the 2002 elections. During the time Kenyatta and Moi were mistreating Raila and his father, Odinga, Kibaki was serving loyally and quietly as Minister and Vice President. He never raised his voice in defence of democracy and pluralism, nor did he advocate for any type of reforms to make Kenya a better country. He believed in KANU's infallibility, and was better remembered for his ill conceived comment that: "trying to remove KANU from power is like cutting a *mugumo,* a fig tree, with a razor blade."[84] He believed it was impossible to change the government of the time, not just in the present, but forever. It was not difficult to understand why Kibaki was so sentimental about KANU. He was one of its founders—having abandoned his teaching career at Makerere University in Uganda—and spent years moulding it into the monster it later became.

Another reason why the *Kibaki Tosha* declaration was baffling was because Kibaki and Raila were two extreme opposites: Kibaki was conservative and gentlemanly, who waited for things to happen, while Raila came across as "too aggressive and too much in a hurry."[85] While Raila was happy in trenches, Kibaki was most comfortable in a well-furnished office with files piled up high on his desk. Kibaki was a consummate technocrat, Raila an astute politician. Moreover, Kibaki was fourteen years Raila's senior, a student of the old school that believed in the supremacy of age. And if that was not enough, Kibaki was a golf enthusiast, Raila a football buff. Other than their love for public service, the two had absolutely nothing in common.

84 Mwai Kibaki.

85 Salim Lone, Babafemi A. Badejo's Raila Odinga: An Enigma in Kenyan Politics, Yitab Books, p. 341.

## Kikuyu/Luo animosity

The whole issue became even more intriguing when one considered the longstanding animosity and mistrust between Luos and Kikuyus. In the late fifties and early sixties, a political marriage of convenience took place between the two most prominent tribes in Kenya when Odinga, a Luo, became one of the most vocal advocates of Kenyatta's release from detention. Odinga's slogan, *No Kenyatta, No Uhuru*, upset the colonial administrators and intimidated smaller communities. The Rift Valley, Coast, North-Eastern and Western regions viewed him as too self-important for their comfort.

Even before then, Kikuyus and Luos had enjoyed a rather cordial, albeit testy relationship. In *Not Yet Uhuru*, Odinga talked of his early relationship with Kenyatta during the days of the KAU: how during his first meeting with Kenyatta in Kisumu in 1948, the latter refused to alight from his car to greet him, and that Odinga had to walk to him to shake his hand; and how in 1951, Achieng Oneko a Luo, and one of those who were later incarcerated with Kenyatta, and Mbiyu Koinange, a Kikuyu, had been sent to London to put up Kenya's land case to the colonial government. While Oneko returned home to report to the people, Koinange remained in England to enjoy the good life. Luos took that as a betrayal of the independence struggle. It was obvious that even in those days, the Kikuyu/Luo ties, though mutually respectful, were tactically cautious.

All that notwithstanding and according to his own testimony, Kenyatta's arrest and detention saddened Odinga. Throughout Kenyatta's incarceration, Odinga was the only one who fought tooth and nail for his release, against opposition even from the detainee's own tribe. Odinga later described Kenyatta as "my hero…a giant of a man."[86] Upon his freedom, however, the two sadly found themselves at opposite ideological ends. While Kenyatta had metamorphosed from a freedom fighter to a moderate, Odinga had moved far to the left. He had courted the Chinese as much as he had lured the Russians. Shockingly, Kenyatta used Odinga's closeness to the East to denounce him as a communist lackey.

---

86 Oginga Odinga, His Philosophy and Beliefs, Introduction by Prof. H. Odero Oruka, p. 91.

In 1966, barely three years after independence, in the first public demonstration of hostility, the former detainee edged Odinga out of KANU. The man who liked to wear a colourful beaded cap and loose below-the-knee pants was never to trust Kikuyus again. But the final break between the two occurred in 1969 when, during a visit to Odinga's home town of Kisumu, Kenyatta was stoned by angry pro-Odinga supporters, prompting security officials to open fire and kill several people. Within the following twenty-four hours, Odinga was arrested and placed under house arrest for four days before being hauled to detention, where he spent one and half years. Kenyatta had relied on intelligence reports from British officials who were constantly spying on Odinga and giving Kenyatta exaggerated information about his communism links.

Another good example of Kikuyu/Luo shaky co-existence emerged in 1992 during the FORD elections when Odinga clashed with Matiba over who was to become Chairman of the party. Matiba was one of the richest Kenyans, with properties extending from hotels to real estate to high-end schools and media. He had entered politics after a chequered career in government service that had started in the mid-sixties, and had spent time as a top soccer administrator. For the record, he was the first African Permanent Secretary in independent Kenya. But his entry into politics was not welcomed by Moi who saw him as among those in the Kikuyu community who wanted to perpetuate the legacy of the *House of Mumbi*. Odinga, on the other hand, saw Matiba as a jonnie-come-lately who was obsessed with power. He was not going to give in without a fight.

The FORD Constitution was clear that whoever was the Chairman, he or she was the automatic nominee for the presidency. So, the disagreement between Odinga and Matiba was more about the leadership of the country than the stewardship of the party. It was also about ethnicity and cultural prejudices. In the bitter debate that raged, Central Kenya leaders coalesced around Matiba and came out strongly against Odinga, with appeals to Kikuyus and Kenyans in general to reject him because he was "an uncircumcised person (a *kihii*)."[87] As a general cultural rule, Luo men do not circumcise, and the reference to *kihii* represented the ultimate insult on the Luo traditions. With that insult, the line had been drawn, and the

87 B.A. Ogot and W.R. Ochieng, Decolonization and Independence in Kenya 1940–1993.

contest was no longer between the two individuals, but between two of the country's most powerful tribes.

Odinga had banked on the Kikuyus to support him as a payback for his advocacy over Kenyatta's release, but he was utterly wrong. "Odinga believed that since he had supported Kenyatta (earlier)… (Kikuyu) leaders would be willing to support his bid for the presidency this time (1992). But he was mistaken…and soon discovered that most of the Kikuyu leaders who had rallied around him during the formation of FORD were now ready to fight him to the bitter end…." Soon, Raila joined the fray by declaring "no" to any choice of another Kikuyu president.[88]

The Kikuyu/Luo wars did not end there. During the 1992 general elections, when Paul Muite, a Kikuyu and FORD-Kenya Vice Chairman was contesting a parliamentary seat, he garnered 38,416 votes for himself, while his Chairman Odinga who was contesting the presidency, got only 3,246 voters in the same constituency. This clearly showed that the Kikuyu were not up to supporting the Luo in a political contest, and that Odinga's role in the liberation struggle and in the Kenyatta release issue had long been forgotten. In the presidential election, Odinga came fourth behind Moi, Matiba, and Kibaki, the latter two being Kikuyu. Interestingly, the role was somewhat reversed in the 2007 elections when Raphael Tuju, a bitter Raila foe but Kibaki's top point man in Luoland, received over seven thousand votes in parliamentary elections in his Rarieda constituency while Kibaki, running for president, got less than three hundred votes there.

When Raila vied for the presidency in 2007, the troubling political relations between the two major tribes had only slightly changed. As late as July 2007, Kikuyus were still branding Raila unelectable because of his tribe.

So, the question was: why did Raila support a Kikuyu for president?

Political analysts theorised that the choice of Kibaki was a strategy to split Kikuyu votes between Kibaki and Uhuru and thus deliver victory to the opposition. Could that have been the true reason why Raila settled

---

[88] Ibid.

on the more experienced, but unassertive Kibaki? Or, was it because he wanted to mend fences with the Kikuyu in exchange for their support in future?

## Candidates nominated

As the opposition went on with its rally at Uhuru Park, Moi and his delegates were at Kasarani Sports Centre anointing Uhuru as the heir apparent. Unlike the *"kichinjio"* of March 18, this latest convention was peaceful and uneventful. It was conveniently choreographed to please Moi and to demonstrate a sense of party unity. By embracing Uhuru, Moi did to Uhuru what the Kenyatta family did for him after the death of the founding father. The Kenyatta family supported him against intense opposition from powerful forces within the Kikuyu community who did not want him to succeed Kenyatta.[89] Moi, commonly referred to as "*Nyayo,*" Footsteps, because of his professed commitment to follow Kenyatta's policies, was returning a favour to the fallen leader, but he was also buying a life insurance policy to protect himself from possible prosecution should a hostile successor take over and indict him for the many political evils he had allegedly committed over the years.

Even as Moi tried to put up a brave face at Kasarani and exude the confidence of victory, it was clear to everyone that he was under siege and his preferred choice, Uhuru, isolated. Most of the founding top officials of KANU had left, and the once giant ruling party was now a pale shadow of itself. The rapidly changing political atmosphere overwhelmed Moi, who for most of his years in power, had lived more or less in a comfort zone. He had been feted as the absolute ruler, Farmer No. 1, Educator No. 1, and so on, and had assumed other titles only a despot would.

A few weeks after the Uhuru Park rally, Kibaki was formally declared the opposition flag bearer, paving the way for NAK and LDP to enter into a formal MOU on power sharing. In the MOU, Kibaki was to be President,

---

[89] A group of mainly Kikuyu elite wanted the Constitution changed to remove a clause that allowed the Vice President to assume office for ninety days pending elections in case of the death of the President. Fronted by the GEMA, the group wanted another Kikuyu to succeed Kenyatta. But its efforts failed after Moi was backed by Attorney General Charles Njonjo.

Wamalwa, Vice President, Raila, Prime Minister, Kalonzo and Saitoti, Vice Presidents and Charity Ngilu and Kipruto Arap Kirwa, Deputy Prime Ministers. By that time, the disagreements in the Rainbow Coalition had petered out, somehow, and leaders had expressed willingness to work as a team to depose KANU from power. Since the Constitution allowed only the positions of president and vice president, the two parties agreed to work on a new Constitutional dispensation within the first one hundred days to create the post of premier for Raila, as well as positions for the rest of the leaders by June 2004. It was also agreed that positions in the diplomatic, the judiciary and in government institutions would be shared on a fifty–fifty basis. But as we will see later, the much-hyped MOU was another example of political betrayal that was to cause a lot of grief in NARC, leading eventually to its early demise.

# CHAPTER 5
# Terrorists strike

It was a balmy day following days of incessant rains; the sky was blue and the white clouds were scattered and formless. The birds sang from treetops, and the swishing wind, fuelled by swaying coconut trees, produced amazing musical notes that permeated through the villages in a falsetto of transcendental calmness. But that state of tranquillity was suddenly shattered by a huge sound of explosion coming from the direction of the Indian Ocean. The blast was so huge that its deafening noise was heard many kilometres away. It didn't sound like an explosion from a burst car tire, nor the kind of thunder usually associated with dynamites from the quarries dotting the stone-rich Kenyan coast. It was crudely loud: like a sound in a war zone. I was on my way to Kilifi, farther north from Mombasa, and had just passed Kikambala, a semi-urban enclave with an abundance of mangos that dangled from shapeless tree branches like coloured kidneys.

As I cruised along the highway leading to the historic town of Malindi and to the majestic island of Lamu, I heard the shattering sound accompanied by a pungent whiff of metal. At that early hour of the morning, the thought of a bomb attack was far from my mind. In any case, Mombasa and the whole of the coastal strip had not seen any major war-like activities and had been peaceful since the British forcefully kicked out the Portuguese in the seventeenth century.

Other than scattered minor tribal skirmishes here and there, the whole area had experienced nothing but tranquillity. People from different regions, tribes, and religions had co-existed with minimal confrontations, a true haven of peace. I passed the vast Vipingo sisal estate—producers of the world's best quality sisal fibre—breezed through the pristine Swahili town of Takaungu, on the right, lumbered over Mbogolo Bridge as the fast flowing river waters rumbled below, and emerged at Mnarani's Kilifi Plantation, a colonial dairy farm owned for generations by a white British family, the Wilsons. I was the Rainbow Coalition's parliamentary candidate for the area, and just as I was settling down for a meeting, a call came informing me that terrorists had attacked an Israeli-owned luxury resort at Kikambala and instructing me to drop everything and rush to the scene.

Although relatively new in the north coast, the Paradise Beach Hotel had established itself as an exclusive retreat for Jewish visitors. It abutted the blue waters of the Indian Ocean. From some of the windows of the spacious rooms, residents could see infinitely into the heavenly horizons beyond. Kibaki, Raila, Kalonzo Saitoti, and others, who were navigating through the bone-jarring tracks of dirt roads in a nearby constituency made a quick about-turn and sped at high speed towards the site of attack.

My body was shaking and I was confused, as I whizzed past speeding *matatus,* mini-vans, and trucks carrying raw salt from pits farther north. I asked myself many questions on my way back. What went wrong? A bomb! Were there any deaths? If truly a terrorist attack, who was responsible? Ordinarily, the road journey between Kilifi and Kikambala takes forty-five minutes on moderate speed, thanks to the innumerable potholes of various sizes and shapes that had transformed the once smooth highway into a killer road. On this day, it took me only thirty minutes to reach Kikambala. My small Toyota saloon was literally dancing over the craters, shaking to the disembodied ocean winds.

The massive blow-up, I was soon to discover, shook adjoining hamlets and sent villagers rushing to the scene, followed by a large contingent of uniformed police officers and detectives. When I arrived, smoke was bellowing from the reception area and ambulances were busy ferrying the injured. The hotel gate and the front section of the hotel were completely ripped off, and pieces of human flesh were scattered amidst mangled rubbles. Relatives of the victims, most of them from the adjoining village, including one family that had lost four of its members, were wailing uncontrollably, while dozens of frightened Israeli guests, huddling on the fringes of the coral stonewalled complex and clutching whatever they could urgently salvage, were awaiting evacuation.

As expected in such a state of confusion, security forces had a difficult time controlling the curious crowds. A quick assessment showed that the device used, whatever it was, had caused maximum damage to the front office area. I knew then that many lives had been lost. When a visibly upset Kibaki and his colleagues arrived, I led them around for a closer inspection, and that is when I realised innocent Kenyans had died, victims of a conflict they knew nothing about, or its place of origin thousands of kilometres away. Three Israelis, including two children were among the victims. "These are terrorists," an aggrieved Kibaki told those gathered at the grisly scene, "they are killing innocent people and no one should show sympathy. As a nation we join all peace loving nations in condemning this type of terrorism."[90]

Three suicide bombers in a sports utility vehicle had gate crashed through the heavy metal grills and had detonated a powerful device at the reception area, where a group of traditional dancers had gathered to welcome new arrivals from Tel Aviv. Thirteen people were killed, ten of them local dancers who were trying to eke a living the best way they could. The three attackers also perished. Most victims of that diabolical attack died instantly while eighty others were taken to hospital with injuries. A group of Israeli tourists, which had arrived at the airport to begin a two-week holiday and was on its way to the hotel to replace another one that had just been dropped at the Moi International Airport, was re-routed back to the airport.

As the 757 Boeing plane of the original departing group soared into the air on that clear morning on their journey home, a group of terrorists hiding in the grassy fringes of the airport released six blasts of surface-to-surface missiles—one missing the plane by just a few meters. Eyewitnesses saw a speck of red as the missiles flashed past the aircraft. If any of the devices

90 VOA, November 29, 2002

had struck its target, the two hundred and seventy-one Israeli tourists plus the crew would most likely have perished. The airport terrorists gathered their deadly arsenal from the thicket and vanished into the busy highway nearby. Later, twelve suspects, including some foreigners, were arrested for alleged involvement in the attempted attack on the airliner.

Israeli investors built the Paradise Hotel to cater for Jewish visitors wanting to sample the Kenyan coastline and to enjoy the country's famed wildlife heritage in the interior of the country. The hotel was so exclusively Jewish that it regularly flew in kosher foods and drinks from Israel and employed ethnic chefs from the Holy Land to satisfy its clients' palates. To give its visitors a taste of Kenyan culture, it featured locally crafted four-poster beds, wildlife sculptures and paintings on its walls, and provided a varied entertainment programme that was unique in hotel establishments catering for foreign tourists. Because of the nature of the soiled relations between the Jewish state and militant Arab regimes, the hotel had installed a comprehensive security network to ensure safety of its guests and facility. However, as the events on that hot morning confirmed, the security measures in place could not stop a doggedly suicidal trio of bombers from advancing their evil intentions.

The Kikambala hotel bombing was, until then, the third major terrorist act in Kenya. On the eve of New Year in 1981, a bomb extensively destroyed the Jewish-owned Norfolk Hotel in Nairobi, allegedly planted by operatives of the Palestine Liberation Organisation, (PLO). Some reports indicated that the attack was carried out to punish Kenya for allowing Israelis use of its airspace following a hostage rescue saga at Entebbe Airport, Uganda. Fifteen people were killed and eighty-five were injured in that attack.[91]

---

91 The raid on Entebbe by the Israel Defence Forces (IDT) took place on the night of July 3 and 4, 1976, after a terror group linked to the Popular Front for the Liberation of Palestine, had hijacked Air France flight No. 139, and threatened to kill the hostages after forcing it to land at the Ugandan airport. IDT commissioned Operation Thunderbolt that rescued all the hijackers. Three hostages and forty-five Ugandan soldiers were killed. The then ruler, Idi Amin, blamed Kenya for colluding with the Israelis in the rescue operation, and for allowing the hostage plane and Israeli aircrafts to re-fuel in Nairobi. After the rescue, Idi Amin went on a rampage and reportedly killed many Kenyans in Uganda.

In August 1998, suspected Al Qaida terrorists who simultaneously bombed the American Embassy in Dar-es-Salaam, Tanzania bombed the American Embassy in Nairobi. Two-hundred-fifty people were killed in Nairobi and hundreds others injured. In 2003, Kenya was once again targeted by Al Qaida terrorists when a truck-bomb and an explosive-laden plane, apparently intended for the temporary American Embassy along Mombasa Road in Nairobi, were discovered. The plane was to take off from the neighbouring Wilson Airport and was programmed to ram into the Embassy, less than two kilometres away. A suspect caught by Kenyan authorities named some of the same individuals who had planned the Paradise Hotel attack as having been involved in the planning of the failed assault at the American Embassy.[92]

As the news of the Kikambala bomb blast spread like wildfire along the coast, beach hotels rapidly emptied as thousands of tourists rushed to the airport to find planes home. In Tel Aviv, the government assembled a team of dozens of doctors, sniffer dogs, and security personnel and flew them to Kenya within hours of the attack. In no time, all international television networks were airing the assault, and travel agencies across the globe were busy cancelling tours to Kenya and arranging alternative destinations for their clients. Western embassies were put on full alert, while security units ringed both international airports in Mombasa and Nairobi. In New York, a few weeks later, the UN passed a resolution condemning the attack as a threat to international peace.

The NARC leaders experienced firsthand the terrorism challenges facing them should they take over government. Their visit to the crime scene only hours after the blast was a public relations coup and portrayed them as compassionate and caring leaders. It was not until the following day that Moi—who had been in Arusha, Tanzania, attending a meeting of the East African Community— visited the area.

Terrorists have targeted Kenya for attacks because of its close ties with the US. In 2000, President Bush labelled Kenya a "strategic regional pillar" in the American national security strategy, and renewed airbase, port access and over-flight arrangements with the country. According to the Encyclopaedia of the Nations, Kenya received between fifteen and twenty

92 Combating Terrorism Centre at West Point, a Case Study.

million US dollars for counter-terrorism activities in Africa. On the other hand, Israel and Britain have always maintained a significant military and economic presence in the country. Its strategic port of Mombasa has traditionally been used to supply American and British forces in the Indian Ocean and the Persian Gulf. Israel, its Embassy being the most heavily guarded foreign mission in Nairobi, has clandestinely used the Kenyan airspace for forays into enemy territories.

But there are other reasons why Kenya is attractive to terrorists. The country is the most developed in the region, even though it lacks adequate and efficient border surveillance mechanism. Corruption among immigration officials at border points and along its porous borders makes it easy for unwanted characters to move in and out of the country at will. Its geographical proximity to the failed state of Somalia, where several international terrorism cells are in residence, and the fact that Kenya has a huge population of people of Somali origin, are also major contributing factors. In addition, Kenyan authorities have shown little interest in arresting, investigating, and jailing terrorists, a factor that has entrenched impunity and allowed suspects to go scot-free.[93] For example, out of the six suspects taken to court for alleged involvement in the Kikambala bombing, only four faced trial, and those were eventually acquitted for lack of evidence. Only one was jailed for a weapons offence.

## The fragile tourism

Tourism is one of Kenya's most important economic sectors, and attacks such as those mentioned above have the net effect of destroying the sector. At the time of the latest two bombings, tourists were bringing in an estimated five hundred million US dollars annually, representing twelve percent of GDP. After the attacks, the country lost an estimated one million US dollars per day for at least the following two years. Although Paradise Beach Hotel bounced back to business, the aura and ambience surrounding it will for a long time be tempered by the monument to the dead that occupies the very spot at the reception area where the bomb exploded. It is covered with plants and flowers so as not to evoke the sad memories of that October day.

93 Combating Terrorism Centre, West Point, a Case Study.

As much as Kenya values its tourism assets, a lot could be done to upgrade its hospitality industry. Many roads to game parks are still in deplorable condition; hotel facilities are well below international standards; the general state of cleanliness along the beaches is wanting; and industry personnel are less than courteous. The presence along the beaches of makeshift kiosks that sell everything from handicrafts to drugs, and of criminal elements posing as tour guides and beggars, considerably hurt Kenya's image as a safe international tourist destination. The state of decadence is inexcusable in such an important economic sector. Add sex tourism to that mix and the country is weighted down in a social quagmire.

A study by a British organisation, called End Prostitution, Child Pornography, and Trafficking (ECPAT), showed that thirty thousand Kenyan children were exposed to sex tourism along the Kenyan coastline. "On the beach resorts of Mombasa," the report says, "both boys and girls appear to be sexually abused by male and female sex tourists." The sight of old European ladies in the hands of young African males, and of old white men with under-aged village girls with tight clothes and heavy make-up, is too common along Kenyan beaches. And tourists do not shy away from expressing their outrage. Internet blogs by overseas tourists tell it all: "The town (Mombasa) itself is dirty and full of people trying to sell you everything..." One tourist said: "Another singles out beach boys as the menace hurting tourism in Kenya: I didn't once see any hotel guest sun-bathing on the beach because of the constant hassle they got from beach boys."[94]

The government is fully aware of what goes on in its tourist resorts but has chosen to ignore it, allowing foreigners, among them international criminals, to put up hundreds of private villas under whose roofs these vices take place unchallenged. In addition, the governments have failed to comply with local and international protocols, such as the Convention on the Rights of the Child, and its own Children's' Act of 2002, exposing young people to pimps and child abusers.

Kenya must learn from the US on the way beach resorts are run and how reserves are managed. During a visit to the beaches of Miami in 2009,

[94] Fantastic Scenery, July 24, 2001.

I marvelled at the tranquillity, the efficiency of service, the cleanliness of the beaches, and the absence of hawkers along their tourist resorts. The Miami beaches are some of the cleanest in the world; rescue teams are always on alert in case of an accident; and service is world class. The Everglades National Park in Miami, Florida—dubbed the largest sub-tropical wilderness in the US—attracts eight million people annually to its sanctuary of rare and endangered species of animals and birds. In comparison, Kenya with its famed game reserves such as Masai Mara lure less than one million visitors per year.

It is also widely acknowledged that the country's perennial unstable political climate badly affects tourism growth in Kenya. The attempted coup of 1982, the political wrangles in the NARC Government in the early 2000, the explosion of post-election violence in 2008, and sporadic ethnic clashes, all conspired to paint Kenya as a high risk security nation. When visiting a destination, visitors want to feel secure. A country that does not offer security is unlikely to sustain its tourism industry. In Kenya, visitors fear to venture out on foot from their hotel premises for fear of attacks by marauding glue-sniffing youths and petty thieves. Pestering beggars are everywhere, and so are carjackers. Even in New York's Harlem, considered one of the more insecure places in the US, tourists roam freely without any guides or security. They take trains and public means to reach historical venues scattered all over the vast inner-city neighbourhood without worries at all. In Kenya, the Tourist Police, which was formed to deal with security issues along the beaches, has been unable to enforce law and order, forcing guests to spend time sequestered within the precincts of their hotels.

No wonder the American government for years has continued to warn its citizens to stay away from Kenya. Although those warnings have not deterred adventurous visitors from visiting, they have slowed down growth of tourism from North America. To avoid terrorist attacks like those that took place in the country, the Kenya Government must tighten its border security, especially along the frontier with the unstable Somalia, and end rampant corruption in the immigration department, whose officers are often compromised to allow entry of even known international criminals and terrorists.

# CHAPTER 6
# Another Kikuyu president?

With one month to go before the 2002 general elections, the Rainbow Alliance was faced with the conundrum of how to successfully sell another Kikuyu president to a country that was seemingly Kikuyu-fatigued. Many in NARC knew that a second Kikuyu president in four decades was a hard sell in a country with forty-two tribes. The first President was Kenyatta who was a *Kikuyu*; the second was Moi, a *Kalenjin*. In Kenyan popular lingo, therefore, the Kikuyu and the Kalenjin had already had their share. It was now time for other tribes "to eat." Given this scenario, it became difficult for party strategists to predict how the majority of voters would respond to Kibaki at the ballot box, given his ethnic background.[95]

Moreover, Kibaki had been rejected twice before, partly because of his inherent rigid personality, and partly because of his uninspiring leadership style. Even though he was the second longest-serving parliamentarian after Moi, and had a long stint as Vice President, his local travels rarely went beyond the confines of his Nyeri district in Central Kenya. Though many had heard of Kibaki, not so many had seen him in flesh. It was as if he was allergic to local travels. If he was not at his ministerial office, the man variously described as aloof and disengaged, and "serene and unbothered"[96],

[95] Ethnicity plays a significant role in the social, economical, and political life of Kenyans.

[96] Professor Makau Mutua, Sunday Nation, December 27, 2009.

was at Muthaiga Golf Club, playing the eighteen holes or lounging at the club bar enjoying his favourite beer.

Many felt, therefore, that 2002 was too soon for Kenyans to forget the Kenyatta regime. Apart from its reputation as corrupt, nepotistic, and pro-rich, the regime was also notorious for land-grabbing. Throughout his rule, Kenyatta used land for "patronage purposes—to solidify support and build alliances."[97] He *Kikuyunised* thousands upon thousands of acres owned by Africans, Europeans, and Arabs around the country; he created settlement schemes supposedly to settle the landless, but most of that land was largely dished out to Kikuyus to decongest the crowded Central Province. He used a little-known provision in law that stipulated a sixty–forty percent allocation ratio between indigenous people and other Kenyans to short-change locals and deny them full use of the schemes.

And if that was not enough, beach plots along the Indian Ocean Coast were given as rewards to influential personalities who in turn, either sold them to foreign developers to put up hotels and villas, or built mansions for themselves. Those plots eventually fell into the hands of European investors, turning the tourist resort towns of Kilifi, Malindi, and Lamu into foreign enclaves, where drugs were peddled and prostitution was widespread. Most of the streets and shops in the resort towns bear foreign names and markings, and the strange behaviours of the foreigners are having an adverse effect on local cultures.

During Kenyatta's time, senior civil service jobs were routinely reserved for the tribe of *Mumbi*[98] and, when the *Africanisation* policy took effect in the 1960s intended to open doors for Africans to venture into business, retail, and wholesale shops in major cities were allocated mostly to people from one tribe. The Cabinet Minister in charge of the programme was

97 Unjust Enrichment, The Making of Land Grabbing Millionaires, the Kenya National Human Rights Commission, Living Large Series, p. 1.

98 The legend is that at the very beginning of life, there was a man called Gikuyu (Kikuyu in Kiswahili) and his wife, Mireia (Mumbi) who were placed upon the slopes of Mt. Kenya. The duo gave birth to nine daughters, who were later married to nine young men from whom the Kikuyu nation arose. The Gikuyu people, therefore, are said to belong to the tribe of Mumbi.

nicknamed Mr. Ten Percent because of the percentage of bribes he routinely demanded from would-be entrepreneurs.

Perhaps the most tragic cases of Kenyatta excesses are evident in the Lake Kenyatta Settlement Scheme in Lamu and in Taita/Taveta district, both at the Coast, as well as in the Rift Valley. In the seventies, thousands of Kikuyu peasants were uprooted from Central and Rift Valley Provinces and settled in Lamu, amidst protests from the landless indigenous communities. The relocation campaign did not take into consideration the centuries-old conservative Moslem traditions of the Lamu people. Upcountry Kenyans brought with them habits that were a taboo in Lamu: noisy bars and nightclubs, care-free accoutrements, and a proliferation of Christian churches that most Moslems considered a nuisance. This caused resentment and anger among the locals and acculturation became slow and arduous. In Taita Taveta, two families grabbed most of the land: the Kenyatta clan and the immigrant Criticos from Greece. In the land, people toiled for poor salaries at snake-infested sisal plantations and drudged away at crude mines for semi-precious stones. Most of the aggregate benefits went to middlemen, leaving workers in abject poverty.

After independence, Kenyatta encouraged his fellow Kikuyus to form land-buying companies, which benefitted from attractive loans advanced by politically correct banking institutions. "Borrowing money from Kikuyu banks and Kikuyu businessmen, tapping into the expertise of Kikuyu lawyers, the President's fellow tribes-people rushed to buy land of departing whites under a million-acre resettlement scheme subsidized by London. Descending from the escarpment, they flooded in their hundreds and thousands into the previously off-limits Rift Valley, seizing land the Kalenjin and other communities regarded as having been temporarily appropriated by the white man, but rightfully theirs. Given a selling scheme based on the principle of willing buyer, willing seller, there was little the poorer tribes could do."[99] Some of the transactions were voluntary ones, encouraged by the colonial government. "The British permitted Kikuyus to buy land in the Rift Valley, and Kikuyus, using official title deeds saw themselves as the rightful owners of that land.[100]

---

99 Michela Wrong, It's Our Turn to Eat: The Story of a Kenyan Whistle-Blower, p. 112.

100 University of Colorado at Denver: Africa: Majimboism and Indigenous Ideology.

It has been estimated that three hundred thousand hectares of prime land have been seized through dubious means by politically accepted individuals and companies since independence. To most Kenyans then, Kibaki was a leftover from the Kenyatta era, a person who participated actively in the mismanagement of the country, a person who believed in promoting the interests of his people. His nomination by NARC as its presidential candidate was, therefore, a gamble. True, Kenyans wanted change: change in political leadership, change in the Constitution, and change in the bureaucracy. They loathed corruption and wanted it ended. They wanted jobs, affordable universal health care, and equitable distribution of wealth, quality schools, and good infrastructure. They wanted land reforms to deal with past historical injustices, and economic transformation to end poverty. They were not sure initially that Kibaki, surrounded by special interests groups, was the right person to provide that change.

## Land clashes

Land conflicts have been at the centre of Kenya's political life since 1991 when tribal clashes erupted in the Rift Valley only months to the 1992 general elections. Kalenjins in the Tinderet division of Nandi district—incited by politicians anxious to drive out non-Kalenjin voters out of the area to tilt the voting balance in their favour—attacked Kikuyu, Luo, Kamba, and Luhya settlers using bows and arrows, spears, *pangas*, swords, and clubs. According to the report of the Judicial Commission on Tribal Clashes commissioned by Moi in the late 1990s and chaired by Justice A.M. Akiwumi, the attacks were not only meant to drive the settlers out of the Kalenjin areas but also to "cripple them economically and to psychologically traumatise them."[101] The report said the attacks left a trail of destruction, suffering and disruption of life hitherto unknown to Kenya because of "conflicts over land, cattle rustling, political differences and ecological reasons…."[102]

Similar clashes occurred in Western, North-Eastern and Coast Provinces. Since most of those clashes arose out of historical injustices, solutions appeared difficult to attain, meaning that decades after

---

101 Report of the Judicial Commission on Tribal Clashes in Kenya, p. 60

102 Ibid

independence, millions of Kenyans are still landless and homeless. For example, up to eighty percent of the rural population in the Coast Province of three million people are, legally speaking, squatters in the land of their birth while children of absentee landlords born and bred in the Arabian Peninsula own land without even visiting the country, says lawyer Wanyiri Kihoro. The former legislator and political detainee has studied and written extensively about the coastland phenomenon, and blames the Land Titles Ordinance of 1908 for the dispossession of land from indigenous coastal people. Under the ordinance, says Kihoro, all claims to land held under the African customary law or Moslem tenure were to be adjudicated by an administration tribunal, determined, and titles issued where the land claim was proven. Where no title was proven, the land would be deemed "unoccupied" and would become crown land. "The process was intended to ensure that land would become a marketable commodity,'[103] Kihoro says. Thus, large parcels of land reverted to the government, which eventually dished them out freely or at a small cost.

## Kibaki demobilised

On December 3, 2002, while on a campaign tour of Eastern Province, Kibaki was involved in a serious road accident that left him with broken limbs and psychological trauma. That was a big blow to the nascent opposition, but it did not dampen the fighting spirit of the remaining NARC leaders. With a large cadre of campaign aides, media backing, and populist reform promises, the Rainbow Coalition divided itself into campaign groups with the top leaders combing towns in search for votes. A huge corps of second tier campaigners also joined in. At opportune times, they all converged for joint rallies. The vote hunters travelled by road and in choppers and, to traverse difficult, water mass areas, such as the Tana River, for example, canoes were used.

The campaign was conducted as professionally as any, complete with a think tank, marketing, and publicity teams. Party strategists came up with the idea of regional manifestos that highlighted issues and solutions for each area. The manifesto for the coastal region, for example, emphasised the chronic

---

[103] Wanyiri Kihoro; Why the Government Should Intervene Directly to Abolish "Absentee Landlordism" at the Coast.

problem of squatters and landlessness, and suggested ways of how the NARC would tackle those issues, while the manifesto for the northern region listed measures the new government would take to deal with shortages of water and infrastructural development. The regional manifestos demonstrated NARC's focus on crucial socio-economic matters that were of direct concern to rural populations, strategically placing it far ahead of its rivals.

After the initial treatment at the Nairobi Hospital, Kibaki travelled to London for further expert treatment. Kenyans monitored his progress closely even though the government was economical with information. When he returned home on December 14, he was welcomed by thousands of people who had jammed the Jomo Kenyatta International Airport in Nairobi, and had lined along the route to the city centre, to have a glimpse of their returning hero. The tumultuous welcome was reminiscent of the return from a yearlong medical tour of London by Matiba of FORD-Asili in 1992. Awaiting Kibaki was a major political rally at Uhuru Park.

Although he had made some progress in recuperating, the Kibaki that people saw on that day was not the same one they knew. They had expected to see a fully recovered team captain ready to take on the campaign mantle from his subordinates, but as it turned up, he was in no shape to resume work. He looked tired and in great pain. The usual sparkle had gone, replaced by a sorrowful sight. The NARC leaders who met him at the airport could only whisper their worries. One of them looked at the feeble Kibaki, as he was being carried into a van and dropped some tears. "It can't be, it can't be," she repeatedly kept on mumbling to herself.

One analyst was to put it more dramatically: "His right ankle in a cast, his right hand in a sling, and his neck in a protective brace, Kibaki painted a picture of a broken leader. Escorted by a motorcade of 1,000 vehicles, he went straight to Uhuru Park for a rally where a crowd of 120,000 was surprised by Kibaki's condition as his wheelchair was lifted to the dais." All eyes were on him, the commentator said, "but although he spoke forcefully, his remarks lasted no more than three minutes…without stirring the anxious crowd. Suddenly he seemed to lose energy, abruptly ended his speech, throwing the crowd and NARC officials into confusion."[104]

[104] Centre for Strategic International Studies, Africa Notes No. 12, December, 2002.

What could have been a major comeback speech ended in an anti-climax. Short of breath and in obvious agony, the presidential nominee was bundled back into the van and driven away, leaving Kenyans asking themselves whether this was the man to rule them. The obvious fact was that Kibaki's injuries were far more serious than had been thought. The initial prognosis was that he had fractured his arm and sprained his ankle, but at seventy-one years old, Kibaki's injuries turned out to be far more debilitating. He had a high blood pressure condition that worsened with the accident, and blood clots that had to be removed from his legs. What irked Kenyans was the secrecy that surrounded his real condition. Officials said little, and even lied sometimes about his state of health. From the very beginning, Kenyan officials handled Kibaki's sickness as if he was a private citizen with no jurisdiction over a people. That conspiracy of silence and misinformation continued well after he was sworn in as Head of State.

And it was not just Kibaki's health that was hidden from the public. Kenyans will perhaps never know what killed Vice President Wamalwa. I had to raise a question in Parliament once about Wamalwa's hospitalization in London before the government could part with information. His medical records were sealed, so were those of Cabinet Minister Karisa Maitha who collapsed while on a trip in Germany.

When Raila was admitted to the Nairobi Hospital in June 2010, his minders attempted to hide the truth by announcing casually that he had been admitted for fatigue, but that "doctors have assured us that the Prime Minister is in good enough condition to come to office and work as usual…."[105] It turned out that the workaholic politician had already been operated on to relieve pressure from his brain to correct a potentially serious condition called subdural haematoma. In the meantime, rumours were circulating. It was only after his medical team reassured Kenyans that the Premier was out of danger that Kenyans sighed with relief. It took him weeks before he could resume work.

The pattern of secrecy over the health of important people was not restricted to Kenya. Many African leaders die in office without the citizenry knowing the course of death. The worst example of Africa's paranoia over their leader's wellbeing was demonstrated in Nigeria when President Umaru

[105] Daily Nation, June 30, 2010.

Yar'Adua fell sick. He was secretly transferred to a hospital in Saudi Arabia only to be sneaked back into Nigeria at night when his situation worsened. Apart from a few chosen officials, no one, including his deputy who later succeeded him, Goodluck Jonathan, saw him alive. He died pitifully and was speedily buried in accordance to Moslem tradition.

## Raila takes over

A few weeks after his arrival in Kenya, Kibaki had to be re-admitted to Nairobi Hospital for treatment of complications arising from a clot on his leg. His diary had to be cleared of all commitments, including a scheduled meeting with the visiting British Minister for International Development, Clare Short. From that moment, NARC leaders concluded that Kibaki would not be of much help in the campaign. Not that Kibaki had any remarkable campaign skills that were to be gravely missed, but with his absence, the task of selling him became trickier and rested on his lieutenants in NARC. Leaders concentrated on selling the NARC dream of comprehensive reforms, and focused on getting Moi and his surrogate Uhuru out of power. Whether by design or sheer belly power, the charismatic Raila immediately claimed the captaincy of the team and, together with all the others, put up a national face to the campaign. The NARC's national manifesto contained most of what Kenyans wanted to hear: "free primary education, a new Constitution, zero tolerance on corruption, creation of half a million jobs annually and revival of collapsed industries and infrastructure."[106] There were also commitments to better health care, affordable housing, and equitable distribution of wealth.

The cancellation of the scheduled meeting with Short was a big disappointment to the British Government, which had wanted to repair relations with Kenya after years of low-key ties that had worsened during the last year of Moi's tenure. Moi had related well with Prime Minister Margaret Thatcher, and was honoured to be the first Head of State to meet her in 1979 after Kenyatta's death. That was partly because Thatcher cared less about Kenya's human rights violations, but John Major and Tony Blair who followed her, pegged aid with progress in democracy and

---

106 Walter Oyugi, Peter Wanyande, C. Odhiambo-Mbai, The Politics of Transition in Kenya: From KANU to NARC, 2003, p. 37.

the fight against corruption. That was when diplomatic relations between London and Nairobi were at their lowest ebb. At the end of January 2003, Baronness Valery Amos, Minister for Africa, was able to meet the wheel-chaired Kibaki, and the damaged ties were put back on track.

## Bracing for the big fight

As NARC was regrouping, Moi and KANU were sharpening their propaganda apparatus and consolidating their personal and state resources. Both Moi and Uhuru were people of considerable personal and family wealth worth billions of shillings. To get a propaganda edge, the government quietly directed state media organs to subdue opposition coverage and focus on the Uhuru campaign. Selected journalists in the independent media were identified and commissioned to write positive editorial and opinion articles about KANU. The KANU mouthpiece, *Kenya Times*, went into overdrive with articles that exalted the achievements of the party and the potentiality of Uhuru. Grandiose promises were made and development pledges given. In some cases, the government ordered electricity poles and water pipes delivered to hostile areas to show official commitment to provision of electricity and water, only for the material to be carted away after the KANU candidates lost.

Around that time, opinion polls showed Kibaki leading Uhuru. The International Republican Institute poll projected a sixty-eight percent win for Kibaki if elections were to be held then, while Uhuru took only twenty-two percent. Even a confidential KANU poll painted a grim picture for Moi's surrogate son: It showed Kibaki ahead by fifty-two percent with Uhuru trailing at thirty-one per cent. The only way Uhuru could win, surmised analysts, was for Moi massively to rig the elections, a practice he was known to have mastered over many years. However, given the gloomy situation presented by opinion polls, the Kenyan President had a premonition for defeat.

In December, Moi travelled to Washington, DC for meetings with President Bush to discuss security threats posed by international terrorists after the Nairobi and Kikambala bombings. During their talks, issues relating to the upcoming general elections, and Moi's retirement were discussed. The Kenyan leader assured Bush that he would respect the voters' verdict, and that he would hand over power to whoever is elected.[107] Interestingly, while there, in his hotel room, the Kenyan leader reportedly called in a few officials, among them Foreign Minister Marsden Madoka and Head of the Civil Service and Secretary to the Cabinet Sally Kosgei, and gave them what appeared to be a *wosia*, the final word given to close relatives by a dying parent: "You people," he reportedly told them, "you should put your things in order because going into an election is like going to war…Anything can happen you know. We should be ready for any eventuality…"[108] It was as if Moi was preparing them for defeat.

On his way home from America, Moi also stopped over at the London hospital where Kibaki was recuperating. His remarks to his political foe that "only God knows what is in store for tomorrow"[109] were interpreted as an admission of political surrender. The visit to Kibaki, the American-based Centre for Strategic International Studies said in a report, "was seen by the media as heralding Moi's personal acknowledgement that Kibaki would be his successor."[110] The general elections were only two weeks away and Uhuru's chances were not looking good. The BBC correspondent in Nairobi was convinced too that a win by Uhuru was impossible: "Kenyatta is too young, too inexperienced and too dependent on the powerful clique who has brought Kenya to the brink of ruin"[111] to be endorsed by Kenyans, he said in one report.

## The rigging option

As KANU resigned itself to fate, one option remained—rigging. Administration officials at the local level who previously had fears of being detected canvassing for votes, now went full throttle to interfere with the process. At the Coast and in some parts of the Rift Valley, especially Marakwet district, government officials openly campaigned for the KANU, and even selected "known KANU supporters to serve as district electoral officers." Local chiefs were intimidating opposition

---

[107] Centre for Strategic International Studies, Africa Notes, No. 12, December 2002.

[108] Mwenda Njoka, Ugnet, Kenya, January 11, 2003.

[109] BBC, December 9, 2002.

[110] David Throup, CSIS Africa Notes,No. 14, p. 2, January 2003

[111] Ibid

supporters and going house to house to bribe voters with money.[112] In some cases, illiterate voters were threatened with punitive action if they voted for the opposition.

Rigging of elections has been a common feature in Kenyan poll history. From the discredited queue voting of 1988 to outright theft of votes in 1992 and in 1997, Kenya stood out as a country with one of the worst reputations in elections management. That was not the only matter of concern to Kenyans. A more serious one was the presence in the voters' register of an estimated one million names of dead individuals. The opposition feared the names could be used to rig the elections. In addition, many individuals were confirmed to be holding more than one voting card. NARC leaders petitioned ECK, which agreed to delete names of the dead, as well as the other extra entries. International, other African and Kenyan election observers in their thousands arrived to monitor the polls. With all those eyes cast on the process, KANU's plans to steal the election were rendered difficult to accomplish.

What had began as an innocuous miscalculation on Moi's part to gamble with the presidency, had now turned into a case of political myopia that was threatening to hurt the President's legacy, and Uhuru's political future. Weeks before the elections, it was axiomatic even among KANU's diehard supporters that the game was over.

While KANU struggled with diminishing options, NARC was enthralling crowds with its reform agenda. Both sides were pouring fortunes into advertising: major highways were awash with billboards, and newspapers and radio were inundated with promotional materials. Hate leaflets and perhaps millions of nasty phone messages were criss-crossing the country. As days to the polls approached, it was clear to everyone that the once formidable KANU election machine had collapsed. The hitherto KANU strongholds, including Moi's own Rift Valley region, found themselves buckling under the weight of political euphoria favouring the opposition. For the first time in the country's history, the ruling party faced an inglorious defeat. Even before the last vote was counted, Raila was calling on Uhuru to concede defeat and to facilitate a speedy transition. And, in readiness for the worst, Moi, as the Commander-in-Chief, hastened

112 Centre for Strategic International Studies, Africa Notes, No. 12, December, 2002.

to Langata Army Barracks outside Nairobi, to bid a symbolic farewell to a contingent of troops drawn from the Army, the Air Force, and the Navy, from where he exhorted the armed forces to support whoever was to assume command. That ceremony had been slated to take place during the first week after elections, but was fast-tracked after it became clear that a change of government from KANU to NARC was inevitable.

When results began to filter into tallying centres, revealing Vice President Mudavadi had lost, it was clear that KANU was in big trouble, and that the coalition was headed for a clean sweep. At the end, Kibaki got 3,647,658 or 61.3 percent, against Uhuru's 1,836,005, or 20.2 percent of the votes, thus bringing to an end almost four decades of authoritarian KANU rule. NARC won one hundred and thirty-two seats with LDP taking fifty-nine of them. The prediction of some party stalwarts that KANU would rule for one hundred years had come a cropper. In a tribally sensitive country, Kenyans had swept aside their ethnic differences and, for the first time, had put their future in the hands of an opposition candidate who just happened to be a Kikuyu. Hope was rekindled that if Luos could vote for a Kikuyu almost to a man, Kikuyu could do the same to a Luo candidate, in later elections.

As jubilation and disappointment ran through the various political parties, Moi and his close advisors went into a closed-door meeting in State House to ponder over their next course of action. There were only two options on the table: accept defeat, or hang on to power as many despotic African leaders tended to do. Some party hardliners wanted Uhuru not to concede but go to court to challenge the result. However, moderate elements felt such action would trigger violence and plunge the country into an uncertain future. Tension was high, but there was no indication that the armed forces had any interest in intervening to save the ruling party. Interestingly, Moi himself was clear that nothing more could be done to save KANU. After consultations with his confidants, he made several phone calls, including one to Uhuru's mother, Mama Ngina Kenyatta, whom he held in very high esteem.

Eventually it was agreed Uhuru should concede. Before the ECK could formally announce the results, the obvious loser appeared at a press conference at the Serena Hotel, and said he had "accepted the choice of the people, and in particular, I now concede that Mwai Kibaki will be the third President of Kenya." He blamed his defeat on the perception that KANU was not for the change Kenyans wanted. "But we take it up from where we are, and we look positively towards the future,"[113] he told the country.

## Celebration and panic

All over Kenya, except in KANU strongholds and in Uhuru's home area of Kiambu in Central Kenya, masses went into a frenzy of celebration. NARC had achieved what many had failed to do since pluralism was introduced in 1992—defeat KANU. Unsure of what was in store for them, Moi's supporters in government panicked; some deserted offices in a hurry, while others, smelling possible revenge, went into hiding. Many traders had already boarded their business premises and left for the safety of the neighbouring countries of Tanzania and Uganda, and some had even gone to Europe and North America. The normally dependable Presidential Press Service also became invisible, confused, and uncertain about its own fate. The government-owned KBC did not know how to treat the news, and its top officials went underground, leaving juniors to make crucial decisions. Officials at State House and the Office of the President, whose presence would have been required to facilitate a smooth hand over, were nowhere to be seen.

Sally Kosgey, the Head of Civil Service and Secretary to the Cabinet, and one of Moi's most loyal servants, remained among only a handful of officials who made themselves available for the transition of power. A few weeks earlier, in anticipation for a change of guard, the Attorney General, Amos Wako, had appointed a three-person committee to oversee the transition. Apart from himself and Kosgey, the other member of the committee was Chief Justice Benard Chunga. Kibaki had objected to the appointment of Moi allies, but when time came, he had no alternative but to let the team coordinate the handing-over. The military, which for days had been practicing at a local stadium for the ushering of a new regime and the new Commander-in-Chief, quietly retreated behind barrack walls, while the intelligence community, which until then had been reporting to Moi, waited patiently for the new leader to take office.

113 Mwenda Njoka, Ugnet: Kenya, January 11, 2003.

The mass confusion prevailing in government was evident to Kenyans and the international community at Uhuru Park during the swearing-in on December 30, when diplomats could not find seats, the public address system broke down, and the VIP security collapsed, allowing even street urchins to venture into the main dais. When his time came to hand over the sword of honour and to make his final speech as Head of State, Moi was diplomatic amidst insults and mounds of dirt thrown at him by the rowdy crowd: "The people of Kenya have spoken…You have elected a new President and a new Government. Over the next five years they have the responsibility of living up to the trust that you have shown in them. May they be worthy of it." There was a spattering of clapping but nothing dramatic for such a historical farewell speech.

Although government arrangements were in a state of chaos, the day was one to behold. Rainbow colours were everywhere and the crowds were in a singing, dancing mood. Kibaki, his limb still in a plaster and dressed in a designer suit, a white shirt and a colourful tie, displayed a deportment of comradeship and congeniality to his colleagues unseen before in a man known for his indifference. He was ecstatic, even in his immobile position. Even his speech, delivered in a clear, high-pitched tone exuded not doom but optimism for the future of NARC and the country. The only stinging jabs were reserved for Moi, who sat pensively, as his successor described the departing regime as corrupt and inept. His speech was sharp and poetic:

"I was woken up this morning by rays of sunlight," he said, "which had bathed my room in such brilliance that it felt completely new. I began to notice things around me in great details. It was as if the room had been given a facelift. I looked out of the window and, behold a cloudless sky. The trees danced lazily enjoying the early morning breeze. I looked far into the horizon and the beauty of what I saw around me stirred my soul. It was as if I was standing atop Mount Kenya surveying the landscape. I said to myself 'Oh, what a beautiful country!'"

But it was the current state of the nation and his plans for the future that dominated Kibaki's inaugural speech. "I believe that Government exists to serve the people and not the people to serve the Government. I believe that Government exists to chart a common path and create an enabling environment for its citizens and residents to fulfill themselves in life. Government is not supposed to be a burden on the people, it is not supposed to intrude on every aspect of life and it is not supposed to mount road-blocks in every direction we turn to in life.

"The true purpose of Government is to make laws and policies for the general good of the people, maintain law and order, provide social services, that can enhance quality of life, defend the country against internal and external aggression and generally ensure that peace and stability prevails." Saying that he was inheriting a country badly ravaged by years of misrule and ineptitude, he assured the nation that corruption will now cease to be a way of life in Kenya and that the economy "which you all know has been underperforming since the last decade," will be his priority, he said, amid wild cheers. Songs, whistles, and horns punctuated the speech, as President Benjamin Mkapa of Tanzania, Yoweri Museveni of Uganda, and Levy Mwanawasa of Zambia, looked on, and as a white-washed Moi frowned.

At the end of the ceremony, Moi left Uhuru Park a forlorn self and proceeded to State House, accompanied by only a small group of trusted associates, to collect his baggage for the last journey home. A newspaper photo of a sorrowful Sally Kosgey, shedding tears as Moi's helicopter lifted off from State House grounds for his Kabarak home in the Rift Valley, would forever remain an archival gem. Kosgey later became an MP and Minister in Kibaki's second Government.

## Kibaki celebrated

In 1974, Emilio Mwai Kibaki, then a forty-three-year old technocrat was nominated by one of America's most prestigious newsmagazines, TIME, as one among one hundred people in the world with the potential to lead. He was then the Finance Minister and at the prime of his political career. Kibaki was not a big name in the country then, but was among the first crop of intellectuals straight from institutions of higher learning expected to help move Kenya from seventy years of British rule to a truly independent nation.

That early group of technocrats was highly educated. There were people like John Michuki who had graduated in Administration and Finance from the Worcester College, Oxford, UK, who later became a powerful Minister in Kibaki's Government; Tom Mboya, a fiery trade unionist and a gifted politician; Philip Ndegwa, a Makerere University graduate, who later became a senior economic and planning adviser to the government and also Governor of the Central Bank; and several others including Matiba. Kibaki himself had graduated with a BA Honours degree at Makerere University, had joined the London School of Economics, where he was the first African student to graduate with a First Class Honours Degree, and had lectured at Makerere before returning home to found KANU in 1960. Kibaki, in those early years in government, did not display any ambitions for higher office. He was a straight-laced technocrat, just the type of person Kenya needed to propel it to greater development heights.

Although TIME magazine recognised his potential early, few Kenyans could have predicted that Kibaki—whose hobby when young was to trap moles and rodents, and who was fond of warm beer, golf, and English chequered jackets in his later years—would one day be the Kenyan President. Those who knew him from childhood say Kibaki was always aloof and liked books more than friends. He was calm and calculated when sober, but intellectually argumentative and stubborn when drunk. His political rise was meteoric from the time he joined KANU as the party's Executive Officer, to the time he served in Moi's government in various positions. He was Minister of Finance, then Vice President and Minister for Home Affairs, then Minister of Health. Spotting a bald patch on a well-rounded head crowned with pitch-black hair, Kibaki was a fair golfer. He had influential friends in the business sector, who had introduced him to the prestigious Muthaiga Golf Club, a colonial hang-out, where he mingled with rich and powerful business personalities over cold beer and expensive whisky.

The year he was nominated by TIME also saw him move his political base from Nairobi, where he was the MP for Bahati (now Makadara), to his rural constituency of Othaya. Though educated locally up to high school, Kibaki spent most of his young adult years outside Kenya, and as an MP, he appeared uneasy with life in the sprawling constituency in the capital city, with all its slums, high crime, and social problems. He was virtually a stranger to the political culture of the ethnically mixed constituency and felt his future would be better guaranteed in Othaya, an agriculturally thriving area with valleys and hills filled with tea and banana plantations and inhabited by people who spoke his language and understood his customs. While he continued to advise the party on economic matters, he served in Othaya as the KANU Branch Chairman, a post he used to build his grassroots support in the area.

Between 1969 and 1981, when he was Minister for Finance, the economy grew rapidly. The gross domestic product was close to seven percent per annum, agricultural production for export expanded, and the horticulture industry made its debut. Manufacturing grew substantially, while tourism emerged as a major foreign exchange earner—even as the country weathered the storm of global oil crises. By the time of his departure from the ministry, economic fortunes had begun to plummet due to a decline in agricultural production.

On 10 December 1991, section 2A of the Kenyan Constitution which barred pluralism—remember it was Kibaki who tabled the motion in Parliament—was repealed, and soon thereafter, Kibaki resigned from KANU and, together with others, went on to found the DP. His departure from the government and KANU to chart a course away from the party he helped nurture, shocked his friends, but proved that he had matured and was ready to leave the nest for a new, independent abode. In 1992, he contested the presidency on a DP ticket, but came third after Moi and Matiba. He tried again in 1997 but again lost to Moi. The following year, Kibaki entered Parliament as Leader of the Opposition, where he was expected to champion opposition causes, but his performance was below average as he spent more time drowning himself in alcohol than in fighting Moi. Records of parliamentary proceedings during that period give a picture of a man who was disengaged from the political realities of the day, making him a regular subject of cartoons and jokes: a fence sitter, a coward general who could not lead.

After the two demoralising defeats, it became clear to Kibaki and other oppositionists that no single party could beat KANU under Moi. The DP was a Kikuyu-dominated party with no impact outside the Central Province, making a Kibaki presidential win impossible without the support of other political parties. The party's close association with GEMA, a business-social organisation run by rich, influential Kikuyus, did not help much. The Kikuyu, Embu and Meru felt they "were under threat from the other tribes…"[114] GEMA had money but nothing else. It dominated politics in Nairobi, in the Central province, and in the Kikuyu Diaspora, but its clout was missing in the rest of the country. That is why the DP had to engage with the FORD-Kenya and the NPK to come up with the National Alliance for Change (NAC), later renamed the National Alliance Party of Kenya (NAP-K). After that, Kibaki was on the road to success.

The question about Kibaki was whether the man, who helped found KANU and spent most of his years protecting the deplorable status quo under Kenyatta and Moi, was a reformist. Several factors must be recorded. When Moi demoted him from Vice President to Minister of Health, Kibaki was too scared to complain and seemed oblivious to his humiliation.[115] And when he eventually resigned from government, he did so only after being taunted by his buddies, who also prodded him into leading the newly founded DP. It was not his idea to form DP, and Njenga Karume says so in his autobiography.[116] In 2002, Kibaki had to be coerced into running for the presidency on a NAK ticket. He had gone underground and appeared not to want to be bothered. He had to be fished out by Wamalwa and Ngilu and marched to Raila to join the Rainbow Alliance. Again, when Raila made his *Tosha* declaration at Uhuru Park, Kibaki was as surprised as any. He had no clue that he was to be nominated to the highest office in the land. He had not asked for it. It was Raila's creation.

The pattern of dithering on Kibaki's part did not end there. In 2007, when he could not decide whether or not to go for a second term, it was Lucy, his wife, who made the announcement as he stood stone-faced at a public meeting. That display of decisiveness showed Lucy as the person in charge of major decisions in Kibaki's life. Also, it was after some of his close allies threatened to leave him that he decided to announce in September 2007—only three months to general elections—that he would be contesting the presidency on the PNU ticket. He watched unconcerned as the ruling party NARC under his leadership faded into oblivion. All those were watershed events, but Kibaki was not the person to plunge head-on into the unknown. He was, as many commentators have said,

---

[114] Njenga Karume, Beyond Expectations, From Charcol to Gold, Kenway Publications, p. 158

[115] Ibid. p. 260.

[116] Ibid., p. 263.

a hands-off individual, who did not want to soil his hands. Even as politicians in his coalition government wrangled; even as the country teetered on the brink of a Constitutional crisis; even as the country was invaded by two foreigners known as the Armenian brothers; even as the *Standard* newspaper offices burnt; even as Mama Lucy threw tantrums and embarrassed the presidency; and even as violence engulfed the country after the 2007 elections, Kibaki remained unmoved. That was the way the man was always.

Reformists take risks; they endure harassment, imprisonment even death in defence of the cause. There isn't a single incident in Kibaki's long political career that point to Kibaki having put his political life on line. He was, therefore, not really a reformist. "You cannot label Kibaki a reformist," says a writer, Charles Wachira, "he is a conservative. He does not symbolise change. He relies on old and archaic power bases, notably patronage connections and ethnic support."[117]

So, TIME was right in choosing him among the one hundred people in the world with the potential to lead, but potentiality to lead is not the same as leading from the front.

---

[117] Sunday Standard, June 27, 2010.

# CHAPTER 7

## Kibaki betrays, again

The period between Kibaki's swearing-in on December 30 and the announcement of the Cabinet on January 6, 2003, was characterised by confusion, intrigues, and behind-the-scenes manoeuvres as people scrambled for positions and others struggled to take advantage of the President's poor state of health. The person at the centre of gravity as the new government assumed office at the beginning of 2003 was an old friend and school-mate of Kibaki, Matere Keriri, the President's Chief of Staff, otherwise known in Kenya as the Comptroller of State House. Keriri, a restless individual with thick lips, was an economics graduate from Makerere University like Kibaki. He was credited with crafting the NARC manifesto, and was Kibaki's campaign manager in 2002. He had been an MP but had lost his seat. He was now at the very centre of power at a most crucial moment.

Kibaki's friends from the DP days also played a significant role in shaping the new government, among them Chris Murungaru and David Mwiraria, and seasoned activist lawyer/politician, Kiraitu Murungi, all of whom later became influential ministers in Kibaki's first Government. Then there was the bunch from Muthaiga Club: politician Amos Kimunya; entrepreneur Joe Wanjui; former Catholic priest George Muhoho; and an old friend, John Michuki. Njenga Karume who founded DP with Kibaki was also an insider. There were others who, either collectively or selectively came to be known as the Mount Kenya Mafia, an ancillary of hard-core business tycoons and political wheeler-dealers. Largely, these people initially guided Kibaki in reshaping the future of the country. The only common thread running through all them was that they were all wealthy members of the Kikuyu community.

After inauguration, Kibaki did not immediately move to State House, his official residence, but operated from his private mansion in the posh northern Muthaiga suburb of Nairobi, not far from the American Ambassador's residence. Officers from the dreaded paramilitary force, the GSU, had taken up positions around the residence to ensure only vetted individuals were allowed access. His medical condition was still a matter of great public speculation, and his doctors had advised him to remain indoors and to avoid strenuous activities, but there were appointments to be made, ministers to be sworn-in, parliament to be inaugurated, and, foreign dignitaries to be received. Kibaki was not yet in his element to perform all those activities given his medical condition. In their MOU, NAK and LDP had agreed that the party *Summit,* composed of the party's top leadership would meet immediately after the inauguration to agree on appointments to the new government. The two sides had also agreed that the Cabinet would have twenty-two officials, eleven from each side.

On the evening after the inauguration, a Kibaki aide called Moody Awori, the *Summit* Chairman, and requested him to send a list of LDP officials to be appointed to the Cabinet. The LDP top brass had already met and had agreed on its officials. On the morning of the following day, the usually affable Awori arrived at the President's residence clutching a satchel of papers for his first meeting with the new Head of State, but security officers stopped him at the gate. A man of gentle mien, the septuagenarian businessman, recognised for his wide brim hats and an infectious smile, was the longest serving Assistant Minister, and had joined LDP from KANU as Moi's Government crumbled. An elected MP, Awori, who came from a famous family that stretched into the neighbouring Uganda, was now head of the top most NARC consultative body.

Then he discovered, to his surprise, that the congenial atmosphere that had existed among party officials since the campaign started had suddenly vanished. The newly appointed presidential aides had become hostile and uncooperative. After waiting in vain for what looked like hours, he gave up, left his list of proposal with a senior official, and departed crest-fallen. He reported his tribulations to the party leadership, which tried in vain to reach Kibaki. The telephone lines, which they had used for weeks to communicate with him, had been disconnected. They blamed Keriri for the showdown, but the State House official denied that he ever blocked anyone from seeing the President.

The feeling of LDP leaders was one of anger, frustration, and betrayal, but that was not all. When finally the President announced his Cabinet, LDP was shocked that out of the twenty-five ministerial positions, fifteen had gone to NAK, and only eight to LDP, with the rest to smaller partner parties. Almost immediately, hell broke loose in the nascent Coalition. LDP was outraged by the turn of events and said so publicly. It was clear now that the power sharing agreement was out of the window. Some names proposed by LDP had been left out and fresh ones had been included. Raphael Tuju, a Raila foe, and a wavering LDP MP, was appointed Minister for Information and Communication, a move that was a direct slap on the LDP leader.

On January 5, after all attempts to reach Kibaki had failed, the LDP Chairman, Joab Omino, called a meeting of newly elected party MPs. Twenty-six of them gathered at Nairobi Club to plan a reaction. At the end, the meeting issued a stinging statement, formally accusing Kibaki of dishonesty and blatant betrayal. Some members called for street protests, but that idea was shelved, and instead, Awori was asked to pursue a meeting with Kibaki by all means to get him to expand the Cabinet and appoint LDP officials who had been left out, and also to seek reassurances that there would be no more violations of the agreement. That effort was unsuccessful. Raila did not see Kibaki until the day of the swearing-in ceremony at State House on January 6. By that time, it was too late for any changes to be made. Failure by Kibaki to honour the MOU was the first indication that the road ahead was going to be bumpy for the coalition. It also underscored the clout of the Mount Kenya Mafia in the affairs of the new administration.

Nevertheless, battle lines had been drawn, heralding the beginning of internal wrangles that were to remain the hallmark of the NARC Government for all its five years. We had expected that during his first encounter with Kibaki at State House, Raila would pursue the party's hard-line position on the MOU, but he was diplomatic and only expressed hope of better relations between the two sides. He had read the public mood correctly. Kenyans made it clear that they were tired of unnecessary politicking and wanted the new government to get straight into the business of mending their fractured nation, caring less about who got what in Government. Grumbling by LDP over positions backfired as Kenyans accused it of greed and ungratefulness.

Two sets of MOUs—with slight variations—were signed between NAK and LDP but only one, drawn on the morning of October 21, 2002, was made public. The other one, signed during a private ceremony later that day was kept locked up in a lawyer's safe. The document had stipulated that the *Summit* would be convened immediately after the elections to discuss the appointment of the Cabinet and the distribution of ministerial duties; that membership to the Cabinet would be determined on a fifty/fifty power sharing formula; that the NAK would be allocated one position of Vice President and two positions of Second and Third Deputy Prime Ministers; and that LDP would get the second position of Vice President, the Premiership, the First Deputy Premiership, and one position of Senior Coordinating Minister. Most of those positions were to await either a Constitutional amendment, or a new Constitution to be enacted. But after winning the elections, Kibaki trashed the document. As a result, the alliance, hailed by Kenyans as the most promising change-vehicle in recent history, had virtually collapsed even before it had started work.

Two days after announcing his government, Kibaki hosted a luncheon at State House for volunteers who had contributed their time and money to the NARC victory. Flanked by Vice President Wamalwa, Raila, and the Chairman of Kibaki's *Council of Elders*, Joe Wanjui, the President went into great pain to explain his government's plans against corruption. He made it clear that in the process of dealing with the vice some people would get bruised. "It is not possible," he said "to fight corruption without some people having to be declared unneeded, redundant and actually dangerous to the nation." It was, undoubtedly, an intimidating statement demonstrating the new regime's commitment against an evil that, for over two decades, had eluded the Moi government.

But as it would be seen in this book later, the commitment towards a sleaze free nation was easier said than done. In Kenya, corruption had been described variously as a 'dragon', a 'monster' that involved both the big and the small fish; the highest in government and the lowest in society. Those of us who had expected Kibaki to mention the prevailing coalition problems were disappointed because, at that function, he avoided the subject altogether. Raila also played it safe and made no remarks that could be construed as belligerent, and instead, talked about the positive plans the government had in store for Kenyans.

To underscore his determination in fighting corruption, Kibaki almost immediately appointed John Githongo, a youthful, heavy-set reformer to take over the task of spearheading the campaign against sleaze. The bespectacled forty-three-year old former journalist had worked with the Kenya chapter of Transparency International, where his father was one of its founders, and had made a mark as an independent human rights crusader. To the majority of Kenyans, however, he was relatively unknown, even though his weekly column in the *East African*, an up-market Kenyan publication owned by the *Nation* Group was widely read. Githongo's appointment was received well by Kenyans, and hailed by the international community as a fresh dawn in the fight against graft.

To demonstrate his seriousness in fulfilling his election pledges, Kibaki also announced compulsory free primary education for all Kenyans. Within weeks, more than one million children who had been shut out of school had enrolled in classrooms all over the country. Makeshift classrooms were built to take in the overflow, while many children in remote areas of the country had to do with tree shades as classrooms. The generally acceptable teacher-to-pupils ratio of thirty to one reached a new high of up to one hundred pupils per teacher. Although educators complained of a possible decline in the quality of education as a result of over-crowding and fewer teachers,[118] the government was not fazed. The programme endeared Kenyans to the new administration but that did not stop the LDP from continuing with its protests.

On February 18, with the aid of a walking stick, Kibaki shuffled into the National Assembly to open the first session of the Ninth Parliament. That was the first time since the accident that Kenyans were seeing Kibaki walking on his two feet. All eyes were on him to see how he walked, how he reacted to the MPs, and even how he sat on his grand chair next to the Speaker. He was pale and appeared in pain as he struggled to take his position, his broad shoulders stooped and his limbs trembled. The

---

[118] Najum Mushtaq, IPS, October 16, 2008.

Parliament's opening ceremony had been delayed for weeks due to his ill health, and the country was anxious for normal legislative activities to resume. As care free LDP MPs sat on the government side, Kibaki returned to his favourite subject of corruption, saying in a quivering voice that his government had already gazetted legislation to establish a code of conduct for public officials to govern public procurement and strengthen audit systems. He also announced that it had published legislation to establish an Anti-Corruption Commission with powers to investigate and prosecute cases of corruption.

While NAK MPs stamped their feet in joy when Kibaki talked of his determination to complete the Constitutional review process and to reverse "the current negative economic trends," LDP MPs remained doggedly quiet in their seats, not sure whether to believe him or not. Tension was evident in the Chamber. LDP had made it clear that in view of the MOU violation, it would make life difficult for the government in Parliament.

The first major showdown came the following month in March 2003, when, with the support of KANU, LDP galvanized support and passed a motion by nominated MP Aloo Aringo authorising the establishment of a Budget Office. The objective of the motion was to entrench Parliament's oversight role in the preparation, management, and allocation of the budget, and to provide MPs with technical expertise to analyse the budget and to have meaningful control over the process.[119] Legislators knew that the motion, which the government opposed, would not be implemented, but the stage had been set for many more parliamentary upsets that were to significantly embarrass Kibaki and his government. The previous year under Moi, Aringo had proposed a similar motion, but it was defeated on arguments by the government that the creation of such an office would go against the principle of separation of powers between Parliament and the Executive.

Four months later, thinking the situation had changed for the better, the government sent to Parliament the Suppression of Terrorism Bill for debate. The bill was meant to give sweeping powers to the government to conduct searches and detain people suspected of involvement in terrorism

[119] Collins Odote; Too Near Yet Too Far: The State of Constitutional Development in Kenya, 2002.

activities. It was to make it a criminal offence to collect, make, or transmit e-mail or use any other telephone method likely to be useful to a person committing or preparing to commit an act of terrorism. The government would also have powers to confiscate property and detain suspects indefinitely. In addition, anyone found with cash exceeding ten thousand US dollars without valid reason was to be forced to surrender the money on suspicion that it was meant for terrorism.

Sections of Kenyans heavily criticized the bill as they believed it was directed at the Moslem community. Non-governmental groups lobbied extensively to have it thrown out. Amnesty International described it as vague, because of its broad definition of terrorism, while others claimed it was a replica of the 2001 anti-terrorism Patriotic Act[120] of the US, a claim the American government refuted. At the time, Washington was being criticised for allegedly deploying FBI agents to Moslem-dominated areas of Kenya ostensibly to look for terrorists. There were claims of selective raids and arbitrary arrests of suspected terrorists, with some of them being sent off to foreign detention centres while the Kenya government looked the other way. The LDP played a major role in putting pressure to have the bill dropped.

Following intense criticism, the bill was withdrawn, and the government undertook to review it. When it eventually found its way back to Parliament three years later in 2006, the Committee on Administration and Legal Affairs, which was required to initially debate it, said it would only engage it after the US took full responsibility and compensated families of victims of the 1998 terrorist attack at the American Embassy in Nairobi, something Washington had refused to do. The US Ambassador to Kenya, Michael Rannenberger denied accusations that it was pushing Kenya to enact the bill. He claimed his government had evidence that Kenya was among forty countries in the world about to be attacked by terrorists. The Parliamentary Committee, on the other hand, warned that

---

[120] The Patriotic Act was signed into law on October 26, 2001, and allows the American Government to search telephones, e-mail communication, financial and medical records, among others; regulates financial transactions, especially involving foreign individuals and entities; and gives the Government powers to detain and deport immigrants suspected to have terrorism links.

the bill threatened to tear apart the nation's fabric, and offered a fertile ground for inter-religious animosity.

The failure of the government to push through the controversial bill was a major victory for LDP, which now felt confident enough to challenge the government on other legislative matters. So, when the Forest Bill (Kenya) 2004, came along, LDP was there to challenge it. The Front Bench gazed in shock as Parliament rejected the legislation meant to rationalize the utilisation of forest resources; essentially protecting forests from illegal loggers. There was nothing substantially wrong with the bill, but its rejection by a combined force of LDP, FORD-Kenya, and KANU legislators, was meant to hit back at the government's arrogance. It was not until Kalonzo, an LDP Member, became the Minister for Environment and Natural Resources that the bill was brought back to Parliament, passed, and finally endorsed by the President in November 2005. With the passing of the legislation, Kenya was now able to fight off illegal loggers and protect its forests whose cover had shrunk from ten percent at independence to one point seven percent.[121]

## Who is in charge?

For the most part of the first two years, Kibaki's poor health prevented him from taking complete charge of the day-to-day activities of the government, allowing his amorphous *Council of Elders*, or the so-called Mount Kenya Mafia, to manipulate policy matters, a development that piqued Coalition partners. The *Summit*, which had been expected to play a leading role in directing government programmes, was completely sidelined. In fact, the *Summit* never met during the first six months of the NARC government. It was difficult to figure out who was actually running the country. Was it the ailing Kibaki, or his powerful wife, Lucy? How deep was the influence of the Mount Kenya Mafia? Was the Vice President in the loop or was he an innocent bystander?

Perhaps a hint of who may have been in charge of the government during that delicate period could be found in comments made years later by the then forceful Minister for Internal Security, Chris Murungaru, who

121 AFP, August 17, 2005.

allegedly told a *Nation* reporter that, "he was the de facto Prime Minister in 2003 when the President suffered a stroke."[122] However, I want to believe that a cabal of people within the very inner circle, among them Keriri, Strategic Advisor Stanley Murage, and the President's Personal Assistant, Alfred Getonga, was responsible for the functions of the Administration alongside the Mt. Kenya Mafia. Questions about who actually was running the government were relevant because journalists who had covered Kibaki before and after the accident said they had seen two Kibakis: the early Kibaki, engaged, focused, (and) acute; and the later Kibaki, vague, distracted, and struggling to maintain a coherent chain of thought.[123]

That was the time when foreign envoys described Kenya as a new boat sailing without a functional captain. Edward Clay, the British High Commissioner, who had keenly observed Kibaki as he struggled to recuperate, said Kibaki "had a genuine problem carrying on a train of thought from one meeting to another, particularly if there wasn't a witness. Some days were better than others." He added that he didn't think Kibaki was himself again until early 2004.[124] The Head of State was sometimes so disoriented that he could not remember names of his family members, never mind those of his Cabinet. Rumours were that he had suffered a stroke that was responsible for his slurred speech. On several occasions at public functions, he was unable to read his prepared speeches, and often mixed pages to the great embarrassment of his listeners. Many believed it was at that time of his incapacitation that high-level corruption took root in the new administration. Githongo, Kibaki's corruption adviser, was convinced things were not right in the government during the first six months following Kibaki's hospitalisation. He talked of a "lacuna during which all sorts of underhand activity had flourished uncontrolled."[125]

His health problems notwithstanding, Kibaki lumbered on, avoiding overseas trips, but participating as much as possible in the simple day-to-day activities. He officiated at National Days celebrations, and opened and closed private sector meetings. While Raila continued to accuse Kibaki of

---

122 Emeka-Mayaka Gekera, Nation, January 5, 2010.

123 Michela Wrong, It's Our Turn to Eat: The Story of a Kenyan Whistle-Blower, HarperCollins, p. 71.

124 Daily Nation, August 6, 2007.

125 Michela Wrong, It's Our Turn to Eat: The Story of a Kenyan Whistle-Blower, HarperCollins, p. 181.

treachery and dishonesty for reneging on the power sharing agreement, Kibaki went about business as if nothing had happened. Short of staging street demonstrations which the party had disapproved, LDP used every available platform to attack Kibaki, prompting Kibaki's trouble-shooters, Murungaru, Mwiraria, and Murungi to return fire, dismissing Raila's demands as selfish and provocative.

## In comes Wamalwa

From a political point of view, Kenyans now looked to Vice President Wamalwa to provide political guidance and maintain harmony in the tenuous Coalition arrangement. Wamalwa was a patient listener and an independent thinker. Wamalwa, with curious eyes and a soft engaging voice, had worked with the maverick Masinde Muliro of KADU and had deputised for Odinga in FORD-Kenya in the early nineties. Naturally, LDP viewed the Vice President as the best-placed person to pacify NAK hard-liners opposed to rapprochement with LDP. Moreover, he was a Luhya, the Bantu community in Western Kenya, known for its tolerance and humility.

So, when the party *Summit* resolved to hold a two-day retreat at Mt. Kenya Safari Club on April 3 and 4, 2003, to discuss the political impasse in the Coalition and that Wamalwa was to lead it, LDP was more than happy to attend. In total, one hundred and thirty MPs showed up at the resort on the foothills of Mount Kenya amidst an atmosphere of tension and mistrust. When LDP MPs assembled on the morning of the meeting to strategise on the pending contentious issues—including the status of the MOU and the Constitutional review process, which had remained in abeyance despite a plethora of promises by Kibaki to fast-track it—it was clear the retreat was going to be stormy.

The Constitutional issue was crucial because it was through that law that the post of the Prime Minister would be established as per the MOU. Raila was anxiously waiting on the wings to take up that position. Also, LDP felt the peremptory manner in which Kibaki had handled its partner was against the spirit of the Coalition and wanted its overall relationship with NAK reviewed. Some Members suggested a walkout if NAK refused to honour the MOU, but moderate legislators counselled patience. The consultations were heated, and it was not until Raila arrived late that morning that tempers were temporarily calmed. Raila felt LDP had not exhausted all available options to engage in protests and suggested that members should wait to see how the plenary progressed before making any hasty decisions.

When the retreat finally opened two hours late, Wamalwa delivered his most inspiring speech so far as Kibaki's deputy. He talked about Raila in exalting language, using terms like "*Raila-phobia*" and "*Raila-mania*," to describe how NAK and LDP supporters differently perceived Raila. "My brother Raila excites such passion as those who love him love him into death and those who do not are always suspicious of his intentions," he said, amidst a deafening applause. Then in a change of tone, he implored leaders to leave behind their acrimony and instead soldier on for Kenya's sake: "I am beginning to feel some disquiet among the Kenyan people. I am beginning to feel that power may be getting into our heads and subverting our noble goals. I am beginning to feel that we may run the danger of losing our main aim." It was a classic speech delivered with decorum and authority.

Raila, on the other side, had pacified his troops adequately enough to keep them relatively controlled. He narrated the journey Kenya had gone through in its quest for freedom, democracy, and equality, and said that the journey was not complete. "As leaders we cannot afford to fail," he said, "but we must also be truthful to each other. This Coalition is based on trust and that trust must be honoured by all," amid rounds of clapping.

With their intervention, the Vice President and Raila had saved the day. The bitter inter-party emotions that had existed prior to the meeting, cautiously subsided, and an amiable cloud of harmony and tolerance descended, permitting the meeting to continue with few hitches. LDP felt more encouraged about the future of the Coalition when the retreat endorsed a key resolution of reaffirmation from NAK to establish the position of Prime Minister through changes to be made at the National Constitutional Conference (NCC) scheduled to start soon thereafter. Although not specifically stated in the *Nanyuki Accord*, the NCC was also to be asked to create the other positions, namely, the two deputy Vice Presidents and the two Deputy Prime Ministers, in line with the MOU. NAK also promised LDP a new beginning in the conduct of Coalition matters, with assurances that any future appointments in government would be made through consultations.

There was another matter of contention in the NAK/LDP relationship; the dissolution of parties. It was NAK's view that partner parties should disband to form one monolithic party. That matter was at the centre of discussions during a second meeting at Mt. Kenya Safari Club, a year later. By that time, Wamalwa had died and Awori had been appointed in his place. Other than NAK, all the other partners opposed the proposal of disbandment and rooted for NARC to remain a Coalition of parties. The second meeting, chaired by Awori, endorsed eleven resolutions and agreed to form an eight-member committee to look into the party constitution and to make recommendations on the matter. LDP felt the idea of dissolution was part of a conspiracy to end the growing influence of leaders seen to be a threat to Kibaki. There was also worry that with KANU's national support dwindling fast, the transformation of NARC into a mega party could threaten democracy and return the country to a one-party state.

As relative truce reigned, Kibaki on April 9 chose an unfamiliar method of talking to his people. He released a fifteen-minute radio and television message to reassure Kenyans of his willingness to meet his side of the bargain in the Coalition arrangement. The occasion was to mark the first one hundred days of his Administration. "I say, lay your fears to rest…We have made promises and are in the process of keeping them. Where there are delays, these are sincere. We are not a Government that makes promises it does not intend to keep." The message was particularly reassuring to LDP and raised hopes of a more harmonious co-existence between the two fighting sides.

A week later, the President invited all NARC MPs for a delectable lunch at State House to try to promote a common front both in and outside Parliament, and to take stock of the recommendations of the Nanyuki retreat. Representatives from fourteen affiliate parties attended the sumptuous five-course meal. No longer relying on a cane, a more confident Kibaki attempted to persuade MPs on the need to disband all affiliate parties by March 2005 to give way to one united NARC. Kibaki also stood firm by the Nanyuki resolutions to have the membership of the *Summit* increased. The matter had been raised earlier but had generated mixed reaction. He further told LDP to stop grumbling over government positions and instead to concentrate on working, reassuring LDP that the positions they wanted would be regularized through Constitutional amendments. "Getting these jobs," he said, "is like playing a card game, some win and others loose,"[126] He further told the MPs to put the interest of the public ahead of their own personal desires. Surprisingly, and quite unlike him, Raila only had flattering words, describing the lunch invitation as "historic and a great pleasure and honour. You took over power in a wheelchair," he told Kibaki, "and you have ruled us well so far. The MPs came here from Mount Kenya retreat more united and focused."[127] But was it really that cosy in the Coalition?" And, was Kibaki really that sincere?

Political disagreements were not the only challenges facing Kibaki in his first term in office. His government had been too busy fighting itself to pay any attention to growing sleaze in government, compelling people to conclude that old corruption was fighting back! There were also other urgent problems, such as drug and human trafficking, drought, and hunger, as well as judiciary and police reforms. The economy was not doing well, either. Nairobi's reputation as a gangster town remained a challenge to law enforcement agencies, as thugs harassed, raped, and killed innocent civilians. Carjacking and abductions were a nightmare to motorists, and heists were a real threat to business establishments.

Moreso, Kenyans were disappointed that a new Constitution had not been enacted. The process that had begun as Moi departed was marooned by unending discussions over procedures and conduct. Kibaki, who had been expected to fast track reform measures, had become a victim of political shenanigans. A commentator[128] lambasted Kibaki for portraying himself as an 'everyone's technocrat' to capture the image of Kenyans, but that he had failed to live by the expectations of the people. "In 2003, the country was rated by international agencies as one of the most optimistic nations, but by 2005, corruption had reached such levels that some people were saying they had been 'conned.'"[129]

---

126 Robert Orlale, Nation, April 15, 2003.

127 Ibid.

128 Samuel Sanders, Los Angeles Times, May 25, 2005.

129 Ibid.

Also, Kibaki's first term was hit by a series of mishaps that left many wondering whether or not the NARC Government had been jinxed. Within weeks of the Cabinet inauguration, and before the euphoria of victory dissipated, a freak plane crash in the west of the country left the Labour Minister, Ahmad Mohamed Khalif dead and several other government officials injured. Weeks later, another minister in the office of the President, Geoffrey Parpai, died. Another MP, David Mutiso, was swept by floods as he tried to cross a river. As if that was not enough, on August 23, Wamalwa, who had served Kibaki faithfully as his principal assistant, succumbed to unspecified complications in a London hospital; leaving behind a chaotic Coalition he had helped form and nurture. The loss of the officials in quick succession was a big personal blow to Kibaki, since most of them were in his inner circle. During the funeral of his dependable deputy, Kibaki could not restrain tears from rolling down his cheeks.[130] During the first term, another cabinet minister, Karisa Maitha, collapsed and died while on an overseas trip.

## Disbandment of parties

As the country prepared to end the year, Kibaki, on a tour of the coast, made a rather startling declaration that, once again, rattled the relative harmony in the ruling Coalition. He revisited the issue of an all-powerful NARC, and announced that all parties affiliated to NARC would henceforth be rendered "obsolete," a declaration meant to end the life of partner parties and transform NARC into a monolithic party with one leader, one manifesto, and one ideology. The President also called for party polls to elect branch officials and a single national leadership team.

The announcement caused an immediate uproar as affiliate parties threatened to defy the President and delink their parties from NARC if the proposal was implemented. To underscore the seriousness of the announcement, legal experts warned that Kibaki had no statutory powers to take such an arbitrary action. Only the Registrar of Societies had such powers, they said, and only within limits allowed by the Constitution. The

---

130 More officials including two Assistant Ministers, Mirugi Kariuki and Titus Ngoyoni, and four MPs, among them former Minister Bonaya Godana, were killed in a airplane crash in Northern Kenya in April 2006.

proposal was, however, supported by a number of party leaders inside and outside the Cabinet, who told legislators opposed to the idea to toe the line or resign and seek fresh mandate. The issues of disbandment, holding of branch elections and the expansion of the *Summit* became so contentious that the *Summit* had to take them up.

On beefing up the membership of the *Summit* from eight to sixteen, LDP felt the expansion would advantage the NAK and undermine their interests. Already LDP was in the minority in the *Summit* since Awori, Makwere, and Saitoti, who were initially LDP registered members, had crossed over to Kibaki's side and were no longer subscribing to the party. In fact, during a meeting of its top leaders, LDP resolved to terminate Makwere's membership, settling on me to replace him in the *Summit*. But Makwere was adamant. At Awori's palatial residence in the leafy Lavington suburb where the *Summit* meeting took place, both Makwere and I showed up. The showdown almost derailed the meeting and ended only after Awori—with the concurrence of the LDP delegation—requested that I withdraw to another room for the duration of the meeting, pending further consultations. In the LDP's view, my membership in the *Summit* remained valid even though the expansion initiative never materialised due to NARC's internal wrangles and opprobrium. Nevertheless, it took considerable diplomatic skills on the part of Awori to bring order at the parley, which was rocked by a bitter confrontation between Makwere and Raila over the former's continued claim as an LDP representative.

That same day, seeing that the Coalition was on the brink of near disintegration, LDP called a press conference to demand the appointment of an arbitration committee to resolve the wrangles. It invoked a section in the party Constitution that allowed intervention by Catholic, Anglican, and Moslem leaders in case of irreconcilable differences. I was one of two officials—the other was Kamotho—who were sent to the Nairobi Diocese to ask for the participation of the Catholic Church in the arbitration initiative, and the response was positive. Officials were also sent to other denominations. However, NAK dismissed it as unnecessary and refused to cooperate, rendering the arbitration process untenable.

As if that was not enough, some elements in NAK began an exercise that threatened further disharmony in the party. During a meeting south of Mombasa, two NAK Ministers, Karisa Maitha and Chirau Ali

Makwere, launched a controversial registration exercise intended to recruit individual members into NARC in violation of the Nanyuki agreement. That exercise, however, became a talking point for days, not because of the number of members it managed to recruit—only a handful—but by the number of bulls that were slaughtered and the amount of rice that was prepared to entice people into attending the event. The arbitrary action of the two officials violated the spirit of cooperation, and went against the party resolution that no registration of any kind—either for individual or corporate members—would commence until the eight-member committee appointed at Nanyuki to resolve the matter finished its work.

Nevertheless, the dire-hard NAK officials vowed to continue with the registration exercise. Soon thereafter, we at the LDP called a press conference at Parliament Buildings to urge NAK to stop the exercise. We also suggested that an emergency meeting of the eight-person committee be convened to have the offending clause in the party Constitution amended to reflect the feeling of affiliate parties, which favoured corporate membership. NAK ignored the protest.

All along, LDP was looking at different ways on how to engage the physically restricted Kibaki over the matter of the broken MOU. There was talk of invoking Chapter 2, 12 (1) of the Constitution to declare Kibaki unfit to lead for "reasons of physical or mental infirmity." But for such a provision to succeed, the Cabinet would have to pass a resolution to be taken to the Chief Justice, who would then have to appoint a tribunal to rule on the health of the President. In a Cabinet dominated by Kibaki cronies, any thought that such a resolution could pass was far-fetched. And even if it did, there was no reason to believe that the Chief Justice, also a presidential appointee, would be willing to form a medical tribunal to investigate his own boss. The option of a no-confidence vote against the President was also fraught with risks. The Constitution was clear that removal of the President must automatically be accompanied by the dissolution of Parliament. No MP wanted to go home that early, meaning that such a motion—if brought before Parliament—would not get the requisite two-thirds majority to pass.

The only option left, therefore, was to try to amend the Constitution to make it possible for Kibaki to singularly go home without affecting lawmakers. Authored by the never-say-die nominated MP Oloo Aringo,

The Constitution of Kenya (Amendment) (No. 3) Bill was to come up with convincing reasons to justify Kibaki's early retirement. The proposed bill was also meant to strip him of powers of determining the calendar of the House, as well as powers to prorogue, summon, and dissolve Parliament. It was suggested that some of those powers would go to the PSC. The bill further wanted the Speaker, and not the Vice President, to take over temporarily in case the President was incapacitated.

The proposed bill opened a new opportunity for conflict between LDP, which supported the proposed bill, and NAK which vowed to oppose it. Impeachment of a President in any country is a grave matter. In Kenya, however, the incessant internal wrangling provided fodder for such action. The inner thinking in LDP was that although the country could not afford another election less than two years down the line, the motion would serve as a warning that continued violation of the MOU would have consequences. LDP, therefore, considered the impeachment warning an effective tool to arm-twist the President into toeing the line. But like in 2000, when Aringo first introduced the bill during the Moi era, the motion faced hurdles in the House Business Committee, the body that sets the diary for the House. Consequently, it collapsed mid-way and never reached the floor of the House.

# CHAPTER 8

## Should Moi be prosecuted?

As Moi flew out in a military chopper from the State House grounds in Nairobi for the last journey home, the new Kibaki Administration began to ponder over what to do with the departing President and the long list of corruption scandals that had taken place during his twenty-four-year watch. Under Moi, corruption and impunity had become a way of life. There were mega scandals, among them the Goldenberg and Anglo-Leasing, which consumed millions of shillings of public money through questionable dealings and faulty procurement schemes.

Then, there were others, relatively smaller ones, but with a huge economic impact, such as the Mahindra jeeps saga in the mid 1990s, in which the government imported low-standard vehicles for police use at a price six times more than what the government would have spent if it had bought them through local dealerships. There was also the irregular purchase of boilers in which the government spent 3 million US dollars. Under an agreement with a local supplier, the boilers were to be sourced from the US, but for unexplained reasons, they were bought from India. Then there was the planned construction of NEXUS, a highly secret communication centre intended for use by the military. More than 2.5 billion shillings were paid to a phantom Dutch company for the construction of the facility outside Nairobi. The tendering process was circumvented and the company, Nedermar Bv Technologies, could not be traced. The list of scandals was long.

Of all of them, however, the Goldenberg scandal was the one that shattered the conscience of Kenyans. In 1990, when the lucrative tourism industry had virtually collapsed due to general insecurity, and the government had embarked on economic reforms, Moi came up with the idea of an export compensation scheme to boost foreign exchange coffers. The scheme allowed investors who deposited American dollars with the Central Bank of Kenya to be rewarded with an equivalent of the money in local currency plus twenty percent of the total deposit.

A little known Kenya Asian businessman by the name of Kamlesh Pattni jumped at the opportunity and registered a gold and diamond export company, the Goldenberg International Ltd (GIL), even though Kenya did not mine the two commodities. Government officials, allegedly at Pattni's request, hiked the compensation ratio by another fifteen percent, meaning that GIL was to receive a whooping thirty-five percent for every dollar it deposited with the government. By 1993, when the scandal was exposed, the country had lost an estimated 600 million US dollars, equivalent to ten percent of the GDP. Goldenberg, said one Kenyan economist, "was a high level conspiracy…by senior officials of the Moi Administration together with local and international wheeler-dealers who ostensibly capitalised on the government's desperation for foreign exchange, and through greed of Moi's cronies."[131]

The scandal, which stretched from 1991 to 1993, created so much heat from Kenyans and donors that Kibaki, barely weeks in office, had to appoint a commission to investigate how such colossal sums of money were paid out from the Central Bank and to find who the principal players were. Later, he extended the commission's mandate to include seizure of assets that were acquired using Goldenberg money. The commission was headed by a Court of Appeal Judge, Samuel Bosire, and took two years of public hearings and more than one hundred witnesses before recommending that several officials, among them former Vice President George Saitoti, should face criminal charges and that Moi himself should be investigated further for his alleged role in the scandal. Kibaki had to step in because "Moi and KANU were not only reluctant to have the scam investigated, but they

---

131 Peter Warutere, Occassional Paper No. 117, September 2005.

also interfered with the machinery of justice to shield the perpetrators of the economic crime from being prosecuted and convicted."[132]

The Bosire commission found that four hundred and eighty-seven companies had been involved in Goldenberg transactions and a total of 158.3 million shillings paid to GIL alone. During one of a series of cases that dogged Pattni, the Asian businessman alleged that he had given 22 million shillings to silence Oginga and another senior opposition politician. Both of them denied the allegation. It took almost ten years from the time the scandal was discovered to the time Pattni and his associates were indicted for defrauding the government. The delay, according to the Bosire Commission, was caused by political interference by the ruling KANU, which had arranged for guards from the dreaded GSU to provide round the clock security for Pattni and thus, prevented service of summons. It was only after the intervention of the Central Bank of Kenya that the guards were withdrawn. Even then, the Attorney General refused to press charges, prompting the Law Society of Kenya to move to court.

Moi was alleged to have played a part in the scandal. When they were taken to court to answer charges related to the gold scheme, two senior government officials, Prof. Philip Mbithi and Wilfred Koinange, implicated him. Said Koinange to the Commission: "I telephoned the President and told him I had been informed by Professor Mbithi that I should pay out all the amount outstanding to Goldenberg International, and the President said yes, (and that he had already)… spoken to Prof. Mbithi." Koinange told the court that he was instructed by Moi to organise payment of 76 million US dollars to GIL. However, Moi, through his lawyer, Mutula Kilonzo, denied involvement, even arguing that the Bosire Commission had cleared him. "He may have made mistakes. He may have led his Minister of Finance to mismanage the economy. I am not aware of any law he broke, and Judge Bosire would have said so if he found it."[133] Moi refused to take blame and instead faulted his Ministers whom he held responsible. "…money cannot leave the Treasury without someone authorising the transaction. Those whose signatures are on the documents have no choice but to explain to Kenyans," he fumed[134] It was a typical

---

132 Ibid.

133 Guardian News & Media, March 2, 2006.

134 Standard Online, February 10, 2009.

Kenyan blame game where the top blames the bottom and the bottom blames the top. Wouldn't it have been easier for Moi to take responsibility for the mess instead of passing the buck? The way Kenyans do business, the Treasury could not have cleared transactions of such magnitude without Moi's knowledge.

But that was not all that dogged Moi's administration. In September 2007, a damning report on corruption during his era, released by Kroll Risk Consultancy of the United Kingdom, claimed 2 billion US dollars in Kenyan public funds had been stolen through "shell companies, secret trusts and front men." The document further claimed that the money was used to buy properties in England, the US, South Africa, and Australia.[135] Although it was reported that the report was prepared on the request of the Kenya Government, Nairobi officials immediately dismissed it as a political gimmick that could not hold in court.

The extent of corruption in Kenya during Moi's time featured at the Africa Presidential Round-Table in Johannesburg in 2009, two years after he had left office. The Roundtable is a gathering of former African leaders who meet yearly under the sponsorship of educational and other non-governmental organisations to discuss African-related issues. At the Johannesburg conference, African leaders were put on the carpet to explain their role in graft. For the record, this is the verbatim account of Moi's brief interview on the subject:

*Q. Mr. Moi, corruption in Kenya, any regrets? (The audience applauds but also chuckles when Moi pretends not to have heard the question, asking it to be repeated).*

*A. Of course, corruption is a deadly thing that has destroyed many nations.*[136]

He went on to say that the fight against corruption should continue. Moi's inartful and vague reaction to that direct question underscores the dilemma facing leaders when under public scrutiny over matters related to abuse of power. Taken by surprise, the Kenyan leader had no answer to a basic question that required no more than a yes or a no. But through a

[135] London Telegraph, September 1, 2007.

[136] Bate Felix, IPS, April 23, 2006.

thoughtless answer, he allowed himself to become an object of mirth before a distinguished panel of imminent people who must have left convinced of his culpability. Corruption is not just "deadly"—because it takes away food from the mouths of babies and the poor—but it is evil in its very nature because it promotes egocentrism and fuels impunity.

## Other evils

During Moi's rule, several assassinations of prominent figures took place and remained unsolved as he departed State House: Ouko's disappearance and murder was the most prominent, but there were also the mysterious deaths of some of his most virulent critics, among them Bishop Alexander Muge who perished in a suspicious road accident after issuing a scathing attack on the government. He had declared that the Church had a moral obligation to "protest when God-given rights and liberties are violated."[137] For that he died gruesomely. Another victim was Catholic priest John Kaiser, who was shot in the back soon after offering evidence before the Akiwumi Commission on land clashes that implicated senior government officials. Here was a white priest who had worked in some of the country's most difficult dioceses for twenty years, and who had spent years agitating for land rights for marginalised communities, eliminated for resisting eviction of internally displaced persons from a refugee camp in Ngong, outside Nairobi. Earlier, when the priest had complained about mistreatment of the displaced people, he was brutally beaten, then arrested by security forces.

Moi also stood accused for the Wagalla massacre in Wajir's northern Kenya, where government agents killed dozens of people in 1984 following feuds between the Degodia and Ajuran clans. Military personnel allegedly rounded up Degodia villagers, put them behind a chain link at the local airstrip, and kept them in hunger and neglect for days. When some of them tried to escape, soldiers allegedly opened fire, killing dozens of them. The government eventually admitted fifty-seven people had been killed, although villagers put the number at almost three times that.

---

137 Korwa G. Adar and Isaac M. Munyae, Human Rights Abuse in Kenya under Daniel Arap Moi, 1978–2001, African Studies Quarterly.

Moi was most incensed by political critics. By 1986, more than one hundred people said to belong to foreign-based rebel movements including *Mwakenya* and the *February Eighteenth Movement*, as well as local politicians and civil society officials had been rounded up. Mwakenya was formed in 1986 by exiled Kenyans abroad, while the FEM and FERA began operations in Uganda in 1997. Religious organisations, which attempted to fill the vacuum left behind by fleeing and detained political activists were not spared either. Other members of the clergy, among them Bishop Timothy Njoya, were mercilessly assaulted in an attempt to silence them.

But that was not all. Under Moi, dozens of Kikuyus occupying senior positions in government were sacked and replaced with mainly Kalenjin technocrats. Throughout Kenyatta's rule as we saw earlier, Kikuyus enjoyed preferential treatment in appointments, but when Moi took power, the whole civil service was turned upside down. That does not absolve Kenyatta from blame. Any form of discrimination, including ethnic cleansing, should be condemned. This time round, however, the situation was far more serious. The *Kalenjinisation* of the civil service was so rampant that even tea girls in government offices were brought in from the Rift Valley, in the pretext that that region was marginalised during the first regime.

To please Moi, many corporations and multinational companies also recruited Kalenjins to senior positions as managers and directors, as a way of currying favour with the President. The usually reticent people of the valley suddenly gained confidence and began to trade vigorously to gain economic power, which had eluded them even with Moi as Vice President. They invested in banks, insurance, farming, manufacturing, and the media. Along with genuine trading, came shady deals. Some civil servants took government money and invested it in shady financial institutions that soon collapsed. In one such financial institution, the Euro Bank, an estimated 14 million US dollars mysteriously vanished leading to the bank's collapse in 2003. Several other banks went under.

The level of corruption was so high that in 1993, the European Union (EU) withdrew funding for the proposed Turkwell George hydroelectric plant in Moi's home region of Rift Valley, alleging that the project was fraught with sleaze. An agreement signed between the Kenyan Government, the French Government, and a consortium of banks on one hand, and a contractor, Spie Batignolles, on the other, was so tainted that the EU commissioned a study, which returned a guilty verdict on Kenya. "When Kenyan politicians and top civil servants form an alliance with foreigners to take billions in hard currency abroad while knowing that the country is dying of lack of foreign exchange for the importation of drugs and other essentials, that is outright war against one's own country and people," said a report by Mr. A. Katz.[138] In his book, *Africa: Dispatches from a Fragile Continent*, Bill Harden, a media correspondent formerly based in Nairobi, wrote that corrupt officials took home twenty seven million US dollars of the estimated cost of the dam of two-hundred and-seventy million US dollars. Still, in Moi's home area, the government injected eighty-four million US dollars of public funds into the construction of an airport in the farming town of Eldoret, even after the World Bank and other donors had warned that the project made no economic sense. It remained a white-elephant for years.

## A Good Start

Moi's rule began reasonably well when he took over the government in 1977. His first major act was to release all the twenty political inmates in detention camps. He followed that with a strong declaration of commitment to deal with tribalism, corruption, and smuggling of goods across borders. To demonstrate his resolve to clean up government, he fired several top government officials, among them the Police Commissioner, Bernard Hinga, for alleged dereliction of duty. Unlike Kenyatta who loved the company of close associates he had come to know during his long stay abroad, Moi opened up State House to all manner of people. It became a place where important and nondescript KANU officials went for tea and handouts. Moi was an extremely generous individual and dished out money freely, and had no qualms about sharing meals with whoever happened to be at State House during meal times. It was during those private meetings that politicians took the liberty to request for favours, ranging from jobs, to tenders, to political patronage and land. He dished out large parcels of land to friends, relatives, and political associates. Land officers took advantage of the huge land transfer traffic to participate in illegal acquisitions.

---

138 The Index of Censorship, August 1990, p. 19.

The Ndungu Commission of Inquiry into Illegal Allocation of Public Land, which was appointed by President Kibaki in July 2003, came up with a shocking indictment of the ruling class during Moi's time. Its report, handed to the government in January 2004, painted a picture of gross mishandling of land resources. The report was so revealing that when it was discussed in the Cabinet, a decision was made not to release the volume that contained names of alleged culprits for fear of a public backlash.

In explaining its refusal to release that portion of the report, the government cautioned that the matter was sensitive. One official warned that the report had the likelihood of plunging the country into a civil war because it "touches the very heart of Government and the opposition. When finally the media revealed names, almost the entire political leadership, past and present as well the top hierarchy of the military and Government were on the list."[139] A total of seven-hundred-and-fifty-thousand acres of forestland was irregularly hived off and given to politically correct individuals, the report said. The three-hundred-and-sixty-thousand-hectare Mau Forest Complex in the Rift Valley was the worst hit as politicians plundered it without care, even though they knew it served as a water tower for the rest of the country.

More than four hundred settlement schemes, which were established to settle the landless and thousands of acres of trust land belonging to communities, were not spared either. In one particular case, forty-five hundred acres of land meant for allocation to six hundred families of the local Ogiek community was instead allegedly diverted to Moi who built a tea factory. In Kisumu, the report alleged, the allocation of one-hundred-and-twelve hectares of the Kisumu Molasses Project to Spectre International Limited, a company owned by the Odinga family was also illegal, an allegation that has been contested fiercely by the family. The Commission detailed how simple words "Approved by the President" accompanied by the President's signature, deprived the poor of land and made millionaires out of senior government officials, despite provisions in law that barred the President from dishing out public land. The Commission recommended that all the land illegally distributed be repossessed, but no action was taken.

---

[139] Standard, October 1, 2004.

In a front-page story entitled: Land: Who owns Kenya? *The Standard*, quoting various sources, identified the Kenyatta family as one of the biggest landowners in the country. The extended Kenyatta family alone, the report said, owned an estimated five hundred thousand acres. The paper said most of the holders of the huge parcels of land in question were concentrated within the seventeen-point-two percent part of the country that was arable, while the remaining eighty percent of land was mostly arid and semi-arid land. Most of the grabbed land was "acquired for little money then resold, most times for a fortune," the report said.

The Commission found that state corporations, local authorities, and ministries were the biggest losers of land to crooked dealers. "Such land transactions were often highly secretive, and procedures required by law were rarely followed in their acquisitions."[140] At one time, three pieces of prime beach plots in the pristine south Coast measuring about fifty acres, which had been allocated to Moi under questionable circumstances, caused a public uproar, forcing him to surrender them back to the community.

The greed with which people in Moi's government were going about the business of plundering the country did not spare public-run institutions. In the early years of independence, the government established what came to be known as ADC farms, intended to be used to increase productivity and guarantee food security. Influential personalities grabbed thousands of acres belonging to those farms; some were turned into ranches; others sub-divided and sold for profit. The Ramisi sugar factory and the cashew nut plant, both at the coast, were forced to close down as a result of mismanagement and corruption. Also run down were the Nyayo Bus Corporation, a public transport company, and the Nyayo Assembly, which produced the first vehicle prototype in the country. Many others went under.

Kenyans were, therefore, relieved when Moi's rule came to an end. They saw a new dawn. They hoped for more equitable distribution of resources; an end to tribalism and nepotism; more political and social freedoms; a truly corruption free environment; and a real democratic nation. They were inspired by what they heard from Kibaki at his inauguration; that there

140 Benson Owuor Ochien'g, Maurice Odhiambo Makoloo, Collins Odote Oloo, Legislative Environmental Representation in Kenya, Appraising the Role of Parliamentarians in Representing Rural Voices, p. 10.

would be no "sacred cows" and that his government would end impunity and prosecute those caught looting the state. People were now eager to see how Kibaki would handle the financial scandals of the past regime, theft of public land, political assassinations, and so on.

## Work cut out

Out of the Cabinet appointments made by Kibaki during his first term, none was more important than that of Kiraitu Murungi, a legal nerd with a drawling, monotonous musical laugh. As Minister for Justice and Constitutional Affairs, Murungi was the right person to lead the government in investigations and arrests of corrupt officials in Moi's government. Together with the anti-corruption czar Githongo, it was expected that it was just a matter of time before some senior government officials would be hauled to court to face corruption charges, but that could not happen because of friction between the two senior government officials. Instead of working in harmony, the two witch-hunted each other and undermined any intentions by the government to advance its anti-corruption agenda. Kiraitu was a seasoned lawyer and a skillful politician. A Harvard University graduate, he spent years during Moi's rule fighting injustices, human rights abuses, and sleaze; and to make it even more interesting, he was himself a victim of Moi's tyranny. He was now thrust at the nerve centre of advising the new administration on what to do with the former President, and how to sustain the commitment towards zero tolerance on corruption.

When in 1986, Murungi and another prominent lawyer, Gibson Kamau Kuria, went to court to challenge the detention of Raila, state security boys went full throttle to make their life unbearable. Their movements were monitored and their telephones were jammed. They had to flee the country. Later on—years after pluralism had been introduced— at a rally at Uhuru Park in 1997, convened to agitate for Constitutional reforms, Murungi was among those thoroughly beaten by police and hospitalised with serious injuries, an incident that triggered three days of street riots in Nairobi. One can understand then that when Moi exited, Murungi did not have kind words for him. He dismissed the former President as a spent force and advised him to "go home to herd his goats and watch on TV to see how a Government is run."[141] At another time, the powerful minister and a very close associate of Kibaki, warned Moi to keep off politics or lose his generous pension of tax-free allowances. His work was cut out.

Way before NARC took over from KANU, Murungi was among those who believed Moi should face criminal charges after leaving office. Another advocate of that view was Dr. Moustafa Hassouna, a Middle Eastern regional analyst in conflict, democracy, and governance, who was certain the Kenyan leader would face court cases "regarding the way he has amassed wealth as well as lots of queries about his friends."[142] Now Murungi had a choice: either go for revenge, or let bygones be bygones.

On the sidelines, Kenyans waited with baited breath to see whether or not the Kibaki government, which had vowed to crash corruption, would take to trial the man whose rule experienced some of the most disturbing financial scandals and the most virulent human rights abuses in the country's history. At one time, the Kibaki government—in an attempt to show off its seriousness—thought of dragging Moi to a police station to get him to write a statement as the first step towards prosecution, but no one wanted to throw the first stone. Kibaki didn't want to be seen to be anxious about prosecuting him, fearing possible repercussions from Moi's Kalenjin community. During his reign, Moi may have *Kalenjinised* the civil service, but he went to great lengths to protect the economic interests of Kikuyus. While he opened doors for the Kalenjins, he did not interfere with the Kikuyus' unquenchable thirst for business opportunities. It was just proper that Kibaki should reciprocate.

However, not everyone was amused by the clamour to charge the former President. Some argued that for corruption to be fairly dealt with, investigations had to start from the time of Kenyatta's regime, when sleaze and political murders were also prevalent. But that proposal was shot down when Parliament passed a piece of legislation called the Statute Law (Miscellaneous Amendment) Bill in 2003, allowing for amnesty for all those who participated in corruption before 2003. That decision of Parliament was very unpopular among Kenyans, who felt it was trying to protect personalities within itself. "What Parliament has done," said

---

141 Verbal statement to the media.

142 Stephen Mbogo, Africa Files, December 1, 2002.

KACC boss Aaron Ringera, "will make Kenya a laughing stock in the eyes of the international community....They have given aid, comfort and succour to corrupt individuals."[143]

The first to warn against any action on Moi was Uhuru, who said as a country, Kenya's future would be determined by how people recognised and treated their past leaders. The idea of hauling a former head of state before a court of law to be judged by one or more of his own appointees was mind boggling, to say the least. Some thought such an action could set a dangerous precedent in a nation as tribal as Kenya. Suppose Moi's Kalenjin warriors took arms in protest, wouldn't that lead to a blood-bath? Moi, after all, was only following *Nyayo.* Didn't he say that was what he would do, follow the footsteps of his predecessor?

Outside government, some others were already warning of dire repercussions if Moi was arrested. "There would be chaos," one KANU official warned, when pressure mounted for Moi's prosecution. "People will die to protect Moi's dignity."[144] A Nairobi lawyer, Albert Mumma, summed up the dilemma facing Kibaki thus: "Well, he's damned if he does, and damned if he doesn't."[145] But it was Raila's statement delivered at the tail end of the 2007 general elections that revealed the inner thinking in government at the time. On September 25, 2007, Raila told Moi not to panic over rumours that the ODM leader planned to avenge against him. "They (NARC Government) wanted to take him to court, but I stood in the Cabinet and said No!"[146] Raila told a business luncheon.

Available options on what to do with Moi were fraught with difficulties. Letting Moi go scot-free would go against NARC's declared commitment to stamp out corruption and would render its election promises hollow; while hauling him to court could trigger a civil war. Even out of office, Moi was still widely popular, especially among his Kalenjin people who largely benefitted from his rule. At three million people, the Kalenjin were the second largest tribal group after Kikuyus. They had a huge presence in the civil service, the army, and the police. Moi's grip on the intelligence

---

143 Reuters, September 13, 2007

144 Darren Taylor, Inter Press Service, February 16, 2005.

145 Ibid.

146 Nationmedia.com/Kenya Today, September 25, 2007.

community was also well known to his detractors. The Catholic Archbishop of Nairobi, Ndingi a'Nzeki, recommended caution, saying Moi "deserved some measure of protection."[147]

Professor Makau Mutua, Chairman of the Task Force appointed to look into establishing a Truth and Reconciliation Commission for Kenya, weighed in by asking that Moi be treated differently even if he had been implicated in corruption: "Kenyans do not want to set a precedent in which the former President, as it were, was undressed in public."[148] John Githongo, Kibaki's anti-corruption czar concurred. "I agree that a lot of evil things happened under his leadership, but a deliberate choice, which we are willing to defend, has been made not to target President Moi."[149] That coming from a man who was being paid to fight corruption shocked many, but it was perhaps the most intelligent option available.

One reason why the government was so ambivalent about the Moi case was because the Cabinet itself was divided, since some in the Kibaki Cabinet were themselves guilty by association. They knew that any action against Moi would eventually trickle down to them as accessories to crime. After months of quiet consultations, Murungi finally declared that the government had no plans of prosecuting Moi, "owing to respect accorded to the position of the former President."[150] The government chose the softer option, but in doing so, exposed itself as weak and indecisive, a government that condoned impunity. In refusing to prosecute Moi, the government was pandering to threats of civil war, something that had no qualitative basis at all.

Not everyone was happy though with the government's back-pedalling on the matter. "Seeking to hold the former President accountable for past actions is not meant to humiliate him, but to make sure that future Presidents will respect the law," a Kenyan lawyer said. "If Moi is given blanket amnesty for his alleged breaking the law, then

147 Ibid.

148 IRIN, May 16, 2003.

149 BBC, December 2003.

150 In September 2009, Kiraitu invited Moi to his constituency and praised his leadership.

future Presidents can simply break the law with impunity."[151]

An infuriated British envoy Clay revealed he had given the new government twenty instances of possible graft through fraudulent contracts and dubious procurements, which he expected the government to investigate, some of them with Moi's footprints. Observers saw Clay's statement as intended to incite Kenyans into pushing Kibaki to act. After all, relations between Nairobi and London had worsened during the last few years of Moi's government and Clay's remarks were seen from that light.

The decision not to prosecute Moi, therefore, was based more on security concerns than on any legal reasoning. Buoyed by support from his vast Rift Valley, and the magnanimity of the Kibaki regime, Moi was able to escape justice. Again, Kenyans were not sure what hauling such a leader into prison would mean to the future stability of the country. Like Kenyatta who forgave the British for his detention—"I will forgive but not forget"—Kibaki decided to forgive Moi unconditionally for his transgressions.

Ironically, Murungi, the man who had been expected to press charges against Moi, would himself be a victim of corruption allegations when his name was mentioned in the Anglo Leasing scandal. It was alleged that Murungi's voice was caught on tape by Githongo, making comments that appeared to be coercing the Anti-corruption Chief not to press charges in return for the suspension of a debt of 30 million shillings owed to the government by Githongo's father. But Murungi described the recording as "insufficient and inadmissible" to form the basis of any action. Nevertheless, on February 13, 2006, Murungi was forced to resign as minister to allow for investigations into that scandal. He was reinstated to the Cabinet eight months later after he was exonerated.

## Moi escapes, others nabbed

Just as Moi was being let go without even a slap on the wrist, other African leaders were being hounded with charges of corruption elsewhere

---

[151] Darren Taylor, Inter Press Service, February 16, 2005.

in the continent. President Frederick Chiluba, who had ruled Zambia for a decade from 1991 to 2001, was arrested on allegations of stealing nearly 500,000 US dollars of public money. The case dragged on for eight years before he was found not guilty of the charges. However, his wife, Regina, was not so lucky. In March 2009, she was jailed for three and half years on five counts of failing to account for properties estimated at millions of dollars suspected to have been stolen. The arrest of the two former occupiers of State House, Lusaka, was due to the determination of Chiluba's successor, Levy Mwanawasa, to seriously deal with widespread corruption in the country. Parliament had to remove the immunity from criminal and civil proceedings to allow criminal charges against Chiluba. Unlike Kibaki who remained uncommitted to going full throttle against certain forms of corruption, Mwanawasa was committed to catching both the big and the small fish, and many of the latter, just as many of the former, were sent to prison. It was only on appeal that Regina was set free and the prison term quashed late in 2010.

Other high profile corruption-related cases against African leaders included the one that almost got the then Deputy President of South Africa, Jacob Zuma, imprisoned for an alleged arms deal with a French company linked to fraud and bribery. The charges led to his dismissal by President Thabo Mbeki and the imprisonment of his close ally. However, the case was dropped in 2009 on technical grounds. Bakili Muluzi, the former President of Malawi was also arrested in 2006 on accusations of corruption involving millions of US dollars of public money allegedly deposited in his accounts.

Cases of corruption involving big shots have led to prosecution and jail terms in many countries. We are still to see that in Africa, and Kenya, in particular.

# CHAPTER 9

# Commercialisation of politics

The introduction of pluralism in Kenya at the end of 1991 was a giant step towards entrenching democracy, but it was also the beginning of a unique political phenomenon in party politics: political commercialisation. Until then, Kenya was a *de jure* one-party state and KANU was the ruling entity. Like the single party establishments in communist countries, KANU was both totalitarian and inclusive. Only those considered most loyal to the party leadership were approved for nominations for elective office and the presidential candidate faced no opposition. The party was also egalitarian in the sense that all Kenyans had to belong to it, and any attempts at wavering or defiance were met with arrest and, sometimes, imprisonment. A good example was that of Odinga. When he left KANU in a huff in 1966 to form KPU, his political fate was sealed. Kenyatta rushed through Parliament the Preservation of Public Security Bill, and within weeks, eight of Oginga's confidants[152] had been arrested and detained without trial.

Others like legislator Martin Shikuku who bravely stood in Parliament and said KANU was dead, and Jean Marie-Seroney, the Deputy Speaker, who retorted in the same vein that there was no need to substantiate the obvious, were picked up from the precincts of Parliament and detained. Things were no different after Kenyatta's death. The events that followed the 1982 attempted coup ingrained KANU further as a vehicle for human

---

152 They were: O.O. Mak'Anyengo, P.O. Ooko, Oluande K'Oduol, J. Moyangi, O. Arigi, W. Rading, Dennis Akumu, and V. Wachira.

rights abuses. But now, years later in 1991, thanks to an unrelenting campaign by civil society groups, individuals, and the donor community, the section outlawing parties other than KANU had been removed, and people clamouring for democratic space were now free to register parties of their choice without threats of punishment.

A number of political parties, prominent among them the FORD, were registered. In the next ten years, the number had reached one hundred and sixty,[153] and more were being registered daily. That situation continued unchecked (at one time the number had passed three hundred) until 2008 when Parliament passed the Political Parties Bill, instituting tough rationalisation reforms that reduced the number considerably. But even then, the field remained crowded with parties that had no hope of winning seats in the Legislature or the local government. Most of them were ethnically or regionally-based and almost all were individually controlled. Some analysts, Kenyan lawyer Donald B. Kipkorir being one of them, believed such a trend may have been caused by historical events, in which tribes looked for father figures to lead them. "Maybe, because of our historical past in hunting & gathering or when we were engaged in cattle and women raids, our DNA is wired to look for a warrior-king to lead our tribes."[154]

The genesis of district-based political parties was entrenched during pre-independence days when the colonial government banned nation-wide organisations, the idea being to stop Africans from organising a national movement. Each region had its own party, but even after national parties were permitted in the run-up to independence, the pioneer parties, KANU and KADU, could not escape the ethnic tag. While the former belonged to the majority Kikuyu and Luo, the latter was a conglomeration of smaller tribes from the Coast, Western, and Rift Valley provinces. When KANU splintered in 1966, Luos left with Odinga to found KPU, while Kikuyus remained with Kenyatta in KANU.

The ethnic divide manifested itself again in 1992 when FORD—which was originally a national party—split into two factions. Kikuyus went with Matiba to FORD-Asili, and Luos and their neighbours, the

153 James Shikwati, The African Executive.

154 Sunday Standard, September 26, 2010.

Abaluhyia, stuck with Odinga in FORD-Kenya. Later, the Kisiis emigrated with Simon Nyachae to form FORD-People. On the other hand, the DP, which was founded by Kibaki immediately after the introduction of pluralism, remained predominantly a Kikuyu party, while NDP, which briefly merged with the KANU, was Luo dominated. KANU remained perhaps the only truly nationalistic party until NARC was born in 2002. Later, NARC split, with Raila taking along with him a good chuck of a multi-ethnic membership, while Kikuyus went ahead to form their own coalition, the PNU. And again, when ODM-Kenya fractured in 2007, the Kambas left with Kalonzo, while the majority of tribal groupings remained with Raila in ODM. All that time, smaller parties plodded along joining fragile alliances and succumbing to buy-outs. A German non-governmental organisation said in a report that "…all of Kenya's significant parties represent ethnic Coalitions of convenience and commitment, and, thus, ethnic parties." [155]

Before the Political Parties Act was enacted, parties were registered under the Societies Act through the Office of the Attorney General. Since the Societies Act was meant for all organisations and not exclusively for political parties, stringent regulatory measures were lacking to supervise the conduct and administration of political organisations adequately. Thus, the majority of the organisations established under that act felt they were under no pressure to follow the law. Most of them were run by individuals or families—hence the title, briefcase parties—with neither registered offices nor political ideology. And because the process of monitoring and evaluation was lacking, most of them progressed into consumer products on the rack to be hawked to the highest bidder. With the exception of a few leaders, who had previously made their mark in mainstream organisations and civic societies, many founders of those parties were journeymen and women, comprising a mixture of religious fanatics, petty politicians, and businessmen, whose sole objective to form parties was to eventually trade them for money.

They were not alone. Even the so-called mainstream parties were not explicitly clear about where they stood ideologically. They shifted planks to suit the exigencies of the moment. In the early 1950s, for example, they were agitating for independence, then in the 1960s, for multi-party democracy and human rights. "First it was the British, and then it was

155 Sebastian Elischer, Institute of Global Area Studies, February 2008.

Moi's dictatorship. In 2002 it was Moi himself," a report prepared by a German foundation, Konrad-Adenaiuer, said of the shifting ideologies. "After the goal had been attained, the fight reverted to one for political power and state resources." The report averred that this was one of the reasons why many parties did not emphasise institutionalisation, a factor that hastened their rapid disintegration. Take NARC for example. Its sole aim was to topple Moi by defeating Uhuru. Once that was done, it disintegrated for lack of ideology.

In more developed nations, ideologies are true foundation of parties. "In the United States, for example, both the Republican and Democratic parties share an ironclad commitment to the military and economic supremacy of America in the world," says a Kenyan scholar. "Similarly, political parties in Kenya ought to be guided by an irreducible, incontestable core of national values and interests."[156] Party manifestos in Kenya also do not generally guide the membership. Other than serving as propaganda tools, manifestos are usually rich in empty promises but poor in constructive substance. To make it worse, the contents of those documents are invariably never implemented. Parties launch manifestos in posh hotels to kick-start their campaigns, only to discard them after elections; they would then be tacked away in Cabinets only to be fished out, dusted, and re-issued with basic modifications for the next elections.

"…Each political party drew up a manifesto that articulated its objectives, philosophy, ideology, and values, but these were mostly for the purposes of registering the party and legitimising candidates. Party manifestos once written and presented to the registrar of parties, make good reading for students of political science. But as people we had not matured politically to the point of using elective politics to debate philosophies, ideologies, and values, or of looking to the common good, rather than for narrow ethnic advantage,"[157] Nobel Laureate Maathai wrote in her autobiography. Similarly, party offices would be opened with pomp, but after elections, they would be closed, and activities put on hibernation until the next polls.

---

156 Professor Makau Mutua, The Role of Political Parties in Transition, Kampala, Uganda, May 15, 2004.

157 Wangari Maathai, Unbowed, Anchor Books, p. 258.

One analyst opined that in Kenya, parties were only used as election vehicles to ensure their owners perpetually stayed in Parliament and government. "Parties have no membership… When membership cards are available, they are bought by individual politicians for distribution to their supporters, or to deny their opponents' supporters access to party machinery," he said. "It is therefore normal to find a voter with membership cards of two or more parties."[158] The same applies to the much coveted life membership. Because it is so common for people to migrate from one political party to another, it is similarly common for people to hold multiple life membership certificates. Kipkorir argues that "unlike in civil democracies where political parties are real homes of the members, in Kenya, political parties are vehicles driven by our tribal chiefs and we change them as many times as he changes them."[159] Lack of originality is another common trait missing in Kenya's political system. Parties would plagiarise manifestos passing them as their own; or they would just cut and paste provisions borrowed from different constitutions, just enough to cobble a document that the Registrar would accept.

## No difference

In May 2004, I represented LDP at a workshop in Kampala, Uganda, on the role of small parties in transition. There, I learnt that most of the problems plaguing political organisations in Kenya were also inherent in political parties in the neighbouring countries of Uganda and Tanzania. In Tanzania, where the Tanganyika African National Union (TANU) and later the Chama Cha Mapinduzi (CCM)—the Revolutionary Party—dominated the political landscape for many years before the introduction of pluralism; and in Uganda, where the Uganda Peoples' Congress (UPC) reigned before it was toppled in 1968, opening up space for more parties, promotion was never considered an integral part of party management. Most of the parties did not reach out to "the political market" to sell their platforms, and most remained a "one-man-show."[160]

---

158 A Konrad-Adenauer-Foundation Report.

159 Sunday Standard, September 26, 2010.

160 Sengondo Mvungi, Role of Political Parties in Transition, Kampala, Uganda, May 15, 2004.

In all the three East African countries politicians and non-governmental organisations had to agitate for reforms to force the governments to provide a level playing ground for all players. Like in Kenya, vote rigging was also common in Tanzania and Uganda, and electoral bodies were manipulated to favour rulers of the time against any attempt by the opposition to gain power. There was also lack of internal democracy in most organisations, with the party leader being the unquestionable supreme head.

Lack of a clear and definitive ideology also meant that parties were often not consistent in the way they projected themselves to the public. For example, while KANU prided itself as being "the party of peace", a study by the Central Depository Unit, which analysed electoral violence in 2002, showed it recorded the highest number of violent incidents involving intra-party conflicts and fights between KANU supporters and those of other political parties. The same scenario applied to NARC and FORD-People, which did not have any instruments of educating their supporters on electoral violence, but whose members were found to have participated in violent activities. The worst example of the failure of political parties to control their charges was evident during the post-election violence in Kenya in 2008, when unruly party youths ran amok, killing people and destroying property without any restraint from their leaders.

## Money makers

Commercialisation of political parties is most prevalent during election period. This is harvest time, when candidates open their purses, and voters drop everything to chase easily available cash. In the 2007 general elections, candidates spent 14 million shillings on bribes even before the campaigns kicked off, "a lot of it stolen from the State, some donated by private companies that want to secure contracts with the Government in future."[161] Millions of shillings were also spent on days preceding the elections and on polling day itself. "It is a travesty. We do not have democracy. What we have is a group of rich people buying their seats in Parliament,"[162] complained one analyst. In parliamentary by-elections that took place in

[161] Derek Kilner, VOA, December 3, 2007.

[162] Charles Otieno, Coalition of Accountable Political Financing, December 3, 2007.

September 2010 in three constituencies in Nairobi, candidates reportedly spent millions of shillings to be elected. One candidate boasted spending more than 10 million shillings in billboards alone, with an aggregate expenditure amounting to 150 million shillings while his official earnings for the two years remaining term was estimated not to exceed 20 million shillings. The question is: what motivates the moneyed to go for elective office? Is it power or is there some sinister reasoning? In Kenya, it is power as well as the expected opportunities for self-enrichment. Cases have been cited of legislators who entered Parliament in deplorable financial condition but who soon became business magnates owning prime real estate and expensive vehicles.

Lack of statutory expenditure caps means that Kenyan politicians can spend freely to influence voters through bribery.

Another form of commercialization is through the purchase of voters' cards by candidates especially in their opponents' strongholds. Once purchased such cards are then destroyed as a way of tilting the results. Candidates also bribe voters before elections and at polling stations and hire youths to disrupt and carry away ballot boxes from polling stations where their preferred candidates are seen to be fairing badly. The disbanded ECK was notorious for vote rigging, urged on by an unfair electoral system. However, the by-elections held under a new electoral body after the poll violence of 2008 were seen, to a large extent, to have measured up to internationally accepted norms.

Election time is also when party owners earn fortunes through nomination fees and membership cards sold to candidates and members. As part of normal business in these parties, candidates can buy nomination certificates thus avoiding competition in primaries. Parties open temporary offices to sell their wares, only to close them immediately after polls. Some of the parties offer themselves for sale to politicians who want to escape the fuss of registering new parties. Registration procedures in Kenya have normally been tedious, frustrating, and expensive. Rural folks wanting to register parties have to travel all the way to the capital, and have to make many more fruitless repeat journeys before they are able obtain certificates.

Raila's acquisition of NDP in 2001; his buyout of LDP in 2002; and his dramatic procurement of ODM in 2007, were classic examples of how easy party acquisition is in Kenya. In the case of NDP, originally owned by Steven Omondi Oludhe, the party changed hands "in exchange for half a million shillings and his used Mercedes Benz."[163] The party was available and Oludhe was personally known to Raila. On the other hand, the acquisition of LDP from Dennis Kodhe, a journalist, occurred when Raila and his allies were looking for a party after disagreeing with Moi on the Uhuru project. Chirau Ali Makwere, who later became a Minister in Kibaki's Government, had just retired as an ambassador, and was tasked by Kalonzo to look for a friendly party that could be used as a vehicle against KANU. Makwere talked to a number of registered parties and finally settled on LDP whose Secretary General was Kodhe. Makwere reported his finding to Kalonzo, who then briefed Raila. According to author Babafemi A. Badejo, there were negotiations between Raila's emissaries and Kodhe and at the end "an unpublished sum was paid and the party changed hands."[164]

However, that transfer of LDP had a little more drama than the simple explanation offered by Badejo. The acquisition of LDP was meant to be a normal business transaction, in which case certain procedures, including submission of returns to the relevant authorities, were to be met. But in that particular case, those procedures were inadvertently overlooked. For months on end, a tug-of-war raged between Kodhe and his group on one side and Raila and his people on the other, over the change of ownership. As a condition of surrender, Kodhe demanded nomination to Parliament. He also demanded to retain the right of association with the Liberal International, (LI) a worldwide European-based organisation dedicated to the protection of liberalism from totalitarianism and communism. The LI was already in collaboration with LDP under Kodhe. While that particular request was easily granted, and Kodhe was allowed to continue as a regional representative of the LI, no one, including Raila, was ready to promise Kodhe anything else until after elections.

---

163 Babafemi A. Badejo, Raila Odinga: An Enigma in Kenyan Politics, Yintab Books, p. 178.

164 Ibid., p. 226

In the meantime, Kodhe co-operated fully pending formalisation of ownership. Unfortunately, Joab Omino, who was chosen to chair the new outfit under Raila, died before the transfer could be finalised. By the first quarter of 2004, Kodhe and his group increased pressure for financial compensation. When finally money was found, Kodhe and his associates were invited to a meeting at Mayfair Hotel and a briefcase containing an unspecified amount of money handed over to them. Only Raila and Kodhe know exactly how much money was in that briefcase.

## LDP reborn

The transfer of LDP from Kodhe to Raila was smooth, done publicly at Uhuru Park on the day the Rainbow Coalition was launched. As a political strategy, thereafter, the party decided to nominate two of its officials to run the party on a daily basis. That is how Larry Gumbe became Chairman and Mumbi Nga'ru, Secretary General of the LDP. With the two now in charge at the Secretariat, the party grew fast and became a major threat to the other more established parties, such as KANU and FORD-Kenya. Gumbe, an engineer by training was an intelligent and independent thinker, courteous but forthright, a valuable political strategist with talents and skills that went beyond the classroom at the University of Nairobi where he taught. LDP could never have chosen a better chairman.

Conversely, Nga'ru was a tough-talking politician, ruthlessly blunt and shamelessly undiplomatic, with a carefree attitude, capable of giving and taking the worst in any given situation. A terrific organiser and mobiliser, she was the only high-ranking Kikuyu in a party dominated by people from outside the Central province. By identifying with Raila, Nga'ru took a major political and personal risk, but her resoluteness and loyalty combined to make her one of the most visible officials in the party. The two lustrous officials gave LDP the balance between the radical stance of Nga'ru and the moderating influence of Gumbe.

The duo was staunchly pro-Raila, forbidding any chances of Kalonzo upstaging or even undermining Raila on party matters. It was also difficult for Kalonzo to plot an action that determines a political course.[165] Gumbe

165 Dennis Onyango, Africapress, August 11, 2007.

and Ng'aru were now in a strategic position to influence the registration of members and the election of branch officials to bolster Raila's popularity at the grassroots and increase his chances for his presidential bid in 2007. The party leader was able to receive up-to-date intelligence reports from within the headquarters, as well as from all parts of the country. But even with the non-MPs at the helm, the need was felt for a political secretariat to deal with day-to-day political issues. Consequently, politicians were named to handle parallel party tasks. David Musila took over from Omino as Chairman and Joseph Kamotho became Secretary General. The *Summit* was named so was the NEC. This unique form of parallel leadership was necessary, but the dual arrangement had its own disadvantages. For one, it created grey areas that raised questions as to which of the two groups was the "real leadership."

As registered officials, Gumbe and Nga'ru were the legitimate and legal signatories of all party transactions: bank accounts, minutes, local and international protocols, inter party agreements, and so on. They were the only ones recognised by law to enter into talks with any government or non-governmental bodies over any matter connected with the party. The political wing was, therefore, technically subservient to the *de jure* leadership, although the former had a more enhanced political profile. The political officials had no grounding, either in the party Constitution or in law under the Register of Societies Act. They were amorphous, in the sense that they could only articulate political positions but had no technical responsibilities.

While the Secretariat was empowered to run the party—and did so with vigour—the political wing remained glued to a utopian belief of self-esteem. That explained why Raila was not worried about the composition of the political wing, convinced that his clout lay with the two officials he had chosen to run the Secretariat. In many occasions, Chairman Musila was by-passed on crucial party decisions mainly because he was considered a Kalonzo ally. That state of affairs caused friction within the inner stratum of the organisation. "Gumbe and Mumbi (Nga'ru) would not bulge on anything unless it was from Raila despite Musila being the Chairman," MP Franklin Bett said. "They made life very difficult for Kalonzo."[166]

166 Dennis Onyango, Africapress, August 11, 2007.

Consequently, a section of the party (allied to Kalonzo) wanted Mumbi (Ng'aru)) removed, allegedly because she favoured Raila[167]

Having Musila, a fellow Kamba as Chairman, did not sufficiently offer Kalonzo comfort. He remained deeply perturbed by the omnipresence of Gumbe and Nga'ru at the Secretariat. Feeling apprehensive and yearning to protect his interests in the party, Kalonzo brought in Mary Mbandi—a former small town mayor—to counter-balance the power of the two and to serve as his "eyes and ears."[168] This was done unilaterally and the NEC was not formally informed about it. The coming of Mbandi—who had no specific official duties, and whose salary came directly from Kalonzo—was a classic example of the kind of power games that played out between Raila and Kalonzo. It was Mbandi's duty to keep Kalonzo informed of all activities at the party offices. "When they (Kalonzo people) wanted to know anything, they would call her, not Gumbe or me. She would relay their instructions to the Secretariat,"[169] Ng'aru said.

That atmosphere of distrust and suspicion significantly impacted the day-to-day operations of the office and led to frequent communication breakdowns and rifts, as interests clashed and competing individuals fought for control of party affairs. Nga'ru and Mbandi could not stand each other, and disagreed and quarrelled at every available opportunity. Both were characteristically overbearing and both were former town mayors, Ng'aru having served in the industrial town of Thika in Central Kenya. Those disagreements filtered down to the executive level and into NEC. As the *de jure* Secretary General, Nga'ru had every right to attend NEC meetings. Mbandi, on the other hand, had no official station, but insisted on being present at those crucial meetings, taking notes of everything that was going on and serving tea and coffee to members.

Soon, the NEC meetings became the new battlefield for power within the party. There was a clear divide between pro-Raila and pro-Kalonzo people regardless of what issue was on the table. Ethnicity became a major issue, as NEC members from Nyanza province threw their full weight behind Raila, while those from the eastern region

167 Ibid.
168 Ibid.
169 Ibid.

fiercely protected Kalonzo's interests. The among us who were neither Luo nor Kamba were often amused at the ethnic drama unfolding before our eyes and remained uncommitted on many issues. Although much care was taken by the NEC not to make a public display of prevailing disagreements, it became obvious that the party was headed for a major challenge, especially given the fact that branch elections were only months away. The conviviality and camaraderie often displayed during press conferences after NEC meetings painted the LDP as united when, in fact, the party was unravelling at the seams. The LDP is "on fire and the public show of unity among its leaders is only but a public relations gimmick,"[170] said one writer at the time.

## Now, Luo vs Kamba

When Kalonzo marked his twentieth year anniversary as a Member of Parliament, he invited all MPs, but Luo legislators dramatically stayed away although Raila sent his wife, Ida, and the Chairman of the Luo Council of Elders, Meshack Riaga, to represent him. It was clearly a revenge snub because a few weeks earlier, Kalonzo had boycotted Odinga's memorial ceremony, and had given a wide berth to the first anniversary of the death of Joab Omino, the Luo LDP Chairman. Raila's absence from Kalonzo's event was not taken lightly by the latter's camp, and the conflict spilled over to a Parliamentary Group/NEC meeting at a Naivasha hotel in the Rift Valley that following month.

A simple argument over room allocation turned into a physical fight between MPs Ayiecho Olweny who was allied to Raila and Moffat Maitha who was on Kalonzo's side. The argument was why Mbandi, Kalonzo's "ears and eyes" had not been allocated a room at the lodge where the meeting was to take place. Nga'ru, who was responsible for bookings and allocation of rooms, saw no reason of providing accommodation to Mbandi, since according to her, the Kalonzo aide had not been invited and had no role in the discussions to start the following morning. Maitha, a Kamba, charged that the exclusion of Mbandi, also a Kamba, was deliberately meant to humiliate her and to undermine Kalonzo. Other MPs from his region supported Maitha.

---

170 Daily Nation, April 23, 2006.

The argument soon led to pushing and shoving, throwing of ashtrays and very abusive ethnic epithets. Kamba MPs insisted that unless Mbandi was allocated a room, they would boycott the retreat and return to Nairobi. Although she was finally given a room, the poisoned atmosphere created by that incident threatened the fate of the meeting. So, when Raila and Kalonzo arrived that evening, legislators spent hours at the lounge—over beer, whisky, and copious cups of tea—trying to salvage the talks. We finally managed to bring temporary peace, and the meeting proceeded as scheduled the following morning.

It was at that meeting in Naivasha that Kalonzo fulminated against the media over references of Raila as the *de facto* LDP leader. "The party has no supreme leader and the media's continued reference to Raila as the *de facto* leader of LDP has no basis," he said angrily to the assembled participants. Raila men countered by saying at no time had Raila described himself so, adding the title was a media creation. The reference had become common in media coverage, but had gone unchallenged until then. Kalonzo viewed the leadership reference as an attempt to portray Raila as head of the party when, according to him, the two were equal members of the *Summit*. The confrontation mirrored the poisoned atmosphere at the retreat and underscored the extent of deterioration of relations between the two principals. It appeared at the end of the day that they had been reconciled, but there was more drama, of a different kind the following day.

Minister Raphael Tuju stormed the meeting to confront party leaders who had wanted him thrown out of the LDP for allegedly collaborating with NAK. Both Tuju and another Minister, Suleiman Shakombo, an LDP MP, had voted with Kibaki's party during a parliamentary vote on the Constitutional review against party directives. Some LDP officials wanted them expelled, but Tuju boisterously defended his membership in NAK, told off those present, then walked out without care. A few days later, Tuju announced that he no longer considered himself a member of LDP. It was clear from that moment that Tuju had killed his golden goose. Since Raila commanded a near fanatical following in Nyanza, and that anyone disagreeing with him risked voter rejection, Tuju's tantrums were to become politically costly.

The youthful Tuju was the MP for Rarieda in Raila's Nyanza Province, and for years, his relations with Raila had been stormy. The reason: Tuju had refused to acknowledge Raila's political supremacy in the region, saying he was unwilling to pledge loyalty to another politician regardless of political dangers. Without Raila's express support, Tuju, nevertheless, managed to capture his parliamentary seat, a feat that infuriated the Nyanza kingpin. The situation was exacerbated when he was appointed to the Cabinet against Raila's wishes, taking the place of another nominee Raila had recommended. A few months earlier in the lakeside town of Kisumu, Raila's stronghold, Tuju had been ejected from a meeting by rowdy youths who denounced him as a traitor. His principled obstinacy eventually cost him his seat in 2007 after a relative newcomer allied to Raila trounced him. Tuju, it appeared, had not learnt a crucial lesson open to Nyanza politicians: don't dare cross Raila's path. He should have taken note of what happened to James Orengo, Dalmas Otieno, and Aloo Aringo, all of whom underwent distressing political moments when they attempted to chart their own independent course away from the kingpin. It was only after the three atoned for their actions that they were rehabilitated and allowed back into the fold, the first two serving as Raila's appointees in the Grand Coalition Cabinet of 2008.

By the middle of 2006, Raila had not announced his intention to vie for the presidency. That indecision was driving Kalonzo crazy since Raila was his biggest stumbling block to State House. The former had tried various methods to win the latter's endorsement. Firstly, he toned down his hostile criticism and started to refer to Raila as "my brother." Secondly, he sent messages to some of Raila's men urging them to convince Raila to drop his quest for the top job. That did not seem to work. At a meeting in his constituency, Kalonzo made a brave attempt to win Raila's nod by appealing, not only to his wisdom, but also to the emotions of party members. "I hope my friend Agwambo," Kalonzo said, his voice quivering, "is ready to die for me in the same way I am ready to sacrifice my life for him." In other words, Kalonzo was asking Raila to drop his ambitions for his sake. Raila never responded to that weird plea. How Kalonzo expected Raila, a much more popular politician, to forgo his plans for the presidency baffled pundits.

## Branch elections

The atmosphere surrounding the LDP branch elections was tense to say the least, with rival groups fighting for control of the party at the grassroots level. Physical fights were reported in a few places, and in some instances, officials dissatisfied with the manner in which the elections were conducted made threats of defections to other parties. Subsequently, in many branches, rival officials submitted more than one list of purportedly elected officials. In some cases, supporters known to be allied to either Raila or Kalonzo were locked out of polling areas; in other instances, polling stations were conveniently shifted to new locations at the last moment and without notice in order to confuse voters; yet in others, no actual polling took place, and names were handpicked. In Nyanza, where rampant irregularities occurred, those opposed to Raila were locked out of the exercise by being denied membership cards, the pre-requisite instrument for voting.

The election process was seriously compromised and as a result, election disputes were registered in more than half of the two hundred and ten branches, many of them in Luo Nyanza, Rift Valley and the Coast. At the Coast, almost all of the twenty-one branches submitted two parallel lists of officials, one representing Raila's preferences, and the other representing Kalonzo's people. As a compromise, NEC ordered repeat elections in nineteen branches throughout the country, and results from sixty-one branches were rejected. Committees appointed by the NEC to reconcile quarrelling branch officials failed in their work because some of the reconciliators were supporters of either Raila or Kalonzo. For that reason, the grass roots elections failed to achieve their intended purpose of strengthening the party. Instead, they yielded acrimony.

While branch officials were quarrelling, those at the top were also venting their own frustrations. The working atmosphere within the party had become intolerable and some officials considered resigning. Internal democracy was lacking and consultations were infrequent and inadequate. The political wing of the party complained the Secretariat was sidelining it on major decisions. Allegations were also made that the Secretariat was operating bank accounts unknown to the rest of the party officials.

As a last ditch effort to salvage the organisation from imminent disintegration, some national officials asked for a meeting with Raila, hoping that such a meeting would resolve a number of acrimonious issues. Because of difficulty of access, Minister Ochillo Ayacko—who hailed from Raila's backyard—was tasked to make an appointment with Raila. Kalonzo, Musila, Kamotho, Ligale, and I attended, but Raila did not show up at the Nairobi Club, although we were informed he had confirmed attendance. We soon learnt he was somewhere else having lunch with a visitor, meaning the meeting could not take place. Although Ayacko undertook to arrange another meeting the following day, it was generally felt that such a meeting could not achieve much under the prevailing cloudy atmosphere.

Sometimes in August, I was invited to a meeting at Ukunda in the South Coast where local leaders expressed frustrations at the treatment they were getting from mainstream parties and announced intentions to support an indigenous Coast-based party that would be better placed to fight for their interests. I immediately expressed interest in joining such a party, an announcement that infuriated my party bosses in Nairobi who quickly called an NEC meeting at which a decision was made to discipline me for going against the party. The NEC made no effort to hear my side of the story. I, therefore, felt my rights had been violated. It wasn't long after that that I issued a statement declaring that I had lost confidence in the higher echelons of the party and announced my resignation as Vice Chairman. Chairman Musila and Secretary General Kamotho followed suit a year later.

## The enigmatic Raila

In the history of independent Kenya, no one individual has attracted the kind of magnetic admiration from Kenyans than Raila Amolo Odinga. While Tom Mboya was intellectually intimidating and self-important and J.M. Kariuki complaisant and populist, Raila conflated all the bad and good qualities of leadership: intelligence, charisma, and courage, but also over-bearance, intolerance, and tactlessness. Raila could be humble and forgiving one moment, but moody and brusque another. Politician Paul Muite likened him to German's notorious and murderous Hitler. "He is someone who would destroy a country if he sees power… But he must be stopped from seizing power."[171] The question is: Can anyone stop Raila?

Raila honed his political skills under the feet of his legendary father, Jaramogi Oginga Odinga—"who taught me to be a true patriot"[172]—and primed his ideological thoughts in the communist East Germany and in cold detention cells, where he read the Bible religiously and the Koran thoroughly. One American commentator described him as a man with a "clear reputation for courage and for integrity and for change."[173] When speaking during the launch of his autobiography by Babafemi A. Badejo: *Raila Odinga: an Enigma in Kenyan Politics* in July 2006, Dr. Tom Namwambah, a University lecturer, offered the most flowery description of Raila. "Amolo," said Namwambah, "is Kenya's voice of reason; courageous captain; isle of ingenuity; voice of the voiceless; shield to the defenceless; patriot pan-Africanist and above all, Kenya's beacon of peace."

Not everyone will agree with that fulsome description of the man who has come to symbolise the country's quest for democracy and reforms, but none would dispute the fact that Raila is an erudite individual; a great mass mobiliser; and, a true nationalist. He is gifted with an encyclopaedic memory of events and people that often baffles his colleagues. He could narrate minute details of activities that happened years ago with utmost accuracy. Commentator Mutahi Ngunyi, however, calls Raila "a slow punctured revolutionary…He has the gut but not tact…who thinks the Government as more important than the people."[174] But some say Raila means well for Kenya even though he is often misunderstood.

His heavy sway over Luos may sometimes overshadow his deep nationalistic credentials. One writer says Raila's dominance of his community may be "a blessing and a curse," because "it gives him a solid ethnic base but also detracts from his nationalistic credentials."[175] Raila deliberately refused to contest in his home turf specifically because he wanted to shed off any insinuation that he was a tribal leader. His Langata

---

[171] Babafemi A. Badejo, Raila Odinga: An Enigma in Kenyan Politics, Yintab Books, p. 339.

[172] Evans Wafula, AfricaNews, September 3, 2007.

[173] Bryson Hull, Reuters, November 14, 2007.

[174] Mutahi Ngunyi, Sunday Nation, August 8, 2009.

[175] Kenya Talk, August 7, 2007.

constituency is as cosmopolitan as any in Nairobi is, with a heavy tribal and racial mix. Only a few minutes from the slums of Kibera, where children often craft footballs from newspaper scraps, is a stadium where the rich, on horse backs, spend their weekends playing polo and drinking expensive whiskies at a private club house. His constituents are the jobless and the downtrodden, as well as the wealthy and the privileged.

But even the cleverest of politicians blunder. In late 2007, Raila made the mistake of inviting Dick Morris, an American poll specialist and commentator to join his campaign team. What he did not know—or knew but did not think much of it—was that Morris had a dark past in his own country, which was unknown to most Kenyans. It was not until Raila appeared publicly with him and announced that the American had offered free consultancy services that the media began to take a closer look at the visitor's background.

Morris was President Bill Clinton's consultant during his re-election campaign in 1996, but was forced to resign after an American newspaper printed an expose' of his alleged relationship with a prostitute, amidst claims that he had a sexual fetish of toe sucking, a rather strange behaviour for a man of his status.[176] In addition, the Department of Revenue Services had also allegedly named and shamed Morris in the American state of Connecticut as one of the top ten tax evaders. All this information was readily available and a simple background check by Raila's people could easily have revealed the true Morris, but they allowed themselves to be embarrassed by associating themselves with a disgraced character. "Either (Mr) Odinga is unaware—which is difficult to believe—of the man's background, or he chose to ignore it, which is a political mistake"[177] said one Kenyan commentator at the time. Morris entered Kenya on a tourist visa, and according to immigration regulations, was not allowed to engage in any form of work-related activity. By announcing that he was offering Raila pro bono services as a campaign consultant, Morris attracted the attention of authorities who were willing to do everything to stop Raila from winning the elections. When Kenyan newspapers exposed him for what he was, he quietly left town. That blunder temporarily staggered Raila's campaign.

---

[176] Morris's escapade was featured in TIME magazine, September 9, 1996.

[177] Peter Mwaura, Daily Nation, November 17, 2007.

Raila's big plus was his charming relations with the media. Among the three Presidential candidates in 2007, Raila excelled in the use of the Fourth Estate by making himself accessible and easy to interview. Although his party spent 152 million shillings for mass media against Kalonzo's 6 million shillings, it was his charisma and connections in the media, rather than his financial might that kept Raila's name constantly in the public eye. His abrasiveness and defiance of authority, his availability and openness, all combined to endear him to the media. Invariably the media built Raila to what he later became. Had the media ignored his perceived role in the 1982 coup attempt; had they downplayed his detention without trial and his flight to Europe disguised as a Moslem; and had they disregarded his reform credentials, the man who later became the second Prime Minister of Kenya would not have survived the unmitigated irritations of Moi and Kibaki.

# CHAPTER 10
# The Orange Movement

As expected, the town of Kisumu on the shores of Lake Victoria was in a joyous mood. *Boda-boda*, operators, their bicycles decorated with old posters of Raila and decked with tree branches were roaming the town in celebration of their son's homecoming. At the local stadium, thousands of people from all walks of life turned up: traditional dancers, acrobats and clowns. Party leaders were in their orange shirts and hats, while *wananchi* wore decorative bouquets of real oranges; some draping their shoulders with garland formations, while others had fruits sown on brim hats. It was September 2005, and the joint rally of the LDP and the KANU was on. The Constitutional referendum on the government-supported Kilifi Draft was only a month away, and the two parties were determined to defeat it.

A few weeks earlier, the KANU Chairman Uhuru had announced that his party would join LDP in opposing the proposed dispensation because, he said, the Draft did not represent the true sentiments of the people. He re-emphasised that point in Kisumu, saying Kenyans deserved a better Constitution. The Kisumu rally was one of many the newly found LDP/KANU alliance planned to hold throughout the country. Speakers poked holes on one aspect or another of the document. They were unhappy about the excessive powers bestowed on the presidency; were dissatisfied over the distribution of resources; did not feel sufficiently comfortable about land rights; and felt the people's views on devolution of power had not been adequately addressed.

The meeting progressed well until one of the presidential candidates, Najib Balala, took to the podium, and in a surprise move, announced that the "Orange" Movement was to be transformed into a political party. "We are today transforming the Orange Movement into a full-fledged political party to fight Kibaki," he said in Kiswahili. "From here, we'll traverse the country to convince Kenyans not only to reject the Government-imposed Constitutional Draft, but to vote out Kibaki in the next General Elections," he added, amidst jubilation from the over-crowded stadium. I looked at Uhuru, who was seated next to Raila but saw no surprise on his face. Raila, on the other hand, sat quietly trying to absorb the impact of the announcement. Few could understand the abrupt announcement, especially the manner in which it was made, prompting frantic consultations between some leaders at the podium. Such a critical announcement, some felt, should have been made after exhaustive consultations and debate, not only within LDP itself but also with possible allies like KANU. In the absence of such a dialogue, some KANU and LDP officials present could not immediately understand why it had to be made at that particular meeting.

As far as I knew then, no discussions had taken place, and the issue had not arisen at any LDP forum. As Balala continued with his speech, Raila could only tell those who enquired at the time that he would brief them later. It emerged days later that Balala had in fact consulted with Anyang Nyong'o, Uhuru, and Raila as the meeting progressed, but that Raila had expressed reservations about an announcement at the time. Kalonzo and party Chairman Musila were opposed to the transformation arrangement and said so after the meeting.

The rally ended cordially and everyone returned home, but discussion on the future of the Orange Movement continued. For KANU, the issue was fundamentally sensitive. It touched on the very heart of its existence and its future functions. Moi, the outgoing party chairman, had already made it clear that he was totally opposed to any dalliance with any other party, believing that the forty-year old organisation was strong enough to recapture power on its own.

To clear the air, some LDP MPs pressed for a PG meeting to get an explanation from party officials as to how the party had arrived at such a crucial decision. They argued that the NEC and PG had not met to authorise the change. A joint NEC/PG meeting did indeed take place at

Continental House. Members were allowed to air their views freely, and they did. Some criticised unnamed party officials of habitually making unilateral decisions on crucial party matters. Others asked whether the Kisumu declaration meant that LDP and KANU were working towards an alliance beyond the referendum. On that matter, some MPs felt KANU could not be trusted and reminded Raila of the failed KANU/NDP merger in 2002. "*Mheshimiwa*, KANU let you down in 2002. Do you want that to happen again," one asked.

Balala, on the other hand, defended his action on account of the strong position the party was in ahead of the referendum. "It was clear we were headed for a win, but something had to be done to send a message that LDP was ready for the battle beyond the referendum," Balala said, in an interview for this book. "To team up with KANU we needed a strong LDP, so I decided to bulldoze my opinion through, and it was accepted by most of my colleagues."[178]

At the NEC/PG meeting, Raila listened attentively, as he always did when put on the spot. Finally, his time came, and although he did not clearly defend Balala, he was left with no alternative but to try to save the party's face. He said he had heard everyone but saw no need for panic. He spoke of Kibaki's betrayal on the MOU, took the meeting through the ensuing wrangles, and blamed NAK for the hostility in government. He told the legislators that he had received intelligence reports that LDP ministers would be dismissed for opposing the plebiscite, and warned that the last thing the party wanted was division among its ranks. "This is not the time for us to fight amongst ourselves. We have bigger fights ahead," he added.

Instinctively, Raila rubbed his left eye—damaged during his days in incarceration—with the back of his palm, looked around the rectangular table like a matador preparing for the fight of his life, and then gasped, "We either wait to be vanquished by Kibaki and NAK," he said, "or we regroup to defeat NARC in the referendum and prepare for elections in 2007. It's our choice," emphasising the point. Over the issue of consultations, Raila admitted that none of the party organs had been consulted over the

178 A phone interview, June 15, 2010.

issue, but said discussions had taken place among a section of the party membership and that the idea had been accepted.

He reached into his trouser pocket, took out a white handkerchief, wiped his brow and, as is customary for Raila when challenged to explain himself on a tricky situation, twisted his lips slightly, then took up from where he had left off. "This matter was sensitive, and we did not want it to leak beforehand. I want to plead with you, ladies and gentlemen, to understand and not to condemn." As he finished his speech, some of his critics nodded in approval. He did not apologise as some had wanted him to do, but he explained himself fully, believing his point had reached home. Balala remained silent after Raila's explanation, and saw no need to ruffle the feathers. At the end, we were left with two options: either to trash the Kisumu declaration and proceed to strengthen LDP, or to find a way to accommodate the new development.

The NEC/PG chose the latter and resolved that the Kisumu declaration was proper despite lack of prior widespread consultations. Consequently, the proposal to form an Orange party was unanimously endorsed. The discussion then moved to the name itself. Should it be a "movement" or a "party?" Why "democratic?" "Why not just the Orange Movement Party of Kenya?" one member enquired. But it was all semantics. The fact that the organisation already had the popular "Orange" brand in the title satisfied many of those present. The orange brand was borrowed from Ukraine where, in 2004, following a disputed election there masses of people took to the streets to protest against electoral malpractices that allegedly denied Victor Yushchenko victory. The movement was disbanded immediately after a revote in which Yushchenko won. In Kenya, it assumed a particularly patriotic nuance. The meeting finally settled on the name, The Orange Democratic Movement Party of Kenya. However, MPs made it clear that even with that decision; they would not endorse any proposal to dissolve LDP. It was further agreed that KANU would be informed accordingly of all the decisions.

I came to know later that Raila, Kalonzo, and Ruto did actually meet at the Nairobi Club on August 16 and discussed in detail the matter of legalising the movement. Uhuru, who had been invited, did not attend. However, information available was that even at that meeting, Kalonzo raised objections about an immediate announcement, preferring instead to wait until it was closer to elections, but he was overruled.

The actual transformation did not take place until the following August, when leaders converged at a resort in Eastern Province to discuss sharing of interim positions within the party. Uhuru, who had participated in some of the group's functions since the Kisumu declaration, attended but left the meeting early, proving right those MPs who had doubted KANU's sincerity in a joint arrangement. Despite his absence, ODM-Kenya officials went ahead and announced a Coalition of KANU, LDP, and other smaller parties. From the very start KANU had made it clear that any coalition arrangement would have to be based on corporate membership—to give KANU the option of retaining its brand name and functions—as opposed to individual membership that would have led to the weakening and even disbandment of affiliate parties. The new party went ahead and nominated its officials. Henry Kosgey was named Chairman, Anyang' Ny'ongo Secretary General, and Omingo Magara Treasurer.

The following month, ODM-Kenya officials retreated to Naivasha to discuss structures and to strategise on the coming general elections. The meeting, however, was mired by sharp differences, as those allied to Raila insisted on the individual system of membership, while those associated with Kalonzo took KANU's position and rooted for corporate membership. Elsewhere, the long-standing KANU Chairman, Moi, cautioned Uhuru about being involved in alliances with other parties, and directed that Uhuru should not chair any KANU forum unless he pulled out of ODM-Kenya. So, as Uhuru danced with ODM-Kenya, he was aware of how far he could go.

# CHAPTER 11
# ODM-K nomination impasse

Altogether, nine ODM-Kenya candidates[179] from seven of the eight provinces had declared interest in the 2007 presidential race. Of the nine, only the North Eastern Province did not field a candidate. Towards the end of 2005, and before anyone in the party had declared interest, Kalonzo was leading the Steadman Group ratings with a thirty-five percent lead ahead of the others. At number two was Uhuru at seventeen percent, while Raila mastered a measly four percent. As for the incumbent, he was rated at twenty-seven percent. If the elections had been held then, Kalonzo would have swept all the eight provinces except Central, and would have been neck-to-neck with Kibaki in Eastern.

The clean-cut Kalonzo was a fresh entrant into the big league of national politics, but his overwhelming showing in the early opinion polls gave him a significant personal and psychological boost. That was the time in 2007, when Kenyans were looking for young, fresh blood to take over from Kibaki. Kalonzo had been in politics for almost two decades and had held important positions in Parliament and in the two previous governments. Now, he wanted the biggest of the prizes: the presidency, but like many over-confident politicians, Kalonzo was a victim of self-

179 Raila Odinga (Nyanza); Kalonzo Musyoka (Eastern-Ukambani) Najib Balala (Coast); Musalia Mudavadi (Western); Julia Ojiambo (Western) Joe Nyagah (Upper Eastern); William Ruto (Rift Valley); Nazlin Omar (Nairobi); and Uhuru Kenyatta (Central).

inflicted hubris. He was too self-centred and too much of a loner. He had not taken time to build a strong grassroots network, and was misled into thinking that his previous KANU connections alone would be enough to secure support from all the eight regions. What he didn't realize was that he needed a structured campaign machine to promote his policies and aspirations, but at that time, he felt no need for any such broad-based campaign apparatus, believing individual MPs would best serve his interests. That was his undoing. His popularity was ephemeral and a year later tables had turned, and Raila had rushed from behind and had overtaken him with a seventeen percent vote lead, while Kalonzo had tumbled to fourteen percent. The battle of wits had begun.

By July 2007, Raila had increased his lead to twenty-five percent against Kalonzo's eleven percent. With an impressive forty-five percent overall lead, the incumbent Kibaki was still the most favoured presidential candidate among Kenyans. Kalonzo's rapid slump from the top of the charts to the bottom of the ladder was a wake-up call for the former KANU rubble rouser, and the situation never reversed.

There were two other reasons why Kalonzo's popularity nosedived so quickly and so dramatically. For years, the people of Rift Valley and Ukambani had enjoyed cordial, almost brotherly relations, thanks to the African Inland Church (AIC). The Church first entered Ukambani from England in 1895 before penetrating into the Rift Valley years later, where it gathered a substantial following. The two branches of the Church shared a single hierarchy and cooperated closely in religious activities. Kalonzo did not belong to AIC but the bond between the Kamba and the Kalenjins was rock solid. The commonality between the two Bantu tribes did not end there. During the First World War when the British Government opened its first military base in Kenya, it recruited foot soldiers mainly from the Kamba and Kalenjin tribes because of their loyalty and willingness to take orders. Consequently, the two tribes dominated the King's African Rifles that accompanied British soldiers to various countries during the Second World War. During years of service in the trenches of Burma and Abyssinia (Ethiopia), the two peoples developed a long lasting friendship that was to endure well beyond the war years.

As expected, at independence, the military found itself dominated by Kambas and Kalenjins, with the former providing the first three Army

Commanders, and the latter taking control of key ranks.[180] Those two factors combined to bind the two communities and the bond was sustained. So when Kalonzo declared his intention to vie for the presidency—in the absence of Moi—the populous Kalenjins were prepared to support him. They knew Moi and Kalonzo had been close. What they did not fathom was that relations between the two had collapsed when Kalonzo refused to support Uhuru for president. Traditionally, Kalenjins vote as a block, and their support is crucial for anyone to win the presidency.

By abandoning Moi at the height of the Uhuru Project, Kalonzo had automatically lost the support of his mentor, and in effect, of the AIC. Moi was a powerful figure in the Church who played a major role in the election of its leaders. He was still extremely popular in the region, even after leaving office. His influence was enormous and anyone crossing his path was unlikely to get the support of the Kalenjins. Another trait about Moi was that, like an elephant, he never forgot. He, therefore, had not forgotten that day in 2002 at a public rally in Ukambani when Kalonzo told him to his face, that come what may, he would not support Uhuru. Never before had anyone dared to embarrass the President openly before his subjects. The young politician had killed the goose that lay the golden eggs, so to speak.

So, when Uhuru lost the presidential race, Kalonzo was undoubtedly among those who were in Moi's black book. Within a matter of less than three years, the bond that had sustained the close ties between Kalenjins and Kambas had been unglued, and with the encouragement of Moi, Kalonzo's support in the Rift Valley had been wiped out. He was no longer received in the region as "our son," but as an outsider trying to capitalise on old ties. There was one more reason why Kalonzo lost his initial support in the Rift Valley.

After Moi retired, the person most likely to take over the region's leadership was Nicholas Biwott. He was the senior most Kalenjin leader at the time. Reserved and soft spoken, Biwott was a feared man during the time of Moi. He was Moi's chief adviser. During his peak, if you wanted to get to Moi, the man to talk to was Biwott. He called himself the Total Man, and the name stuck. While Kenyatta had Mbiyu Koinange, Moi

---

180 Brig. J. M. Ndolo, Brig. J.K. Mulinge, and Maj Gen. J.K. Nzioka.

had Nicholas Biwott. On top of that, his enigmatic persona and peculiar habits were often the subject of constant talk among fellow politicians. Few people knew where he actually lived in Nairobi, and stories were told of how he changed cars several times during the course of a journey, ostensibly to shake off potential security threats. He rarely dined out and when he did, he exercised extreme care over where and what he ate. He was known to avoid *a la carte* menus, instead preferring buffet spreads from where he would carefully choose and pick.

I came to know Biwott a little more personally when I worked as a senior protocol officer in the Ministry of Foreign Affairs. A regular companion of Moi during his many trips abroad, he always insisted on a senior official to serve as his personal assistant. On several such trips, I was assigned to him, my job being to make sure he was comfortable and his official needs were met. Travelling with him in the same car in foreign lands, I found him to be an extremely amiable individual who often talked about family matters, something that contrasted the picture often painted by the media of aloofness and self-centredness. On one occasion, I remember, he even talked about his children and love for education. Biwott served diligently under Moi until he was briefly detained on suspicion of involvement in the murder of Foreign Affairs Minister Robert Ouko in 1990, after which he was dropped from the Cabinet. When he was reappointed two years later, his power base had waned. In 2007, he lost his parliamentary seat to a greenhorn, signalling a new era in his political life.

With Biwott out of the running as the regional kingpin, the only other possible successor was Ruto, a forty-one-year old former youth leader, known to be independent and ruthlessly ambitious. It was Ruto, a General Science graduate from the University of Nairobi, who took over the docket of Home Affairs when Saitoti was sacked as Vice President and Minister for Home Affairs a few months to the 2002 general elections. In Ruto, the Kalenjin had found a worthy candidate as their leader. While many deserted Moi, Ruto stuck with KANU during and after the collapse of the merger with NDP, and supported Uhuru throughout his campaign for the presidency. Together with Uhuru, he joined Raila in opposing the Kilifi Draft, and when ODM-Kenya was formed, he was one of the founder members and remained there against Moi's advice. In January 2006, Ruto announced his presidential bid and joined the long list of contenders from ODM-Kenya. If there was one single action that sealed Kalonzo's fate in the Rift Valley, it was that announcement. Like soldiers responding to a cue, the region, wholesomely shifted its support to their kinsman, Ruto. Kalonzo was never to redeem those votes, which eventually went into Raila's poll boxes.

## Uhuru goes his way

Of the nine candidates, only four were considered most promising: Raila, Kalonzo, Mudavadi, and Uhuru. The rest were fringe candidates, who tagged along expecting to benefit from the winner. Even as he strived to be recognised as a serious candidate, Uhuru was, at the same time busy, trying to shield KANU from being swallowed by ODM-Kenya. He wanted KANU to be allowed to field its own candidates against others in the Coalition, and a forty percent share of all senior positions in a future ODM-Kenya Government, but Ruto saw mischief in Uhuru's refusal to commit fully to the Orange party, and warned him either to play ball or leave. Uhuru was facing too many hurdles in his journey to the presidency; inexperience, lack of broad support, and the Kenyatta family tag all worked against him. Mudavadi, on the other hand, did not appear serious enough and was willing to support Raila as long as he could be assured of a second tier position. That left Raila and Kalonzo as the two big opposition guns in the 2007 elections.

Until early that year, the party had not found a solution on how to select its presidential flag-bearer. Two main selection methods were discussed: A consensus approach, where presidential candidates would themselves sit and agree to field one of their own; and a delegates' system, where representatives from branches would be brought together to vote for the popular candidate. The consensus method excited a degree of passion among members, even though a section of the candidates opposed it, claiming it would not provide a fair playing ground. Others felt the delegates' system was easy to manipulate and expensive to run. They argued delegates could be bribed to vote for a particular candidate; thus, rendering the whole exercise undemocratic. While Raila was for consensus, Kalonzo favoured the delegates' system.

The stalemate continued for weeks on end and raised serious questions about the preparedness of the Orange team for the elections. Fears were mounting that the two top contenders were hardening their positions and drifting apart, making it even more difficult to achieve an agreement. In an attempt to restore harmony, ODM-Kenya leaders retreated to Naivasha to discuss and agree on the best nomination procedure. The meeting proceeded smoothly until Kalonzo abruptly left the hall without telling anyone that he had a television interview in Nairobi—two hundred and ten kilometres away. When he was finally traced, he requested that the final resolution be postponed to await his return, a request the participants rejected. When he turned up the following day, he once again left early to address a rally elsewhere. It emerged later that Kalonzo was angry with Raila, whom he accused of allegedly sponsoring some of the candidates in a conspiracy to torpedo his bid. There were strong rumours that Raila sponsored many of the ODM-Kenya candidates, who were expected to eventually drop out and support him, but those rumours could not be verified. At the end, the meeting failed to break the stalemate on the presidential nomination issue.

## The Council of Elders

In April 2007, after weeks of failure by the party to agree, MP Mohamed Yusuf Haji, a lanky six-footer with a red-dyed goatee came up with a bright idea. He suggested a collegiate approach, where sober-minded legislators from KANU and LDP would meet and deal with the matter. When he approached me with the idea, I immediately agreed, and within a few days, we had recruited twenty MPs and had picked MP Fred Gumo—the Assistant Minister in the President's Office, the one who was fired from the government on the same day as Minister Joseph Kamotho—as Chairman. The group comprised some interesting characters. Reuben Ndolo, dark, heavy in muscles was a former boxer. David Musila and Andrew Ligale, lucid and focused, were ex civil servants. Henry Kosgey, toothy and ill tempered was the ODM-Kenya Chairman. William Ntimama, a combative Masai warrior, and Gideon Ndambuki, easily mistaken for a wrestler, were once Moi's close buddies. Marsden Madoka, soft spoken and meticulous, was at one time Kenyatta's aide de camp. Amina Abdalla and Abdul Bahari, both eloquent and fastidious, were from the nomadic clans of Northern Kenya. The towering and amiable Joseph Nkaissery was a retired military officer. Nyiva Mwenda, wife of former Chief Justice Kitili Mwenda, who helped launch Kalonzo's political career, was gracious and motherly. Omingo Magara was an Indian trained accountant. The plump Naomi Shaban was a qualified dentist. Chris Okemo was a former finance minister, and Oburu Odinga was Raila's elder brother and protector. Our job was to facilitate dialogue among the competitors and to recommend the fairest system of selection. Our self-styled title: the *Council of Elders*.

At our first meeting at the United Kenya Club, we agreed that all our deliberations would be kept secret and would be made public only after a decision had been reached. Gumo was the only one we authorised to brief the media on the general progress of the discussions. However, we soon realised that conducting Council business in total secrecy was not easy in a group as big as ours. All our meetings were leaked to the media, giving critics an opportunity to question the direction of our deliberations. None of us knew who was responsible for the leaks. It got so bad that someone at one time suggested that members take an oath of secrecy, but the idea was shelved, because it was argued, the participants were "*wazees,*" elders, who were expected to behave responsibly.

Initially, the majority of Council members favoured the consensus approach because it was easier to accomplish and cheaper to implement than the delegates' selection process, which was cumbersome and expensive. The consensus method was also less acrimonious, as the candidates would select one of their own, while the other method of winner-take-all could generate splits. Critics of consensus argued that the method was undemocratic and would undermine majority opinion. As a result, the Council was divided over the two options. Again, the Council felt the candidates were too many, and that a method needed to be found to trim the number. Some of the candidates highly criticised the idea of an elimination process, and they argued it would favour certain candidates. They wanted everyone to be given a fair chance in an open, competitive process.

In a follow-up meeting, all aspirants were invited to offer views on the work of the Council. Apart from a few complaints from Uhuru and Ojiambo that the composition of the group did not fully represent all candidates, the Council was endorsed as a legitimate body mandated to carry out the exercise of nomination. Party Chairman Kosgey, who was a Council member, was asked to ensure that the draft party Constitution was amended to recognise the existence of the Council to avoid legal problems in future.

After the elimination idea was thrown out, it was decided to implement a resolution passed by the party plenary a few months earlier, to increase the non-refundable nomination fee from 1 million to 2 million shillings. This was another attempt to rid the field of what the Chairman called "pedestrians,"[181]—those with the least chance of winning the election. While the Council struggled with incessant leaks of its business, another much more serious challenge suddenly erupted.

On June 10, Kenyans woke up to an article in the *Sunday Nation* reportedly extracted from a confidential document that suggested that the Council had finally identified Kalonzo as the party presidential nominee. The content of the report bore very close resemblance to that of a document presented to the Council a few days earlier by MP Chris Okemo. Entitled *The Orange Democratic Party – Kenya: Strategic Nomination of the Presidential Candidate*, the report contained information on the voting trends in three past General Elections in 1992, 1997, and 2002, as well as an analysis of ODM-Kenya voting patterns during the 2005 referendum. It further speculated that those who had voted for the party in the previous polls would most likely vote for the ODM-Kenya in 2007. The report also analysed the popularity of each of the presidential candidates in their areas of representation and provided an analytical forecast of regional voting trends for 2007.

Okemo—a former Cabinet Minister with bushy grey hair dyed black, and priestly features—had submitted a nicely-bound report, which the Council was informed, had been prepared by independent analysts desirous of helping the party reach an agreement on the nomination impasse. Okemo did not divulge, nor was he questioned, about the authors of the report. The Council received it in good faith, believing it was the effort of genuine ODM-Kenya friends. In his characteristic scholarly way, Okemo laboriously took members through the report, and finally asked them to decide whether it could be used as the basis of a solution to the party's nomination dilemma.

The Council was stunned by its conclusions; that of all the party candidates, Kalonzo was the only one who could beat Kibaki; that he would win outright in four of the eight Provinces—Eastern, Rift Valley,

[181] Election News, April 27, 2007.

Western, and Coast—and would share Nairobi with Raila who will only take Nyanza. The report—which contradicted all opinion polls—was very categorical about Raila's negative chances. It gave Kalonzo a fifty-three-point-four percent lead against Kibaki, Ruto fifty-point-eight percent, and Raila fifty-point-five percent. Uhuru, the report added, would get only forty-eight-point-six percent if he were to go against the incumbent, while Musalia would garner forty-seven-point-four percent. The report predicted a victory margin of only 412,763 votes against the competition, and suggested that efforts be made to get more people to turn out and vote in ODM-Kenya strongholds of Nyanza, Rift Valley, and Coast. The key to a win, the report further added, hinged on all the ODM-Kenya candidates staying together, warning that any fall-out would give Kibaki victory. Interestingly, in its survey that same month, the Steadman Group had shown a completely different scenario. While Kibaki had continued to lead at forty-five percent, Raila had increased his lead by eight percent to twenty-five percent while Kalonzo had dropped three points to fourteen percent.

The *Sunday Nation* report was received with a mixture of interest and anxiety by party supporters, some of whom felt it did not represent the true position on the ground. They wondered how Kenyans could have favoured Kalonzo over Raila whom, they said, had more widespread support in the country. They described him as fearless and aggressive, and the only one who could bring change and restore national pride after years of notorious KANU rule. Kalonzo, they said in radio talk shows, represented the retrogressive past, lacked charisma, and was ambivalent on some critical national issues.

When the Council met two days later, the report was inevitably on top of the agenda. While everyone accepted that the newspaper report was similar to the document tabled earlier before the Council, they could not understand how it had found its way to the media. "This report has caused a lot of damage to our credibility," a furious Chairman Gumo said, his choleric temper very much at play. "What I want to know is who leaked it. And let me add that I am not joking." He made it clear that the Council had not made any decision over whom the presidential candidate would be. "So everything that has been published is speculation, and to me, that speculation is in bad taste," he added menacingly, while scanning the room.

Several members made comments, most of them condemning the leak. Allies of Raila dismissed it as the work of the intelligence community intended to confuse voters and project the opposition as a divided house. They claimed that similar documents were circulating widely in the country and were meant to undermine the party. "I want us to be very careful," one said. "There are people out there who do not want to see Raila's name on the ballot. They are using some of us to divide the Orange family. We should not allow them to succeed." Raila allies charged that Kalonzo was a late comer to the reform movement and could not be entrusted with presidential responsibilities; while Kalonzo's argued that the position of his foes was based on personal rather than party interests. Consequently, the Council formed a sub-committee to study the report more carefully. Okemo chaired it and it included three other members, but the raging controversy made it difficult for the sub-committee to conclude its work successfully. It met only twice, and its third meeting was cancelled due to lack of a quorum.

In the meantime, members began to question seriously the origin of the report. Interestingly, Okemo was unwilling to shade much light on where he got it, leaving the members in a quandary. The Council wondered too about who could have leaked the report. Was it one of the elders? If so, who and what was the motive? Or, was it leaked at source by an overzealous typist or messenger? The Council reached no conclusion since it could not find evidence to implicate anyone in particular, even though fingers had been pointed at one or two members of the Committee.

Other than Okemo, who had custody of the document at all times, no one else was known to have had complete access to the report other than during meetings. Okemo was the custodian: he would bring copies to the meeting and collect all of them back at the end. It is possible the leak could have emanated from anyone among those who initially handled the document: typists, copiers, and so on, or, it could have been released deliberately by an insider to cause confusion in the party. Moreso, it could have been the work of people in the intelligentsia, as had been suggested. Whoever did it; he or she succeeded in causing irreparable damage to relations among the candidates, and helped to hasten the demise of the *Council of Elders.*

But more surprises were in the offing. On June 29, the Council once again invited the presidential hopefuls to a meeting. After Okemo had taken members through the report, Raila became visibly enraged. He questioned the origin and authorship of the report, and claimed government agents had infiltrated the Council. He viciously attacked those who were spreading information that he was unelectable because he was a Luo. "If we are talking about sacrifice, the Luos have sacrificed a lot for the independence and democratisation of this country. If Luos cannot lead Kenya where do you want them to go, Uganda?" he asked. When he began to speak, the room went quiet, but that silence soon turned into gloom, as those present could no longer look at him directly: most bowed their heads uncomfortably. That Raila was intensely wounded by perceptions based on his ethnicity was only evident to those present in that room at the United Kenya Club on that day. To illustrate how melodramatic the situation was, once he took out his handkerchief and wiped his eyes. The following day the media quoting sources within the Council, referred only to "emotions running high," unknowing that the events of that day had marked the turning point in the presidential race.

After the *Sunday Nation* exposé, it became clear that the Council could no longer enjoy the unfettered confidence of the presidential candidates. What worsened the already frayed nerves in the party was to come later, when Gumo appeared next to Kibaki—ODM-Kenya's arch foe—at a public function in his constituency and heaped praise on Kibaki's leadership. That incident upset some in the party and raised questions about Gumo's loyalty. An angry Balala—who had not been happy with Gumo and his Council—finally got his chance to pummel the man, describing him as a leader without a stand, and said the Council was "as good as dead."[182] In view of the widespread dissatisfaction with the Council among some party leaders, a retreat planned for Naivasha that would have once again brought together all the presidential aspirants, was called off. That was the last time the Council was ever heard of again. The collegiality had vanished. Just as suddenly as it came, the committee fizzled out and died a natural death. Thus, with the seeming failure of the consensus method, the party decided to concentrate on the delegates' system of nomination.

182 East African Standard, July 11, 2007.

About that time in mid-July 2007, a ceremony was planned at Kapkatet in the Rift Valley to anoint Mudavadi, a Luhya, as the Kalenjin community's presidential candidate. Son of Moses Mudavadi, an influential politician during Moi's era, the young Mudavadi, from Western Province, had expected support from the region because of his father's long relationship with the Kalenjin. The ceremony was, however, cancelled at the eleventh hour after organisers withdrew, fearing reprisals from a section of Kalenjin leaders. Ruto took advantage of Mudavadi's unplanned absence and addressed the crowd to promote his own candidacy. Thirteen Kalenjin MPs publicly supported his presidential bid.

Not too far away in Eldoret town, another Kalenjin group led by the ODM-Kenya Chairman, Henry Kosgey, a Kalenjin, held a press conference to drum up support for Raila. Kosgey assured his people that Raila was the right candidate who would ensure a just Government that would put in place an equitable distribution of resources, and build a non-tribal society for the benefit all Kenyans. The two parallel meetings heralded a major split among Kalenjin leaders over whom Kalenjins should support: their own Ruto or Raila, the man they fondly called Arap Mibei, the man from the lake. The split among the Kalenjins also infuriated Moi, who could not bear seeing his community disintegrate. No longer in working terms with Ruto or Raila, Moi pleaded with his people to stay put in the KANU, but many ignored him.

A few days after the last meeting of the *Council of Elders*, Raila took his case to the people by convening a meeting at Kamukunji grounds in Nairobi. It was at that meeting that he blasted his fellow aspirants for undermining him, and confirmed for the first time, that his bid for the presidency was unstoppable. He said his 'Luoness' was not a factor, and described those opposed to his candidature as tribalists. Raila's categorical declaration staggered Kalonzo who had expected a "Kalonzo tosha" announcement like the one at Uhuru park some years earlier.

## Raila's secret MOU with Moslems

After Raila had made clear his stand on the presidency, he proceeded to sign a controversial treaty with a section of the Moslem community. Moslems are a significant constituency in Kenya. At about twenty percent of the population, their vote is crucial for anyone who aspires to win the presidency.

The MOU with the National Moslems Leaders' Forum (NAMLEF) was meant to cement relations between Moslems and the prospective future Raila Administration. In exchange for support, Raila was expected to meet certain obligations, including ending alleged discrimination, intimidation, and harassment against Moslems. The two sides agreed that the agreement would be based on mutual trust, honesty, integrity, transparency, and good governance, and that a commission of inquiry would be set up to investigate incidences of human rights abuses, marginalisation, and injustices on Moslems. In addition, Raila was to accord the Moslem-dominated northern and coastal regions budgetary priority in roads, telecommunications, water, housing, education, and health.

Because the MOU was signed and kept secret for months, it elicited a lot of speculation in the media and internet outlets, and caused uneasiness among Christians who saw it as an attempt to introduce stringent Sharia Laws in the country. But all that speculation ended when Raila called a press conference towards the end of November and revealed what turned out to be nothing but a benign agreement of mutual interest. Moslem leaders said they had tried to sign a similar agreement with Kibaki and Kalonzo, but the two had turned them down.

As a result of that agreement Raila received the bulk of the Moslem votes but two years after the inclusion of Raila and ODM in the Coalition Government, it was obvious Moslems had received little gains as a result of the MOU. There was widespread feeling that they had, once again, been forgotten and relegated to the periphery.

# CHAPTER 12

## Cracks in the opposition

In early March, 2007, Kenyans in the Diaspora organised a meeting in London and invited the ODM-K presidential aspirants for a bonding session. ODM-Kenya officials overseas, mainly friends and supporters of Raila planned the meeting "to showcase the human face of the party leadership".[183] Those in the Diaspora shared the same frustrations as many of their compatriots at home over the party's inability to agree on one suitable presidential candidate. They felt that the contestants should be given an opportunity—away from the prying eyes of the Kenyan media—to sort out their internal squabbles and to move on with the business of galvanising support for the coming elections. The climax of the visit was to be a gala dinner event in which each of the candidates was to be given a chance to explain his or her vision for the country. Tickets for the event were offered at between 100 to 1000 pounds Sterling,[184] depending on the proximity to the candidates. The price of sitting next to Raila, for example, was to be much higher than that of sitting, let us say, next to Nazlin Omar.

The meeting was important for another reason: to provide an opportunity for opposition supporters abroad to raise funds for the struggling party. Kibaki and his wealthy friends had stashed millions, perhaps, billions of shillings for use in their presidential campaign. For them, it was a do or die

183 An ODM-K UK press release.

184 1 pound sterling approximated 120 shillings.

affair. It, therefore, was imperative that ODM-Kenya should find money, lots of it, from every available source, to fund its campaign. Raila was to arrive in London from the US where he had gone on a private visit, while the rest were to take the seven-hour flight from Nairobi to arrive there in time for initial meetings with the organisers. However, when he landed in London, Raila was informed that the rest of his colleagues would not join him for the rendezvous. He felt betrayed since only the previous day, the party headquarters had confirmed their attendance.

It was a tense moment for Raila, who kept on phoning his key aides in Nairobi, wanting to know the truth. In Kenya, some of the candidates had assembled at a Nairobi hotel, preparing to hold a press conference. Mudavadi and Balala were busy with other engagements, and had indicated their inability to travel. A furious Raila phoned and lambasted each one of them individually for letting down their hosts in London. "He was talking to them like he was in charge, like someone who didn't want to tolerate indiscipline in the ranks," said someone present when Raila made the calls. Each of the candidates gave different excuses for their no-show. It was obvious that ODM-Kenya was facing its first major leadership revolt, and Kalonzo was suspected to be the master-mind. Although there was no indication that Balala and Mudavadi were enjoined in the conspiracy, their absence was a matter of much speculation. Ruto, on the other hand, did not give much of a reason, but later denied reports that he had been denied a British visa because of an alleged case pending in court. On his part, Kalonzo was reported as saying he was staying back in solidarity with Ruto. According to rumours circulating in Nairobi, the gathering at the hotel had planned to distance themselves from the event.

In the preceding days before the London meeting, reports had circulated that Raila had arranged the meeting to declare himself "*tosha*" as he did to Kibaki at Uhuru Park on October 14, 2002. That, coupled with reports that the controversial Bishop Gilbert Deya was the main financier of the event, upset the others. A Luo and an acquaintance of Raila, at the time, Deya was embroiled in child trafficking allegations, an excuse the candidates also used to skip the trip. They now claimed the event had been "hijacked by people with ulterior motive."

The only meaningful reason for the snub was that the rest of the candidates were scared of Raila's growing popularity and feared that the event could cancel out any attempts at finding a presidential candidate through a democratic process. It was actually an attempted coup d'état that collapsed only after the tough talking Raila warned them he was ready to go it alone. That conspiracy did not stop the dinner event from proceeding as planned, and gave Raila an enviable opportunity to challenge his colleagues' leadership credentials.

Without naming names, but clearly directing his remarks at Kalonzo, Raila declared that, "he who does not want to be with the rest of us should walk out."[185] He accused his imaginary opponent of working to destabilise the party. Nyagah had expressed similar sentiments a few days earlier in Nairobi and he repeated them in London: "Steve (Kalonzo) is my friend….I repeat it today that anybody who does not want to work with the rest of us must leave the party now."[186] Having clearly fingered his target, a determined Raila returned to Nairobi and quickly began work of mobilising the rest of the ODM-Kenya team against Kalonzo, painting the Kamba leader as weak, cowardly, and easily manipulated. In the following weeks, media articles were written dismissing Kalonzo as a Moi protégé who had nothing to show in the struggle for democracy.

The London letdown filliped Raila to surge on with a lot more confidence than he had before the trip. For the second time since the Kamukunji meeting, Raila announced he would not endorse anyone for the presidency, sending a clear message that he was ready to wrestle against anyone who dared to block his way. As the battle between the two contestants raged, fatigued Kenyans—through newspaper columns and radio talk shows—started to air views about a possible compromise presidential candidate. They were tired of the infighting now threatening the future of the party. The name of Mudavadi popped up frequently, and so did that of Mutava Musyimi, then Secretary General of the National Council of Churches of Kenya. Mutava's name had come up once before prior to the 2002 elections but fizzled out after Kibaki was selected to take on Uhuru. The name of the House Speaker, Francis Kaparo was also being mentioned along the corridors of Parliament as a possible compromise candidate.

185 East African Standard, March 12, 2007.
186 Ibid.

It was obvious now that the power struggle between Raila and Kalonzo was tearing the party to pieces. Determined as ever to realise his dream of occupying State House, Kalonzo retreated to his home ground of Ukambani, and cheered on by a large crowd at a trading centre, declared that he would never step down for Raila. He boasted of possessing the right leadership qualities and said he was the best candidate for the job. The crowd, primed for the ultimate confrontation at the ballot box, heard Mutula Kilonzo, the local MP, accuse Raila of applying "guerilla tactics"[187] in his quest for the presidency.

Apart from those presidential shenanigans, another latent war was boiling under the party's wings: the control of ODM-Kenya. During a NEC meeting, a bitter argument ensued over the control of the party. Daniel Maanzo, who was the *de jure* Chairman and Kalonzo's ally, declined to hand over party instruments to the *de facto* Chairman, Kosgey, ignoring a resolution passed at a party plenary two weeks earlier. Since only the registered Chairman was allowed to sign nomination forms for aspiring election candidates, party bigwigs feared Maanzo could use his position to undermine pro-Raila candidates, so they wanted him to vacate office. Maanzo, on the other hand, argued that Kosgey had no legal standing to act on behalf of the party.

Another point of contention at that NEC meeting related to the custodian of the party registration certificate, which was, until then, in the hands of Maanzo. In order to have full control of the organisation, Raila wanted the certificate transferred to the *de facto* Chairman, but Maanzo vehemently refused. That NEC meeting was marred by an ugly confrontation between Maanzo and Kosgey, watched by Raila and Kalonzo. As the standoff progressed, Kalonzo took Maanzo out of the meeting for a tête-à-tête, supposedly to soften his position, but even after he returned to the meeting, Maanzo maintained his hard-line stand and refused to budge on the two issues: signing of nomination papers and transfer of ownership documents. From his remarks, Raila did not believe Kalonzo and Maanzo were not reading from the same script, prompting him to make a rather telling comment that "there were many political parties and (that) ODM-Kenya was just a name."[188] That statement was loaded in meaning and

---

[187] Africanpress, July 28, 2007.

[188] People Daily, July 4, 2007.

indicated for the first time that Raila was thinking of ditching the ODM-Kenya and registering his own political party. It was clear to party officials that the whole issue of ownership had become tribal: it was Kamba verses the rest. Kalonzo believed he had finally cornered Raila.

The events that followed showed that Maanzo was not yet finished with his mission to frustrate Raila. The combative *de jure* party Chairman wrote to two local banks asking them to freeze party accounts and to stop all transactions with the Raila group. "I am the Chairman of the party," he said in his letter to the institutions, "and wish to inform you that any such accounts were opened in contravention of the party Constitution and the relevant provision of the law." Maanzo wondered how the banks could allow unregistered party officials to open and operate party accounts without reference to him. Maanzo's action to close down the accounts was viewed by the Raila group as belligerent, bordering on treachery. About that time, Maanzo ally, Chepkonga, the party's registered Secretary General, who had not been seen in public, surfaced for the first time at a press conference attended by Kosgey and other high ranking party officials allied to Raila, to claim he had resigned from his position at ODM-Kenya and now supported Raila.

But in a bizarre performance no one could explain, the same Chepkonga re-appeared before newsmen a few hours later in the company of Maanzo to denounce his earlier statement, saying it had been issued under duress. That latest development threw both sides into a spin and raised questions about Chepkonga's credibility. Was he compromised, first by the Raila faction, and then by the Maanzo group? Or, was he merely confused as a result of excessive media attention? Simply, the semi-illiterate Chepkonga, who had been enjoying Maanzo's handouts all along, had developed cold feet, and had decided to make an about-turn. After that awkward display of obfuscation, the former lowly paid worker was spirited away by Kalonzo allies to an unknown safe house, where he was housed and given a small stipend to keep him away from the media. It was then that Maanzo reported receiving death threats. He did not explain whether the threats were coming from inside or outside the party.

In the meantime, Kalonzo, Ruto, and Uhuru, declined to submit their nomination papers to the party Secretary General Ny'ongo, claiming he was a Raila sympathiser, making it known that they would only offer the documents to a fully constituted Election Board, which at that time was short of the required fourteen members. It was not until the Board was revamped that the candidates agreed to oblige. All those events left Kenyans distraught, unable to comprehend exactly what was going on in their party. Time was running out, yet leaders were still squabbling over simple operational matters.

# CHAPTER 13
# Plot against Raila

On a chilly evening, six men and two women made their way to the boardroom of Uhuru's private offices at the Chancery Building along Valley road, Nairobi. It was July 4, 2007. Earlier that day, several top Kenyan leaders had been at the residence of the American Ambassador, Michael Rannenberg, to mark the US Independence Day. Among them were Vice President Awori, Raila, and Kalonzo. The cream of Kenya's diplomatic and business community was there, so were US Marines, in their resplendent light khaki uniforms, an absolute show of power in what was, indeed, American territory. A group of American students from the International School of Kenya was there to sing the National Anthem as the Star Spangled Banner was hoisted high on top of a mast. A sumptuous selection of Kenyan and American delicacies was spread over several tents, including *nyama choma,* as well as burgers and shish kebabs, to be washed down by frothy beer and choice wines.

That morning, Kalonzo and Uhuru had talked and had agreed to meet to discuss party politics and their own future in the ODM-Kenya. As I made my way out of the envoy's residence, Kalonzo pulled me aside and told me of the evening's rendezvous, just at the precise time when Raila and his wife were bidding farewell to the host at the main entrance. It was to be a secret meeting of the two leaders' closest aides. No agenda was immediately revealed, but there was a sense of urgency in the way Kalonzo was delivering the invitation. For weeks, since the leaked report that had favoured him against all his other colleagues, Kalonzo had been under siege. His detractors wanted to isolate him; to make him a pariah in ODM-Kenya. At selective night-time meetings in restaurants—from Palacina in town to Rusty Nails in the Karen suburbs—Kalonzo was the subject of discussion. A strategy was worked out to malign his reputation and to paint him, not like the angel he claimed to be, but a land grabber who had stolen from the landless. He was accused of illegally snatching a piece of land in Ukambani that had been allocated to squatters. Of course, he denied the accusations. The allegations left Kalonzo acutely stressed, and the volleys were not coming from Raila directly but through his hard-core lieutenants and supporters.

The Chancery building is an impressive office-cum-business address, just up the hill from the Nairobi Business District. Directly across the busy street is the huge Nairobi Pentecostal Church, which Kalonzo often used to go to for divine intervention ahead of a major event. On several occasions, he retreated there to seek solace in prayer and peace of mind. The general area where the Chancery building is located is commonly referred to as the Hill, and although not specifically up market, it boasts important landmarks, such as the Kenya School of Law, the highly secured Israel Embassy, and the Integrity Centre, headquarters of the Kenya Anti-Corruption Commission, the original site of the once famous Starlight Night Club. It is from a suite of upstairs offices at this prestigious address that Kenyatta's vast empire—of real estate, farming, communication, and tourism—was managed. When Kenyatta died, the empire was left under the care of his reclusive widow, Mama Ngina, even though it was commonly known that most of decisions were arrived at through family consultations.

After parking my car in the secure basement, I was chaperoned by a security aide through several well-secured doors into Uhuru's boardroom. July is usually a cold month by Nairobi standards, and as we drank hot tea to wade off night chills in the well-furnished suite, with Kenyatta's portrait looking on, it became clear that Raila was the main item of discussion that evening. Kalonzo and Uhuru had agreed to bring to the meeting three officials each. Kalonzo brought in MPs David Musila, Nyiva Mwenda, and me, and Uhuru came with party leaders Dalmas Otieno, Marsden Madoka, and Naomi Shaban.

The general elections were six months away and nomination wrangles in ODM-Kenya were shearing the party apart. Although Raila and

Kalonzo were the leading contenders, the former was leading in opinion polls. Uhuru, on the other hand, remained an outsider, unhappy about KANU's continued association with ODM-Kenya, and had threatened to pull out unless his party was recognised as an independent coalition partner. KANU and ODM-Kenya had joined ranks two years earlier to oppose the Kilifi Draft at the referendum, and had continued to cooperate against Moi's wishes.

Daggers were drawn that evening at Chancery House. Neither the son of Jomo nor the son of Mairu had kind words for Raila. After all, Raila had masterminded Uhuru's defeat at the 2002 elections, and he was now frustrating Kalonzo's quest for the presidency. Had Raila accepted Moi's designs and not lead a rebellion, Uhuru would probably have become the third president of Kenya. But Raila's palace coup had halted midstream the political career of the young man, and had embarrassed Moi. So, it was not surprising that Uhuru was coming out strongly against Raila, accusing him of masterminding a campaign to destroy partner parties by denying them an opportunity to field candidates in elections. "I am certainly not happy with the kind of treatment KANU is getting from ODM-Kenya," Uhuru ranted. "Raila has become uncontrollable and the only way to deal with him is to isolate him." That evening I saw Jomo in Uhuru, complete with the former president's menacing eyes. He was lashing out at Raila, just as his father did to Odinga way back in 1969. The only time I saw Uhuru angrier was after his name was linked to the 2007 post-election violence in a report by the KNCHR, in July 2009, which made him labour ardently to exonerate himself.

Uhuru said he had called the meeting to discuss possibilities of forming a powerful movement against what he called Raila's "dictatorial" ways. He suggested that the Third Force could initially include himself, Kalonzo, and Ojiambo. Attempts, he added, would also be made to bring in William Ruto, a leading light in the populous Rift Valley region. "This alliance must be formidable enough to stop Raila, otherwise, this man will give us trouble," he said. Uhuru explained that the history behind his party would not allow the KANU to be subservient to any other organisation. "KANU is the independence party with structures much stronger than any other, with a membership more widespread than LDPs. We need respect here," he said angrily. He also complained that Raila men in the Coalition were difficult to negotiate with. "These are not the people I want to conduct business with. We will never agree on anything."

The tempo of the meeting had been set, and the first seed towards the collapse of ODM-Kenya had been planted. The abrasive Raila was the target. The question was whether Uhuru, a relatively inexperienced politician, and Kalonzo, "an avowed opponent of democratic reformers and an unwavering proponent of the one-party-state"[189] could call and sustain a bare-knuckled political fight with a hardened former political prisoner, who had waged an aggressive campaign for democracy and human rights in the country. Were Uhuru and Kalonzo up to the kilter or were they digging their own political graves?

Kalonzo, who had more deep-seated and immediate problems with Raila than Uhuru did, felt that Raila was not a team player. "He is acting like a prefect and treating all of us like children, behaving as if he is already the party's presidential nominee." It would be dangerous, he said, to trust Raila with the leadership of the country. "Can you imagine what Raila will do to all of us? He will step all over the rest of us after he becomes president. We should not allow that to happen." Kalonzo said the idea of a Third Force was brilliant, and he promised to bring on board MPs from Ukambani. At the same time, Kalonzo rubbished opinion polls that showed Raila closing in on Kibaki, leaving him at the bottom of the pile, and warned that unless the trend changed, "we could see this man in State House." He also attacked those in the party, whom he did not name, of frustrating his ambition to become president, and pilloried Luo Nyanza MPs who had asked him to drop his bid in favour of Raila. He said those advocating for his surrender had mischievous designs. "I will be on the ballot box whatever they say," he assured us.

Dalmas Otieno, a dashingly tall individual, and the only person from Raila's Luo Nyanza present, joined his colleagues in supporting the idea of a Third Force. A long-standing KANU loyalist and an intense thinker, Otieno was one of Moi's top advisers, who had his own strong views about the domination of Nyanza politics by the Odinga clan. As Raila stormed out of KANU to join the Rainbow Alliance, Otieno dutifully remained with Moi and Uhuru. He too supported the idea of an alternative movement to take on Raila, but insisted that for such a force to succeed other parties must be brought in, among them the Coast-based Shirikisho Party of Kenya (SPK), and the Western Kenya-based Kenya African Development

189 Professor Mutua Makau, Sunday Nation, July 25, 2010.

and Democracy Union (KADDU). Although he did not personally attack Raila, he appeared in no mood to protect the ODM-K leader from the salvos thrown at him by the two leaders. He admitted Raila's popularity was because of his past sacrifices as a political detainee. "People identify with him because of the sacrifices he made for this country," he said, "but that notwithstanding, a properly coordinated grouping should be able to turn tables against him." Otieno came out as a truly KANU stalwart who was willing to stick to the party and Uhuru. The meeting agreed that Mudavadi, who was closely associated with Raila, would be left out of the proposed scheme for the time being because he could not be trusted.

The meeting resolved that Uhuru would approach Ruto with the idea. Kalonzo would work on Ojiambo, and I would woo the SPK. To start with, we agreed that Uhuru and Kalonzo should make joint appearances, beginning with a breakfast meeting the following week. We felt this would send a message to Raila and his supporters that something powerful was in the offing.

The mood in the room was hostile and both Kalonzo and Uhuru appeared spoilt for a fight. Nevertheless, they knew that Raila would not be easy to wrestle. Their only option was to try to isolate him and make sure he did not get the party's nomination. By that time, Kalonzo's popularity had stuck at around ten percent and Uhuru had yet to recover from the 2002 defeat. Because of his earlier association with Moi, whose regime had been blamed for most of the problems in the country, Uhuru's credibility had suffered a severe blow. His independence had been shattered and his ego bruised. His chances of a comeback in 2007 were virtually nil. Therefore, the so-called Third Force offered him the perfect vehicle to remain politically relevant while awaiting another presidential attempt in future.

## Ruto tricks Kalonzo

Before Kalonzo and Uhuru could embark on their next move, something interesting happened. Ruto convened a breakfast meeting at his residence in Karen to try to cobble up a power sharing agreement. He had invited Raila, and while Raila was there, he called Kalonzo and invited him to the meeting. Although Ruto was himself eyeing the presidency, he was at that time working with Kalonzo. Raila, on the other hand, had already made up his mind about going for the big seat, and had started a countrywide tour to popularise his bid. He had gone to Kisii in Nyanza and then to the Rift Valley. His meetings were well attended and had begun to cause ripples among his colleagues. The success of those meetings most likely got Ruto to seek a power deal.

It took only a few minutes for Kalonzo to drive to Ruto's palatial home, since his own residence was only a short distance away, in the same locality. The first thing Kalonzo saw as he drove into the compound was Raila's car parked on the driveway. There, his worries began. Had he been set up? What could be happening? As the two adversaries sat opposite each other, Ruto dropped the bombshell that stunned Kalonzo: withdraw your presidential bid and accept the vice presidency. Let Raila be the flag-bearer, Ruto told Kalonzo. Ruto himself was prepared to take any other position. Kalonzo's mood immediately changed; he was upset, and did not want to encourage further discussion. Telling the two that he wanted time to think about it, he excused himself and left.

From Karen, Kalonzo got in touch with Mudavadi, and the two agreed to consult other MPs on the next course of action. The group met at the Serena Hotel, and thereafter addressed a press conference. The MPs among them, Nyiva Mwendwa, Andrew Ligale, Kenneth Marende, Charles Kilonzo, David Mwanzia, and I, faulted Raila for trying to divide the party by holding rallies without involving the others. We suggested that, henceforth, the NEC must agree upon all party meetings and that they must be announced in advance. Raila hit back, saying he would not be held back from talking to Kenyans. That acrimonious meeting and the events that immediately followed were a turning point in ODM-Kenya. Within no time, new alignments had emerged. Ruto and most of the Kalenjin MPs who were initially for Kalonzo, and Mudavadi and most of the Abaluhyia legislators sided with Raila, while Kalonzo moved away to consolidate an alliance with Uhuru.

## The cracks go public

On August 6, Uhuru, Kalonzo, and Ojiambo appeared publicly for the first time as part of the strategy to intimidate Raila. The event was a meeting with SPK officials at a Nairobi hotel. What made things worse was the fact that the trio remained tight-lipped about what they had discussed with the coast-based officials. SPK was formed in 1997 to agitate for federalism and for land rights, but it had failed to make an impact at the national level, meaning its inclusion in the Third Force was not going to have a major impact. Nevertheless, its support was important, from a psychological point of view, to intimidate the enemy. Given the murmurs of disapproval that followed from Raila's people, the strategy had succeeded. Kalonzo strategists were pleased with the results and proceeded with plans for another public display of friendship between them. That was accomplished a few weeks later, when Uhuru and Kalonzo went on a road show through the densely populated Mukuru slums on the fringes of Nairobi. Exuberant crowds lined the dusty thoroughfares as a large convoy of vehicles snaked its way on narrow streets to the soccer field at the centre of the vast estate. The road show, in expensive four-wheel vehicles, gave the presidential hopefuls an opportunity to come face to face with abject poverty in one of Kenya's biggest shanty towns.

The unemployed and those at the lowest ranks of society inhabited Mukuru. This slum and others provide day labour to firms in the city's nearby industrial area. The open sewerage system, harbouring millions of flies and dashing rodents; the smoke from *nyama choma* grills bellowing from shacks; and the stench emanating from pit latrines and open dumpsites, are dominant features throughout this slum area. For people like Kalonzo and Uhuru, who were used to well-tended gardens and multi-story mansions, Mukuru turned out to be a reality check. Before addressing the crowd, they donated food and clothing to victims of a recent fire tragedy that had left some residents in the area homeless and hungry. A large crowd attended and was happy to see the two together. "What you are seeing today," Kalonzo told the people, "is the beginning of a lot more appearances between the two of us. When you see me here with Uhuru, you have to figure out yourself what is going on." Uhuru cryptically alluded to an upcoming alliance between the two but revealed no details. The Uhuru/Kalonzo/Ojiambo alliance was, however, short-lived. Shortly thereafter Uhuru convened his party's NEC meeting and declared that KANU would pull out of ODM-Kenya and support Kibaki for president. The proposed alliance disappeared into thin air. ODM-Kenya condemned Uhuru's decision and felt betrayed by a man who, all along, had promised KANU's support for the movement.

In arriving at that decision, Uhuru had underestimated the opposition from the rest of his party officials. Secretary General Ruto told Uhuru to stop making "unnecessary demands" on the Coalition. "KANU cannot give ultimatums to the party," Ruto said. "We are not going to be bound by resolutions of KANU. Uhuru should be bold enough and say I'm out."[190] The open confrontation between the two who had worked closely for years signalled the impending split in KANU that eventually led many other senior officials to join Raila in ODM-Kenya. Dalmas Otieno, who was KANU's Vice Chairman left in October to join ODM-Kenya, saying his party had made a grave mistake not to see signs of the times. With Uhuru gone, Kalonzo was left exposed and vulnerable. He was angry that Uhuru had failed to follow through on their alliance arrangement, allowing himself to be pushed around by Ruto. "I am beginning to think Uhuru no longer has control of KANU," he privately told aides.

## Kalonzo's hurdle

While Uhuru struggled to sort out his own problems, Kalonzo shifted strategy. He realised that his fights with Raila were not earning him any additional support since poll figures were not showing any significant improvement. He grudgingly decided to go along with Raila. Sometimes in September, the ODM-Kenya NEC met and agreed on a timetable for countrywide solidarity rallies. The idea was to reassure people that the party was united—despite internal rifts—and that it was ready and capable of meeting the challenges posed by the upcoming December elections. Among the first rallies to be scheduled was one at Khadija primary school in Mombasa. The town has a rich cultural history dominated for years by alternating occupation by the Arabs, the Portuguese, and the British. Fort Jesus, a huge structure overlooking the entrance to the harbour, is a monument from the slave trade years, originally a prison, but was now a museum. Settlements that used to settle freed slaves still existed in neighbouring areas and one of them, Freretown, was only a stone's throw away from Khadija. It was here that Kalonzo came face to face with angry ODM-Kenya supporters for the first time since the campaigns began, in an incident that almost threw into pieces the fragile relations between the two principal party contenders.

190 East African Standard, July 12, 2007.

The well-attended meeting was buoyant and peaceful at the beginning, but things changed when Kalonzo took the microphone to address the people. Deep in the crowd was a shrill that tore through the crowd like a sharpened blade: "Traitor! You are a traitor." Then another shouted from a corner, "Go away!" Those immediately facing the podium flashed out wooden hammers, (a distortion of the Hummer vehicle which Raila had imported into the country only a few weeks earlier), held them high as they shouted insults at the speaker. Others in the clamorous crowd accused Kalonzo of undermining Raila by sticking to a race he knew he could not win, while others asked him to leave the party. "Why don't you resign?" At one point during the confusion, and as he struggled for attention, Kalonzo made the mistake of asking the crowd whether or not he should cut short his speech. The hecklers answered in the affirmative.[191] The noise became so uncontrollable that Kalonzo lost his temper, mumbled something inaudible into the microphone, and descended from the podium with his head down. All that time, Raila and the other ODM-Kenya leaders sat amusedly. The fracas was brief but the sting was politically lethal for the young lawyer. Whether the goons were hired to cause mayhem and embarrass Kalonzo was at that time beside the point.

The perception created by that charade was that Kalonzo was untrustworthy and an undeserving of the leadership of the country; that he was more concerned about Raila's defeat than his own victory. That evening, Kalonzo complained to his allies that Raila had set him up for the showdown. It emerged later that the heckling was, indeed, planned and that young people were paid to show up at the rally and cause trouble. But the damage to Kalonzo's image was irreversible.

The incident at Khadija sent an ominous message to Kalonzo that he faced a real challenge in ODM-Kenya. He tried desperately to have the meetings suspended pending an agreement on ground rules, but his colleagues insisted the meetings would continue. In a damage control move, Raila called a press conference in Nairobi to appear to apologise to Kalonzo for the ugly incident. He regretted the incident but urged Kalonzo to abandon his protest. Seeing that he was alone, Kalonzo agreed, and that weekend joined the rest of the ODM-Kenya aspirants at a rally in the Rift Valley town of Nakuru. In the meantime, his advisers went back

[191] Africa News Update/East African Standard, July 9, 2007.

to the drawing board to see how to deal with the apparent antagonism from some of his colleagues. Their verdict: tone down attacks on Raila. Worried that Kalonzo's confrontational attitude was costing him support, they advised the presidential candidate to be tolerant until the end of the nomination process, after which he could look at other options depending on the results, but Kalonzo saw nothing wrong with his *modus operandi.* Not too long after that, he admitted to a close ally that his days in LDP might soon be coming to an end.

## NARC days are over

In the meantime, things were not rosy in NARC either, the coalition that ousted Moi and KANU from power. There were serious leadership problems within the coalition. It did not, therefore, come as a surprise when in May 2007, a large group of Kibaki supporters called a press conference in Nairobi and announced the formation of NARC-Kenya, a new outfit that was rumoured to be Kibaki's vehicle in the 2007 elections. Vice President Moody Awori announced that Foreign Minister Raphael Tuju was to chair the party at the head of eight vice-chairmen and an NEC of fifty-eight members, mostly cabinet ministers and MPs.

The decision to form the splinter group was unprecedented, for it was the first time in Kenyan history that the ruling party was effectively disbanding itself while in office. Although Kibaki was not immediately identified as the brain behind the pullout, it was clear from the participation of his senior ministers that he had sanctioned the move. Some described the move as lawful but called for fresh general elections, but others were blunt. "Everyone knows that NARC is dead, killed by the government,"[192] said Kalonzo.

It was just a matter of time, observers predicted, before Kibaki would come out to declare his departure from the NARC. For some unexplained reason, however, his dalliance with NARC-Kenya was short-lived, and for a period of several months no one could pinpoint his political affiliation. Come September and he proclaimed the formation of the Party of National Unity (PNU), a union of close to a dozen small parties.

---

192 The Free Library, undated.

# CHAPTER 14
# Kalonzo on the move

Towards the end of July, Kalonzo finally made up his mind to part ways with Raila as expected, and commenced talks with Dr. Julia Ojiambo on the finer details of decamping to LPK. He kept the negotiations confidential making it difficult, even for his closest supporters, to know there was a new re-alignment in the offing. Five years of incessant quarrels with Raila had worn him down. He was no longer the confident, tenacious individual he had been at the start of his close relations with Raila. He had made too many enemies in ODM-Kenya, and finally, he had been convinced that his chances of being nominated by the coalition had evaporated. With Raila on an unstoppable spin, there was no longer room for Kalonzo in ODM-Kenya unless he was to play second fiddle, something he didn't want to do. His goal was to be the president of Kenya.

On July 30, barely six months to the general elections, he was ready to make the watershed decision to part with Raila. That morning, he arrived at his campaign headquarters earlier than usual, smart in a dark suit, ready for the big announcement. In an upstairs office, as the morning traffic snarled along the busy Ngong road, Kalonzo called several of his top allies and asked them to drop by for consultations. A call came to me at eight am, and within no time, I was sitting across from his black leather swing chair, sipping from a cup of tea, and listening to the reasons why he had decided to leave the party he had helped found. I was lost for words! That he could arrive at such a momentous decision without first consulting his closest allies was beyond belief. I looked at him closely and saw an astonishingly forlorn individual with tired, sleep-deprived eyes, who was trying hard to look cheerful. He was lackadaisical and inscrutable.

Unlike five years earlier when he joyfully left KANU to join LDP as part of a mass exodus of officials, this time round Kalonzo was lonely and sad. He struggled to explain his decision, saying it was the best considering the discordance in ODM-Kenya, assuring me that his chances of ascending to power through LPK were much higher than via LDP. "Don't you think so, Joe?" I looked askance at his small frame on that oversized luxury chair, scratched my scalp as if to evoke wisdom, and compulsively responded: "I really don't know, Steve. This one hasn't sunk in yet." Soon after, I walked downstairs and left him to consult with others, mingled briefly with the large crowd in the compound, and left, as Ojiambo and her entourage arrived for the big press conference.

Some of the MPs from Kalonzo's Ukambani backyard quietly strolled out of the complex too in a show of disagreement while a few grumbled but stayed put. I wanted to neither be captured on camera nor be present at the press conference. Even Kalonzo's closest advisers could not understand the rationale of that sudden move. Among those who were called in by Kalonzo for a brief was Lucas Maitha, the ODM-Kenya's Organising Secretary who admitted later that he was disturbed by the sudden change of events. Other MPs—among them Jebii Kilimo—also came into the party compound, went in for a brief meeting then hurriedly left, citing other engagements.

## Ojiambo arrives

Pint-sized but chivalrous, Ojiambo looked elegant in her well-coordinated African-print dress. Brimming with excitement, she ambled into the compound, with a happy group on tow, like a queen on coronation day. She always boasted about her party's nationwide branch network, but in the scheme of things, the LPK was latent and insular, depending heavily on support from her own Western region. But even there, competing forces were so entrenched that it was difficult for LPK to shine. The big tent, mounted in the open space of the fenced property to shield supporters from the sun, was packed with media people and well-wishers. Kalonzo looked circumspect but composed. After recognising Ojiambo's achievements in academia (she has a PhD in nutrition) and in politics, and thanking her for accommodating him in LPK, he went on a monologue on the significance of the new alliance. "What has happened today," he told the press conference, "demonstrates leadership. By shifting to this alliance, we have shown the resolve to strengthen ODM-Kenya. Remember at the formation of ODM, I said the future is Orange…I want to repeat today that the future is Orange." He said ODM-Kenya was a "party of parties" and welcomed KANU and others to join it without fear. He then ordered the registered party officials who were in his camp to take control of the party, name, and symbol, a final order to render Raila and his group party-less.

News of Kalonzo's apparent switch spread like wild fire. Media outlets interrupted programmes to announce the defection. Blogs went into overdrive. It was as if the whole political landscape had turned upside down. And it had! A fellow presidential aspirant, Najib Balala told the media: "There has been a fall-out. Kalonzo has become a lone ranger." The news of the defection caught everyone by surprise. At the Kalonzo headquarters, the phones rang off the hook; some called to praise the decision, while others expressed pessimism about chances of an opposition win.

After the press conference, the two partners went into private talks then parted ways, satisfied with the day's events. Raila's first reaction was to call a crisis meeting of his top aides and advisers, at the party headquarters. After hours of closed-door deliberations, the group emerged with a statement announcing a decision to go to court to contest the ownership of the party. They saw a government hand in the division and threatened to storm the offices of the Registrar of Societies if Henry Kosgey, the *de facto* Chairman was not registered immediately. A request for change of officials had been filed weeks earlier, but the Registrar had taken no action and Raila people smelt conspiracy.

Separately that same day, two other presidential hopefuls, Mudavadi and Ruto, met with their teams to study the implication of the split, and then both announced their full support for Raila. The key question at *Pentagon* was whether Raila should take legal action to fight for control of the party or move on and find another vehicle. There were those who felt Raila had invested far too much in the party to abandon it without a fight and advised legal action, but others cautioned that time was limited and Raila should register another party. Almost all the leading lights in ODM-Kenya, including what remained of the *Pentagon* stayed with Raila, leaving Kalonzo with only the Kamba MPs, Ojiambo, MP Lucas Maitha and I. I now consider that decision to stay put with Kalonzo my biggest political blunder.

The following day, the *Standard* carried a doomsday headline on its front page: "The Final Fall-out." Finally, the political theatrics in ODM-Kenya had come to an end; there would be no more grandstanding between the two; no more intrigues; no more fights. That morning, however, the Raila group woke up to the realisation that it was party-less. In essence, Kalonzo had run away with the party that had come to mean so much to its followers. People wondered whether the ODM-Kenya's original dream of reforming the country was now over. While some wrote off Raila, at least temporarily, others felt the break up was overdue. Macharia Gaitho of *The Nation* wrote that the split had "played into Mr. Odinga's hands because it allowed him to take charge of his own outfit and start driving his campaign without the distractions provided by Mr. Musyoka..."[193] Another commentator wondered whether Kalonzo's defection was "strategic or political suicide."[194] The move to go it alone was another example of Kalonzo's determination not to lose sight of the big trophy, but with that impetuous decision, he had thrown himself in the deep end, allowing his detractors to label him an apostate and a traitor. To him Raila was a stumbling block, but by leaving LDP and retaining ODM-Kenya, Kalonzo was finally able to take control of his destiny.

## Raila's plan B

Raila did not waste time brooding over the split but immediately began work on plan B, which he speedily found in Mugambi Imanyara. A lawyer by profession, Imanyara saw early that the Coalition was headed for a split. He rushed to the Registrar of Societies and registered a party by the name, Orange Democratic Movement (ODM). So, when Raila was in a logjam, he found solace in Imanyara who offered him his party. During a function on August 14, Imanyara handed over the party instruments

193 Daily Nation, October 2, 2007.
194 Denis Onyango, Africapress, August 11, 2007.

to Raila, among them, the registration certificate, the party symbol (an unpeeled orange), and the party Constitution. It could not be ascertained whether or not Raila paid any money for the acquisition of the new outfit, but what came out in the open was that Imanyara was just as enthusiastic in handing it over as Raila was in receiving it.

"There are very few occasions," Raila said, during the short ceremony at the party headquarters, his voice cracking, "when I lack words to express myself; and this is one of them. ODM is like the River Nile, which starts in the mountains surrounding Lake Victoria and flows all the way to the Mediterranean Sea. Some people were trying to stop it, but it will surely reach the Mediterranean Sea." With those words, Raila once again became the proud owner of a full-fledged political party he could control and run. In return, Imanyara was rewarded with a position in the party's executive committee.

However, Imanyara's over-rated enthusiasm for reaching out to Raila soon landed him into trouble: he was sacked as a director of the Rural Electrification Board, a state body tasked to provide electricity to remote areas of the country. The government viewed his association with Raila as an affront and a betrayal of the trust bestowed on him as a public servant. Imanyara disagreed, but his attempt to get the court to overturn the dismissal failed. It didn't take long before the new party began to outshine and out-budget its rival, ODM-Kenya. Through a series of high profile, well-attended mass rallies across the country, the ODM was blazing the trail and capturing supporters as fast as Kalonzo was losing his. With seasoned politicians behind it, ODM soon became a terrifying force against Kalonzo's ODM-Kenya and Kibaki's PNU.

Kalonzo's transition from LDP to LPK meant that ODM-Kenya now had two presidential candidates to compete for leadership. It was obvious to political watchers, however, that Kalonzo was the senior partner by virtue of the ready-made support from more than a dozen Parliamentarians from his Ukambani area. On the other hand, Ojiambo was a nominated MP without a single legislator on her side. Thus, his entry was a welcome boost to the struggling LPK, which, until then, was considered a junior partner in the Orange party.

The question in the coalition now was: would Maanzo, the *de jure* Chairman be willing to offer ODM-Kenya to his tribes-mate Kalonzo, if so, on what terms? If Maanzo was unyielding towards Raila, would he behave the same way with Kalonzo? It wasn't long before Maanzo made it clear that he would only hand over the party to Kalonzo at a price of a safety net. He wanted to be nominated to Parliament. Without that, he told the presidential candidate, he would not play ball. In the meantime, the party nominated its interim de facto officials, picking MP Samuel Poghisio as Chairman and Mutula Kilonzo as Secretary General. Ojiambo remained chairman of the LPK but a member of the party *Summit.*

Soon, the issue of control of ODM-Kenya boiled over, presenting a tricky situation for Kalonzo who wanted Maanzo to surrender the party for free. Influential Kamba elders tried to persuade Maanzo to budge but to no avail. Weeks passed without a decision from Kalonzo on the fate of the registered party chairman, and seeing that he was not responding quickly enough, Maanzo threatened to throw the candidate out of the party. The situation became intractably embarrassing for Kalonzo, whose campaign momentum had now been disrupted twice, firstly by the change to LPK, and secondly, by the stand-off with Maanzo. Kalonzo had no choice, and finally had to announce that Maanzo's name would be at the top of the list of those to be the nominated to Parliament. The Constitution permitted parties to nominate twelve MPs to represent special interests based on the number of seats each won at elections. Did Kalonzo honour that promise to Maanzo? Of course not! When the time came to fill the two positions reserved for ODM-Kenya, Kalonzo chose two Moslems, fulfilling an earlier promise to the community. It was only after Kalonzo found a job for Maanzo in the civil service that the *de jure* party Chairman agreed to hand over ODM-Kenya to him and peace in the party was finally restored.

## Tussle over running mate

There was another problem for the presidential candidate. In their negotiations, Kalonzo had agreed that Ojiambo would be his running mate and that the appointment in question would be made immediately thereafter. By the middle of August 2007, he had not yet made the announcement, and Ojiambo was getting impatient, suspecting that the team leader was up to something fishy. The two were old acquaintances in

KANU in 1980s and 1990s when Kalonzo was the Organising Secretary and a minister, and Ojiambo was the Women's Leader and an assistant minister. The two were known to get along well, but that was a long time ago. After Kalonzo joined the LDP in 2002, Ojiambo registered LPK, affiliated to ODM-Kenya and declared interest in the presidency. Now, the two had the same ambition of leading Kenya.

The delay in naming Ojiambo as the running mate was causing anguish in LPK. One afternoon in mid-September, as she chaired her NEC, Ojiambo felt she had had enough. She had waited patiently for three weeks for Kalonzo to act, but the tantalising news never came. She called Kalonzo on the phone. Working at his desk at the party headquarters, his response was that he was still mulling over the matter. The seventy-four-year old professor, who had been made to believe that the number two party position was automatically hers was discomfited and could not understand his new partner's sudden change of behaviour. On the phone, Ojiambo was furious, telling him she felt betrayed. Then, she gave him until eight pm that evening to make the decision or risk an LPK pull-out from ODM-Kenya. That news devastated Kalonzo.

Only weeks earlier, he had thwarted expulsion threats from Maanzo. Now he was facing a much more worrisome problem. With little time left until the general elections, he could not afford to be distracted. Moreover, if expelled, Kalonzo would no longer be taken seriously by the electorate; he would be a laughing stock. He called in a few more of his officials to join him at the party office. It was five pm. At eight o'clock sharp, Ojiambo called again to find out whether Kalonzo had made up his mind. He had not! All that time, we sat there weighing the pros and cons of giving the spot to Ojiambo. Some felt Ojiambo was a political lightweight. To counter Raila's popularity in western region, they said, ODM-Kenya needed a much stronger running mate who had strong grassroots support, a national appeal, and charisma. Ojiambo failed in almost all the attributes.

At the time that Kalonzo was considering Ojiambo, he talked to several other leaders, including Cyrus Jirongo of KADDU and Gideon Moi of KANU but they all rebuffed him. No serious politician of substance wanted to play second fiddle to Kalonzo. It was then decided that the only way to handle the Ojiambo issue was not to run away from the problem but to confront it head-on. So, we took the short drive to the LPK offices along the same road to hear Ojiambo out. There, we found the atmosphere in the crowded meeting room unwelcoming and Ojiambo herself in a pensive mood. Her top party officials were there, among them university dons who had stood by her over the years, and who, at that critical moment, only wanted to know the destiny of their leader.

An LPK official immediately went on the offensive. He talked of Ojiambo's magnanimity and how she had sacrificed herself to save Kalonzo, adding that the gesture had to be reciprocated. "Why are you hesitating Mr. Kalonzo? What has changed since you promised her the number two slot?" The questions came in rapid succession like bullets fired from an automatic pistol. From that moment, we knew things would not be easy for us. The official also wanted to know why, apart from the candidate himself, members of Kalonzo's team had not officially defected to LPK. He argued that members of the ODM-Kenya coalition had to belong to a political party, and that, since the defectors were no longer members of LDP, they had to register with the LPK. However, he was quickly reminded that ODM-Kenya was then both a corporate and an individual membership party, and that defectors could choose to be in ODM-Kenya without being members of any other party. The official, however, insisted that Kalonzo had to make a decision on Ojiambo. "Either the professor is in, or we are out," he said, without mincing words.

Others in Ojiambo's camp spoke in a similar manner and tone. One lady with tears lingering in her eyes spoke passionately about Ojiambo's academic and political credentials, and said it was an insult for anyone to suggest—as some ODM-Kenya members had done in the media a few days earlier—that Ojiambo was unsuitable as Kalonzo's running mate. "Why did you join us then if you didn't think much of her," she asked. I looked at Kalonzo and saw the face of defeat. He was no longer the waspish, elephantine gentleman.

If those sentiments from party minnows had deep emotional overtones, Ojiambo's presentation left no doubt that she was determined to get the position by all means. Firm, composed, and obviously frustrated by Kalonzo's indecision, Ojiambo told him that the issue of the running mate was not a matter of discussion at that point, since it had been sorted out in their earlier meetings. What she wanted to know was when Kalonzo would announce the appointment. "I am under a lot of pressure from my party members," she said, "who think I have sold them to ODM-Kenya. We have been patient enough. Now time has come for you to tell us," the tough talking lady said. "So, *Mheshimiwa,* when are you going to announce?" When Kalonzo shilly-shallied, she shot back: "This has to be done by Monday, or I will call my own press conference and announce our pull out from ODM-Kenya," said the fuming lady. It was already Friday night.

Ojiambo's bluntness left Kalonzo ruffled. Where normally Kalonzo would have exploded in a fit of anger, he cringed at the thought of being party-less only two months after decamping from Raila's group. He sat there dejected and numb, a faint sheet of sweat melting on his forehead. "I have heard you, my sister," he interjected. "You don't have to continue." He posed, stroked his neatly padded black hair, and repeated, as if still searching for the correct response. "I have heard you, my sister." He thanked Ojiambo for her beneficiency, and hoped their relationship would be fruitful. However, after a discursive moment that appeared to go on ad infinitum, Kalonzo diffidently told his potential running mate that time was not ripe for an announcement of such magnitude. "There must be a strategy of making such an important announcement," he said, his voice slightly rising. "We cannot just call a press conference and announce. It has to be done within our overall campaign strategy," he said, convinced that he had contained her.

"*Mheshimiwa*, what is this strategy you are talking about," she hit back. "I am your running mate and the only thing you need to do is to get out there and announce." That bruising confrontation revealed the underlying difficulty posed by haphazard party mergers concocted for political, rather than ideological reasons, such as the one Raila entered with Moi.

The meeting ended as nervously as it had begun. The only thing Kalonzo promised was that he would make a decision within a week. As we left, he knew the matter had reached an inscrutable zenith: it had not only become politically precarious, but personally disconcerting. He was caught in a Catch-22 situation; either succumb to Ojiambo's demands or remain with the empty shell that was the ODM-Kenya. While he remained composed, his mind must certainly have been undergoing an overarching feeling of revulsion. Nothing happened within the week as promised simply because Kalonzo still believed there was a much better candidate out there than Julia Ojiambo.

In the hope that the crisis would be resolved amicably, officials of the two sides met to discuss party logistics. When LPK offered its offices as the presidential campaign headquarters, the offer was politely declined with an explanation that Kalonzo was an ODM-Kenya and not an LPK candidate, and that his campaign headquarters had to be situated away from LPK's. Eventually, the two parties agreed to share the various departments, with LPK taking over security and media relations, and ODM-Kenya retaining finance, policy, and strategy departments. The Kalonzo Musyoka Foundation offices remained the meeting venue of the candidate's top heavy think tank of strategists that included two Israelis, one a campaign specialist, and the other a security expert. There was also a British electoral statistician.

## Foreign agents in Kalonzo's team

I first met the foreigners at a Naivasha Lodge sometimes in late 2006 during a retreat, also attended by lawyers, media specialists, marketers, and scholars. The Israelis, I came to know later, were loaned to Kalonzo by an unnamed friend, while the Briton was a polls strategist, whose expenses were met directly by Kalonzo. Apart from me, there were only three other ODM-Kenya MPs present at that secret retreat. Bishop Margaret Wanjiru, founder of Jesus Alive Church, and an aspiring politician who, by then, had not aligned herself to any presidential candidate, was also in attendance. It could not be ascertained whether she attended as a Kalonzo supporter or as a member of the clergy. What I remember most about the Bishop were her highly emotional and apocalyptic prayers that visibly moved Kalonzo to tears as she prayed for God's intervention to ensure his entry into State House. "I beseech You Oh Lord that you hear this man of God, that You may grant his wishes. This country, Oh Lord, is looking not only for political, but also for spiritual transformation, and this man, Stephen Kalonzo Musyoka, is the man this country needs to heal the wounds of tribalism, greed, grand corruption and poverty...." The prayers were powerfully delivered and appeared to uplift the souls of everyone present. It was not long after that that Bishop Wanjiru declared her interest in the Starehe parliamentary seat in Nairobi and chose Raila as her presidential candidate.

Discussions at the retreat covered several issues, among them electoral polling, mass mobilisation, and media techniques. The presidential candidate's strengths and weaknesses were assessed and critiqued. Participants pointed out that although Kalonzo came across as an intelligent, caring individual with a youthful disposition, he was rather reserved and had difficulty connecting with people. "You need to loosen up; be yourself and avoid English when you are addressing rural folk," one attendee told him. Others complained that Kalonzo came out as aloof, didn't mix with his legislative colleagues, never called anyone on the phone unless called, and was stuck in the KANU days, when leaders were perceived to be masters, and citizens as servants. He was told, this had to change. In fact, the phrase "servant leadership", which later became the backbone of his manifesto, was inspired by the conclusions of that retreat. As far as I know, there was no follow-up retreat to determine whether or not any of its recommendations were applied, but the foreign advisers, especially the Briton, continued to attend our brainstorming meetings up to election time.

## Ojiambo picked

Before launching his manifesto in mid-October, Kalonzo finally took the bold step of naming Ojiambo as his running mate. In reluctantly settling on Ojiambo, he considered several issues. One was gender. Women voters would have been offended if Kalonzo had left her out, especially given the fact that none of the other political parties had a woman on their tickets. He knew that was a sensitive matter that could cost him votes. Another reason why Kalonzo chose Ojiambo was her political benevolence at the time when Kalonzo needed help most. True, the two were old acquaintances who knew each other well, but in Kenya, politics and trust are usually strange bedfellows. That for weeks Kalonzo had blown hot and cold on the nomination issue attested to that. Another reason why Kalonzo settled for Ojiambo was that the LPK had its foothold in Western Province, home of Raila's deputy, Mudavadi. It was important to have a checkmate there to avoid a haemorrhage of votes to ODM. But the most compelling reason for choosing Ojiambo, after all, were fears of being thrown out of LPK. If that had happened, his presidential campaign would have collapsed. Looking at Ojiambo at that meeting in her office, I was convinced she was not joking when she alluded to dumping Kalonzo. At the end, what started as an antagonistic relationship ended amicably when, at the party's delegates' conference, Kalonzo was officially nominated the party's presidential flag bearer and Ojiambo his running mate.

When exiting LDP, Kalonzo had refused to use the word defection insisting that he had just "switched rooms"[195] from one ODM-Kenya affiliate to another, an explanation Raila rubbished, saying categorically that Kalonzo had, indeed, defected. The word has negative connotations in Kenyan politics, mainly implying desperation and apprehension, and it's mostly applied to unprincipled leaders who jumped from one party to another. Kalonzo did not want to fall under that category.

## Raila rules the roost

Despite a generous public display of self-importance by the other ODM presidential candidates, Raila was the only serious party nominee. The others were mere praise singers. Mudavadi, who was considered the strongest of all, was unwilling to oppose the man who had saved him from political isolation after he had lost his parliamentary seat in 2002. Raila had convinced Mudavadi to join NARC through the LDP in November 2003. When Mudavadi announced his presidential bid, ironically, Raila was on his side. Notwithstanding the flashy way in which he launched his manifesto, Mudavadi did not demonstrate any serious resolve to challenge his party leader, preferring instead to serve as his deputy.

At the ODM's delegates' conference at Kasarani that same week, Raila received his party's nod after garnering 2656 votes against a token challenge from Mudavadi who received a paltry 391 votes. In accepting the nomination, Raila was ecstatic: "The people of Kenya now have an historic duty to each other and the nation, to rise up together through a popular movement to remove a backward, undemocratic, inefficient, corrupt, authoritarian system, and to usher in its wake a new, popular, democratic order, where the people are firmly in solidarity with each other." With that declaration, the political landscape that had been hazy only a few weeks earlier had now thawed. Finally, Kenya got to know the three most serious contenders for the top job: Kibaki, Raila, and Kalonzo.

Soon thereafter, Raila held a huge rally at Uhuru Park to launch his presidential campaign and to kick-off a series of rallies around the country. The massive attendance at the meeting dubbed the "Thunder,"

---

195 Standard, August 4, 2007.

was reminiscent of the meeting at the same venue on October 14, 2002, when the Rainbow Alliance was commissioned. A huge crowd attended, and speeches loaded with hubris were made by party leaders, sending a clear message to Kibaki and Kalonzo that the race for the presidency would not be a walkover. Buoyed by one opinion poll that placed him at fifty-three percent ahead of Kibaki's thirty-seven percent and Kalonzo's eight percent, Raila accentuated on his favourite subject: change in governance, which he said was long overdue.

Charity Ngilu, a member of Kibaki's NAK, who showed up at the rally in a government limousine, with the national flag defiantly fluttering on the bonnet described Raila as the "new Mandela," and unleashed attacks on Kibaki accusing him of killing the NARC dream. "I am seeking partnership with ODM," she said, to a thunderous applause, "since the party has a team that I believe is committed and capable of carrying forward the NARC dream." The sudden about turn by a woman who had ferociously stood with Kibaki for years was puzzling. It must be remembered that it was Ngilu who coerced the reluctant Kibaki to go for the presidency five years earlier. During the entire first term, she was Kibaki's fiercest defender and often dismissed Raila's frequent attacks on the government as being driven by malice. Now, she had abruptly changed tune and was on Raila's side. However, her dramatic appearance at the ODM rally did not amuse Kibaki, who immediately sacked her as Health Minister. To reward her for courage, Raila appointed her to the exclusive policy-making body, the *Pentagon*.

As Raila was at Uhuru Park, Kibaki was begging residents of Nakuru to recognise his achievements and asking them to give him a second tour of duty. Unlike in 2002 when he was benched because of injuries obtained from a motor accident, Kibaki came out like a wounded buffalo to campaign vigorously for his re-election. His message was precise: Give me another chance to finish my work. He coined the phrase, *Kazi Iendelee*, Let the work continue. He went everywhere, with the exception of Nyanza Province, Raila's fort where security could not be guaranteed. He was attracting large crowds but being a poor speaker, his meetings lacked zest and melodrama.

## The "miracle" rally

That week, the Kalonzo campaign team kept itself busy preparing for what it called a "miracle" rally at Uhuru Park a few days later. The rally was Kalonzo's biggest opportunity to showcase his popularity and to trash opinion polls that had portrayed him as an underdog. Preparations for that rally were intense as the ODM-Kenya worked around the clock to ensure people attended in large numbers. The party went on a bombastic road show through the inner city that week to get people to show up. They did, but it can now be revealed that no miracle actually took place in terms of the huge crowd that showed up; the meeting was as ordinary as any. If a miracle took place, it was the *wananchi* who made it happen! The whole thing was stage-managed since MPs allied to ODM-Kenya were requested to bring in an average of five buses of people from their home areas. In fact, some MPs and big businessmen brought up to ten buses each.

Rent-a-crowd for political purposes is not entirely a new phenomenon in Kenya. It is a tradition that began during Moi's days to guarantee a healthy attendance at presidential rallies. At Moi's rallies in Nairobi, for example, people were trucked in from everywhere and were instructed to bring along entertainment groups and clowns to enthuse the crowd. As KANU's Organizing Secretary at the time, Kalonzo was a central figure in mobilising such crowds, and that experience came handy when the time came for him to re-enact the scene. However, ODM-Kenya went overboard on the "miracle rally" because, although the rally was meant for Nairobians, not many of the city dwellers showed up. Dozens of up-country buses were parked far away from Uhuru Park to avoid detection. People would then walk normally as if they were arriving from localities in the city.

By mid-morning, the Uhuru Park grounds were full of people, making it the biggest rally ever to be held by Kalonzo at any place in the country. "With this huge rally," Kalonzo announced euphorically, "we are re-writing history. From now on, no one should call us *punda,* donkey," (in reference to degrading comments from his opponents over his poor poll results). "We are on the road to state house." Unlike a horse, which is recognised for its grace and speed, a donkey in many African cultures is considered slow and lethargic. With those remarks, a frisson of joy rang out from the crowd. Kalonzo told the meeting that he was the best candidate for the job and asked Kenyans to give him a chance. He also unveiled his manifesto that talked about "servant leadership;" his dream of transforming Kenya into a twenty-four-hour economy; his desire to provide free medical and secondary school education for the needy; and his plans for the marginalised youth and women.

Titled "*Mwelekeo Mpya*", the New Beginning, the eighty-one-page manifesto was, expectedly, fore-worded by a Covenant in which gratitude was offered to God for the plenty, the glory, and for peace and liberty. Then it went on: "A new culture of servant-leaders is what Kenya wants and needs. The time has come to elect to office and to authority, leadership that will positively transform our country and our society, both materially and socially, in a lasting manner. I offer myself for stewardship that is strident and visionary, and that will place service above self at all times and in all circumstances. I bring to you a carefully considered and socially motivated vision that addresses the politics, economy and social welfare of our great nation. I invite you to share in this vision for our country, by supporting my nomination for the presidency." Quite impressive, you'll agree.

For weeks, Kalonzo had tried to persuade Gideon, Moi's son, to support him in revamping his floundering campaign in the ODM-dominated Rift Valley. He had invited Gideon to the "miracle" rally and had expected he would attend as a surprise guest. But instead, Gideon called to say he would not be able to come, but that notwithstanding, Kalonzo courageously went ahead and announced his invitee would attend. The former President's son later denied he had any prior plans of attending the rally, saying he had only sent greetings.[196] It was a fluke that embarrassed the ODM-Kenya leader. Every politician knew that to have a person of Gideon's stature on your side meant support from Moi himself. Gideon did not just have influence but also money, which Kalonzo badly needed.

The "miracle" concept was repeated in Mombasa the following week, and again, it defied all expectations. Though the psychological war had been won, the sad news was that the results of the two rallies, big as they were, did not show in the opinion polls that followed. Kalonzo continued to be placed at third position, at between eight percent and thirteen

196 Nation, October 15, 2007.

percent behind his two challengers. The poor performance in the polls frustrated him immensely, and at one or two critical moments when he was down, he admitted that perhaps he had made a mistake to move away from the original Coalition. Conversely, Raila's party was causing waves, consolidating old support, and gaining new grounds almost throughout the country. When Kalonzo ventured into the ODM stronghold of western Kenya, he received lukewarm support in Ojiambo's constituency of Funyula, but met with hostile youths in Busia, a town on the Kenya/Uganda border. For the second time in his campaign, Kalonzo was heckled and called a "traitor" and police had to escort him out of town for security reasons. Upon his return to Nairobi from that tour, Kalonzo did not have nice words to say about his running mate. "If we can be jeered in Ojiambo's own home place, what chances do we have in Western Kenya?" he asked, rather unsurprisingly. He was finally convinced that he had made a wrong choice in Ojiambo, but it was too late.

During a strategy meeting, I broached the idea of Plan B, but I was brushed away by none other than Kalonzo himself. This is one man, who was at the very bottom of the scale still hoping for a miracle win with only weeks remaining to the general elections. As time got closer, he sobered up to the fact that he faced defeat. Three options were put on the table. The first one was for the ODM-Kenya to negotiate a coalition arrangement with Raila's ODM; the second was for the party to sail alone, face defeat, and bid its time until 2012; and, the third was some form of a working alliance with Kibaki's PNU. Given the pent-up discord between Raila and Kalonzo, option one was quickly discarded. Firstly, it was felt that hardliners in ODM would not support the idea, and secondly, begging Raila to accept Kalonzo back in ODM would be personally humiliating for the candidate. Option two was considered too risky, as members felt five years were too long for any politician to wait on the wings without any substantive platform. Option three, on the other hand, was seen to be the most attractive because Kibaki's position had weakened. We were also convinced that if approached, Kibaki would not be averse to accommodating Kalonzo in his administration, if he won. The last option was considered most viable even though no decision was made as to the methodology of approach.

Of the three candidates, Kalonzo was the most optimistic about bagging the presidency. He truly believed in miracles, not just from a pedestrian perspective but also from a religious context. He believed in the powers of prayer so he supplicated several times a day for victory. By October, however, indications were that Raila was headed for the State House. Seeing the presidency slipping away, government functionaries panicked and quietly sent fillers to ODM-Kenya for a one-to-one meeting between Kibaki and Kalonzo to discuss a working arrangement. But the meeting was difficult to arrange because Kalonzo was flip flopping, unable to take a definitive position on the matter. He worried of leakages and feared damaging his political career, if he was known to be meeting Kibaki. While this was going on, a massive internet propaganda campaign was underway with allegations that he had receiving millions of shillings from Kibaki minders to abandon his presidential bid, accusations I knew to be untrue. It was not easy to fathom who was behind that hateful campaign, but ODM adherents could not entirely be ruled out.

The next few weeks preceding the elections appeared to be the most stressful for Kalonzo. He was often in a foul mood, lacked focus, and looked exhausted. Though not usually a consummate entertainer, Kalonzo, would in normal times, ad lib one or two benign jokes and would laugh heartily at himself, but during this period, he was unblinking. He appeared to have a presentiment for defeat. The black-covered Bible, which he carried along whenever he went, was perhaps his biggest source of inspiration. While away from home, he would read it with reverence and pray on the phone with his religious mentors.

However, the miracle he had prayed for had now turned into a mirage. With the way things were going, he had begun to countenance spending five years on the backbenches of Parliament. Perhaps feeling remorseful for all the attacks he had directed at Kibaki and Raila, or perhaps wanting to atone for his usually belligerent attitude towards his opponents, Kalonzo finally appeared to want to make peace: "There is no bad blood between me and my brother Raila," he said, at the funeral of a onetime technocrat and politician, Darius Mbela. "I will accept defeat if he beats me fairly and he should do the same. I have no grudge with President Kibaki either," he said, as Raila, who was present, put up a subtle smile. Those remarks evoked a mixture of tears and applause from the mourners. Kalonzo had finally seen the light.

## A poor campaign

Unlike Raila who was known to be financially stable, thanks to his early involvement in business, Kalonzo was not particularly moneyed. His wealth declaration forms, which he made public, showed he was worth only 50 million shillings, which included bank deposits of less than 2 million shillings, a few pieces of land, vehicles, and stocks. While Raila came from a fairly well-endowed political family, Kalonzo, on the other hand, hailed from the back waters of absolute poverty. When Raila was busy making money running a gas cylinder company in the early 1970s, Kalonzo was still in high school trying to earn grades to get to University. And during Moi years, when he could have enriched himself through corruption, as many of his friends had done, Kalonzo maintained a fairly virtuous lifestyle and, apart from unproven allegations of land grabbing, he was undoubtedly among only a handful of politicians during Moi's time who were not known to have benefitted from public largesse.

For his campaign, Kalonzo relied largely on donations from the friends he made during his stay in Greece and while serving as Foreign Minister. His close association with Jakaya Kikwete, his Foreign Affairs counterpart in Dar es Salaam, who later became Tanzania's President, was well known. So was his friendship with Southern Sudan's liberation leader John Garang, with whom he worked closely for peace for that oil rich region. Kalonzo maintained those cordial relations with Garang's successor, Salva Kir, after the former's death in an air accident.

Unlike his opponents' campaigns, which were well funded, Kalonzo's presidential campaign was marred by lack of adequate finances right from the very beginning, and as his campaign lumbered on, he made it clear to the ODM-Kenya aspirants for parliamentary and civic seats who had expected assistance from him that: "you are on your own. Don't expect funding."[197] Ngilu, his perennial foe in Ukambani, always chided him about his financial inadequacies, saying Kalonzo was too poor to sustain a credible presidential campaign. His presidential headquarters was packed with mostly young and inexperienced staff, some of them relatives; and as was to be expected inefficiencies played havoc to his plans. Bookings for vehicles, charter planes, and accommodation for the candidate and his entourage were often bungled.

[197] Speaking in Kuria, Nyanza Province, November 21, 2007.

In one instance, when I accompanied him on a tour of Northern Kenya, the plane that had been booked to fly us out of Lodwar, a town in Northwestern Kenya, failed to turn up as agreed, forcing us to borrow vehicles and to travel hundreds of kilometres by road to Lokichogio a far away town, to catch a scheduled flight, thus wasting time that could have been used for campaigns in other parts of the country. In another incident, his hired light plane ran out of petrol in a remote coastal outpost, forcing the candidate to abandon his scheduled tour of the region. The plane had enough fuel to fly to Malindi, a few hundred miles away, where a well-wisher, Abu Kanavu, provided fuel to enable it to proceed to Nairobi. Abu was son to Kalonzo's benefactor, Ahmed Talib, one of those who helped him during his early political career in Ukambani.

There were many times when expensively rented sound systems failed while on the road and at major public meetings, exposing the campaign to ridicule. Because of the expenses associated with travels, Kalonzo was forced to reduce his entourage to a bare minimum, sometimes arriving at public meetings with only two bodyguards and one or two politicians, in contrast to Raila who travelled with most of his *Pentagon* members, and Kibaki, who was at all times accompanied by some of his ministers. All that portrayed Kalonzo's presidential campaign as being poorly financed and grossly mismanaged.

But Kalonzo's campaign was not doomed just by its lack of finance and poor execution of programmes. There was a serious lack of commitment among many of his closest regional allies and supporters. Many Kamba, for example, were torn between supporting their kin and voting for a more adept non-Kamba, for example, Raila, thought to be a more credible presidential material. In Ukambani itself, support was split between Kalonzo and Ngilu, a capricious manipulator who liked to call Kalonzo a "coward" and a Kibaki "spy" who left ODM-Kenya to escape competition from his rivals.[198]

Kalonzo also had to contend with John Harun Mwau, a wealthy former police sharpshooter and once a presidential candidate for the Party of Independent Candidates (PICK), who relished every opportunity to thrash Kalonzo. A combination of Ngilu and Mwau made Kalonzo's dream of capturing his home province block vote impossible. Undoubtedly, those

198 Standard, April 13, 2008.

factors contributed immensely to the Kamba split, making campaigning in his home region a major challenge. Like Ngilu, most Kamba especially the professional lot, saw Kalonzo's campaign as going nowhere

One constituency, which Kalonzo tried unsuccessfully to woo, was the Moslem community. The majority of Kenyan Moslems reside along the Coast, thanks to the influence of Arabs in past centuries, but there is also a large number of Moslems of Somali origin, north of Kenya, along the border with Somalia. Unfortunately, throughout his political life, he had portrayed himself as an ultra-conservative born-again Christian, even though in his early life in Mwingi, he had interacted freely with Moslems and even benefitted from their benevolence. As a result, the majority of Moslems saw him, rightly or wrongly, as anti-Moslem undeserving of their support.

At one time, he met with a group of Moslem clerics and scholars in Mombasa who wanted to know his stand on the Moslem religion and to question him on his lack of interest in Moslem activities. Unlike Kibaki and Raila who had been photographed in *kanzus* and fezs during Moslem festivities, Kalonzo shunned any situation that would be seen to be questioning his Christian faith. Although he denied professing anti-Moslem feelings, he could not explain why his presidential campaign team did not have a single Moslem in a senior position. Seeing his difficulty in coming up with a coherent explanation, I passed him a note telling him to declare there and then that he would immediately name one to his inner team. I expected him to make an unconditional declaration there and then, but Kalonzo failed to take the bait. He read the note and tucked it away in his shirt pocket. On our way out, a Moslem scholar pulled me aside and bluntly told me the man had failed the test because he had not sufficiently convinced them he was a religious moderate who could work with them. He lost the Moslem vote altogether.

# CHAPTER 15

## Violence erupts

As temperatures rose with the fast approaching general elections, signs of violent activities began to emerge. In Mt. Elgon, about five hundred kilometres west of Nairobi, attacks against innocent people were on the increase; houses were being burnt and thousands of people were fleeing their homes for safer areas. Elsewhere, a major supermarket chain reported a sudden increase in the sale of machetes, and announced it was limiting purchases, fearing the weapons might be used in election violence. About the same time, police, on a routine check, stopped an official car assigned to an assistant minister and an assortment of weapons, mainly machetes, was discovered. Soon thereafter, two people were shot dead in two constituencies in western Kenya, and a woman parliamentary aspirant from the same region was murdered in Nairobi in unclear circumstances. Machetes were weapons of choice during the Rwanda genocide in which thousands of civilians were killed in ethnic fighting between the Hutus and the Tutsis.

In Central Kenya, a twenty-two-year old woman was pulled out of a campaign convoy by armed men, raped and then killed. Cases of women candidates being attacked were also reported from many areas of the country. One hundred and twenty women had offered themselves as candidates in 2007, as opposed to twenty-two in the 2002 general elections, a definite threat to male contestants. In Kisii, ODM officials, including Ruto, who gatecrashed a fund-raising event organised by opponents, were attacked by youths firing arrows and hurling stones, forcing the officials to run for their lives. The hosts claimed the officials had not been invited "and we are not to blame for what befell them."[199] The cause of the emerging countrywide violence, the state-funded Kenya National Human Rights Commission (KNHRC) believed, was to prevent certain tribes from voting for their candidates, thus giving advantage to others. Senior political leaders were not spared either. A meeting called by Saitoti in his constituency was disrupted, while Uhuru had to be shielded from a fractious crowd of stone throwers during a meeting in Uasin Gishu after youths from an opposing party invaded his rally.

By early December, cases of campaign-related crime had increased so much so that two dozen foreign embassies issued a statement asking for zero tolerance on campaign violence. Elsewhere in the Rift Valley, dozens of people were killed in Kuresoi, Mt. Elgon, and Molo, forcing thousands of people to move away from their homes for fear of gang attacks. Hate leaflets were discovered on the streets of Keiyo and Kericho districts that led to the arrest of three people. Surprisingly, two of the men caught in the act were alleged to be policemen belonging to the Embakasi Administration Police Training College, outside Nairobi. A local television station was bold enough to publish the names and force numbers of the officers, identifying them as some of the purveyors of inciteful propaganda pitting the indigenous Kalenjins and Kikuyu settlers in the region.

Certain FM radio stations, particularly in the violence prone areas of Rift Valley and central Kenya, began a hate campaign that fuelled ethnic tension to unparalleled levels: "Mongoose has come to steal our chicks"; "Get rid of weeds" were some of the metaphors used by the radio stations to whip up tribal sentiments. The hateful stations were no different from Radio-Television Libre des Mille Collines, the notorious station blamed for contributing immensely to the Rwanda genocide in 1994. Inciteful tribal language songs were also composed some calling leaders "murderers… power hungry…lazy."[200] The KNCHR, which investigated media content during the period leading to elections, admitted that there had been a lot of hate speech, sometimes thinly veiled.

---

[199] Daniel Wallis, Reuters, Sept 22, 2007.

[200] IRIN Africa, alleged lyrics of a song by a Kenyan musician.

In Nairobi, a giant PNU billboard along the busy Uhuru highway near Nyayo Stadium was destroyed by fire and the ODM was blamed for it. Both sides reported many cases of destruction of posters. Allegations of poor performance were also being directed at Raila himself, with opponents suggesting that he had built only two toilets in the toilet-deficient sprawling Kibera slums for all the years he was the area MP. He quickly responded with a full-page advertisement listing all his achievements, including the number of schools, health centres, and roads he had built through state devolved funds. He also said he had built dozens of toilets.

Election violence has been a regular feature during all elections since the introduction of pluralism in 1992. Election related tribal clashes occurred with precision prior and during the elections in 1992 and 1997. In 1998, Moi appointed a Judicial Commission under Justice A.M Akiwumi to enquire into tribal clashes in the country. At the end, the Commission named prominent politicians as some of the instigators of the violence that resulted in the loss of thousands of lives. Between January and December 2002, for example, three hundred and twenty-five Kenyan lives were lost,[201] equivalent to six deaths per week. Isiolo North constituency in Northern Kenya where twenty-three people died was rated as the most violent. Throughout the campaign period in the 2002 election when Moi was campaigning for Uhuru, and the Rainbow Coalition was struggling to end KANU rule, tension was high. "There was the presence of vigilantes, militias, and traditional 'warriors', making some to believe that Kenya would fail the test and go the 1994 Rwandan style: degenerating to genocide."[202]

In the absence of political will and rampant impunity, not a single prominent individual named in that report was ever successfully prosecuted.

---

201 Central Depository Unit (CDU), 2003, p. 12.
202 Ibid., p. 17.

# CHAPTER 16

## Secret mission to Kibaki

While Raila and Kalonzo stomped rural Kenya, Kibaki travelled to the Coast for the second time in two months. With one million votes up for grabs, the region provided crucial swing votes for presidential candidates. For years, the region had been a KANU zone, and even after the introduction of pluralism, it continued to support Moi and KANU, but the pendulum had changed in 2002 when Raila left KANU, took over LDP, and helped form the Rainbow Coalition. Within a few months—from the day NARC was born on October 14 to election time in December 2002—the region had completely moved from being a KANU stronghold into a veritable opposition enclave. The predominantly *Mijikenda* tribes—that for decades had complained of marginalisation—finally found a reason to turn against the independence party, which they had bitterly blamed for their massive poverty, illiteracy, and landlessness. The level of disillusionment against KANU was so high beginning in the 1990s that people at the coast had toyed with the idea of succeeding to form an autonomous region.

In the meantime, radical elements had formed a rag tag para-military group calling itself *Kaya Bombo* that was anchored deep in a forest in Kwale, south of Mombasa. In August 1997, the group armed with arrows and bows, and at least one pistol, burnt down a police station killing five officers and setting free all the prisoners. They destroyed houses and looted personal property.[203] Although they cited dispossession of land as the main

---

[203] Report of the Judicial Commission Appointed to Inquire into Tribal Clashes in

reason for their violent behaviour, it was evident the group had a political agenda. The government, chary that those localised attacks could spread, posted a large contingent of security forces in the area. Indeed, some attacks were reported as far away as the north coast, many miles away from the forest.

As he made his final foray into the region before the general elections, it was obvious Kibaki had all those factors in mind. He knew that the government's inertia, over the years, in dealing with the chronic land issue had driven many voters to the opposition. In earlier visits that year, Kibaki had tried to pacify the people by issuing land ownership documents to hundreds of landless people, but that impetuous decision was inane and certainly inadequate.

It was a mild October, and although the day was hot and humid due to intermittent showers of the seasonal short rains, the cool ocean breeze as the sun set in the horizon, provided a perfect moment of reflection for the seventy-two-year old leader battling for re-election. As was always the case, his Strategic Policy Adviser, Stanley Murage, was at his side, keeping him informed of the fast changing political scenario. Murage, a towering bespectacled figure, had risen from a junior position as a quantity surveyor in government to occupy one of the most coveted offices in Kenya's political scene. His rank was that of Permanent Secretary, equivalent to the chief executive officer in a large corporate entity, but his actual place in government was far more profound and carried much more clout that most Kenyans realised.

Murage entered State House in November 2004 after six years in government. The story was that, his appointment—like those of many others into the high echelons of Government—was carefully vetted by Kibaki's *Council of Elders*. He was appointed to head the newly created Strategic Policy Unit, whose terms of reference were coached in bureaucratic lingo that hardly sounded inspiring: "to elaborate on policy initiatives by the President for communication to relevant Ministries for implementation…to monitor policy implementation and ideas requiring policy initiatives by the President…and to undertake assignments on behalf of the President."

---

Kenya, chaired by Mr. Justice A.M. Akiwumi, July 31, 1999, p. 256.

It was what the job description did not say that gave him the leeway to be centrally involved in all major policy decisions at State House. He controlled the daily diary; coordinated presidential speeches; decided who the President would meet and not meet; and which meetings the Head of State would attend, and which would be delegated. He advised the President on policy and prepared talking notes for transmission to the Cabinet. Many Cabinet Ministers and top government officials owed their appointments and survival to the influential workaholic. He reportedly influenced the appointments and sacking of senior government officials and was revered within government circles. He sat in all key meetings involving the President and took notes, making him the custodian of some of Kibaki's most treasured secrets. In fact, some say, it was Murage himself—abrasive and bulging in raw guts—who engineered his own rise in influence. Within no time, he had become the most important player in executive policy formulation, and remained so throughout Kibaki's first term from 2003 to 2008. Aggressive, and by some accounts stubborn, he was far more powerful and excessively more influential than the State House Comptroller, then a dour, young technocrat called Hyslop P. Ipu. He completely eclipsed Ipu whose role became increasingly opaque, as Murage's soared.

Administratively, he was supposed to report to the Head of Civil Service and Secretary to the Cabinet, but he often felt no need for that since his strategic location within the State House made it easy for him to deal directly with Kibaki. When that was not possible for personal or logistical reasons, Murage would make unilateral decisions that sometimes turned out to be highly controversial, as when he got himself entangled in a matter involving the World Bank Country Director, Colin Bruce, as will be seen later on. I first met Murage in August 2005 when I went to State House, Mombasa, along with other Coast MPs. He impressed me as amiable, aristocratic, and highly intelligent; he had a commanding presence and personality, factors that complimented Kibaki's statesmanship disposition: A few weeks earlier, opinion polls had shown that Kibaki's popularity had dropped significantly in at least six out of the eight provinces. Raila had overtaken Kibaki for the first time with a fifty-three percent lead ahead of Kibaki's thirty-seven percent and Kalonzo's eight percent. That was not good news for the President, and his people feared he could end up as a one-term President whereas his predecessors—Kenyatta and Moi—had spent long stints at the helm.

On that Sunday morning, the President had gone to church with his wife Lucy, and had returned to the palatial palace overlooking the Indian Ocean for a quiet day. Those who saw him in church, however, attested to the fact that he appeared less jovial than normal, more reflective, and a touch more subdued than during his earlier appearances. It is possible his foul mood was caused by recent newspaper headlines that had painted a gloomy forecast of his re-election chances: "Raila Tops Tables"[204] "Raila Stretches Lead over his rivals"[205] some of them had shouted. Undoubtedly, Murage was a worried man. He must have spent many hours thinking of how to save his master from possible humiliation. Kibaki's defeat would mean more than just a personal blow to Murage. It would mean the overthrow of the *status quo* and the end of an era for the enterprising Kikuyu who had benefitted immensely from years of patronage. The idea that enterprising Kikuyu could lose power was scary, and explained the high anxiety within the ruling and professional classes during those last weeks before elections.

For a man who had spent all his life in the rocky world of Kenyan politics, Kibaki was not, however, new to the pain and emotional stress of defeat. He had lost two presidential elections to Moi, in 1992 and in 1997. In 2005, he had suffered a debilitating showdown when the Constitutional Draft of his choice was soundly defeated during a referendum. As a first term president Kibaki's overall performance had been relatively good compared to Moi's: the economy had grown by almost seven percent from zero growth; inflation had been brought under control; and infrastructure development was visible, as major roads were paved, airports upgraded, and telecommunication sector improved. Tourism—one of Kenya's leading foreign exchange earners—was booming, and free primary education, which he introduced earlier in his term, had greatly transformed and rejuvenated the educational sector. The only major bloat in his presidency was his administration's inability to realise a new constitution, which he had promised, would be delivered within one hundred days after taking over.

Sadly in Kenya, incumbents were not always re-elected on the basis of track record and good performance. Kenyatta was re-elected three times mainly out of reverence for his pioneering role in the independence

---

[204] Sunday Nation, September 29, 2007.

[205] Sunday Nation, October 13, 2007.

struggle, while Moi was kept in power for more than two decades through voter coercion, manipulation, and widespread corruption of the electoral system. None of them won re-election because of their development records. If development were the sole defining factor, Kenyatta and Moi would not have enjoyed their long terms in office. Their regimes were corrupt and abused human rights and democratic ideals. The two helped destroy what was once an African economic powerhouse through gross mismanagement, self-interest, and cronyism. At the end of the Moi era, the country was a basket case, relying heavily on donor aid.

## The talks

As opinion polls continued to show Kalonzo trailing far behind the rest, some in ODM-Kenya began to ponder hard and wide about available options. We had looked at several and had concluded that an association with Kibaki was the best option available. By September, Raila was ahead with forty-seven percent; Kibaki was second with thirty-eight percent and Kalonzo still trailed at eight percent. In the early days, when his poll ratings were plummeting, Kalonzo spitefully dismissed them as the mischievous work of his detractors; but as the clock ticked to the finish line, he began to have second thoughts. "Do you think we should believe these polls," he once asked me laconically. "We will be fools to ignore them," I replied with a slight grin.

After settling on Kibaki, we got down to work without, at first, involving Kalonzo. A selected group of senior party officials secretly formed a committee of six, which was eventually trimmed down to three: I was chosen to chair the panel, which also included Johnstone Muthama and Professor Philip Kaloki. We held several meetings, including one at Serena Beach Hotel, Mombasa, which was also attended by Party Chairman Samuel Porghisio, the objective being to work out a mutually agreeable pact with Kibaki to secure Kalonzo's place in government. That entailed meeting personally with the President.

The broad plan was for us to work with Murage who had already expressed interest in such a pact. Initial talks were conducted and the concept of a meeting with the President was agreed. In the meantime, Muthama and Murage were in constant communication on the phone that morning of October. I knew the mission was fraught with risks and political dangers for both the candidate and us. Murage had assured us of confidentiality, but I was not sufficiently convinced that a meeting such as the one we were planning could take place without attracting attention. State House Nairobi was ruled out as venue since it was too "open" and for us to be seen there at a time when the election campaign was on its final leg would raise eyebrows. We agreed the meeting had to take place elsewhere, and that is how State House Mombasa was chosen as venue. It was then that we informed Kalonzo of our mission and he sanctioned every detail. Other than those in the committee and the party Chairman, no one else knew of the plans that were to change the dimension of the political leadership in Kenya. Kalonzo had warned that he would denounce the mission if it leaked, but we assured him that we would take maximum care to have it held as surreptitiously as humanly possible. The only one thing we asked Kalonzo to do to help in covering-up the tracks was for him to continue his political attacks on Kibaki and Raila. That he did with gusto, at one time accusing the incumbent as having ran out of ideas: "President Kibaki and ODM candidate Raila Odinga should know that we are nearing to State House," he told one meeting. "We need inspirational leadership and not politics of hate."[206]

For Kibaki, the proposed mission from ODM-Kenya was a blessing. It gave him hope that something could be worked out to enable PNU and ODM-Kenya to join hands and, together, defeat Raila and his ODM. I was already in Mombasa on the day of the planned meeting. Professor Kaloki could not come along, but Muthama and Justice Kasanga Mulwa arranged to fly from Nairobi that evening for the seven pm meeting. Justice Mulwa, a gregarious former Kenya High Court Judge, left the Kenyan bench acrimoniously in 2004, and was, at the time of the meeting, awaiting his retirement from the East African Court of Justice in Arusha, Tanzania. I have no idea how the judge was recruited into the mission since he was not a party insider, neither was he a member of the committee. I was told he was to serve as our adviser. The flight from Nairobi, however, was delayed and the meeting had to be moved forward. That delay, I found out later, precipitated a minor panic at State House given that the President had to restructure his evening activities. I linked up with the two at a nearby private club for the final briefing before our short drive to State House.

---

206 Daily Nation, October 15, 2007.

We all jumped into a taxi driven by a trusted squinty-eyed, bald-headed ODM-Kenya sympathiser who was told to keep his mouth shut.

The bright lights of the old but well-maintained Toyota Corolla taxi slashed through the dark night, as it rattled past the lighthouse that guides ships into the harbour. The black Indian crows known for their ubiquitous droppings all over the coastal town during the day, had long gone to rest; the streets were deserted; and along State House Road, night *Askaris* were on duty guarding modern dwellings of the rich. The mixed aroma of home cooked Swahili delicacies and flowery-smelling incense floated over the oceanfront from the nearby Swahili Old Town, turning the air into a pot-pourri of heavenly divine. When the bright beams hit the metal gate of State House, three guards dressed in military fatigue jumped up from their secure cubicle. A menacingly looking *askari*, a big gun slang over his shoulders, opened the pedestrian gate and approached us warily. He took one brief curious look, extended a curt greeting of "*Jambo Mheshimiwa*," and confirming we were the expected visitors, gestured to his colleague who had his hand on the lock to open the main gate. We drove slowly along the driveway, past the amphitheatre where Kenyatta spent many nights being entertained by traditional dancers, and came to a stop at the entrance of the huge whitewashed house. The State House Comptroller Ipu stood unassumingly at ease to usher us in. He was the only one we saw in the huge compound that night; the rest having retired for the day. The tide was at its peak, pounding the sides of State House down below and splashing salty, foamy water to the edges of Kibaki's private office on the ground floor. It was quiet at the colonially built structure overlooking the passage way into Kilindini harbour. Apart from the security lights illuminating the vast compound, the only other lights that were on were in the living quarters upstairs, where Mama Lucy, the President's wife, was in residence.

The President's office is relatively small, but attached to it is a sitting area where he relaxes with his visitors. It was drizzling when we arrived at the presidential residence at eight-ten pm. No one was more relieved to see us than Murage. He had tracked the movement of the team from the moment it left Nairobi to the time it landed at Moi Airport. The timing was perfect. It was pitch dark, and we felt covered and safe. Throughout that Sunday, Murage had made not less than five calls to Muthama, a self-made millionaire gemstone dealer. A consummate politician with substantial clout in his Ukambani homeland, he was planning to contest a parliamentary seat during the coming elections and was at that time, coordinating Kalonzo's presidential campaign. He ran a business empire that extended into real estate, construction, and banking, but it was in the mining business that the ever friendly and judicious Muthama made his millions, dealing in rubies, greenstones, and tanzanite from as far away as Tanzania and Congo and peddling them to dealers around the world.

Only a few years earlier, he had been a major financier for KANU and DP, becoming one of the most influential power brokers in Ukambani, first as a financial backer of the maverick Charity Ngilu during her failed presidential bid in 1997, and later as a major contributor to Stephen Kalonzo's presidential bid in 2007. An astute wheeler-dealer, the flamboyant forty-two-year old businessman, with a super ego to boot, always boasted about his close association with the First Lady, Lucy, and, how easy it was for him to procure an instant appointment with the Kibakis. He never talked about how he came to know the First Family so closely. Nevertheless, he managed to secure a meeting, and that is all what mattered then.

On paper, Murage and Muthama were two dissimilar individuals. Murage had graduated as a Building Economist while Muthama had climbed the ladder to financial success through sheer guts. They were both tall and imposing and were widely respected in social and business circles. But now, with all their disparities and similarities, the two needed each other and their point of convergence was their stake in Kibaki's and Kalonzo's political destinies.

Each one of the three top candidates had reasons to occupy State House. The septuagenarian Kibaki desperately wanted to win, if for any other reason, to defy pundits who had given him no chance of a second term. On the other hand, Raila desired the presidency to fulfill a life-long ambition of the Odinga family, while Kalonzo saw himself as representing the fresh voice of Kenyans. He was the "Third Force" in case one of the other two failed to win outright. He would be there to provide the swing vote. But it was Kibaki who had everything to lose. Already considered a lame duck, especially after failing to push for a new constitution, President Kibaki had to prove that despite all his failings, he still commanded the support of Kenyans.

Dressed in a long-sleeved flowery shirt, dark pants, and shoes to match, Kibaki was waiting for us in his office overlooking the sea. A gentleman as always, he stood up as we came in, and gave each one of us a firm handshake and a broad smile. Covertly, he didn't look too perturbed by the political diatribe that was swirling all around him, but inside he must have been going through his own private cavalry. From where we sat, I could see faint shapes of marine vessels anchored miles away in the blue churning sea possibly waiting to enter the port; and by way of red dots, small flickering lights in the horizon representing canoes on their way to routine nocturnal fishing expeditions.

I sat to the right of the President, with my two colleagues Muthama and Mulwa completing the semi-circle. The President and his advisor sat on the opposite side. I was, therefore, face-to-face with the most powerful individual in the country for a tete-a-tete that was unprecedented in Kenya's history. Never before had private individuals been given an opportunity to intercede with the President to have an expected loser considered for the second most powerful post. Kibaki was an executive president with full constitutional powers of appointments. It was his prerogative and his alone, to nominate his principal assistant. He was under no duress when he appointed Michael Wamalwa, then Moody Awori. The circumstances were normal then. This time around, Kibaki was under siege, desperate and petrified of losing the presidency. He was prepared to do anything and to take any measure to preserve his position. My mission was simple: do whatever it takes to secure a Vice Presidential position for Kalonzo. The matter was grave but I wanted the deliberations to be amiable, perhaps somehow casual, but without compromising the weightiness of the subject. I knew at that particular moment that my own personal reputation was at stake. If I could manage to get Kibaki to accommodate Kalonzo in his government, I would certainly ingratiate myself to the party leadership, I thought. A failure would diminish my intrinsic standing and hurt my ego.

The introductions were brief primarily because the President was familiar with all of us. Mulwa was at one time an MP. In 1999 when Mulwa was elected to Parliament, Kibaki was appointed Minister for Finance and Economic Planning by Moi. The two were also acquaintances in KANU. Similarly, as we noted earlier, Muthama had known the Kibakis for years. Before the meeting formally began, we spent several minutes breaking the ice with small talk, ranging from the weather to the impending dissolution of Parliament, which the President said, he would announce soon.

Then I began my pitch: "Your Excellency, as you have been informed, we are here on behalf of a fellow presidential candidate, Stephen Kalonzo Musyoka. We have his mandate to meet with you to discuss possibilities of you two working together."

It seemed everything was at a standstill at that point. I took a deep breath, sized up the immediate reaction from the other side, and saw it was good. The President seemed keen and attentive, so I continued: "Mr. President, every available indicator, from opinion polls to political analyses, point to a possible win by ODM. In recent weeks, ODM has bombarded the media with a lot of propaganda against you and Kalonzo, and this information, misleading as you may think it is, is reaching the people and the people are responding positively. People are asking for change and they see Raila as the person to bring that change. Sir, I am not saying your Government has failed. Indeed, it has not. We now have free primary education, the economy is improving and there is peace."

I paused and looked straight at Kibaki to ensure the message was getting through. "But the truth of the matter is that things don't look too good for either you or Kalonzo, and for your presidency to continue and for Kalonzo to survive politically, the two of you must come together. We may think it's too late, but it's not", I said.

I could feel my heart pounding louder as I struggled to conclude my submission. "Your Excellency, it may not be possible at this meeting to wrap up a comprehensive agreement, but at least we can reach a preliminary understanding on how we can proceed from here."

I thought I had done a pretty good job to set the mood. "Mr. President, I now wish to ask Muthama to say something." We had agreed in advance that Muthama would be the one to make the key proposal. He rubbed his palm softly, and in a respectful way, turned to address the President: "Your Excellency, our main concern is what will happen to you and to Kalonzo if Raila wins. I know for a fact that Kalonzo is ready to work with you, so if you are ready to work with him, then ODM-Kenya would be willing to support you against Raila."

Kibaki looked at Murage, rubbed his hands gently on the arm rests on both sides of his seat, looked up at Muthama and asked: "What do you have in mind? Do you have any specific proposal?"

I looked at Justice Mulwa; he in turn looked at Muthama, and at that point, my head rose as if to command Muthama to go for the kill. He bit his lower lip, took a deep breath, and then blurted out, "Yes we have a specific proposal, Your Excellency: If you allow it, we want Kalonzo to be your Vice President."

At that time, I felt a general sigh of relief, the weight on my shoulders down-loaded like a sack of potatoes from a sweat-soaked back of a porter. Finally, our most critical demand was on the table. My adrenaline was racing and I knew at that moment that the political landscape was about to change forever. The beaming expression on the faces of Justice Mulwa and Muthama did not hide the joy that ran through their veins. A passively relieved Murage adjusted his glasses and gave out a hidden smile.

For the next few seconds the room fell silent; the pounding waves outside became more resounding, and the eerie, ghostly feeling of the colonial relic more ominous. It was during that particular nanosecond, that I imagined the big, cushy Vice President's office; wide-eyed bodyguards standing everywhere; and secretaries typing and filing away top secret documents. I imagined seeing the pint-sized Kalonzo sinking in that huge leather chair; I imagined hearing the faint, angry shouts from afar of, "traitor," "traitor" and calls of protest from ODM. I imagined seeing top-heavy headlines flashed across the front pages: "Kalonzo gets the vice presidency"; "Wiper wipes them all." "He's passed in between them," etc. etc. But in that citadel of power, at that critical moment of great anticipation, I soon found out that all that was an illusion.

Kibaki wasted no time. "If that is what you want, then it's granted," Kibaki said blithely. Just like that? I asked myself quietly. I felt like jumping up and down in joy, but that was not the place and the time to do that. "I accept your proposal," the President said, as if to emphasise the point. That was it; a coup de grace. My heart sank with inner peace. But Kibaki was not just about to offer the job without his own conditions. Yes, the matter was about support in exchange for the Vice Presidency, but Kibaki wanted more: a complete merger between the PNU and ODM-Kenya. Just as he had advocated for a strong monolithic NARC a few years earlier, he was now hinting at an arrangement where ODM-Kenya would disband to join PNU. "We must aim at merging our parties and that process must not take too long," Kibaki continued. "I would prefer that we get to work immediately so that we can have an announcement before the presidential nominations. I am sure Kenyans would be happy with the news. They will celebrate," he added.

Muthama looked at me as if wondering whether this was really what we wanted: A merger? I kept on saying to myself. Then, just as unexpectedly, Kibaki suggested a one-on-one meeting with Kalonzo at the earliest time possible. In fact, he proposed the following Wednesday, which was only three days away. While the three of us tried to digest what was happening, the President ordered Murage to start work on the meeting immediately.

I knew Kalonzo would be happy about the vice presidency, but I was not sure he would readily accept a meeting with Kibaki when the elections were just around the corner. Justice Mulwa who, until then had remained quiet, showed an urge to make a contribution: "Your Excellency, Sir, I have no problem with a face-to-face meeting between you two, but I am worried that if such a meeting leaked, Kalonzo would be destroyed and his presidential bid would end. This is a very sensitive matter and needs careful planning, Your Excellency. We don't want anything to backfire on us. If such a meeting is necessary, it has to be conducted in a highly confidential environment; the venue and the people attending must be carefully agreed." Mulwa who had come along as our advisor was executing his task marvellously. His stolid demeanour and judicious intervention gave us confidence and his presence at the meeting uplifted our spirits. The President did not query why a public servant of such high standing was at State House at that time of the night, engaging in a game of high political stakes. That did not seem important to him at that point, and he treated his officer with reverence; the two even cracked a few jokes.

On the proposed meeting between the two principals, Murage assured us it would be kept confidential and would take place in a safe house away from State House. "Leave that to me. Believe me, there is nothing to worry about." We were left unconvinced, but we let the matter rest for the time being. Murage then suggested that a sub-committee be formed to include party officials from both sides, but Kibaki objected and said that introducing more people would expose the talks, and even get some people to torpedo the initiative for their own selfish interests. "You know," he said firmly, "once you bring these other characters in, nothing will move. They will bring their own prejudices and judgments. We'll not go anywhere. Only the people who are here should carry this matter forward." We agreed. As we concluded the talks, I assured Kibaki that we would keep our side of the bargain if he kept his, while at the same time underscoring, in case of doubt, that we would accept the Vice Presidency. My remarks were intentional given the betrayal in regard to the LDP/NAK MOU a few years ago. Finally, I thanked him for offering his time and an opportunity for a meeting. We left promising to brief Kalonzo fully at the earliest opportunity, and to get him to accept the one-on-one meeting that same week. We left after agreeing to pursue with Murage details of the bilateral talks.

The three of us were satisfied with the talks. Similarly, Kibaki appeared content that a solution to his immediate crisis was in the offing. As I drove home through the poorly lit Mombasa streets and over the Mtwapa Bridge into my constituency, the import of that evening's meeting began to sink in. I began to wonder whether what we had just done was good for the country. I reflected back to 2003 when a selfish Kibaki betrayed the Kenyan people and scuttled the NARC dream by violating a mutual agreement entered in good faith between friends. I thought of the ignominious sacking of LDP Ministers after the Draft Constitution was rejected in 2005. I also cogitated about how Kibaki—despite his declarations about battling graft—did little to save the country from covetous officials. Is this the man I wanted as my leader for another five years? I asked myself. How about Kalonzo? Does he deserve to "win" even in the event that he lost? Why was it so important for me that I should fight for him? Many questions occupied my mind that night and for days thereafter.

Muthama fully brief Kalonzo about the meeting with Kibaki and he was pleased. Now that things had worked in his favour, we advised him to cease direct attacks on Kibaki. No one wanted a situation where the President would change his mind because of careless and invidious remarks made in the heat of a public meeting.

Muthama and I held another meeting with Murage at his private offices in Nairobi in which the broader spectrum of our intended alliance was discussed. What was frightening though, was the speed with which the other side was pushing for the alliance. The President, said Murage, wanted the arrangement soon, completed, and ready for unveiling before the presidential nomination date in a few weeks time, insisting that any support after the elections would be of no use since it would not provide Kibaki with the required physchological boost to win the elections outright.

Like Kibaki, Murage alluded to the disbandment of ODM-Kenya. That was a very bad idea to us, as bad as when we were being asked by Kibaki a few years earlier to disband LDP. It was an idea fraught with dangers. In any case, this was not a decision few of us could make; only the National Delegates Conference could commit the party to such a declaration, and there was no way such a conference could be convened at such a short notice. We agreed among ourselves in the ODM-Kenya that the issue of our party disbanding was out of the question, and that position was conveyed to Murage. Avenues for further discussions were left open, but nevertheless, we were assured that the agreement on the vice presidency would remain.

On October 20, a now intrepid Kibaki unleashed a torrent of attacks against Raila who, together with other ODM leaders, was present at Nyayo Stadium for the Independence Day celebrations. He called them liars following a series of statements they had made about the government. Raila responded by saying that Kibaki was panicking because he sensed defeat. Two days later, the President dissolved Parliament, setting the stage for the much-awaited general elections. By that time, the polls had become a two-horse affair between Kibaki and Raila. The latter had increased his lead, according to one opinion poll to fifty-three percent, while the former had dropped by one point from the September ratings to thirty-seven percent. Kalonzo had not moved an inch from his static eight percent. Things were, therefore, delicate on Kibaki's side. Kalonzo made no move on the question of the merger and the matter remained in abeyance, but deep inside some of us, we knew the deal was sealed and that Kalonzo would partner with the PNU in a coalition government. The planned one-on-one meeting did not take place, but we in ODM-Kenya kept in constant touch with Murage.

In the meantime, to cloud mounting speculation at the time, Kalonzo came out strongly to deny there was any pre-election arrangement with anyone. Rumours circulating in the media to that effect had talked of a possible "secret card" between two of the three candidates. Although speculation was rife that ODM-Kenya was up to something, no one except a few of us knew exactly what was in store. "Would it be Raila whom Kalonzo has repeatedly accused of puncturing his presidential ambition or PNU's Kibaki whom the ODM-Kenya candidate accuses of non-performance?"[207] That secret was revealed four weeks later.

## Kibaki unveils plan

A few weeks earlier, Kibaki had unveiled his new election vehicle, the PNU, signalling his desire to abandon the NARC, the party that propelled him to the presidency. That decision ended months of speculation about his 2007 election plans. In a short span of time, Kibaki had abandoned three political parties—the DP, NAK, and NARC. He was now ensconced in PNU.

Immediately after announcing that PNU was his re-election vehicle, Kibaki launched his vision for the nation, in which he laid down ten pledges that his government would fulfill if elected, among them, free secondary education and free ante-natal care for pregnant women; creation of jobs for the youth, a devolution strategy to ensure equitable share of economic and social development; and a more vibrant economy: "Today we are setting forth a bold platform as the PNU that will change the lives of every Kenyan forever," he had said, at the launch. "We are mapping out a bright future for this great nation that is real, tangible and achievable. We have made commitments, but we are confident of achieving them because we have demonstrated our ability to deliver on the pledges we make to the people. We are therefore here to declare to all Kenyans through our manifesto that the PNU represents the best hope for this nation."

The PNU manifesto was bold on promises, but even with all the reassurances, the situation on the ground was not good. Out of the eight regions, Kibaki could only count on the predominantly Kikuyu-dominated Central Province, the Upper Eastern Province, a portion of Nairobi, and a section of the Coast. The vote-rich Rift Valley, Nyanza, Western and

207 Sunday Standard, December 2, 2007.

Ukambani regions were out of bounds. But that was not all. He had lost two ministers to the opposition in a matter of weeks: Charity Ngilu of Health and John Koech of the East African Cooperation left to join the opposition. In between, Kibaki had been forced to cancel the inauguration of the Sondu-Miriu Hydroelectric plant in Raila's Nyanza stronghold for security reasons, depriving him of an opportunity to talk directly to his opponents' Luo supporters. And if that was not enough, his presidential campaign team of mainly old guard, found it difficult to communicate with the younger supporters. Youthful leaders in the party complained they had been excluded from campaign activities, a situation which eventually cost the party votes.

# CHAPTER 17
# The final moments

The Steadman Group opinion poll conducted in mid-December 2007 showed Raila had levelled at forty-five percent against Kibaki's forty-three percent, making the elections the closest ever in Kenya's history. Kalonzo's count was stuck at a poor eight percent. The country was awash with observers from all over the world ready to assess the polls. The US was well represented, as was the EU. There were also observers from AU and from local non-governmental groups. To political pundits, the 2007 was a watershed election. Two people who forced KANU out of power in 2002, and who fell out due to leadership wrangles in NARC, were now meeting in a bare knuckle contest to test their popularity. Kibaki had the advantage of incumbency, and in Kenya, history has shown, incumbents don't lose. But Raila had a strong machine in the ODM. Within a few months, since the break-up of ODM-Kenya, the party had spread its tentacles throughout the country and had become a major threat to Kibaki. Once again, it was a battle between a Kikuyu who wanted to preserve the *House of Mumbi*, and a Luo who was spoiling for revenge, rekindling the past wars between Kenyatta and Odinga and between Matiba and Odinga.

Because of the high stakes involved and the tightness of the race, there were fears of violence, regardless of who won, but many Kenyans and the international community hoped the elections would end peacefully. Towards the last days before the polls, only a few scattered incidents of violence were reported. Law enforcement officials were on full alert, especially in the volatile Rift Valley, where tribal clashes had previously occurred between Kalenjin and Kikuyu. A huge contingent of GSU officers, regular and administrative policemen, as well as undercover elements, had taken positions in the region On election day itself, everything was peaceful and there was a general feeling of impending stability after the polls, but that was illusory. As results began to stream into the tallying centre at KICC in Nairobi, many people at the centre and those watching live television transmissions felt something was not quite right. It was taking far too long to announce results, especially those coming from the central and north-eastern regions. Rival camps held impromptu press interviews and advanced claims of vote rigging; as a result, tensions rose. By the end of the second day of counting, the commanding lead of more than 370,000 votes that Raila had obtained the previous day had dwindled to 80,000. By the evening, official counts were showing, Raila had 3,341,116 votes against Kibaki's 2,450,871, a lead of 890,245 votes. Immediately, Raila claimed victory, but the ECK chairman, Kivuitu insisted those were not final results. Within hours, however, Raila's lead had vanished in favour of Kibaki, and soon thereafter, public announcement of results was stopped.

Watching live broadcasts of the tallying, Kenyans were alarmed at the confusion, name-calling, and lack of transparency by tallying officials, and within hours, mayhem had broken out in several parts of the country. Throughout the day, Raila had declared that he had won, and when the situation got more convoluted, he went on record to say the elections had been stolen. Interestingly, when that was happening, Kalonzo was asking the ECK to release the results "without any further delay."[208] To him, Kibaki was the winner and there was no need to wait any further. Released at the height of political heat, Kalonzo's statement was insensitive. Was he in too much of a hurry to take up the Vice Presidency? Or, did he think a hurried announcement would halt the ODM's quest for truth? Either way, he was mistaken.

Suspicion was raised further when lights suddenly went out at the tallying centre and para-military police stormed in to clear people from the hall. Immediately thereafter, Kivuitu went into a sealed room and announced that Kibaki had won by 4,584,721 votes against 4,352,993 for Raila, a lead of 231,728 votes. This is how the observer team of the

208 East African Standard, January 6, 2008.

Washington-based International Republic Institute recorded the events of December 29, in its final report:

"The release of constituency results at the constituency level had not resumed, and by late afternoon the crowd at KICC had become extremely tense with arguments breaking out and agents reportedly having exchanged blows. Samuel Kivuitu, the Chairman of the Electoral Commission of Kenya announced a few additional constituency results which were challenged loudly by opposition representatives. GSU personnel were ordered to clear the KICC conference room, and all public broadcasting ceased. It was announced that only the state-owned radio station, KBC, would be allowed to broadcast subsequent actions of ECK. Shortly thereafter, Kivuitu appeared on KBC and announced the final presidential figures naming President Kibaki the winner."[209]

To confirm that the elections had been rigged, the ODM paraded Kipkemoi Kirui, a parliamentary staffer seconded to the ECK, who confirmed that indeed votes were manipulated: "My conscience could not allow me to see what I was seeing and keep quiet," he told mesmerized Kenyans. Kirui's brave revelation shocked the nation and emboldened the opposition into open defiance against Kibaki. From that moment, Kirui's life was in mortal danger, and soon he left the country for safety abroad.

## Secret swearing-in, more violence

The swearing-in ceremony on the grounds of State House, within an hour after the Kivuitu announcement, was a restricted affair, with only PNU officials and their sympathisers attending. Invitees were rushing to the grounds, even as Kibaki was taking the oath of office, a clear indication that invitations were hurriedly sent out. Compared to the events of December 2002, when Kibaki was inaugurated in a ceremony full of pomp and aggrandisement, the State House affair was egocentric and inane, and moreover, the absence of foreign envoys and regional leaders as is often the case, was clearly noticeable. Dressed in a dark suit and a white shirt, Kibaki took the oath confidently, and in his short

209 The International Republican Institute, Election Observer Mission Final Report, December 2007.

address appealed for calm. "I call upon all candidates and Kenyans in general," Kibaki declared, "to accept the verdict of the people."[210] But his appeal was vacuous since ODM had already announced a full-scale protest action.

Almost as soon as the results were declared, the EU expressed doubt over the veracity of the count, declaring that the ECK "had not succeeded in establishing the credibility of the tallying process to the satisfaction of all parties and candidates."[211]

ODM leader called people to mass action to protest the vote results. Across the country, there was an instant violent response. In the slum locality of Kibera, in Raila's constituency, where people had kept vigil for two straight days waiting for the results, thousands of people poured into the streets, waving clubs, burning houses, and interrupting traffic. Chaos soon spread to all Kenyan towns where businesses were burglarised and looted, and those suspected to be Raila opponents beaten or murdered. Kibaki supporters were also attacked and some of them killed. Foreigners scampered to catch the earliest flights out, while those on their way to Kenya, including a group from the US-based Al Buckner International Mission, cancelled their travel plans. International television stations, among them CNN, Al Jazeera, and the BBC, interrupted transmissions for the "breaking news." Kibaki responded by banning all local live broadcasts and 'broadcasting of any inciting or alarming materials."[212] Amidst protests from local media houses, and in the absence of news from their own indigenous stations, Kenyans turned to foreign channels for information about what was taking place in their own country.

The American Government, which had hastened to acknowledge Kibaki's re-election, quickly made an about turn, and instead admitted that there had been "serious problems" during the vote counting process. It was not until more than two years later that Washington admitted that it was not "sure who (actually) won the elections."[213] Ms. Meg Munn, Parliamentary Secretary of State for Foreign and Commonwealth Affairs told the British House of Commons that her government would not recognise Kibaki as the

---

210 Daily Nation, December 31, 2007.

211 TimesOnline, December 30, 2007.

212 Daily Nation on the Web, February 5, 2008.

213 David Ochami, Standard, March 1, 2010.

legitimately elected president and called on the two sides to find a solution through mediation. The Kenya Government was surprised and angered by that British position, saying Her Majesty's government had no business meddling in Kenyan affairs. Some international election observers packed their bags and left but not before ruling that the elections were "seriously flawed." The London *Economist* said the Kenya polls were "a very African coup."[214] "Both sides stole votes," said Julius Melli, one of the officials who witnessed tallying at some polling stations. "But Kibaki stole more, and stole them inside the tallying centre." He added that results were announced even when documents were missing, incomplete, unsigned by officers or party representatives, incorrectly tabulated, photo-copied or forged.[215]

Incidences of destruction of property and killings went on for several weeks, leaving thousands dead and tens of thousands displaced.

In the meantime, between December 30 when violence started, and January 8 when Kibaki named his Cabinet, Kalonzo's ODM-Kenya was in regular talks with the government. Kibaki's lieutenants, including three cabinet ministers, Amos Kimunya, John Michuki, and Martha Karua, met several times with ODM-Kenya officials, Mutula Kilonzo, David Musila, and Samuel Poghisio. There was a lot of pressure from State House to complete the talks and pave way for the announcement of the Cabinet. The meetings were intense and lasted for hours at a time, focusing mainly on the relationship between the PNU and ODM-Kenya and the overall structure of the intended Coalition. Two agreements were finally reached: One, regarding the appointment of ODM-Kenya people to the Cabinet and state organisations, and two, regarding the long-term relationship between the two parties. Towards the end, ODM-Kenya called a press conference to announce details of the agreements but a last minute change of mind saw the conference cancelled. The contents of those two agreements remain a closely-guarded secret between top officials of the two parties.

---

214 Dennis Onyango, Standard Online, January 6, 2008.

215 Shashank Bengali, McClatchy Newspapers, January 31, 2008.

## Kalonzo assembles his troops

On January 6, the Head of the Civil Service, Ambassador Muthaura called Kalonzo to inform him to be ready to join the government. On that same day, Kalonzo summoned his *Summit* to endorse the party's entry into Kibaki's government. At a closed door meeting at Serena Hotel, *Summit* members told Kalonzo he had no option but to join the government. "This is an opportunity," I said, "that must not be missed. We have missed the presidency but between now and the next elections, you will need a platform." "The vice presidency," I continued, "would give you such a platform. If you don't take this offer, you will fade away and nobody will remember you in 2012." As the person who engineered the appointment, I felt strongly that Kalonzo had no escape route. The country was in a state of maelstrom. Kibaki had shown blustering audacity by forming a government in the midst of chaos. This was the time he needed Kalonzo most as a possible stabilising factor.

Mohammed Affey, a former Kenyan ambassador to Somalia who was later nominated to Parliament by Kalonzo, agreed the country was in dire need of stability. "If we support the Government I am sure we'll achieve that stability." Each of the *Summit* members supported the idea of joining the government. A nervous Kalonzo remained attentive, his left hand resting on his chin, during the one-hour meeting. He was relieved when it was over and a unanimous green light was given for him to accept the appointment. He thanked the officials for their support and assured them that he was ready to join the government. At that meeting, no mention was made of other Cabinet positions for ODM-Kenya because it was felt they had been catered for in the pact with PNU.

On January 8, 2008, a day before Kibaki announced his Cabinet, the party top officials assembled again at Serena Hotel, and from there, drove in a motorcade to State House to officially re-affirm acceptance of the vice presidency and somehow to "hand over Kalonzo" formally to Kibaki. In a modest reception room in State House, we were joined by the Internal Security Minister John Michuki, Head of the Civil Service, Francis Muthaura, a member of Kibaki's *Council of Elders*, George Muhoho, the Policy Strategist Stanley Murage and government spokesman, Alfred Mutua. From the ODM-Kenya were Chairman David Musila, Secretary

General Mutula Kilonzo, MP Lucas Maitha, Mohamed Affey, and myself.

The atmosphere was cordial, though there was an air of sadness at the violent turn of events. We reviewed the events surrounding the tallying of votes, as well as the violence that was raging in the country. Some blamed the ODM for claiming victory, which they said, it could not substantiate, and engaging in an exercise that threatened the security of the country. Kibaki beamed when Mutula, one of the party officials present at the tallying centre, assured him that he had indeed won. "Rest assured Your Excellency," "and have no worry whatsoever. We looked at the contentious votes, and I can guarantee you without any fear of contradiction that you won the elections fair and square. If ODM disagrees," Mutula told the lackadaisical President, "they are free to go to court." Kibaki said nothing in response. Given that Raila had already dismissed the option of resorting to courts to sort out the mess, Mutula's congent submission was more political than pragmatic. Raila's view was that the Kenyan Judiciary was too corrupt to be relied upon to make a fair and just judgment over such an important dispute.

Kalonzo, on his part, assured the President that he was ready to serve in the new government, adding that whatever happened during the campaign was now water under the bridge. "I said a lot about your government during the campaign, Your Excellency, but Kenyans know what your administration has done for them during these past five years," he said. Those remarks were in contrast to comments he had made only a few months earlier, when he had dismissed Kibaki as "too old to rule and should pack his bags and go home to rest."[216] Now, as he sat there in front of his prospective boss, those words rang hollow. Kalonzo said the country had to forge ahead. "With our Coalition in place," he said, "the healing process has begun. I want to assure you that I will assist you in every way to restore peace."

Someone advised the President to immediately visit those areas torn by violence to show the government was stable and functioning normally. Within days, Kibaki was visiting affected areas in Cherangani, in the Rift Valley, where he issued a strong warning to his protagonists: "There

[216] Kumekucha, January 26, 2007.

is a government in place in this country which has the responsibility to the people of Kenya for their security. Let no one therefore delude themselves that they can get away with crime."[217] ODM leaders who had continued to make statements urging people to resist attempts to form a new administration hit back saying mass action would continue until Kibaki agreed to their demands.

## FM stations threatened

Michuki—a man known not to mince words—chastised people who were using mobile phones to spread propaganda against the government and accused some FM stations of fuelling ethnic hatred. He said Kenyans were being subjected to rumours and innuendos by opposition forces bent on making the country ungovernable. He said as minister in charge of internal security, he found ODM's handling of the crisis a matter of grave concern. But we were shocked when he requested a presidential permission to ban SMS communication and to shut-down all FM stations spreading ethnic hatred.

The Minister, known for his hard-line position on everything, argued that such irresponsible radio stations had fuelled the Rwanda genocide. "Your Excellency, we should not allow that to happen in Kenya, and if you concur, I will go ahead and shut down all those stations." The room went silent and everyone looked at him in disbelief. "Is he real?" one participant remembered thinking later. Mutula, who is a senior legal counsel, said such drastic action, coming on the heels of restrictions on live broadcasts, would expose the country to international condemnation; would be counter-productive; and would portray the government as being in a state of panic. Only a few days earlier, all live broadcasts had been banned. Others supported Mutula in the room, and the discussion on that matter ended there. Kibaki did not comment on Michuki's proposal.

It was true that hate messages were flying all over the place and recipients were asked to forward them to friends and relatives. Authorities knew that some of the messages were used "to organise and direct attacks against other communities and to spread rumours that fuelled ethnic

---

217 Africanpress, January 10, 2008.

hatred and political animosity, particularly during the chaos."[218] In fact, one individual was taken to court for spreading one such message, but he was eventually freed for lack of evidence. Michuki's suggestion, therefore, made sense only that it was too drastic and backward. What Kenyans wanted at that moment were serious efforts to restore peace. Belligerent actions would only exacerbate the situation and plunge the country deep into civil war. The seriousness of what the minister was saying was demonstrated when the government later pushed for the enactment of the Kenya Communications Amendment Act, 2008, which provided stiff penalties for anyone caught generating or sending offensive messages.

Before the meeting ended, the President encouraged the PNU and ODM-Kenya to continue bonding and dialoguing, and promised to honour any agreement reached between the two parties. He said security forces were in full control at all the trouble spots, and predicted that the violence would end sooner rather than later.

## Kibaki announces half Cabinet

The following day, Kibaki announced his Cabinet of seventeen ministers with Kalonzo as Vice President and Minister for Home Affairs. In the announcement, the President made it clear that the Cabinet was not complete and that there was still room for the ODM to join in as a Coalition partner. Two other ODM-Kenya officials, Mutula and Poghisio were appointed to the Ministries of Nairobi Metropolitan Development and Information and Communication respectively. Kalonzo, who had been transformed overnight from a third place loser to a winner, immediately moved to take up his new responsibilities at Jogoo House.

In the meantime, the government was overwhelmed by the unrelenting violence, and the announcement of the Cabinet did not help matters at all. As for ODM, it confirmed what its officials had thought all along; that Kalonzo was not to be trusted. Instead of quelling violence, the Cabinet announcement made matters worse and emboldened ODM to press even harder with its opposition to the new arrangement. The following day, ODM top officials went into a closed-door meeting to discuss the next

[218] Kipchumba Some, Sunday Standard, October 25, 2009.

course of action. When they emerged, they announced three days of anti-government rallies to be spread in thirty different locations. They warned the government violence would continue unless Kibaki resigned. But the government quickly responded that any such demonstrations would be illegal and would be met with force. The government followed the warning by placing huge contingents of security personnel at suspected venues of such meetings, including Uhuru Park.

During the first few days after his appointment, Kalonzo was visibly uneasy about the sudden change of fortunes. He had talked of miracles, and one had just happened. He had talked of *kupita katikati yao,* passing in between the two, and indeed, he had slipped through unnoticed. However, the general atmosphere at Jogoo House—the official office of the Vice President since independence—as he drove in sandwiched by security vehicles was far from friendly. Lowly civil servants congregated in groups at the parking area, talking in whispers about their new boss; others abandoned work and were curiously peeping down from the iron grill windows upstairs. Prison sentries—as the Vice Presidency also incorporates the Home Affairs docket—saluted as Kalonzo climbed the few stairs to the reception area from where he was met by a senior officer and ushered into the VIP elevator. Two secretaries, carry-overs from the Awori vice presidency, welcomed him into the huge office featuring a red carpet, satin curtains, and a wide ornate clean desk, just as I had imagined.

From his window, he could see the High Court building where he was sworn-in as a lawyer many years back; and below, evidence of the hustle and bustle of human and vehicular traffic that had come to define Nairobi as one of the busiest cities in Africa. Abutting on Jogoo House on the other side is the towering KICC building, once the headquarters of the KANU, upright and defying, where Kalonzo spent most of his political life defending Moi's atrocious policies.

Jogoo House, a grey edifice right in the middle of downtown Nairobi, has an interesting history of its own. It was in the basement of this building way back in 1964 that a large cache of Russians arms allegedly connected to Vice President Odinga were "discovered." Odinga insisted the government with Kenyatta's full knowledge had ordered the arms but that the President had denounced it to paint him as a communist lackey. Top defence officials conducted the raid on the basement in full glare of the media; carried out when Odinga was out of town, leaving him most embarrassed.

Also in this building, careers of many politicians were destroyed. Kalonzo was Kenya's tenth Vice President.[219] Many before him had resigned for different reasons and only two—Moi and Kibaki—had eventually ascended to the next level to become president; Moi having succeeded Kenyatta directly, and Kibaki having resigned before weaving his way to the top from opposition benches. Kalonzo was, therefore, stepping into a hot seat. He was now the President's principal assistant and senior advisor. He was also taking over a Home Affairs portfolio held previously by both Moi and Kibaki.

Now with his half government in place, Kibaki was ready to deal with the election crisis and the resultant mayhem, even though one of his first decisions as President, that of appointing Kalonzo to head a committee to spearhead reconciliation between the two warring sides, was a monumental blunder. It was no different from letting a cheeky predator intervene in a fight over a carcass between a hungry hyena and a prowling buzzard. Kalonzo was an interested party and he could not be expected to be a fair arbiter. Raila was incensed, saying "even Jesus Christ and his disciples would not have sat in a committee chaired by Judas Iscariot." That remark immensely disturbed Kalonzo, who wondered how a man of "undefined religious convictions," such as Raila, could make such remarks against a pious individual of his standing.

Although the Odingas were Protestants by faith, they were not known to be deeply religious. Raila's father, Odinga, professed the Christian faith and even went around villages spreading the word of God during his school days, but he resisted white missionary teachings, as well as Biblical names for himself and his children. At his own baptism, he deliberately failed to bring along a godfather or a godmother and took the names Obadiah Adonijah only after an elder forced them on him. Because the names smacked of colonialism, he did not like them, preferring instead to be called simply Oginga Odinga. Raila, on the other hand was baptised early in life and

---

219 The others were: Odinga (resigned), Joseph Murumbi (resigned), Moi (became president); Kibaki (resigned), Josephat Karanja (resigned), Saitoti and Mudavadi (resigned), Wamalwa (died), and Awori (resigned).

given the names Rayila Amolo Odinga, but years later, when he was already the country's Prime Minister, Rayila now Raila, underwent another baptism ritual as a reconfirmation of his faith. An avowed Christian, yes he was, but certainly not a "born again" adherent. Without the cooperation of the ODM, the Kalonzo reconciliation committee failed to get off the ground.

It needs to be said at this point that Kalonzo's appointment as Vice President was neither an afterthought by Kibaki, nor a patriotic move by Kalonzo to save the country from chaos. It was not a miracle either. It was a deliberate, calculated, and planned affair meant to stop the ODM from winning the presidency. It was conceived, discussed, and sealed more than two months before the elections. It was purely a strategic political move; a sort of pre-election pact between two major political players. It was a survival technique meant to save Kibaki and Kalonzo from possible humiliation.

In our secret discussions with Kibaki, we did not go beyond the issue of the Vice Presidency and the need for an alliance between ODM-Kenya and PNU. We, for example, did not discuss the elections themselves; the mechanisms to be used to stop Raila; nor did we discuss whether part of that mechanism was to be the manipulation of the elections. It appeared though that PNU insiders had a far wider plan, and the plan, whatever it was, was executed with the full cooperation and connivance of the ECK. What happened at the KICC tallying centre—even without thinking about who won or lost—lacked transparency and appeared to be a serious case of collusion involving the ECK and officials at the highest levels of government. It was not a coincidence that the lights went off at the very crucial moment when the results were about to be announced; nor was it necessary for the para-military units to intervene in a what was purely an administrative matter. The entire performance of ECK Chairman Kivuitu and some of the Commissioners was also suspect and without doubt contributed to the violence that followed.

The most important thing for ODM-Kenya is that it achieved what it wanted to achieve, and did so without succumbing to pressure of a complete merger with the PNU. So, when Mutula talked, just before the results were announced, of "informal approaches"[220] having being

220 Sunday Nation, December 30, 2007.

made by PNU and ODM to lure ODM-Kenya into forming a Coalition Government with one of them, the matter was already fait accompli.

## The world worries

Despite earlier expectations in government that violence would cease with time, killings and destruction of property continued in parts of the Rift Valley, Western, Central and Nairobi. Other regions also reported sporadic incidences of lawlessness. At one time, Kibaki extended an olive branch to Raila by calling for mediation talks, but the latter insisted that any such talks had to be held under the supervision of international mediators, a suggestion the PNU leader initially rejected. Raila was particularly incensed by the naming of the Cabinet describing it as a "joke and a gimmick."

By now, the post-election chaos had become a matter of international concern. Messages of restraint were flying from everywhere: from Obama's Administration in Washington, Tony Blair's Government in London, and the EU in Brussels. While Western nations consulted on how best to assist the east African country, Kibaki and Raila engaged in verbal exchanges that appeared to exacerbate, rather than deflate the state of disharmony. Security forces sent to quell violence at hotspots were clearly unable to deal with the volatile situation and resorted to using live bullets to scatter crowds and save their own lives. Many people were killed.

Then, Kibaki invited Raila to join his government of National Unity but the ODM leader declined, offering instead three options as a condition: the establishment of a transitional government; the enforcement of a power-sharing arrangement; or, a recount of the national votes to determine the real winner. Kibaki insisted he won and the results would stand. He dismissed the other options as unnecessary. There was a stalemate. The question then was not how long the mayhem would continue but how deep in the abyss the country would sink. The economy was at a virtual standstill. Many businesses closed for fear of looting, investors fled, and tourists went elsewhere. Roads in affected areas were jammed with people running away for safety. They took refuge in church compounds and in government institutions. Women and children were most affected through rape and displacements, as well as through human trafficking. Then came the torching of a church in Eldoret, in which dozens of refugees were burnt to death. That shocked the country and reminded many of the atrocities in Rwanda.

The African Union, in consultation with the international community, dispatched the Ghanaian President, John Kufuor to Nairobi, while America sent its Assistant Secretary of State for African Affairs, Jendayi Frazier, to help broker peace. Together with former African Heads of State, Benjamin Mkapa of Tanzania, Katumile Masire of Botswana, and Kenneth Kaunda of Zambia, the leaders held separate talks with Kibaki and Raila, but initial results were not comforting.

At that time a mysterious document, allegedly authored by the World Bank Country Director, Colin Bruce, surfaced in a closed door meeting of the two sides. ODM claimed that both sides had negotiated and agreed upon the document but that Kibaki had refused to sign it. However, the government denounced it, saying the President was seeing it for the first time and called the ODM allegations that he had refused to sign it, an attempt to deceive and mislead Kenyans. Foreign Minister Moses Wetangula said Kibaki had not sent any emissary, nor had he mandated anyone to hold discussions with ODM leaders. Bruce's proposal purported to offer a solution to the election crisis. It proposed, "having a credible and impartial investigation into the issues arising from the elections, determine if a re-run was necessary, and if so, provide a time frame on a structure of government until the re-run."[221] According to Mwenda Njoka, an investigative journalist, Kibaki was livid over reports that someone in his government had committed him into a mediation working document he (the President) knew nothing about. "It turned out Murage (was the person who) had been trying behind-the-scenes to cobble together a mediation team." Said Njoka, a senior journalist with the *Standard* newspaper, who added that Kibaki was not amused when he found out that Murage "had decided to make and implement policy rather than to advise on the same."[222] That debacle, it was alleged, is what ended the skillful technocrat's career at State House. Murage, by omission or commission, had become yet another victim of State House shenanigans.

---

221 Cantran Ground Report, August 14, 2008.

222 Standard, January 27, 2008.

Feeling frustrated that his mission was heading nowhere, a flummoxed Kufuor left the country, telling the media that the warring parties had agreed to work with Kofi Annan, a former UN Secretary General, "towards resolving their differences and all the other outstanding issues including the Constitution and electoral reforms."[223] Hopes for a peaceful solution to the election fiasco, and to the continuing violence vanished, albeit temporarily. There was confusion initially as to who actually had invited Kufuor to Kenya. A government statement alluded that the Ghanaian Head of State was just dropping by for tea, which was not true. Similar confusion surrounded Annan's mission, with the Kenya government denying that it had invited the former UN Secretary General. It said the government was not the aggrieved party since it believed Kibaki had won, and saw no need to invite anyone to arbitrate. To drive its point home, the government website announced that Kibaki had won forty-seven percent of the votes against Raila's forty-four percent.

Under pressure from the international community to accept the Annan intervention, Nairobi then quickly backtracked from its earlier position and issued a statement saying it was looking forward to his visit. A day before Annan arrived, President Obama broadcast a taped radio message through a local FM station in which he expressed his sorrow about the events in his fatherland, saying the post election violence bears "no resemblance to the Kenya I know and carry with me." He told ODM to "turn away from the path of mass protest and violence in seeking participation in Government."[224] It appeared from that statement that Obama was holding Raila responsible for the quagmire and wanted him to ceasefire, but Raila was in no mood of doing anything of the sort. By that time, five hundred Kenyans had been killed and two hundred and fifty thousand others had been dislodged from their homes.

When Annan arrived in Kenya at the end of January, his initial assessment was that although the elections had triggered violence, it had evolved into "something else." He was alluding to rampant cases of rape, burning of houses of worship, looting, destruction of infrastructure, and judicial killings by, among others, rogue police personnel. He immediately visited the hardest-hit areas of Rift Valley, after which he talked of "gross

223 KBC, January 11, 2008.

224 Cristi Parsons, Swamp, January 28, 2008.

and systematic abuses of human rights...some form of ethnic cleansing."[225] He said those responsible for the killings and destruction had to be held to account. The following weeks proved the most difficult to handle for the seasoned diplomat. After the two sides had agreed to work together to resolve the crisis, a committee was formed to look at the real issues, and identified a four-point agenda to address the crisis.[226] The committee was represented equally by the two warring sides.

On February 21, after many frustrating moments, Annan announced to the impatient nation that he was finally optimistic that a deal could be on the way. "I am beginning to see light at the end of the tunnel," he announced in a statement, adding that both sides had agreed on a new government structure. However, the fragile talks almost derailed when a PNU member in the committee, Martha Karua, lambasted Annan for allegedly hinting on a transitional government for two years pending a fresh presidential poll. The combative Minister for Justice and International Affairs accused the chief mediator of "misrepresenting" the facts, claiming what Annan was reported to have said had greatly embarrassed members of the dialogue team. What the former UN official had proposed was a grand Coalition Government because of "...the sort of urgent political grievances we seem to have here."[227] In the meantime, Kenya's troubled situation was raised at the African Union Summit in Addis Ababa, and the continent expressed deep concern at the situation in Kenya.

Despite Annan's earlier optimism, the PNU/ODM joint committee appointed to find a solution to the crisis was not breaking any new grounds. There were far deep-seated differences than had earlier been expected. Both sides felt they had been cheated and neither the ODM nor the PNU wanted to cede ground. While Raila felt he had been robbed of the presidency through an inveterate system of manipulation, Kibaki had

---

225 Kenya Times Online, January 23, 2008.

226 Briefly, Agenda One, cessation of violence and restoration of fundamental rights and liberties; Agenda Two, immediate measures to address the humanitarian crisis and promote reconciliation and healing; Agenda Three, measures to overcome the political crisis; and Agenda Four, establishment of local tribunal to try perpetrators of post-election violence.

227 Reuters, February 12, 2008.

become inured to the trappings of power and was unwilling to surrender without a fight.

Consequently, Annan's shuttle diplomacy was facing hurdles as Kibaki and Raila, through aides, frequently changed positions. The only bullet left in Annan's arsenal was a direct meeting with the principals themselves. At that time, Tanzanian President Jakaya Kikwete had been roped in, and it was his wise counsel that finally prevailed. Relations between Kenya and Tanzania had immensely improved in the preceding years, away from the belligerence that existed during Kenyatta and Nyerere's time. Though far apart in age, Kibaki and Kikwete had developed mutual trust and respect between them. On February 28, after a joint meeting with the two principals, Annan emerged from the Office of President, along with Kikwete, Kibaki, and Raila, to announce: "We have a deal." A huge sigh of relief descended all over the country.

The state of intransigence and chaos finally came to an abrupt and successful end. And, while leaders proceeded to form a new government, thousands of displaced people, IDPs, were moved into camps where most of them remained throughout the first term of the Grand Coalition Government.

# SECTION TWO

# CHAPTER 18
# Constitution-making

After several unsuccessful attempts to kick-start the process of drafting a new Constitution for the country, the National Constitution Conference (NCC) finally opened at the Bomas of Kenya—a cultural centre outside Nairobi—on April 30, 2003. Six-hundred-twenty-nine delegates—including all 222 MPS—from all over the country converged in the capital to deliberate on the draft. Professor Yash Ghai, a world-renowned Constitutional lawyer, led the Constitution of Kenya Review Commission (CKRC), which had prepared the ground for the conference by collecting and collating views from all over the country. For more than a year, the focus of Kenyan politics shifted to the new Constitution initiative. The bumpy drive to a new Constitution had been going on for fifteen years. During that time, scores of Kenyans were killed, many others were detained, and yet others had fled the country for safety. Although the original Constitutional Review Act was passed by Parliament in 1997, it was not until 2000 that the CKRC began work minus civil society groups and the opposition. Furious that they had been excluded, the non-governmental organisations formed their own parallel outfit called the Peoples' Commission of Kenya (PCK), which later became the Ufungamano Initiative, giving them a vehicle to drive the Constitutional framework. However, in 2001, the Act was amended, allowing Ghai's group to merge with Ufungamano, thus forming a panel of twenty-seven commissioners.

Unlike Moi, the reluctant apostle of constitution-making before him, Kibaki had said from the very beginning that a new Constitution would be his top priority. He went to Bomas to inaugurate the NCC and pledged his full support. The NCC brought legal experts face to face with rural Kenyans—some educated and others not quite academically endowed—who believed a new constitutional dispensation was necessary to reform the country. The delegates to NCC had been hand-picked by Moi during the dying moments of his government, when pressure for a new Constitution had peaked. Most of the delegates were, therefore, party adherents, retired civil servants, and peasants. Moi did not have a genuine interest for a new constitution, for the existing one gave him unparalleled powers to run the country like a fiefdom. On the other hand, Kibaki looked at the Constitution as the perfect legacy for him after four decades in politics. He was in his element when he inaugurated the conference, paying glowing tribute to non-governmental organisations "for bringing us to this stage, in our review process… The best homage we can pay, to all of them," he said, "is to act in the best interest of our nation and to fight for more democracy and freedom." Then he offered his unconditional commitment: "My government pledges to support this process in every way. We shall not interfere in the review process... It is my wish that this process be concluded as soon as possible."

The *wanjikus* were not so much interested in the legal arguments by delegates as on the practical results of the convention and the realisation of a new dispensation. They knew the current Constitution favoured the rich; that it did not adequately address the critical issues of land, basic human rights, and equalities. They knew they wanted a recall clause to send home non-performing MPs. They also knew they wanted presidential powers in the existing constitution reduced, and so on. Moslems wanted their centuries old Kadhi's Courts preserved, even as a section of the Church wanted them scrapped. The courts have operated since independence and handle the issues of marriage, divorce, and inheritance.

Huge tents were erected to provide room for delegates to tackle each of the various chapters in the draft. Unfortunately, the Bomas conference also came to be used as a platform for the extension of the NAK/LDP wrangles. Kibaki's party wanted a system of government with executive powers bestowed in the presidency while the LDP favoured a ceremonial presidency with a powerful prime minister. Consequently, there were a lot of accusations and counter-accusations, and many near physical fights during the period of the Bomas talks.

No wonder then barely three months after convening, the talks collapsed under the weight of fractional politics and personality cults. The exercise had been reduced to a political duel and jockeying took centre stage, the common good was abandoned and the nation's state of fracture became more evident. The delegates too were polarised on party and personality lines, and as money changed hands, they became cheeky and shifted positions depending on who was paying more. On June 6, the conference came to a stand-still. Chairman Ghai believed a cooling down period was necessary to calm down frayed tempers and take stock of the direction of the talks.

Then tragedy struck. Professor Crispin Odhiambo-Mbai, a University don who had been instrumental in crafting and chairing the Committee on Devolution was killed in his house in what some of his friends believed, was an attack related to his work at Bomas. Devolution had turned out to be one of the hottest subjects in the discussions, for the simple reason that it touched on the matter of equitable distribution of resources, something the ruling class had resisted all along. Mbai, who was believed to be sympathetic to the LDP position of devolving power from the central government to the grassroots, had become unpopular among those who wanted to retain power at the centre. His elimination became political when those arrested for the murder told police they had been paid by a NARC politician to carry out the assassination. When the confessions were published in the local media, three editors of the concerned paper—Tom Mshindi, David Makali, and Kwamachesi Makhoha—were arrested and held briefly by the police. Like many cases before it with political connotations, the murder case remained with the courts throughout Kibaki's first term, and even by the end of 2010, the matter was still unresolved.

As a result of the conflicting positions, the conference was chronically behind schedule. The deadline of June 30, 2004, which the government itself had set as the benchmark for the unveiling of a new Constitution, was months away, yet nothing substantially positive had so far come out of the conference. The LDP insisted that the deadline had to be respected because Kibaki had promised Kenyans so, while the NAK countered that the deadline was non-binding and was only a "target."[228]

---

228 Sunday Standard, June 20, 2004.

Raila declared that it was either June 30 or nothing. "If we don't deliver the Constitution by June 30, we can just as well put it aside, put it on the shelves, and move forward," he said. "I do not see any purpose that will be served by trying to develop any sort of consensus." As a delegate myself, I stressed that point further in comments to reporters when I accused the government of cheating Kenyans over and over again on the issue of the Constitution. "June 30 remains the big lie of the year," I said, "and (the deadline) is still an important political issue for us," adding that the fact the government was unlikely to meet its deadline would undermine its ability to make promises in future. "We at the LDP have to distance ourselves from that lie," I told the media.

After much haggling between delegates allied to various political interests mainly over the so-called contentious issues, it was agreed to restart the talks on August 17 in what was called Bomas II, but again, politics played havoc with different camps sticking to their hard-line positions. The session failed to make headways and was abandoned after only one month.

## Bomas under threat

On December 24, I released the following personal statement to the media on the wrangles in NARC and the Constitutional impasse:

> Continuing verbal exchanges between senior members of the Kibaki Government over issues to do with presidential succession and the future of the Constitutional review process demonstrate the deep-seated political crisis bedeviling the ruling NARC. Never in the history of independent Kenya has a Government, in its early years of governance, faced such a crisis of confidence and been subjected to such internal turmoil as evidenced in the present regime
>
> The political environment is so poisoned, and cracks in the Coalition so entrenched, that the future of NARC as a governing Coalition can no longer be guaranteed. Disillusionment and despair among Kenyans are so widespread, the high expectations for change built during the campaign so dashed, and the Government itself so ineffectual in governance, that the country may be teetering on the brink of social collapse.

> The people of Kenya should no longer expect change in such an atmosphere of discontent, chronic party rivalries, elitist arrogance, and intolerance of opinion. In a nutshell, the Coalition has become untenable, and the option of disbandment should be considered, even if it means seeking fresh mandate from the people. Kenyans will be day-dreaming to think that the economy could be revived, and mass poverty eradicated, when the Government and specifically the Cabinet is pulling in different directions.
>
> In the meantime, I submit that the Constitutional review process should be allowed to continue uninterrupted in its present form. Anyone campaigning to have it stopped or altered in anyway other than in its present format should be isolated and condemned. The review process is not a preserve of a few in the Government. It is an all-Kenyan initiative that must be carried through, away from factional interests.

I released the statement following reports that the government had plans to scuttle the third session of the talks. Immediately after the collapse of the second session, senior Kenya government officials embarked on a campaign to discredit the Bomas Conference. By the end of December, twenty-five MPs belonging to the NAK, led by Lands Minister Amos Kimunya, had petitioned Speaker Francis Kaparo for a *kamukunji* to discuss the future of the talks. One hundred forty MPs, including almost the entire Cabinet attended in a show of might that was rarely seen in unofficial sessions, prompting extra seats to be brought in to accommodate the over-flowing legislators in the tiny Old Chamber of Parliament.

Although Parliament was in recess, the National Assembly building was a beehive of activity as MPs retreated to meeting rooms for consultations. Short phone messages were circulating urging legislators to agree to have the Bomas process disbanded altogether and the process transferred to Parliament. Consequently, the government side wanted MPs to sign a petition to acquiesce to a premature re-convening of Parliament so as to have the changes endorsed. The NAK said it no longer had confidence in the delegates who were pushing for the curtailment of presidential powers. Minister Kimunya who introduced the *kamukunji* was, himself doggy about the intentions of the meeting: “We are not talking about scuttling

Bomas," he told the meeting. "What we are asking is, if the product from Bomas can't work, what next?"[229] His message was clear though: that Bomas is no longer the way they wanted to go!

The highly-charged *kamukunji*, however, failed to produce an agreement for the recall of Parliament, since most of the MPs excused themselves from the meeting for a variety of different reasons, forcing the Speaker to end the discussion prematurely. Raila did not attend the meeting, opting to concentrate on the funeral arrangements for Joab Omino, the LDP Chairman, who had died a few days earlier. What was unusual about the *kamukunji* was that LDP MPs were not given an opportunity to speak, and the meeting became a one-sided affair. It was a well-choreographed meeting intended to get MPs to rubber stamp an idea already agreed by the NAK. That effort miserably failed.

While this was happening, a few MPs in NAK, including some Cabinet Ministers, were busy exploring another option. Instead of the NCC, they wanted a team of experts appointed to complete the remaining work. They claimed that as constituted, the conference "lacks the intellectual capacity and political neutrality to deliver a Constitution for posterity."[230] They further complained that Moi had chosen the delegates, and that most of them lacked understanding of law, adding that some delegates had been disrespectful to MPs: often booing and shouting them down. On top of that, they wanted Yash Pal Ghai, the NCC Chairman—whom they accused of supporting Raila—to resign. Lacking support, the proposal and the group fizzled away.

About that time, a group of principal players in the Constitution review calling itself the Coalition of National Unity (CNU), and fronted by MP Bonaya Godana, convened a meeting at the Safari Park Hotel to tackle a number of contentious issues that had cropped up in the course of the Bomas discussions. I was one of four LDP representatives at the forum, which was attended by religious, civil society, and political party representatives. Although the CNU leaders, who included Nyachae and Uhuru, said the forum was not meant to railroad Bomas talks, it was obvious from the agenda that the government side planned to push for

229 Sunday Nation, January 25, 2004.
230 The People Daily, January 5, 2004.

provisions that favoured a strong President and a weak Prime Minister. That became clear when the meeting rejected the creation of a powerful Prime Minister, stating instead that the President should be the one to appoint the Prime Minister after consultations with Parliament. "We believe executive power must be exercised by one person," the CNU said in its position paper. "We want an Executive President who is elected by universal suffrage by all Kenyans. All other people must be below the President." At the end of it all, the LDP Secretary General Kamotho signed the statement on behalf of the LDP, but it was obvious the proposal would be unacceptable to the party given the LDP's declared preference for a parliamentary system of government. A number of chapters were discussed and approved including: the Bill of Rights, Representation of the People, and the Legislation. However, the sticking points remained the fate of the Kadhis Courts and the form of devolution. A few days later, Raila called a press conference to denounce the proposal on the Executive, saying the party position for a strong premiership had not changed.

But what struck fear in Kenyans over the future of the Constitution was a statement by the Head of State made at that time, which appeared to indicate that Kibaki had lost his earlier enthusiasm for a new dispensation. He attacked those whom, he said, behaved as if Kenya did not have a Constitution in place. "Some people have made the issue of Constitution their daily occupation. This should not be an issue of discussion all the time." He said Kenya had a Constitution and what was being done was just "fine-tuning the document."[231] It was obvious he was not talking about the Bomas Draft which the government opposed.

Meanwhile, some activists went to court to challenge the role of the CKRC, prompting the High Court to bar the Commission from finalising its report and the Draft Bill. In an unrelated case, a Court stated that the entire Draft Constitution be subjected to a mandatory referendum. While this was happening, forty-four MPs formed what they called the Constitutional Consensus Group (CCG) to try to reconcile the various positions on the draft. Several meetings were held but were faced with acrimony. In the meantime, Kibaki convened an inter-party meeting at State House to try to narrow the differences of opinion between the various political parties. I was one of about a dozen officials from different parties attending that meeting, which to my

231 Sunday Nation, January 11, 2004.

view, was a lacklustre attempt by the President to take charge of a rapidly collapsing stack of Constitutional cards. It appeared to me then that Kibaki had completely lost control of the process, and his lethargy at the meeting attested to that. Hard-liners within the inner circles of the presidency who were unwilling to compromise over the contentious issues, specifically on presidential powers, had hijacked the process. Instead of driving the process, Kibaki had become a mere spectator: an unwitting collaborator in high stake political intrigues perpetuated by his self-centered allies.

After efforts had failed to deprive the NCC of the mandate to complete the Draft Constitution, the delegates re-convened for their third session in January 2004, with an undertaking from the government that the new Constitution would be ready by June 30. By that time, Prof. Ghai had resigned—after being accused of plotting to help Raila snatch power "through the back door"[232]—and had been replaced by Abida Ali-Aroni, a fellow Commissioner. Kenyans were now almost convinced that a new Constitution would not be forthcoming as promised. Unlike the earlier two sessions, Bomas III was even more tumultuous: both sides made accusations and counter accusations of bribery of delegates.

On February 15, Murungi and Raila engaged in a bitter verbal exchange in a conference tent at Bomas in full view of delegates. Murungi called Raila a traitor in government out to wreck the review process, while the latter responded by claiming that the Justice Minister had short-changed Kenyans by proposing a defective Constitutional Draft. The encounter almost turned physical, but the two were separated by Minister Godana, among others, before fists started to fly. The following month, Kibaki summoned both of them to State House for a reconciliation meeting that helped pave way for consensus talks.

Catholic Bishop Philip Sulumeti who had been appointed to chair what was known as the Consensus Building Committee to harmonise the contentious issues finally presented his report to the NCC in mid March 2004. Because the recommendations gave executive powers to the President as both Head of State and of government, as opposed to a powerful Prime Minister and a ceremonial President as favoured by the majority of delegates, the report was rejected. When this happened, the

232 East African Standard, March 16, 2004.

entire government delegation, led by Vice President Awori, walked out of the conference. Among Ministers who remained behind was Raila and Balala, and together with three hundred and forty delegates, passed a resolution that the President's powers be stripped off and be given to a Prime Minister. The resolution also said that the premier would nominate Cabinet Ministers, Deputy Ministers, and Deputy Prime Ministers to be appointed by the President. Meeting the quorum threshold of fifty percent, the conference went through all the articles of the Draft Constitution, passing each one of them with ease. The whole idea was a stroke of creative political posturing played in the same manner as when Raila took over a FORD-Kenya's delegates' meeting abandoned by his rival Wamalwa at Thika, and went ahead to elect his own party officials.

The new development left the government side dumb-founded; caught in a web of its own miscalculation. Both Murungi and Ngilu called for the scrapping of the Bomas process, with the former describing it as "defective and unrealistic."[233] That same evening following the walk-out, Kibaki called a Cabinet meeting at State House—minus LDP ministers—and expressed shock at the turn of events. However, he said in a statement that the government would not interfere with the decision reached at Bomas, since an Act of Parliament created Bomas. "It is the government's wish that the new Constitution be a unifying factor, providing a sound framework for lasting peace, stability, and economic and social development for all."

The adoption of the controversial Bomas Draft ended more than a decade of efforts to come up with a new draft dispensation. However, Kibaki was not going to let the Bomas letdown end without a response. Soon thereafter, he reshuffled the Cabinet, demoted LDP officials to junior ministries, and brought on board opposition MPs from FORD-People and KANU. Among those appointed were Simeon Nyachae and Njenga Karume. Uhuru, who was then leader of Government Business in Parliament and Chairman of KANU, blamed Kibaki for poaching his officials without consulting him, saying in a hard-hitting statement that by doing so, NARC had killed democracy. But as was common with Kibaki, he ignored Uhuru's protests, and went ahead and swore-in the officials. The demotion of the LDP-affiliated ministers triggered demonstrations in

---

233 East African Standard, March 17, 2004.

major towns, leading to one death in Kisumu, where tear gas and bullets were used to quell protestors.

Not long thereafter, Paul Muite, Chairman of the Parliamentary Select Committee on Constitutional Reform (PSCCR), called a meeting to discuss the way forward, but the committee of twenty-seven failed to transact any meaningful business because of verbal confrontations that ensued between supporters of the NCC and those who opposed it. Muite had a hard time defending accusations that he had failed to discharge his responsibilities as Chairman of the PSCCR, a factor members alleged had caused the collapse of the talks.

In the meantime, the Ufungamano Initiative released its own draft, which was different in many aspects from the Bomas proposals. It proposed that all executive authority be placed on an elected President with no provision for a Prime Minister; that the Vice President be elected on the same ticket as the President; and that the Cabinet be composed of non-elected professionals to be appointed by the President and approved by Parliament. It also opposed the establishment of the Senate saying an additional House would add no value to governance.

In a dramatic development, Muite resigned from the PSCCR and was replaced by William Ruto after LDP and KANU ganged up and blocked a government-backed candidate. To calm the political temperatures, the President endorsed the Consensus Bill to allow legislators to amend the Bomas Draft. In the original legislation, amendments were not allowed and Parliament could only approve or reject the document. While supporting the Consensus Bill in principle, Murungi objected to a provision that stipulated that the legislation could only be adopted by a sixty-five percent majority of parliamentarians. It was only after that provision was amended to allow a simple majority, that the government supported it. However, KANU and LDP objected to any attempts to "illegally" alter the document and announced they would oppose the bill, but after two days of heated debate, the amendment to the Constitution was approved by one hundred and two votes to sixty-one, but not before twenty members of civil society organisations were arrested for trying to march to Parliament to persuade members to reject it. On the day of the vote, most LDP and KANU MPs stayed away, leaving the legislation to pass almost unchallenged.

By October, LDP had become so restless in government that it successfully pushed for a Parliamentary Group (PG) meeting of all NARC MPs to discuss the state of the Coalition, as well as the Constitutional deadlock. Kibaki initially agreed, but a day before the meeting at the Old Chamber of Parliament, he backed out, claiming a meeting of the PSCCR had been scheduled for the same day, and that some legislators would not be available because they would be attending the swearing-in ceremony of the new Somali President in Nairobi. The LDP saw the cancellation as a further attempt by government functionaries to avoid discussing important national matters. At the PG meeting, the LDP had planned to confront the President on why he had included opposition legislators into the Cabinet while the NAK/LDP Coalition was still in place. By cancelling the meeting, Kibaki avoided a major showdown.

The government side then retreated for two days to the Sun and Sun Hotel in Kilifi, made substantial changes to the draft, and came up with what was later called the Kilifi Draft. While the Bomas Draft transferred much of the power vested in the presidency to the Prime Minister, the Kilifi Draft permitted a powerful Head of State and a Prime Minister with little authority.[234] The opposition vowed to reject the draft, but Kibaki announced he would personally lead the campaign to support the new revised document.

## The private sector worries

In the meantime, a worried private sector convened a series of meetings to try to reconcile the warring NARC partners. Lee G. Kariuki, a former Chairman of the Architectural Association of Kenya and a key leader in the Kenya Private Sector Alliance (KPSA), a confraternity of eminent businesspersons, volunteered to lead a peaceful process of reconciliation between NAK and LDP intended to realise an enabling environment for business in the country. There were already worries that the political feuds were hurting the economy by scaring away potential investors and threatening the stability of the country. The intended talks were to identify the contentious issues in the partnership and to find mutually agreeable solutions. The sessions were held at the Serena Hotel under the cover of secrecy. The first meetings were held with Raila of LDP, Musikari Kombo of FORD-Kenya, and David Mwiraria of Kibaki's DP.

[234] Joyce Mulama, Mail & Guardian, July 26, 2005.

Those meetings were followed by another with a team from LDP, of which I was a member, under the leadership of David Musila, the party Chairman.

The mediators were concerned that the wrangles in NARC were diverting the attention of the NARC Government from fulfilling its election pledges—including the Constitutional review—and had left Kenyans in a state of disillusionment and despair. They warned that unless solutions were found, donors would stop aid, corruption and insecurity would thrive, and the differences could spill to other institutions and arms of the government and disrupt development.

During the session with the KPSA, LDP expressed frustrations at the betrayals perpetrated by the NAK wing of the government, and told the business leaders that the only way to end the wrangles was for Kibaki to go back to the MOU and start afresh. We further reiterated our desire to make life as difficult as possible for the government until our demands were met, a position the entrepreneurs did not favour.

The KPSA then met with NAK leaders after which a joint meeting was to be convened. The latter meeting never came to pass. The differences were too big for the KPSA to handle, and the reconciliation process collapsed. The private sector initiative was certainly a noble one, but the issues at hand were political and needed a political approach, as well as goodwill from both sides. It was clear both NAK and LDP were unwilling to change their hard-line positions; the former believing that the contentious MOU was a closed chapter, while the latter insisting the agreement had to be implemented.

On November 21, 2005, Kenyans went to the polls in a landmark referendum—the first in independent Kenya. The ECK had designated "banana' as the symbol for the Yes camp, and "orange" for the No camp. The predominantly NAK-dominated Central Kenya region voted overwhelmingly in favour of the government draft, while most of the rest of the country supported the No platform. What followed was a devastating defeat for the government and an obvious show of no-confidence in the Kibaki administration. Fifty seven percent of the voters rejected the draft while only forty-three percent said "Yes."[235]

---

[235] Another attempt at constitutional making took place during Kibaki's second tour of duty. On August 4 2010, Kenyans went to the polls in a referendum

The following day, an angry Kibaki dissolved the Cabinet, raising temperatures on both sides of the political divide. NAK felt betrayed by LDP for opposing the draft, while LDP was over-joyed that it was able, once again, to inflict damage on the government's image. However, at the LDP headquarters, we knew that our short, turbulent stint in government was about to come to an end.

Two weeks later, when Kibaki announced his new Cabinet, LDP personalities were missing. Kibaki had finally purged his incorrigibly troublesome ministers. The NARC dream was practically dead; the Coalition in smithereens. However, there was drama when some of those appointed turned down the nominations. Joshua Orwa Ojode, the legislator who had joined Raila in the KANU/NDP government a few years earlier, and who had been named Environmental Minister; and Wangari Maathai, who had been chosen as his Assistant Minister, were among those who declined to take up their positions. Those supporting Kibaki reported happily to their offices, some even before they were sworn-in.

Fearing that many other appointees may fail to show up for the swearing-in the following day, Kibaki called an emergency meeting of his close associates at State House to decide on whether to cancel the ceremony pending fresh appointments or to proceed. A decision was made to go ahead with the swearing in. Eventually Kibaki had to find new allies to complete his Cabinet. At one point, Kibaki had his eyes cast on a number of LDP members to join his Cabinet, but Raila, fearing embarrassment, issued a strong statement calling those considering positions in Kibaki's Government as "crows scrambling for carcasses."[236] That comment was not received kindly within the party ranks and was considered selfish and dictatorial.

In the meantime, LDP convened a press conference and called for snap elections, arguing that the government had lost legitimacy. As usual, Kibaki ignored the call. Just as LDP's top officials were kicked out of the Cabinet, some party MPs were removed from crucial house committees.

---

and endorsed a presidential-style constitution. Sixty-seven percent of Kenyans endorsed the new dispensation that retained a powerful president with checks and balances; removed the post of Prime Minister and reserved cabinet positions to non-Members of Parliament, among many radical changes.

236 Standard, December 13, 2005.

The final ties that bound the two partners had finally been cut off and a full-blown war between Kibaki and Raila had been declared. The Coalition arrangement that had given Kenyans so much hope only a few years earlier had become unsustainable. According to Finance Minister David Mwiraria, the wrangles in government had cost the country 300 billion shillings in foreign aid that could have gone towards the revival of the economy. "They (donors) are scared of the in-fighting in our Government," the minister cried in disappointment.

# CHAPTER 19
## Questions for cash

Sometimes in mid-2004, an individual associated with a cabinet minister called me to a meeting at the Professional Centre, just a few metres away from the Parliament buildings. He told me he had been instructed to "facilitate" me—a euphemism for a bribe in the political lingo—in exchange for my support on a bill that was before Parliament. I was then a Member of the Departmental Committee on Health, Housing, Labour and Social Services, which was responsible for the passage of the bill. The facilitation, he told me, was to be in the form of "fuel money" and employment for a relative who had to be a university graduate. The minister was worried that the bill was unpopular among MPs and feared it could be defeated. The individual further revealed that an MP he did not name, had already been facilitated, and his young relative was already happily employed in the ministry. If I agreed, he told me, we could finalise the deal the following day.

The brazen corruption attempt shocked me. Never before had anyone been so brave as to make such a proposition to me. I told him I would call him back, a response that surprised the individual who had expected an immediate commitment. The following day when my committee met, I reported my encounter with the individual and wondered aloud whether any one of the other members had been approached. They said they hadn't. Soon, that proved not to be true because early the following morning, the same individual called and angrily demanded to know why I had reported our discussion to the committee. I knew at that point that one or more members had been compromised. After that encounter, I was removed from the committee and my efforts to seek intervention from the Speaker and the Chief Whip, who was also a member of the committee, failed. I did not earn another place in any House committee for the duration of my term.

I have narrated the above story to illustrate the presence of corruption in the Kenyan Parliament. So, if one asks whether or not MPs are "bought" to table questions, support, or oppose motions in that august House, the answer would be a strong 'yes'. Unlike in other countries, where sting operations are carried out regularly and legislators are nabbed in the act of receiving bribes, no Kenyan legislator has ever been busted for corruption. In Britain in the 1990s, two Conservative Party MPs were punished for allegedly asking questions in Parliament on behalf of a wealthy Egyptian businessman. That case, and several others that followed, were handled internally, and the MPs were suspended from the House for short periods of time. There have also been innumerable unethical cases involving members of the US Congress, the most prominent being that of New York Democratic Congressman, Charles Rangle who was censured by his peers in December 2010 for violating House ethics and fundraising rules. Although he did not lose his title or power to vote, the public shaming of the fifteen-year term congressman was embarassing.

In Kenya, both local and foreign non-governmental organisations have raised and documented the questions-for-cash phenomenon in Parliament. A Transparency International (TI) report, for example, claimed individuals and organisations paid some MPs to raise questions or introduce motions for political and economic interests.[237] The same report raised the issue of integrity regarding names of officials sent to committees for approval before appointment. Some committee members are paid to support or reject appointments, while others have been accused of spiking reports to favour or disfavour certain individuals or organisations facing parliamentary investigations. Corruption is also known to drive censure motions in Parliament. Members are bribed to "fix" certain legislators, while others are given money to oppose such motions.

It is no secret that dirty money in brown envelopes is routinely exchanged within the corridors of Parliament. Some of it is casually stuffed

[237] Daily Nation, March 18, 2010.

in pigeon holes for MPs to pick at will. With a fee of only several thousand shillings, an interested party can buy an MP's vote on any issue. MPs are bought not only to ask questions, but also not to ask questions. Attracted to an easy source of revenue, some MPs raise questions to intimidate intended stakeholders. Once the money is paid, they disappear on the day of the debate, forcing the Speaker to drop the questions or motions. Apart from cash, legislators are also rewarded with perks, such as vacations, goods, school fees for relatives, and so on. Some companies spend millions of shillings every year for MPs' workshops to try to curry favour on pending laws. Interestingly, invitations for such workshops are channelled through the Office of the Clerk, which encourages legislators to attend. Air tickets are collected from there, making it look as if the events are sanctioned by the administration of Parliament.

In 2009, a daily newspaper carried a report claiming that wealthy politicians and business magnates were involved in bribing a section of MPs to get them to debate or vote in a way that favoured their interests. The report also quoted previous and current MPs as admitting that corruption existed, and that "crucial reports had been adopted or thrown out, motions passed or rejected, and certain clauses introduced or removed from Bills before the House based purely on these partisan interests."[238]

## Is lobbying a form of corruption?

Lobbying is a common phenomenon in legislatures throughout the world. In Kenya, the lobbying sector has grown robustly in recent years due to an expanding economy and the competitive nature of business, but it remains comparatively small compared to that in developed countries. Many non-governmental organisations, multi-national companies, and foreign governments assign officers specifically to lobby the legislature and government institutions. In 2007, for example, a local drinks' manufacturer successfully managed to lobby the Kenya Government to reduce excise duty from ten percent to five percent in that year's budget. It was a win win situation as the government increased tax revenue due to increased sales and the company enjoyed tax reduction.

---

[238] Njeri Rugene, Nation, May 16, 2009.

In the US, lobbying is so big that the US Senate had to draft a comprehensive official definition. In general, lobbying in the US is viewed as the practice of trying to persuade legislators to propose, pass, or defeat legislation or to change existing laws.[239] To regulate the sector, lobbyists in the US—there are estimated to be thirty thousand of them in the capital, Washington, DC, alone—are required to register with the government. They are barred from buying gifts and meals for legislators, and while funded trips by lobbyists are not banned, legislators have to get prior permission from the Congressional Ethics Committee.[240]

In the UK, lobbying traditionally refers to attempts to influence an MP's vote by their fellow parliamentary colleagues, or by one of their constituents, or by any outside organisation. In both the US and Britain, the lobby industry is worth billions of dollars, and employs thousands of workers, whose task is to influence the direction of legislation in a particular way. However, political analysts and scholars also see lobbying as a form of corruption where money, in brown envelopes or through bank transfers, changes hand. If this is the case, isn't corruption through lobbying, being legitimised by the same bodies that are supposed to provide checks and balances?

## The NHIF lobby

One of the best examples of lobbying power in the Kenyan Parliament involved the enactment of the proposed National Social Security Bill, a piece of legislation intended to revolutionize health services in the country. Authors of the comprehensive legislation were the Minister for Health and technocrats at the state-run National Health Insurance Fund (NHIF). The NHIF was established to provide medical coverage for registered members, mostly in the public service. On the other hand, the legislation was meant to empower the fund to provide universal service to every Kenyan irrespective of age, health, economic, or social status. Although the idea had been in the minds of planners since independence, it was the first time a comprehensive health care plan of that nature had found its way to the floor of the House. The Bill was tabled in June 2004, amidst

239 New World Encyclopedia.

240 TIME, April 10, 2006.

controversy over its viability and sustainability, and over questions about the NHIF's capability to effectively and efficiently manage it.

For years, Kenyans had viewed the NHIF as a den of corruption and mismanagement. They accused it of wasting resources and losing money amounting to billions of shillings. The Ndung'u report on illegal land deals singled it out for spending 30 billion shillings in five years for unnecessary land purchases, a function completely out of its purview as a health insurance provider. Most of the land purchases were concluded under highly questionable circumstances. Also in 2003, the NHIF allegedly paid out 1 billion shillings to various hospitals as rebates; out of that, 300 million shillings was allegedly lost through fraudulent claims. The NHIF's Chief Executive at the time, Dr. Adan Hassan, however, was commended for spearheading the new medical scheme, although he did not escape criticisms from sections of the medical and insurance industries.

There was intense lobbying for and against the Bill, an exercise, which started months before the draft legislation reached Parliament. The Federation of Kenya Employees (FKE) joined hands with Avenue Healthcare—a health care provider—to bitterly oppose the scheme, accusing the government of rushing the initiative before actuarial studies had been done and before the NHIF had been properly evaluated. The two organisations also questioned the rationale of introducing such an expensive scheme when the country's economy was struggling. Also questioning the government's ability to sustain the programme was the World Bank—one of the organisations expected to help fund it. Its Country Director then, Makhtar Diop, said it was unlikely the Kenyan budget could afford such an expensive programme. "I do not know of any country anywhere with a domestic per capita income of below 400 US dollars that has attempted such an ambitious scheme,"[241] he lamented.

But the government and the NHIF were unmoved, and went full throttle to try to ensure the enactment of the legislation, which was to cost 40 billion shillings. A portion of that money was to come from the Exchequer through Value Added Tax, Excise Duty, payroll contributions, and donor funding, while the rest was to be availed from the private sector and well wishers. In a press interview, Dr. Hassan, said although

241 Sunday Nation, June 27, 2004.

he understood the concerns of his critics, he nevertheless, believed that the programme was doable and, therefore, vowed to take Kenyans to "the Promised Land."[242]

In the process of promoting passage of the bill, the NHIF held a series of seminars to counter adverse publicity from critics opposed to the fund. The first workshop for MPs was held at the secluded but high market Ngulia Serena Safari Lodge in the Tsavo National Park on April 2, 2004. Representatives from the International Labour Office in Geneva and selected chief executives of social security organisations in other African countries were invited to sensitive the lawmakers on the positive aspects of a health insurance fund. Others who benefitted from subsequent seminars and retreats organised by the NHIF were officials of the Federation of Kenya Employees (FKE) and government officers. A public relations firm was hired to market the initiative. The NHIF also heavily lobbied the Parliamentary Standing Committee on Health, Housing, Labour, and Social Welfare of which I was a member. The NHIF and the Ministry of Health also lobbied the Kenya National Union of Teachers, the Federation of Kenya Employers (FKE), as well as senior civil servants willing to support the scheme. The lobby efforts included both overt and covert monetary disbursements as well as pure public relations.

The marketing initiative was costly to the taxpayer. No wonder critics and the media questioned the use of funds for such efforts. Allegations were made that the NHIF had used millions of shillings to publish large quantities of civic education material for distribution to its branches around the country. There were also allegations that participants to those seminars—who were essentially public officers—were paid allowances against standing regulations; that contracts had been issued to relatives and friends of NHIF employees; and, that tenders worth millions were doled out through favouritism. In most cases, it was alleged, contracts had been given out through single sourcing, a violation of procurement regulations.

While the government and the NHIF were busy promoting the bill, those opposed to the scheme bought advertising space and hit the media circuit. A half-page advertisement appearing in Kenyan press on June

242 Ibid.

17, 2004, headlined: "Ms. Ngilu: Withdraw this Bill!" claimed that the programme was so under-funded that it would do severe damage to existing private health provisions, and that it would increase costs of employment, since companies would be forced to pay higher taxes. "Private insurance will be crowded out as company medical budgets are taken over by NHIF. Benefits that workers currently enjoy will no longer be available. The Kenyan worker's right to choose will be lost and everyone will be at the mercy of a huge, monopolistic, Government boondoggle," the Avenue Healthcare advertisement said. It further claimed that NHIF could not ensure availability of drugs and medical staff and that the whole process will enable "corrupt elements to steal even more, and inefficiencies (will) be magnified." Already, reports were alleging that some power brokers within government were expecting to reap billions of shillings if the scheme materialised.

Indeed, an intelligence report claimed private insurance companies stood to lose up to 7 billion shillings as a result of the new Medicare plan.[243] The money, the report claimed, was what would have been paid by the government to private health providers for coverage of civil servants. The introduction of the public venture, it was claimed, would only benefit some corrupt senior government officials. The campaign for withdrawal of the bill was so intense that the Cabinet—which had been watching from the sidelines—began to take note. At one point, Health Minister Ngilu who was passionately promoting the scheme and who strongly believed that the scheme was good for the public, threatened to resign if the bill failed to pass through Parliament.

It was because the stakes were so high that lobbyists felt compelled to infiltrate the Parliamentary Committee on Health, Housing, Labour, and Social Welfare, whose unequivocal support was necessary to realise the bill's success. Lobbyists were sent to individual members of the Committee to persuade them to back the bill during debate. That is how I came to meet the so-called facilitator.

As accusations of corruption in the proposed NHIF scheme mounted, Hassan came out openly to defend himself. "I am personally not corrupt" he said, and (I) challenge anyone who can prove me wrong to come out and

243 Standard, June 20, 2004.

say so." Conversely, he alleged that some of his critics had in fact attempted to bribe him so that he could abandon the programme but insisted he would not be swayed. At the end of the day, lobbyists opposed to the bill won. The bill sailed through Parliament, but it was denied Presidential assent and was sent back to Parliament for review. That was the end of the plan proposed by Minister Ngilu, who despite earlier threats, did not resign.

# CHAPTER 20

# Greedy legislators

On February 11, 2002, the Parliamentary Service Commission (PSC)—the body that oversees the welfare of MPs and staff—appointed a tribunal to review and make recommendations on the terms and conditions of service for MPs including their salaries, allowances and benefits.[244] The tribunal was also to look into the allowances for staff, as well as salaries, allowances, and retirement benefits for the President, the Vice President, and the Speaker. Chief Justice (Rtd) Majid A. Cockar chaired the tribunal. After nine months of listening to submissions from sitting MPs, public service institutions, professional bodies, and trade unions, the tribunal finally presented its report to the Speaker of the National Assembly, Francis Ole Kaparo, on November 5, 2002.

The tribunal concluded that, "the job of a Member of Parliament is a selfless job for which no amount of money would be enough to compensate for the inconvenience, the risks and the bother the job entails…a Member of Parliament is sometimes seen as a "mobile bank."" The report went further to say that voters go to their MPs when "they run short of school fees, when they do not have enough money to bury their dead or hold pompous weddings. When a roof of a classroom is blown off by wind, the public rush to their representatives." A member's car, the report added, "is

244 Report of the Tribunal on Terms and Conditions of Service for Members of Parliament, p. 7.

sometimes used as an ambulance."[245] The tribunal, therefore, concluded that for MPs to be able to perform their duties effectively, "they should be facilitated to manage Parliament well, and be provided with office equipment."[246] The conclusions arrived at by the tribunal were precise, and reflected the reality in Kenyan politics, but they also raised eye brows from critics who saw them as patronizing and unfair to the electorate in a country where political corruption was encouraged by politicians in exchange for support.

A few weeks into the first parliamentary session under Kibaki, the report was presented to the House for debate, and as expected, it was overwhelmingly adopted, I being among only three MPs to oppose it. Although MPs were constantly under pressure from their electorate for financial support, I felt it was morally wrong for a section of the population to be so heftily remunerated, while the majority lived below the poverty line. My stand was criticised by some legislators, and at least one MP attempted to rough me up along the corridors of Parliament for "denying us what we deserve." A month later, amidst a nation-wide outcry, the bill was adopted without much of a contest, increasing the MPs' salaries from a package totalling 395,033.30 shillings per month to 485,000 shillings per month, 200,000 shillings of it taxed. The package did not include sitting allowances, a three-point-three million car grant, and a winding up allowance of 1.5 million shillings in five years. Together with other allowances, a Kenyan MP became one of the most highly paid legislators in Africa, equalling lawmakers in some of the developed countries.

In addition, MPs with special responsibilities such as the President, the Vice President, Ministers, Assistant Ministers, and Whips also received attractive salary increases, so did the Speaker and his deputy. The PSC defended the proposed package as "appropriate", but the public outcry was immediate and deafening, even as TI came out with a report supporting the MPs pecuniary dilemma. The TI report said the bulk of an MP's expenditure was on handouts to constituents who expected them to contribute to *harambees*, that is, community fund-raising initiatives, school fees, medical expenses, and so on. In effect, the report said, MPs were

245 Ibid, p. 39.
246 Ibid., p. 23.

sustaining an unofficial welfare system, but also contributing to corruption and dependency among communities.

Kenyatta introduced the *harambee* system of raising funds for community projects, such as dispensaries, schools and boreholes, and so on, soon after he became President. It was meant to assist the poor to raise their standards of living. But it soon boomeranged into a scam where monies raised at such functions were pocketed by leaders. The worst example of this con game involved Kenyatta's own pet project—the Gatundu Self Help Hospital in his home village—where millions donated by business enterprises and individuals seeking favours from Kenyatta were squandered. Every week, Kenyatta would preside over such functions at his home; contributors would be asked to sign cheques but leave open the name of beneficiary, making it possible for recipients to insert names of family and relatives. Instead of Gatundu Hospital becoming a modern health facility, given the large amounts of contributions made, it stood out as a stark memorial of the kind of corruption Kenya experienced during Kenyatta's rule. During Kibaki's first term in office, *harambees* were banned by Parliament as part of efforts to curb corruption, and were replaced by devolved funds from the central government paid directly to the grass roots.

It had been expected that with the huge salary increases, MPs would cease to engage in rogue activities, but that was wishful thinking. Bad elements in the legislature continued to engage in stealing taxpayers' money right from inside the Chamber itself by fiddling with attendance sheets and earning illegal sitting allowances. The practice was for MPs to be marked present by orderlies as they entered the Chamber. At the end of each session, the list of attendees would be submitted to the Assembly Clerk, who would then calculate the sitting allowance to be paid to each MP at the end of the month. However, the manual system was manipulated through collusion between some sleazy MPs and crafty parliamentary staff. Some lawmakers paid off staff to mark them present while they were miles away from the vicinity of Parliament. The system of manually marking attendance may have been effective during the colonial days of the Legislative Council when members were fewer, but it was definitely ineffective after the number of legislators had increased so tremendously.

Technical appearances were another method used by MPs to swindle taxpayers. This peculiar art form was popularised by Kenneth Matiba, the FORD-Asili leader after he lost the presidential election in 1992. He accused Moi of rigging him out and announced in protest that he would only make enough technical appearances to comply with the Standing Orders, which required MPs to be present at least once every eight Sitting days. Anyone planning to be absent beyond that period had to seek written permission from the Speaker. Also, since there was no limit as to how long a member was required to be in the House, some lawmakers would show up just long enough to be noticed and marked present. They would then saunter out without concern and disappear into Nairobi traffic, satisfied that their Sitting allowance for that day was safe and sound. That form of booking out was perfectly legal, meaning a member could enter the Chamber five minutes to closing time and still be recognised to have attended that day's session. In mid-2007 close to the general elections, truancy became so serious that no business could be conducted in most days because of lack of quorum. Only thirty members out of two hundred and twenty two were required to sustain business, but even those few could not be realised in most days.

It also became common for MPs to deliberately miss Parliament to protest against matters unfavourable to them. For example, frequent absences during the debate on the Miscellaneous Bill in October 2007 were cleverly stage-managed to force the government to accede to MPs demands for gratuity at the end of their term. Because the government was anxious to have the bill passed, it had to give in by including a provision that satisfied the legislators' demands. That form of blackmail was used successfully to undermine the government during several occasions in Parliament.

MPs had other ways of earning extra income beyond their fat salaries. One of them had to do with overseas travel. Through their house committees, lawmakers routinely planned trips abroad, some of them completely useless, to earn travel allowances. There wasn't a single committee that did not benefit from overseas excursions, not even the Catering Committee, whose members travelled abroad to study how food purchases were managed. Favourite destinations included Europe, the US, and some countries in Asia. South Africa and Botswana were the only countries in Africa that were on the list of Parliamentarians. The higher profile the committee, the more overseas trips it could justify. For example, the Defence and Foreign

Relations Committee had more reasons to travel overseas than, let us say, the Agriculture, Lands, and Natural Resources Committee. Similarly, the Committee on Administration, National Security, and Local Authorities had fewer opportunities than, for example, the Education, Research, and Technology Committee. That was the reason why membership to house committees was always a subject of intense lobbying by Parliamentarians. On several occasions, host countries complained about the size of parliamentary delegations from Kenya and about not being informed in advance of their arrival. Consequently, some host countries were forced to introduced stringent measures aimed at discouraging trips by Kenyan legislators due to costs and protocol concerns.[247] The excesses of the Ninth Parliament were not isolated. During the first eight months of the Tenth Parliament that started at the beginning of 2008, legislators had already exhausted 116 million shillings in overseas travels. In defending their frequent trips abroad, members argued that the trips were necessary as learning experiences. The net effect, however, was that taxpayers' money was being used to benefit the bellies of only a few.

In their quest to maximise on travel earnings, some MPs resorted to some outlandish methods. They would search the Internet for international conventions bearing the faintest connection to parliamentary work, human rights, or global events and would then solicit invitations from those organisations and apply for permission to attend them at the expense of Parliament. A formal invitation from a foreign organisation was all one needed to make an application for authorisation.

But it was not just MPs who yearned for the good life in overseas junkets. The Assembly Clerk and Speaker kept a busy schedule travelling abroad on official business. In May 2005, concerned about their frequent absences, I submitted a parliamentary question directed at the Minister of Finance that read as follows:-

1. *Can the Minister tell the House the amount of money spent by the Government to finance foreign trips by the following officials, between January 2003 and January, 2005:-*
   *(a) The Speaker of the National Assembly*
   *(b) The Clerk of the National Assembly*

247 Daily Nation, March 18, 2010.

2. *Can the Minister give a breakdown of the cost of air-tickets and personal allowances for the two; number of days spent overseas and purpose of the visits?*

3. *Can the Minister also table a list of all foreign trips undertaken by Members of Parliament during the same period showing the cost of air-tickets and personal allowances; period of stay abroad for each Member and purpose of visits?*

The question was rejected on grounds that the matter was a domestic affair and did not warrant public debate. The refusal to allow public scrutiny of the National Assembly's financial portfolio, showed lack of transparency and accountability in an institution charged with safeguarding public coffers, even though it did not mean some form of impropriety had been committed by any Administrator in Parliament.

## Impeaching the Speaker?

In October 2004, a plot to impeach the Speaker was hatched. A section of lawmakers cited the purchase of Continental House whose cost, they claimed, had been highly inflated, as the reason for the rare action. They were to rely heavily on the report of the Ndung'u Commission on Illegal and Irregular Land Allocation, which had concluded that taxpayers had been "ripped off of hundreds of millions of shillings" in the deal. The report noted that the purchase of the MPs' office complex had been conducted in "a highly suspect manner which cost the Exchequer huge amounts of money." When the building was advertised for sale on March 31, 1995, according to the report, the National Assembly was one of several bidders. However, the National Assembly lost the bid to a company called Archway Holdings, which bought it for 225 million shillings. Three months later, the National Assembly bought it from Archway Holdings for 465 million shillings, an amount considered by some legislators to be unreasonable, especially since another 300 million shillings had to be used for renovation.

The Speaker was not amused when a finger of guilt was pointed in his direction, saying he was merely the chairman of a sub-committee that approved the deal. "If Parliament makes a mistake, I cannot be held personally responsible because it will be a case of the collective House making the mistake rather than myself." But the MPs appeared determined.

On October 13, 2004, the MP for Eldoret East in the Rift Valley, Joseph Lagat, filed notice of a motion which read as follows:-

*"That, aware that this House is desirous of a sober and harmonious relationship between the Speaker of the National Assembly and the Members; concerned that the integrity of Parliament as the supreme watchdog institution over the Executive has been questioned due to various suspect quotations for works by the National Assembly through the Parliamentary Service Commission; cognisant of the fact the custodian of the order and the integrity of the Honourable House is Mr. Speaker; this House resolves that the Hon. Francis Xavier ole Kaparo, vacates the office of the Speaker of the National Assembly in accordance with section 37 (2)(C) of the Constitution of the Republic of Kenya."*

That section of the Constitution stipulated that the Speaker shall vacate his office if the National Assembly so resolves, by a resolution supported by the votes of not less than sixty-five percent of all its Members (excluding the ex officio Members[248]). The motion was potentially damaging to the dignity of the House and, in particular, to the reputation of Kaparo, who was considered among the best Speakers Kenya had had until then. As Kaparo threatened to sue if it turned out that the matter had been "actuated by malice," the more liberal members, including myself, called for caution on the part of MPs. I said the motion would raise "the already high political temperatures" and urged my colleagues to find less confrontational ways of dealing with the matter. Kaparo himself described the motion as "misguided and ill-advised." In cautioning MPs about the matter, he noted that it was very hard to build a reputation but very easy to destroy it. "It is very easy to make accusations," he said, "but very hard to prove them." The motion never proceeded as Lagat withdrew the motion before it had a chance to be debated.

---

248 The Attorney General was an ex-officio Member in the House.

## Cancerously corrupt

Allegations of corruption in the administration of Parliament have been made for years. Back in 1996, MP Martin Shikuku, described the House as "cancerously corrupt" as he questioned the tender award for a planned rehabilitation of the House. At the time, MPs were querying a contract worth 151 million shillings awarded to a company that was under investigation by the Parliament's watchdog, the PIC. Members were not happy with the inflated cost of the tender and questioned the credibility of the chosen contractor.

The National Assembly's long history of sleaze, some say, began after the departure of the last white Speaker, Humphrey Slade, in 1969. His exit opened floodgates for some African administrators who followed to raid Parliament with impunity. Buildings soon ran into disrepair, toilets stunk to high heavens, the once sparkling carpets shredded, the quality of food deteriorated, and, generally, the standard of cleanliness plummeted. The catering department stopped purchasing from recognised butcheries and vegetable shops and resorted to sourcing their goods from connected farmers and meat sellers in the fringes of the city. Soon, members noticed that their succulent T-bone steaks had been replaced with inferior quality meat. *Maandazi*, doughnuts, and tasteless beef sausages had replaced the fresh egg and cucumber sandwiches and biscuits that were served during morning and afternoon tea.

At one time, the fare at the cafeteria was so predictable and so monotonous that most legislators preferred to go for tastier *nyama choma* outside Parliament.

## Inside Continental House

The acquisition of Continental House, next to Parliament Buildings—regardless of the controversy surround it—was, undoubtedly, the most notable achievements of Speaker Kaparo. Before that, MPs had no offices and no support staff to assist them in parliamentary work, and had to operate either from the lounges or from their own cars. At Continental House, they have a fully stocked library and conference facilities, as well as a roof-top restaurant.

However, the impression given by the media of a state-of-the-art building with superb facilities, including a well-furnished gymnasium complete with sauna, jacuzzis, and salons, was not entirely true. Although those facilities physically existed, the reality was far from the truth. From the time of installation, the jacuzzis, for example, had never worked and had remained dysfunctional throughout the life of the Ninth Parliament. No one could explain why they were not functioning. Similarly, the saunas were in a perpetual state of disrepair. Either the system would pack up altogether, or the temperatures would be too hot or too cold for comfort. At one time, the administration attempted to persuade the Parliamentary Service Commission to sanction the use of 2.3 million shillings for repair work. This was declined.

The massage rooms did not fare any better. For example, although the administration spent a lot of money for what they thought were the right massage tables, they turned out to be of the wrong dimensions. They were too thin, squeaky, and uncomfortable. The air-conditioning system in the gym, and indeed in the whole building, rarely worked, and users were either freezing or frying in the heat. Compared to many gyms in the country, the exercise club at the National Assembly was a third rate facility at the time I was there. Shower rooms and toilets were often blocked or plumbing was falling apart. And although salons and barber shops were in the initial plans, they could not be activated because of lack of certain equipment. Worried that they could endanger their lives in what was clearly a sordid state of affair given the frequent malfunctioning of electronic equipment, MPs, at one time, protested to the administration and threatened to boycott the gym if repairs were not undertaken speedily. Dissatisfied with the general state of the gym, many MPs preferred to use exercise rooms in five-star hotels in town, where facilities were far superior and the general state of cleanliness much more satisfactory.

The administration spent a lot of money buying customised towels and gowns for all the two hundred and twenty-two members, complete with embossed name tags, when it was obvious that MPs were basically on a five-year contract. By the time I left in 2007, a heap of unused gowns was still collecting dust at a corner in the gym. I wonder what happened to all those gowns belonging to MPs who didn't make it back to Parliament in 2008.

So, while externally, the impression was given of bliss for its occupiers, internally the story was quite different. During the dry season, the offices became unbearably hot and doors had to be left open, while in July, August, and September, the offices were too cold for lack of a heating system. And although the administration always encouraged MPs to acquire computer skills, very few computers in members' offices were hooked to the Internet, yet millions of shillings were used to lay cables between Parliament Buildings and Continental House, and to install equipment in members' cubicles. The only computers that had internet facilities were in the library, but even there the service could not be guaranteed because of connectivity problems.

On the positive side, however, the Continental House was undoubtedly one of the best innovations to have happened in Kenya's Parliamentary history. Its acquisition promoted efficiency and gave members a sense of pride. Unfortunately, however, the offices were not always used for the purpose they were meant for. Some lawmakers turned their cubicles into some sort of lodging facilities and private business centres, where import and export enterprises thrived. The business of selling one brand of vitamin supplements was particularly rampant along the corridors of Continental House. Young, beautiful girls, some brought in from far-flung villages, ostensibly to work as personal assistants, did more than just typing and filing. The heavily made-up girls wore their "personal assistant" badges in a way to be admired and walked the corridors of Continental House without care. There were indeed some respectful and decent workers in the building, but those were highly outnumbered.

The most embarrassing event during the Ninth Parliament was when an MP was accused of raping a woman in his office. The matter was widely publicised and became a subject of unkind jokes by radio disc jockeys. The unfortunate incident required that the accused member write a police statement. At a press conference, which was also attended by his wife, he denied everything. The matter did not go to court, but the incident portrayed MPs as low-lifers, dishonourable, and immoral creatures who use their privileged positions to engage in unbecoming and criminal acts. The reputation of members was further tarnished when it emerged that the sewage system at Continental House had clogged due to careless disposal of used condoms. The blockage, which was reported more than once, forced the administration to post notices on the corridors and in washrooms asking occupants not to dump used condoms in toilets. There was, however, no concrete evidence that the used condoms came from members since so many other people used the building.

# CHAPTER 21

# Corruption in the Media

Matters of journalistic ethics have been the focus of governments and the media from as early as the 1920s, but unfortunately, the issue of corruption in the Fourth Estate has not been adequately addressed. One media practitioner says this is a matter that "one hears all the time but never reads in the papers."[249] Koigi wa Wamwere, a former political detainee and media owner himself, has this indictment to make against the men and women of the media: "In Kenya, the media have failed to shine light on their own scandals and gross exploitation and corruption. As they point at the speck in the eyes of others in society, they do not see the log in their own eyes." According to Joe Kadhi, a veteran journalist, "ethics-related scandals have included conflict of interest, freebies, junkets, intellectual theft, deception, carelessness, kowtowing to advertisers and politicians, use of dubious evidence and outright bias."[250]

That corruption exists in editorial rooms of Kenyan media houses is no longer a secret. Media executives and professional organisations have admitted it, so have laymen, such as politicians and business leaders. Since media practitioners are a creation of an inherently corrupt society, their involvement in sleaze only mirrors the rot and evils that have bedevilled the nation since independence. There have been serious cases of extortion

---

249 Friedrich Ebert Stiftung, March 2000.

250 Ibid.

by media practitioners that have involved not only cash but also threats to human life.

In 2008, the *Nation* Media Group launched what it called the Media Integrity Watch, to try to stop corruption in media circles. It promised that those "found to have flouted our ethical principles will be dealt with firmly." That got the Kenya Union of Journalists to respond with a question: who will be the prosecutor, the judge, and the jury of this "integrity watch?"[251] Very little was heard from the *Nation* about that initiative until May 2010 when the Group put a half-page notice in its paper under the headline, "Protecting the Integrity of Journalism", in which again, it admitted that "widespread corruption within some newsrooms appears to be a major aspect of the perceived erosion of journalistic integrity." It said the matter had been brought up in various fora, and related to journalists and those purporting to be journalists "soliciting or accepting various forms of kickbacks, gifts, cash rewards, or freebies from newspapers in exchange for promises of favourable press coverage."[252] A similar notice was posted in the paper in December 2010 promising that those found to have flouted ethical principles will be dealt with firmly.

On its part, the *Standard*, the other mass circulation paper, also chipped in with a notice on December 2, 2010, with the headline, "Defending the Integrity of the Media", in which it cautioned its journalists not to accept gifts and complimentary offers from newsmakers and for newsmakers not to tempt staff with cash or other gifts in exchange for coverage.

Freelance correspondents who earn peanuts, but who contribute up to an estimated seventy percent of all content in media outlets, are often blamed for promoting corruption in the media, but the problem is much bigger than that, and involves even senior reporters and editorialists. A journalist, Eric Orina believes "the biggest problem of corruption in the media lies with top Editors....They are the gatekeepers, the people who receive sometimes up to millions of shillings in unaccountable funds to ensure a story is either used, twisted or killed."[253] A media analysis report prepared in 2008 by Peter O. Mbeke, a lecturer at the University

251 Africa Files, September 13, 2008.
252 Daily Nation, May 13, 2010
253 Africa Files, September 13, 2008.

of Nairobi, and Tom Mshindi, a media consultant, agreed that there was correlation between poor working conditions and unethical behaviour among journalists. It reported a huge disparity in remunerations between junior staff members and senior editorialists, and admitted that some news sources and corporate organisations often retained some senior editors at a fee to ensure continuous positive coverage of their events and issues.

The 2006–2007 Media Sustainability Index of the International Research Board, which provides in-depth analyses of media conditions in countries of Africa, Europe, Eurasia, and the Middle East, blames lack of will to raise awareness of, and enforce, a code of conduct for corruption in the Kenyan media. "Many journalists ask for transport from organisers of events. Editors ask for money to kill stories or give more coverage to certain people, institutions or businesses."[254]

The problem is so serious that it was featured in 2008 in a documentary called *Uncovering the Media* by Khamis Ramadhan. In the film, the Chairperson of the Kenya Correspondent Association, Oloo Janak, talks of mistreatment by media houses of freelance correspondents who, he says, work under difficult conditions with poor pay. They neither have transport to get around the countryside, nor insurance or communication equipment. Such journalists can hardly be expected to survive on the money they earn for the stories they file, he says. Most of them, therefore, rely on handouts, and sometimes, extortion. There have also been cases where newsmakers write stories and send them with cash to reporters who then bribe editors to get the story printed. This practice is common in the alternative media, but cases have also been reported in the mainstream media, where some stories have raised eyebrows. Tervin Okoko, a journalist, says by looking at a printed story, he can tell which one has been paid for. "I can tell there is something wrong here. Someone has an agenda with that."[255]

What happened in 2005, however, revealed that corruption was imbedded deep in the Kenya Union of Journalists itself. A ceremony to award media personalities of the year was marred by a faulty selection

---

254 Okoth Fred Mudhai, Time to Harvest? Media corruption and elections in Kenya.

255 International Media Suport, July 7, 2009.

procedure, doctored price lists, and conflict of interest, leading to the walkout of a judge and the return of awards by angry recipients.

It would have been expected that the Media Council of Kenya, whose mandate is to enforce ethics in media houses would be in the forefront of fighting graft in the profession, but some journalists have raised doubts about the effectiveness of the Council. "I don't believe it will go far when the people who comprise it are themselves media people." Frank Ojiambo, who has worked in senior positions in the mainstream media, throws in a metaphor. "I mean you don't set a rat to catch a rat; you set a cat to catch a rat!"[256]

One of the most interesting allegations of corruption in the media was made in 1997 by Kenneth Matiba, the individual who was detained with Raila, when he alleged bribing a senior reporter with a car in exchange for publicity during the run-up to the 1997 general elections. The matter went to court, but it could not be sustained due to lack of evidence. Writing his weekly column, *This Week that Was*, in September 1996, Kwendo Opanga admitted that winning the case did not necessarily vindicate the editor since corruption is "fiendishly difficult to prove for it is after all, not a spectator sport."[257]

Opanga was to face almost similar complaints against him years later, although in his case, it was "not directly and conclusively a bribery scandal...."[258] He was forced out of the *Nation* Group on grounds that he accepted 60,000 shillings from agents of the KANU ahead of the general elections in the 1990s. The journalist explained the money was not a bribe but a consultancy fee for a job he did for the party. However, he did admit to a conflict of interest and offered an apology, but he was still forced to quit.[259] Opanga's case did not fail to elicit criticisms from his peers. Joe Kadhi, a long standing editor and communications lecturer wrote in one report that the "fact that such a serious editor could be caught with his pants down on ethical issues simply meant there was a need for

256 Ibid.

257 Okoth, Fred Mudhai, Harvest Media, Corruption and Elections in Kenya, 2007.

258 Okoth Fred Mudhai, Time to Harvest, p. 7.

259 Ibid.

all journalists in East Africa to be reminded of the basic principles of journalistic ethics."[260]

Many of the corruption accusations made against the media in Kenya, unfortunately, have lacked proof, thus making it difficult for the Media Council or anyone else to investigate them. Wilfred Kiboro, Chief Executive Officer of *Nation* Group said just that in an interview in 1998; that it was impossible to take action against culprits in his organisation without concrete proof. "Allegations against editors are not new," he said. "The question is whether there is any proof from people making those allegations...If somebody comes with documentary evidence...then we would take action."[261]

Perhaps the most dramatic of all allegations made so far against the media came from the government spokesman, Alfred Mutua, when he alleged in 2007 that the Fourth Estate had become "synonymous with corruption, and, therefore, lacked the moral authority to accuse others." Responding to a sustained attack on the government over matters of graft, he said in a signed statement that he had evidence that politicians were paying huge amounts of money to have their stories featured on newspapers' front pages. Some of the papers, he alleged, asked up to 250,000 shillings per month to suppress government related news. Although he said he would soon expose the "preach-water drink-wine" culprits, he never did.

A certified fraud examiner and advocate of the High Court, Collins Wandera, writing in the Opinion Page of the *Daily Nation* on December 22, 2008, under the headline "Media Can't Cast the First Stone," admitted that he had been a victim of unethical behaviour from journalists whom he said, asked "for tips to facilitate publication of a good topical issue. I have been asked for bribes by journalists in Kenya, Uganda and Tanzania."

The so-called chequebook journalism is not just a Kenyan problem, but a global phenomenon. Bettina Peters, writing on how the media tries to cover-up corruption in the Fourth Estate, says that journalists are often given free rides and meals to provide favourable coverage. "Many engage in a host of corrupt practices, ranging from "cheque-book journalism"

---

260 Friedrich Ebert Stiftung, March 2000.

261 Expression Today, 1998.

to news tailored to suit advertising or commercial interests."[262] A 1998 report by Aidan White of the International Federation of Journalists, entitled "Caught in the Act", says that, "inside journalism there is so much unethical activity which is itself worthy of wider coverage."[263] Yet the Kenya media, which have been at the forefront in exposing corruption, marital scandals, and personal tragedies, have failed to examine and expose those within who have shamed the profession. An investigative report prepared by Otsieno Namwaya, as part of a fellowship award by the Africa Centre for Open Governance (AfriCog), says that politicians—the most harassed by corrupt journalists—often do not report corruption cases for fear of being victimised and denied coverage. Consequently, politicians suffer silently. I remember an incident at ODM-K party offices where journalists almost rioted after being denied cash after a press conference. They vowed to give the event a black-out and promised never again to respond to future media events at the offices. The situation was saved only after a party official parted with money. Serious as it was, the incident was hushed. "For those of us who have experienced it, there are two levels of corruption in the media, says legislator Martin Ogingo. "First is the petty corruption in which reporters take small bribes as a condition for writing stories, and the second is the corruption involving media owners and editors."[264] Although bribes to owners and editors are said to be commonplace, media executives do not think the matter had reached alarming levels. The truth of the matter, however, is that unless media houses come completely clean on the matter, the Fourth Estate in Kenya would continue to operate under a cloud of suspicion on matters of integrity.

## The state of the media

The Kenyan media has grown by leaps and bounds since the pioneering days in the 1940s of Oginga Odinga's *Ramogi*, Francis J. Khamisi's *Mwalimu* (Teacher), and Henry Mworia's *Mnyenyereri* (The Caretaker), among many others. From crude, slow manually driven presses to computerised printing systems capable of producing thousands of copies of newspapers per hour; from television scanners to live video pictures, the print and electronic

262 The Media's Role: Covering Up Corruption, November 27, 2002.
263
264 Otieno Namwaya, AfriCog,

media have made a quantum leap from Stone Age to the era of Information Technology, where news is now disseminated in real time across a much wider territory. For decades, the only major print medium in Kenya was the Standard Group, a conservative establishment nurtured and sustained by British settler interests. Two broadsheets, *The East African Standard*, an English daily, and *Baraza,* a Kiswahili weekly were in the Group. When in 1960, His Highness Prince Karim Aga Khan decided to launch The *Sunday Nation,* followed a few months later by the *Daily Nation*, the country began a historic journey of media transformation that was to change the entire face of mass communication in the country.

Although radio broadcasts had started way back in the 1920s, it was not until 1960 that a modern broadcasting facility, KBC, began nationwide transmissions, but Kenyans had to wait until 1964, a year after independence, to watch television programmes. At that time, KBC had been renamed VOK, a title that was to change once again back to KBC in 1989. Privately owned television and FM stations were then unheard of, giving the state-owned station control over the gathering, selection and dissemination of news, as well as the choice of entertainment. In the absence of an official news agency, state communication was managed by the Department of Information, which was headed by *wazungu.* It was not until 1964—two years after independence—that Africans began to make an appearance in government newsrooms in a substantial way. Boaz Omori—one of the early Editors-In-Chief at the *Nation*—was hired to Africanise the VOK newsroom. He recruited three young reporters: Arthur Chang'awa from the Information Department, Shadrack Sikobe from the *East African Standard*, and me from the *Nation,* to pioneer the African presence at Broadcasting House. In many ways, that was the nucleus of the state-owned Kenya News Agency, which grew to employ thousands of workers throughout the country.

Once a week, a reporter would go to Gatundu, Kenyatta's rural home, to cover the President as he received delegations that came to pay homage and seek advice. Despite his many years abroad and a long stint in detention, Kenyatta was still a down-to-earth person when he became the country's Prime Minister and later President. He liked to meet people and hold consultations and Cabinet meetings under a shady tree in his compound. He had a deep voice, a big laughter, and red penetrating eyes, and was as fatherly as any wise *mzee* one could find in an African village.

A great lover of traditional Kikuyu delicacies, especially *mbuzi choma*, roasted goat meat, Kenyatta spent hours listening to cultural music and praise songs.

He was also fond of the media, and that relationship grew after he held his first Government-organised international press conference in 1961 while imprisoned at Maralal in Northern Kenya. He held another major press conference after his release to debunk fears that he planned to avenge the British for his detention. In fact, he jolted Kenyans when he assured his erstwhile nemesis, the British, that he would forgive but not forget, and that when put to a leadership position, he would be the leader of *all* Kenyans. The story received global coverage and projected Kenyatta to the white settlers not as a "leader of darkness and death"—as the colonialists had labelled him—but of light and hope.

One day much later, when I was at my desk at the Government Press Office, the phone rang and a deep voice boomed through the gadget: "This is Kenyatta." My first reaction was one of shock, then disbelief, then panic. I didn't know whether to put the phone down and shout for my senior to come, or to be calm and calculated; but he settled my nerves when he said he was only inquiring about the whereabouts of a senior ministry official. I was left trembling. It was not unusual for Kenyatta to call people directly without going through the usual official red tape.

While the *Nation* was liberal, bold and pro-nationalists, the *East African Standard* was brazenly conservative, with a colonial attitude of hate and disdain for Africans. The more the *East African Standard* leaned to the right to support white interests, the more the fast-paced *Nation* moved the other way to identify with African aspirations. As a trainee reporter, I found white editors under Kenneth Bolton to be notoriously rude to African reporters, just as they were snobbish and arrogant to African leaders of the time. Conversely, the atmosphere at *Nation* House was friendlier, and the editors helpful.

The Aga Khan knew, from the very beginning, that the only way to sustain his business in Kenya was to stay on the good side of Kenyatta even as he struggled to stave off political interference from the same individual. In its book, the *Birth of a Nation: The Story of a Newspaper, the Struggles of a Country*, a story is told about how Kenyatta pressurised the Aga Khan to employ one of his relatives as chairman of the Group, and how the company successfully managed to wriggle itself out of that dilemma without hurting relations between them. Interestingly, the *Nation* was excited when Kenyatta released his Press Secretary, George Githii, to take over from Hilary Ngweno, as the paper's second African Editor-in-Chief. Githii, whose trademark was a spotted bow-tie, was a no-nonsense, if not daring journalist, who loved to front-page his editorials, and who didn't mind ruffling feathers, as long as he was able to put his views across. He took on the highly and the lowly and, instead of supporting the government positions as had been expected, he often criticised them. Githii was an ardent yoga adherent, and the joke was that he only wrote editorials after a session of meditation. But the cordial ties Aga Khan had built with Kenyatta proved too costly for the organisation when the paper got itself embroiled in an embarrassing situation that was to affect its reputation for years.

In 1975, the *Nation* reported in bold, front page headlines, that J.M. Kariuki, a former freedom fighter and a popular parliamentarian—who had been reported missing for days—had not disappeared, after all, but had instead travelled to Zambia for business. It quoted a dangerously misleading statement delivered in Parliament by Home Affairs Minister Moi to that effect, without making any effort to counter-check its veracity. If the sensational report was meant to calm a disturbed nation, worried stiff about the safety of one of its most outspoken law-makers, it did completely the opposite. It created panic and fuelled speculation about a possible government cover-up, propagated by the *Nation*. No one in Kariuki's family knew of any planned travel by the legislator. When his burnt body was eventually traced to Ngong forest, the truth was laid bare, throwing to the wind the reputation the paper had built over the years. Humiliated and exposed, Githii left to settle overseas.

Meanwhile, as years went by, and as his rule came under intense criticisms from the international media over corruption and intolerance of alternative views, Kenyatta's initial love for the media began to wane, and he became increasingly suspicious of the Fourth Estate. It was not uncommon for government officials to call newsrooms to complain about the manner in which this or that government story was covered or not covered, or to lament about how the media favoured Odinga. It became necessary for newspapers to censor themselves to avoid a clash with an over-sensitive government. A good example was when Kenyatta's health began to weaken. Newsmen knew the man was on his last leg, but they could not print the information for fear of retribution. Their silence almost plunged the country into a civil war when Kenyatta suddenly died and a power struggle ensued.

When Kibaki took over, many thought media mistreatment would cease, but that did not happen, at least not during the first phase of the NARC Administration. Every attempt was made by the Kibaki Government to frustrate media attempts to achieve true independence and enhance freedoms and professionalism. One year into his government, police arrested vendors and confiscated copies of several titles seen to be critical of the government. Those newspapers—the *Weekly Citizen*, the *Independent*, *News Post*, and the *Summit*—more like newssheets—were popularly branded the alternative press, and were printed on four by four sheets that were easily concealable in a jacket pocket. Most of the information contained in those publications was highly seditious and scandalous, but did provide juicy reading for Kenyans tired of the usually predictable political news. At one time, masked men stormed the offices of the *Weekly Citizen* and took away computers and other essential equipment. That same year, a local FM station, KISS, was put to task by a government minister, who accused it of defamation. A government task force appointed to probe the allegations was later dismissed by a court, which said, it had no basis in law. That was not all.

To show its determination in reining the critical press, early in 2006, the government arrested three journalists—Denis Onyango, Chacha Mwita, and S. Savula—over a story that alleged that Kalonzo had held a meeting with Kibaki, reportedly to lobby to be appointed Vice President. The *East African Standard*, which was seen by many to be leaning towards Raila, described the story headlined, "Kalonzo, Kibaki in Secret Meeting," as one of the most sophisticated political manoeuvres by the President yet. However, the government responded by accusing the paper of "muddying the integrity of the President." Kalonzo also denied such a meeting took place. The case against the three journalists was eventually withdrawn, but the incident underscored the government's intolerance of the Fourth Estate.

## Media invasion gone mad

The most dastardly act of media transgression, however, occurred on a morning in early March 2006, when a group of masked thugs carrying AK47 assault rifles raided *The Standard* newspaper offices in the industrial area of Nairobi, burnt down its printing press, then drove five kilometres into down-town and shut down its sister television station, KTN. The middle-of-the-night assault was a "commando-style operation,"[265] and although the officials denied involvement, the government could not explain how such an attack could have taken place without its knowledge. *The Standard* claimed the raiders were police personnel, while Raila, at a press conference, said the attack was "aimed at instigating fear and diverting the attention of the public from real issues facing the country." It was not until much later that the government admitted the raids had been carried out to protect state security.

"If you rattle a snake," John Michuki, the Minister for Internal Security said in an often quoted remark, "you must be prepared to be bitten by it."[266] That was a clear challenge to the media to keep off government matters and to report only what was pro-establishment. Whether or not the case of the arrests of the journalists a few days earlier and the raid at *The Standard* were connected, no one could tell, but the criminal act brought the country to its lowest ebb in the eyes of those agitating for complete press freedom, "a sad day for the Kenyan people, for the impartiality of the Kenya police force, and for the freedom of the media in Kenya,"[267]

Only a few weeks earlier, Raila had revealed that two foreign individuals, Artur Margaryan and Artur Sargasyan, had arrived in the country to carry out an assassination plot against some opposition leaders. Although the reaction of the government was initially one of denial, it turned out later that the two were actually in the country. What raised further suspicion about their intentions was that the raid at the *Standard* took place about the same time that the presence of the

---

265 Pan African News Agency, February 3, 2006.

266 Media interview.

267 Maja Daruwala, Commonwealth Human Rights Initiative, March 3, 2006.

two foreigners was confirmed. For those with inquisitive eyes, a closer look at the video, which was repeated infinitely by television stations, showed features of some of the raiders to resemble closely those of the two Caucasians. Although the two were first identified as Armenian brothers, they were actually not Armenians and not brothers at all, and Armenian authorities discounted their claims of kinship to a leading politician of that country.

On June 9, the duo was deported after they were deemed a security risk. An investigation on the activities of the two by a parliamentary select committee revealed "they were conmen and international drug traffickers." The report, released in 2005, further revealed that during their stay in Kenya, the Artur brothers enjoyed official protection and that their presence was part of a conspiracy to commit atrocities. The committee also recommended that Mary Wambui, a political activist who alleged affinity to Kibaki, and her daughter, who was allegedly linked in a love affair with one of them, be investigated. Conversely, the report of another probe team, the Kiruki Commission, appointed by the government to investigate the same matter, was not released to the public.

Despite assurances from the Kibaki Government that it cherished press freedom, all indications proved that was not the case. For example, on August 2007, the Minister for Information introduced a bill intended to establish a media regulatory board and a media advisory board in place of the independent Media Council of Kenya, which was formed in 2004. The new initiative meant that the government would register all journalists, a task universally undertaken by professional organisations. In addition, the government was to appoint officials of the board, a move construed to mean that the body would be under the control of the state. The most contentious issue, however, related to disclosure of sources. The bill, if passed, was to force editors to reveal their confidential sources. The *Daily Nation* described the clause as "offensive and a threat to democracy."[268] A few days later, hundreds of journalists took to the streets of Nairobi with their mouths taped to illustrate the gagging of the media, but their action did not stop Parliament from passing it with only twenty-nine votes in the House of two hundred and twenty-two MPs.

268 Daily Nation, August 23, 2007.

Perhaps because of criticisms from local and international organisations, or as a result of advice from the Attorney General, Kibaki refused to assent to the bill, and a week later sent it back to Parliament, objecting to the same clause which was at the centre of controversy. The offending provision said: "When a story includes unnamed parties who are not disclosed and the same becomes the subject of a legal tussle as to who is meant, then the editor shall be obligated to disclose the identity of the party or parties required to." In his Memorandum of Objection to Parliament, Kibaki felt the clause was ambiguous and could be misinterpreted because, he said, "unnamed parties" in the clause had not been qualified or restricted, adding that it could be construed to include the subjects of the story, as well as the sources of information. Parliament agreed to delete the clause and the bill was taken back to State House, and Kibaki assented to it.

About the same time, the government withdrew another piece of draft legislation called the Kenya Communications (Amendments) Bill 2008, which was to empower the government to restrict media ownership and to control content on both television and radio. Several journalists were arrested during street demonstrations against the bill, and when they tried to protest during the Independence Day celebrations on December 12, several of them were arrested. Despite widespread protestations, Parliament passed the bill after a heated argument. It was widely alleged that the MPs endorsed the legislation to hit back at the media for demanding they pay taxes on their huge allowances, but the legislators said they were only doing what was right for the country. Raila tried to explain that the bill was crafted before the formation of the Coalition Government and that the sitting government was only supporting it based on the principle of collective responsibility. That view drew sharp media reaction with one newspaper accusing the government of dragging the country "back to the days of dictatorship."[269]

Kibaki went ahead and assented to the bill early January 2009, saying that the controversial clause was not part of the bill he signed. He assured Kenyans that his government was still committed to the ideals of press freedom and democracy, and that "it would not roll back on the

[269] Standard, December 17, 2008.

gains we have made in this regard."[270] The media was outraged: "With this Act," one newspaper editorialized, "MPs attacked freedoms earned through blood, sweat, toil and tears of generations for which *wananchi* fought and died in this country's unforgiving streets."[271] The good news was that after intervention by Raila and the input of media organisations, the government later published amendments, deleting the controversial clause.

---

[270] AFP, January 9 2009.
[271] Standard, 12 December 2008.

# CHAPTER 22

## Devolved funds

One of the biggest successes of the Ninth Parliament was the enactment of the Constituency Development Fund (CDF) Act in 2003. The legislation, which sought to correct imbalances in regional development, allowed the government to devolve a specified amount of money every year directly from the Exchequer to the people on the ground, without passing through the traditional methods of government bureaucracy in the regions. It allowed the allocation of two-point-five percent of government ordinary revenue to all the two hundred and ten constituencies, where seventy-five percent of that money would be distributed equally and the remainder as per poverty levels. All in all, the Fund was a godsend and was an innovative way of devolving funds from the centre to the grassroots.

The Act was very strict in the use of the money; it barred any use of the funds for political activities and stopped MPs from signing cheques. To cap it off, a stiff prison term of five years, a fine, or both were designated for those caught to have misappropriated the funds. Further, the people at the grassroots level were to be involved in the selection and implementation of the projects under a constituency committee, and project committees were to be set up by the MPs through proper consultations at all levels. Nevertheless, all those rules and threats of stiff punishment did not stop crooked politicians from interfering in the affairs of the fund and dipping their hands into the kitty. Instead of being a boom for the poor, the Fund opened a plethora of loopholes for crafty individuals to steal from the public. MPs loaded their local committees with close relatives, including spouses and tribes people, and awarded businesses to their friends and political cronies. They also awarded themselves tenders for the supply of materials. I knew of a legislator in a far-flung area of the country who owned the only truck and the only hardware shop, and had artisans and labourers. Project committees under his chairmanship, would buy building materials from him, hire his truck to haul materials to sites, and provide the workers. You can imagine the monetary yields.

Misuse of CDF funds was common. Noble projects meant to ease hardships and help reduce poverty among people were unfortunately manipulated and hijacked by greedy elected officials, and turned into cash cows.

Bahari Constituency, which I represented for five years from 2002–2007 was like many of the two hundred and ten constituencies in Kenya: poor, semi-illiterate, water deficient, with a high mortality rate due to poor health services; and a school drop-out rate that was one of the highest in the country, especially among girls, who became pregnant early or got married off. There was also a chronic problem of landlessness, meaning that approximately seventy percent of the people were squatters. But Bahari was also blessed with a long stretch of the Indian Ocean, and tourism and fishing were major activities.

Bahari was the first constituency in the country to come up with a clear road map to development using the devolved funds. Through financial and technical assistance from Action Aid, an international non-governmental organisation, constituency leaders began by assessing the development needs of the area via meetings with grass-roots leaders, youth, women, and business organisations. The result was the adoption of a strategic plan. Three main problems were identified for immediate action: education, water, and health. The choice of the three priorities was logical because one, they intertwined, and two they were relatively straightforward to deal with. Of the three, education was the pillar. Without education, even the simple action of getting people to boil drinking water to avoid water borne diseases; of engaging in unprotected sex; or, even of using mosquito nets to protect them from malaria, could be difficult to achieve. A good example was when villagers in one part of the constituency returned hundreds of free-supplied mosquito nets to authorities following rumours that the nets were magnates for devils. A vigorous civic education campaign had to be undertaken urgently to crush the rumours and calm nerves, before people could accept them back.

By the time the CDF Act was implemented in 2004, the Bahari Constituency Committee was ready to manage projects, and had the capacity to monitor and evaluate them. Issues of transparency and accountability were stressed for proper management, and people on the ground were sufficiently briefed on how to select and supervise projects in their areas. It was also agreed, from the very beginning, that politics would have no place in the development agenda; and those chosen to execute the programmes would be upright leaders free of corruption. Early in 2005, the Vice President, Moody Awori, officially launched the Bahari Strategic Plan.

Our priorities included building four additional secondary schools to meet immediate needs of the people in areas not served with such institutions; construction of a secondary school to cater for the deaf; increasing the number of dispensaries in rural areas; and building wells and initiating piped water projects in specific areas of the constituency. By the time the Ninth Parliament was disbanded at the end of 2007, fourteen hundred projects had been initiated and only seventeen of them had not been completed because of time. Every year, ten percent of the Fund's yearly allotment was dedicated to bursaries for secondary school-going pupils. Another two percent was kept aside to help the very poor parents who could not afford to have their children admitted to Form 1, the first year of secondary school. This funding allowed poor qualified students to enter institutions while waiting for their applications for the main bursary to be processed. Hundreds of students, who would otherwise have failed to meet the entry deadline at Form 1 because of lack of funds, benefitted from this facility.

In 2006, the National CDF Committee rated Bahari as the country's best constituency in terms of project management. The constituency was lauded for "its contribution of constructive engagement approach…where the Bahari CDF capacity was developed to deliver on their mandate as provided for in the CDF Act of 2002." Throughout my term in office, Bahari received the largest amount of disbursement and undertook more projects than any other constituency in the country. The area's CDF activities were featured and constantly updated at w.w.w.baharikenya.com, an initiative I supported with my own personal funds. Because of the positive publicity in the media, the constituency became a popular destination for visiting CDF committees from throughout the country desiring to study the Bahari model of management. In July 2008, the Constituency hosted a delegation of Tanzanian legislators and researchers who wanted to study how the programme was implemented and monitored.

Because the people themselves selected and managed the projects, they succeeded without facing too many hiccups. However, there were instances when the population was slow in absorbing the impact of projects in their areas. A good example was a secondary school in Roka Ward, which took more than a year to attract pupils to the institution. For months, only a few determined students showed up. The situation was so grim that at one time, the community thought of turning the school into a village polytechnic to save the buildings from going to waste. By the end of my term as the area MP, the school had become so overcrowded that more streams needed to be built, thanks to a campaign to encourage parents to cooperate. The CDF was, undoubtedly, the most brilliant initiative to come out of the Kenyan Parliament.

# CHAPTER 23

# Women in Parliament

Soon after Wangari Maathai returned home after receiving the Nobel Peace Prize in Oslo, Sweden, in 2004, crews of filmmakers and journalists arrived to record the life and tribulations of the first woman Peace Laureate. The sixty-four-year old was then an MP and an assistant minister for Environment and Natural Resources. She was a member of the ruling party NARC led by Kibaki, a person who hailed from her district in Nyeri. Despite regional connections, however, her relations with the President were not particularly warm especially since Maathai had spent years fighting injustices in the Moi regime, of which Kibaki was a senior member. When the latter left KANU in 1991 to form DP, Maathai did not join him there but decided, when the 1997 elections came, to contest the presidency under the banner of the Liberal Party, a small, unknown outfit. Kibaki came third while she came fifth in a contest won again by Moi. By the time she won worldwide recognition, the first African woman to earn a PhD had spent decades in public life as a lecturer, an environmentalist, and a politician, while simultaneously struggling to manage a difficult marriage and a busy schedule as founder of the Green Belt Movement.

The documentarists, with the Speaker's permission, recorded Maathai as she spoke to the world from the floor of Parliament on the dangers of climate change and the need to conserve the environment. She was passionate and eloquent, stressing that the world's survival depended on sound and sustainable management of the environment. Today, the videos of that village girl who rose from humble beginnings at a scrubby village of Ihithe in the Central highlands are available in libraries throughout the world, yet she remained almost a stranger in her own country.

While laureates in other countries were being treated as national icons and sought after for advice on a myriad of international and regional matters, Maathai was being treated shabbily at home. Travelling abroad, she is honoured with red carpet treatment and feted by presidents and kings, but at home she is treated as an ordinary *mwananchi*, perhaps in response to the years she spent taunting the authorities in power. It needs to be noted that when she stood for elections in 2002, she won ninety-eight percent of the vote in her Tetu constituency, but when she entered the 2007 primaries to seek re-election she was unashamedly rigged out.

Kenya is traditionally a chauvinistic society where the male race lords over people of the opposite sex. It is not surprising therefore that very few women have risen to higher positions in government and in political parties. Though their numbers in the National Assembly have increased steadily in recent years, statistically, women still represent a tiny minority. The situation is worse in political parties.

The first woman to enter Parliament was Grace Aketch Onyango in 1974 as MP for Donholm, the seat vacated by Kibaki after he chose to return to his home district of Othaya. Since then, the number of women lawmakers has gone up, thanks to a renewed sense of aggressiveness among the educated class. Compared to other African countries, however, Kenya remains at the bottom in terms of parliamentary representation. During the first multi-party elections of 1992, only six women were elected to Parliament, but that year, the country got its first woman cabinet minister, MP Winfred Nyiva Mwendwa, who was appointed to the Culture and Social Services docket. In 1997 two women, Charity Ngilu and Wangari Maathai became the first women to contest the presidency. Both did poorly, but their entry was a pragmatic demonstration of how far women could rise in Kenya's political system.

Out of the two hundred and twenty-two elected and nominated members in the Ninth Parliament—from 2002–2007—eighteen were women. Unfortunately, Parliamentary Standing Orders of the time were discriminatory against women lawmakers and did not adequately cater for their welfare. They were not allowed to carry handbags into the

Chamber and were not entitled to maternity leave, among other things. Those discriminatory regulations were, however, abolished in the Tenth Parliament after they staged protests and walkouts.

Even as they continued to fill parliamentary benches, their legislative impact, especially on issues of women and children, remained negligible. Most of the women legislators in the Ninth Parliament, for example, were inactive, even though in that Parliament they managed to pass the largest number of bills so far, a total of three: the Sexual Offences Bill by Njoki Ndung'u; the Cotton Bill by Julia Ojiambo; and the Gender Policy by Alicen Chelaite, the last a landmark gender-sensitive legislation that mandated that thirty percent of all jobs in the civil service be allocated to women.

While women Parliamentarians made some gains in boosting the clout of women at the political level, they failed miserably in fighting for the empowerment of rural women. More than fifty percent of Kenyans are women, but the majority still live in inhuman conditions, subjected to gender abuse and denial of social rights. Most rural communities still do not allow women to inherit property and many women suffer silently through marital rape. Since many communities deprive girls of education, early pregnancies are common in many areas. Cases of child trafficking and abuse at work places are rampant. Women are also subjected to what in many countries would be considered hard labour: collecting firewood, digging wells, and building houses while most men whiled away their time in drinking dens. Therefore, there exists a long list of issues Kenyan women leaders could tackle to ease the suffering of rural women, but they have failed to address them.

In Parliament, the numerical majority of men over women have for years, worked to the disadvantage of the latter. During debates, women legislators had to endure sneers and snippets of degrading comments from their male colleagues, sometimes making their contributions inaudible. On many occasions, the Speaker had to intervene to protect female Parliamentarians from embarrassing interventions from some of their chauvinistic male colleagues.

A perfect example of male misbehaviour against women manifested itself during debate on the Sexual Offences Bill, 2005. The bill sought to impose maximum penalty for rape and defilement, bar female genital mutilation, and offer counselling and medical treatment to victims of rape. It also wanted to outlaw wife inheritance and sexual harassment. For the duration of the debate, public galleries were full of women who came to offer support, but they were disappointed by the unbecoming attitude of male legislators towards their women colleagues. From the very beginning, it was clear that male legislators were uncomfortable with, and suspicious of the good intentions of the bill. They complained that the legislation was intended to punish men for practices that were generally condoned by traditions, and appeared uninterested in the broad objectives of the legislation.

Cases of abuse against women have been on the increase in Kenya in the past few years; children as young as a few months, and women as old as eighty-five have been raped and subjected to inhuman treatment. Penalties allowed under the existing law were shamefully inadequate. The bill, therefore, provided the only hope for the suffering women to get justice and be treated with respect.

Almost collectively, male legislators opposed provisions to give magistrates unlimited powers of sentencing, arguing that a runaway court could issue sentences of up to life in prison; thus, defeating the societal objective of reforming as opposed to punishing offenders. Male parliamentarians also feared that the bill could be used by jilted women to frame men, and saw mischief and vindictiveness on the part of the mover, a lawyer and an award winning crusader of women rights. Women lawmakers were constantly interrupted by catcalls and endless points of order. "They are not taking it seriously," said Jane Onyango, director of the Kenya office of the Federation of Women Lawyers, after observing the misconduct of the male legislators on the first day of the motion. "They were very noisy when Njoki moved the motion. Some were whispering from the floor that she ought to withdraw it,"[272] she complained.

However, what triggered a major uproar of protest from women was a seemingly flippant comment made by MP Paddy Ahenda who called women "'shy creatures' who did not make sexual advances, further saying that in African society, women would say no when they meant yes." The legislator was criticising a provision in the bill that, he claimed, would criminalise making advances at women. He said that endorsing that

272 Voice of America, April 27, 2006.

provision would be tantamount to making marriages illegal. Women MPs were incensed and walked out of the House, prompting women visitors in the gallery to follow suit. They described the remarks as "chauvinistic" and demeaning to women. When the members eventually trooped back into the Chamber, they pointed at the Parliament's motto embossed on a wall of the Chamber that said, "For the Welfare of Society and the Just Government of Men," and called it "stupid," prompting one male legislator to demand that they be ejected from the Chamber for disorderly conduct. The Executive Director of CRADLE Children's' Foundation, Millie Odhiambo, who was later nominated to the Tenth Parliament, accused the MP of trivializing debate on the Bill and "poking fun"[273] at the pain victims were undergoing.

When the bill was put to vote the first time, it was overwhelmingly defeated by two hundred and four votes against eighteen. By the time Parliament finally adopted the bill on March 31, 2006, it had been heavily amended to appease male legislators, and lacked the original sting intended by the mover. Parliamentarians had chopped off several provisions from the original draft, including those dealing with marital rape and female genital mutilation.

In general, issues of gender were treated with sarcasm in Parliament. Even matters of the kitchen were not spared. At one time, a male member who was appointed to serve in the Catering Committee refused to take up his position, saying his culture did not allow men to "cook" never mind that the committee was not about cooking, but about setting and maintaining standards in the cafeteria. The comment, some women legislators remarked, was clearly meant to debase women implying that the role of women was only in the kitchen. Such is the dilemma of women lawmakers in the male dominated Parliament in Kenya. Ndungu had this to say about her parliamentary experience: "The most memorable anecdote was one politician cutting me short, reminding me to concentrate on typing, and stop distracting men's contribution."[274]

---

273 Voice of America, April 27, 2007.

274 Standard on Sunday, December 5, 2010, a quote from Women and Political Leadership in Kenya, Dr. Nyokabi Kamau.

In August 2007, the Kenya Women Parliamentary Association began a campaign for affirmative action by staging street demonstrations to gather one million signatures to push for fifty reserved seats through a constitutional amendment bill. But when the bill came up for discussion, the male-controlled House rejected it. To make matters worse, the Association did not succeed to get women to chair any of the House Committees during the Ninth Parliament. Also, up until then, no woman had been appointed to the membership of the crucial Parliamentary Service Commission.

Gender inequality is not just limited to Parliament. Political parties in Kenya have failed to include women into top party positions. In the 2007 general elections, only ODM-Kenya, among the three major political parties, had a woman on the presidential ticket, but only after the candidate, Ojiambo, had threatened to throw its principal, Kalonzo, out of her LPK party. Women who protested against their exclusion in ODM and PNU were given peripheral positions, most of which were quickly created to silence them, prompting a newspaper columnist to complain that women had been short-changed.

Another good example of male bias against women in the legislature manifested itself in January 2007, when small political parties proposed Njoki Ndungu, the proposer of the Sexual Offences Bill, as a candidate for the Speaker's position in the Tenth Parliament. When the elections were held, she did not get a single vote, not even from the women parliamentarians. As a result, Kenya missed an opportunity to make history by failing to elect the first woman Speaker in the country since independence.

# SECTION THREE

# CHAPTER 24
# Who killed Ouko?

Following a successful motion in Parliament by MP Eric Gor Sunguh, a Select Committee was formed on March 26, 2003, to investigate the unsolved murder of former Minister for Foreign Affairs and International Cooperation, Robert Ouko. However, public hearings did not start until February 17, 2004, the delay having been occasioned by a tug-of-war between the National Assembly administration and the committee over procedures and hiring of counsel. I was one of the original fifteen members of the committee, but changes in membership became necessary later as a result of attrition, resignations, and appointments to Cabinet. The Ouko Select Committee was the second such committee in Kenya's parliamentary history to investigate a murder of one of its own.

The first one was constituted in 1975 after MP J.M. Kariuki was killed and his remains found by a Masai herdsman—his fingers chopped and his eyes gouged—in a thicket in Ngong Hills, west of Nairobi. The Sunguh committee was also the fifth attempt to probe the mysterious disappearance and murder of the fifty-eight-year old Ouko, whose charred body was found on February 16, 1990, a short distance from his rural home at Koru in Kenya's Nyanza Province. Police had carried out investigations immediately after the murder, but the government felt further investigations were necessary to get to the bottom of the crime and, had therefore, requested the assistance from England's Scotland Yard. Six months later, and to the surprise of Kenyans, President Moi halted the probe by the British team led by Detective Superintendent,

John Troon. The team also had Detective Inspector Graham Dennis, Detective Sergeant David Sanderson, and Forensic Pathologist Ian West. Nevertheless, the officers went ahead and prepared a preliminary report detailing their partial findings, which they handed over to the government in September 1990.

The contents of Troon's report were so compelling that the government established a Judicial Commission of Inquiry a month later on October 2 under the Chairmanship of Justice Evans Gicheru of the Kenya High Court. The commission heard testimony in public for a whole year, but Moi, feeling uncomfortable with revelations that appeared to implicate his officials, disbanded the commission after only two hundred and sixty days of deliberations saying he was "not satisfied that it was the correct thing to do at the time." The stoppage of the Troon and Gicheru investigations confirmed the feeling of many that Moi was only playing to the gallery, and had no serious intention of pursuing the killers of the flamboyant minister, murdered only days after the presidential delegation returned from a National Prayer Breakfast in Washington, DC, on February 4, 1990.

However, in an attempt to impress the Kenyan public that his government was genuinely committed to finding the truth, Moi established yet another probe, this time comprising five senior police officers under the chairmanship of Mr. C.W. Ongoro. Ongoro and his team were directed to undertake deeper investigations into the allegations made by Troon on the roles of cabinet minister Nicholas Biwott and Internal Security Permanent Secretary Hezekiel Oyugi. Others who attracted Troon's interest during his investigations were civil servant Jonah Anguka, politician Joab Omino, and a senior government administrator Julius Kobia. This investigation led to the arrest of Anguka, who was eventually charged with the murder. He was, however, later exonerated and freed. Troon, who had read his team's entire investigation report to the Gicheru Commission, had named two senior government officials as prime suspects in the murder.

The soft-spoken Ouko became victim number five in a series of political assassinations in Kenya dating back from the first decade of independence. Within a span of less than forty years, five prominent politicians had been killed under mysterious circumstances. Two of them were assassinated during Kenyatta's regime, while the other three were eliminated during Moi's administration.

The Sunguh Committee hearings were often stormy given the critical nature of the probe and Sunguh's temperamental persona. Sunguh came from Ouko's Nyanza region, and his constituency was within the same district that Ouko represented in Parliament for twenty years. Ouko was elected as the MP for Kisumu Rural in 1979. In 1988, the holder of an honorary degree from Pacific Lutheran University in Seattle, Washington, US, moved to Kisumu Town, which was later split into West and East. Sunguh, a plump no-nonsense type who played football and managed the Parliament's football squad, Bunge FC, always talked about how anxious his constituents were to have the murder resolved. For him, the matter was not only of moral value but of political significance. "I must crack this nut," he kept on repeating to us. But it took ten months, from the day the committee met and elected Sunguh chairman, to the time hearings started. Bureaucratic red tape—ranging from delays in confirming the lead counsel, to clerical support, to budget cuts for investigative work—initially slowed down the committee's work, leading to frequent verbal confrontations between Sunguh and the National Assembly clerk, Samuel Ndindiri. There were unconfirmed reports of a conspiracy allegedly hatched between "senior officials in Parliament and prime suspects in the murder, in an effort to obstruct the quest for the truth."[275]

The Parliamentary committee had plenty of witnesses to call once the hearings got underway: government officials who accompanied Moi and Ouko to the US, office and domestic staff, family members, as well as investigators and medical examiners. Moi, for reasons best known to him, declined to appear before the committee and an affidavit he sent through his lawyer, Mutula Kilonzo, was rejected. On his part, Anguka attracted a lot of interest from investigators because of his suspicious movement on the day of the minister's disappearance. However, when sittings commenced, he had already fled the country and the committee was unable to interview him. But it was able to interview Troon and other witnesses during hearings held at the Kenya High Commission in London in early February 2005.

---

275 East African Standard, February 17, 2004.

Unfortunately, an estimated one hundred potential witnesses, who had earlier collaborated with the Scotland Yard team and the Gicheru Commission, and who would have been useful to the committee, had died, most of them, allegedly under mysterious circumstances: Paul Shikuku, the herds-boy who was identified as the first one to stumble on Ouko's burnt body just vanished and was later declared dead; Oyugi, the Permanent Secretary for Internal Security who was placed at Ouko's home on the night of the murder died shortly after his arrest and interrogation by the police. Many detectives and staff who would have been useful in shedding light on the events surrounding Ouko's disappearance and murder died under different circumstances.

But all the five probes: the initial police investigations, the Scotland Yard, the Gicheru Commission, the Ongoro probe, and the Sunguh Committee left more questions than answers. They all named names, some of them of senior government officials, but no one was ever successfully prosecuted. The murder joined a string of unresolved killings that had taken place over the years.

The then Kenya Ambassador to Washington, Denis Afande, told the Sunguh Committee that he had advised the government, through a telex message, against Moi's visit to Washington because of security concerns and the fact that no bilateral matters were to be discussed. Relations between the two countries were at that time poor, due to increased American criticisms of human rights abuses in Kenya; and possibilities of street protests in the American capital could not be ruled out. The ambassador was, therefore, uncomfortable with the visit, but was informed by the late minister that preparations were at an advanced stage and the visit could not be cancelled.

It was the Foreign Affairs Permanent Secretary, Bethwel Kiplagat, who shocked the committee by saying in evidence that he was not "privy" to the Ambassador's message, prompting the committee to express concern that as the administrative head, Kiplagat could not confirm or recall the message. So, the question was: Was there a message or not, and if so, how come Kiplagat did not know anything about it? And most importantly, if the message was received, why did the government ignore the ambassador's advice?

As to what really transpired in Washington during the presidential visit between January 30 and February 4, 1990, witnesses offered contradictory evidence. For example, did Biwott sarcastically refer to the Foreign Affairs Minister as "Mr. President" following the latter's outstanding performance at an international press conference? Was it true or false that as a result of that performance, President George W. Bush suggested to Moi that Ouko should replace him (Moi) as President? In testimony, Biwott denied that he made any such reference. Was there, or was there not, an altercation between Ouko and Biwott? Ambassador Afande and Permanent Secretary Kiplagat told the committee they were not aware of any scuffle involving the two. Afande said the two shared the same vehicle. But other witnesses including Ouko's brother, Eston Barrack Mbajah, told the committee that the differences in Washington had led "to a near confrontation..."

A woman, Herrine Ogembo, who claimed to be Ouko's second wife, said the late minister told her of a scuffle between the two when the minister called her from Washington. In a hand-written report, which she gave to Troon for submission to the Parliamentary Committee hearings in London in February 2005, Ogembo said Ouko was called to the White House to meet with President Bush, who told him that he was not happy with the corruption involving top Kenya government officials. "Bush even praised Bob (Ouko) that he was an honest man, clever and hardworking and wondered why Bob could not be the leader of Kenya," she quoted the minister telling her during a rendezvous in Nairobi after the Washington visit. "However, Bob told me he told Bush that he appreciated what he had said...but was happy and satisfied with the post of Minister for Foreign Affairs." Ogembo further narrated that Bush responded that he was not happy with Moi's commitment to fighting sleaze and, therefore, was not going to waste his time seeing him. It was alleged that Moi had requested Ouko to book an appointment with the American official.

When Ouko went back and informed Moi that Bush did not want to see him because of other commitments, Ogembo said in her report, the Kenyan President pleaded with him to go back to persuade the American leader to see him even "if it was just for a few minutes." Eventually, according to Ogembo's written testimony, Ouko managed to convince Bush to agree to the meeting, and that was when Moi was able to see the

American leader. Bush repeated to Moi what he had earlier told Ouko: "He told Moi that, you are now aged and your country is running well economically, you have the Minister for Foreign Affairs who is capable, why don't you step down for him," Ogembo said quoting Ouko. The remarks, according to the witness, made Moi very sad but the Kenyan leader remained diplomatic. According to her, that incident might have been the genesis of Ouko's problems, because after that, "Biwott started abusing him (Ouko)."

Reports of an altercation between Biwott and Ouko were also confirmed in the testimony of Malacki Odenyo, the Director of Administration in the Ministry of Foreign Affairs, and in testimonies of Ouko' wife Christabel, and his sister, Dorothy Randiak. Witnesses testified that Biwott was unhappy about Ouko's press conference in Washington, DC at which the Foreign Minister strongly defended the government against accusations of human rights abuse, bad governance, and corruption. George Otieno Ndege, a police officer and Ouko's former bodyguard, testified that Biwott had allegedly accused Ouko of fronting "himself as the best Cabinet Minister in Kenya."

However, it emerged in the committee that the animosity between the two cabinet ministers might have started long before the Washington visit, fuelled by business rivalry, political supremacy wars, and jealousy. During the 1988 general elections, Biwott allegedly supported Ouko's rival, Joab Omino in the contest for the Kisumu Town constituency seat. The only reason given to the committee for Biwott's interest in the Kisumu Town seat, situated many kilometres away from his own home in Keiyo district, was that Ouko had begun a one-man crusade against corruption—some of it involving senior government officials. Ouko was said to have been preparing a report for submission to the government on corruption in the Kisumu Municipal Council on irregular plot allocation, and was probing sleaze at the Turkwel Gorge Hydro-power Plant, which was then under Biwott's Energy Ministry. Witnesses alleged that Biwott and Oyugi did not want Ouko to win the parliamentary seat and, therefore, campaigned intensely to get Ouko rejected by voters in favour of Omino.

Then there was the controversy over the revival of the Kisumu molasses plant, which was situated in Ouko's constituency and which

Moi had ordered rehabilitated. In her testimony on August 26, 2004, Ouko's personal secretary, Esther Ruvaga, claimed Biwott and George Saitoti, then Finance Minister, allegedly opposed the revival of the plant, and on many occasions, the latter "refused to approve (decisions on the plant)..." It was further alleged that Ouko had wanted the contract for the feasibility study of the project to go to an Italian company with the acronym BAK, but according to Marrianne Brinner Mattern, a BAK director, who appeared before the committee on December 2 and 3, Biwott instead allegedly wanted the contract awarded to a Canadian company.

The Kisumu molasses plant was built by donor funds in 1970s, but its mismanagement led to its collapse; and in 1987, Ouko who was then Minister for Industry, got permission from Moi to have it revived. However, in 1988 when Dalmas Otieno became Industry Minister, Mattern alleged, he commissioned a study that concluded that the plant was only fifty percent viable, and as a result, ordered that it be dismantled and transferred to Mumias Sugar Factory. She further alleged that Saitoti failed to present a proposal for its funding during a subsequent bilateral meeting between Kenya and Italy. Consequently, donor funds that had been earmarked for the rehabilitation of the plant were allegedly diverted to a water project called Noolturesh in Saitoti's Kajiado North constituency.

What startled the committee were Mattern's allegations that several cabinet ministers and a businessman said to be very close to the power barons, Mohamed Islam, had demanded commissions of between five percent and ten percent for any contracts involving the BAK. The allegations—serious as they were—were not corroborated and the committee viewed them with suspicion.

Another intriguing contradiction brought before the committee was whether or not Ouko travelled from Washington to Kenya in the same aircraft as Moi. The late minister's bodyguards testified that Ouko was not among those who disembarked at Jomo Kenyatta International Airport from the plane carrying the Kenya delegation on February 4. They told the committee that the minister had arrived "long after the former President and his entourage had arrived." Interestingly, Permanent Secretary Kiplagat could not remember whether or not Ouko travelled separately from the rest of the delegation, while Biwott testified that he 'personally saw" Ouko seated next to the President on the return flight. Biwott tried to table a copy of the airline manifesto to prove his point, but the committee rejected it saying the document only represented names of those on the government-prepared passenger list.

On the other hand, Achieng Adala, another former senior Ministry of Foreign Affairs official who was at the airport, "presumed" that the late minister disembarked from the same plane. Evidence was adduced that although Ouko's plane arrived earlier; he did not leave the airport but stayed put until the presidential entourage arrived, then walked to the executive pavilion to join the rest of the group. Police officer and former Ouko bodyguard, George Ndege put a spin on the whole issue when he said he had been forced to lie that the late minister returned in a separate flight from Moi. He did not specifically tell the committee who, in fact, forced him into that conspiracy but testified that a senior police officer had coached him on how to record his statement to authorities.

According to his bodyguard, Ouko's fate appeared to have been sealed at the airport when he was led "to a seat several rows behind the former President" when normally, he said, he would have been placed next to the President. Moreover, security sentries allegedly barred the late minister's vehicle from entering the pavilion area, even though other ministerial vehicles were allowed in. Ouko's staff only reached him after Moi's motorcade had left the airport area, his driver said. According to evidence, another indication that Ouko was in serious trouble with his boss was when his passport was confiscated by immigration officers and his security detail withdrawn without any explanation, even though he was scheduled to leave for Gambia a few days later on official duties. Foreign Affairs official Adala told the committee that he was not aware about the passport hitch, but remembered receiving Ouko's passport from the minister's personal assistant on February 14, a day after his body was allegedly found by a herds-boy. As for the withdrawal of his security, Kisumu's topmost cop, Emmanuel Mwachiti Chiti, under whose jurisdiction the Koru home was, pleaded ignorance.

Worried about his security and political career, Troon and Mbajah, Ouko's brother, told the committee in separate testimonies, the minister then decided to appeal to Moi's fatherly passion by taking his two children to Moi's residence at Kabarnet Gardens in Nairobi that same afternoon of February 4, in the hope that Moi would be moved by the presence of the children and forgive him for whatever wrong he had committed. But the former President allegedly refused to see them. Now in a state of desperation and confusion, Ouko visited Oyugi at his Nairobi residence that same evening. In the absence of Ouko and Oyugi, both deceased at the time of the hearings, the committee could only speculate about what actually transpired at Oyugi's home.

If the events that took place at the airport did not raise the red flag about the dilemma facing Ouko, then what happened at State House the following day left no doubt about Ouko's impending fate. After escorting the Canadian High Commissioner to State House for a meeting with Moi, the President allegedly ordered him to proceed on leave to his Koru home. Why did he specifically instruct him to go to Koru? And, in any case, why send him on leave when the rest of the ministers who were in the entourage remained at work? Was he being set up?

Cabinet ministers rarely go on leave. Moreover, it had been expected that Ouko would be busy at work preparing for the Gambian assignment. In his report, Troon surmised that Ouko "was sacked immediately after the Washington visit." According to testimony of several people including his wife, Christabel, Ouko, after he was let go, the minister took the unusual step of travelling at night by road from Nairobi to Koru on February 6. While in Nyanza he allegedly confided to his mother, Susan Seda, in *dholuo,* that "there is a Kalenjin (name withheld), and a son of South Nyanza, (name withheld) who are conspiring to kill me." That information could not be confirmed since Ouko's mother was already deceased by the time the committee met. Three days later on February 9, Ouko left his home early in the morning to travel to Kericho, where he intended to seek intervention from the district commissioner over the seizure of his passport by immigration officials. He had hoped that the official, Peter Lagat, being a Kalenjin like Moi, would be able to secure its release.

However, on his return from Kericho, Ouko's self-driven car was involved in an accident with a tanker at Awasi along the Kisumu-Kericho road. Police Inspector Achesa Litabalia, testified that the minister's double cabin vehicle lost control and hit the rear part of the trailer, which was travelling on the opposite direction. A shaken but uninjured former minister had to take public means to the traffic police offices in Kisumu to report the accident. It could not be established in the evidence whether or not the accident was a normal one, or an attempt on the minister's life. Up to that time, Ouko's Gambia trip was on schedule and the minister had even instructed one of his bodyguards to prepare to travel to Nairobi with him on February 13. From that point, things took an ominous turn. On the day of the travel, the bodyguard could not find Ouko when he tried to locate him.

When asked by the bodyguard about the whereabouts of the minister, Samson Odoyo, a house servant at Koru, said he had left him sleeping, although Selina Were, another servant, reported that the minister had left early in the morning in a white car. On being reached in Nairobi, Susan Anguka, Ouko's secretary, said she did not know the whereabouts of the Minister. Strange enough, as the bodyguard lodged a report with the police on the disappearance, an intelligence officer, Francis Onsano Omwenga, told the Committee that a herds-boy by the name Paul Shikuku, reported seeing a dead body; that while in the area of Got Alila Hill on February 13, Shikuku had seen smoke, and on closer examination, had discovered that the smoke was coming from a human body with "flames around the chest and stomach area."[276] He reported the discovery to his employer who subsequently reported it to the area assistant chief. As it turned out, that report was suppressed by junior officers, or higher authorities refused to take action upon being informed of the strange discovery. It was not until the evening of the following day, that the District Commissioner and Chairman of the Security Committee, Godfrey Mate, were allegedly informed of Ouko's disappearance. A similar report was received at the provincial police office from police headquarters in Nairobi.

On February 14, police moved into the minister's house at Koru and conducted a thorough search of the premises. Christabel, who had been staying in Nairobi, left for Koru upon hearing of the disappearance and arrived there at dawn on February 15. According to her testimony, police were everywhere searching for "some papers," while others were

276 Troon Report, paragraph 38.

combing the homestead. She instructed her workers to help in searching the compound because she had been told nobody had seen the minister leave. From the very beginning, she said, she suspected political motives, especially after she came to know that there had been ill feelings between Ouko and Biwott. Testimony was given that Christabel had ordered workers to look for Ouko "in the ceiling, store, bushes, and surrounding farms." According to Chiti, the Kisumu police boss, police also ordered searches in major hotels in Kisumu. Jesse Gichuru Muhoro, a civil servant, felt the government "had lied' when it announced on February 15 that the minister had disappeared when in fact the body had been found by Shikuku two days earlier on February 13. That evening of February 15, Christabel allegedly talked on the phone to Oyugi, but the contents of that discussion were not divulged to the committee.

However, Philip Rodi, a store man, reported seeing some people in the compound on the night of Ouko's disappearance, among them Hezekiah Oyugi, and a short, fat, black man was standing at the veranda of Dr. Ouko's house hiding behind a pillar. He alleged that the description of the man who stood behind the pillar "fitted" that of a cabinet minister. Questioned on why he did not mention the minister in earlier statements, the store man said "he feared the consequences of death." He alleged that Selina (Were) wanted him to implicate only Oyugi and Anguka (not others) in exchange for money. It could not be ascertained who was to pay the money. Dickson Ogada, another worker in the household gave an almost similar account saying Ouko "was forcefully taken away...and that those present at the home that night allegedly included a Minister (name withheld)."[277]

A further testimony on the events of that night came from police officer Daniel Mukhwana, who mentioned the names of a lawyer, a campaign official, and a district commissioner as the people who allegedly collected Ouko on the pretense that they would assist him to flee the country to Uganda. In a later testimony, however, Mukhwana disowned his earlier testimony, leaving the credibility of his whole evidence in doubt.

---

[277] Others, alleged the witness, were Kisumu PC, Julius Kobia; the then Kisumu District Criminal Investigation Officer (DCIO), Omwega; Biwott's driver, Arap Chuma; Officer Commanding Station, Kisumu, Wilson Karithi, a former campaign manager, and a district commissioner.

House help Selina also told the committee of a power blackout on the night of February 12, and of hearing a loud bang "that sounded like a gun shot," which woke her up. When she peeped through the window, she saw some people in the compound she allegedly identified as two senior government officials. She also allegedly saw store man Rodi tiptoeing in the compound in the company of people dressed in jungle uniform. At that point, she noticed a white car with dim lights driving away towards Koru. Although there were dogs in the household, she did not hear them bark. She went back to sleep and when she woke up, discovered the minister was not in the house. She concluded that he must have left in the white car.

The contradictory testimonies of what actually transpired in the household on the night Ouko disappeared introduced a serious element of mystery in the whole saga; the white car; the presence of senior government officials including a man behind the pillar; people in jungle uniforms; the sound of gunshot, left me convinced that not everyone was telling the truth. Either some of the witnesses had been carefully tutored to avoid the truth, or they were out rightly lying to the committee. No one actually testified seeing Ouko leave the house either voluntarily or forcefully; and unless he was drugged, any forceful eviction would have resulted in a commotion, which in turn, would have aroused the attention of the workers.

By that time, the country was in a state of panic and the government was under pressure to tell Kenyans the truth. The story had become front-page material for days and anxiety, even among foreign Governments, was building up. On February 15, the government released its first statement of the missing person: "The family of the Minister for Foreign Affairs and International Cooperation, Dr. Robert Ouko, has reported that the Minister left his Koru home last Tuesday, February 13, in the morning, and has not been seen." the statement said. "Could Dr. Ouko please contact his family or the nearest police station…" Following that announcement, according to testimony, fifty police officers were deployed to search for Ouko around Koru and its environs even though a senior police officer "Mwachiti (Chiti) gave indications that the deceased might have been dead already." The search continued the following day.

On the morning of February 16, the government issued its second statement, this time attributed to the President: "I wish to express my sadness and grave concern on the sudden disappearance of my Minister for Foreign Affairs and International Cooperation, the Hon. Dr. Robert Ouko. This Government is committed to protecting the life of each and every Kenyan and no effort will be spared in achieving this intention."

That same day, Ouko's body, lying on its back, a revolver, a jerri-can, a jacket, and a torch, neatly arranged next to the remains, was found by a search team of police officers. Additional items that were carefully arranged near the body, according to District Commissioner Mate who visited the scene immediately after the discovery, included a brown leather jacket, a pistol holster, a paper bag, and a *kitenge* shirt, a pair of jean trousers, a Somali sword, and a matchbox. The Scotland Yard officials later reported that because of poor preservation of the crime scene by Kenyan officials, a lot of valuable evidence had been destroyed. They believed, for example, that the minister had been transported by car to the murder scene, but tyre marks had been destroyed by people and vehicles that had descended on the place.

On the evening, a third statement was released by the government, this time, formally announcing the minister's death: "It is with profound sorrow that I have to announce today the death of the Hon. Robert Ouko, Minister for Foreign Affairs and International Cooperation and Member of Parliament for Kisumu Town....Dr. Ouko's partly burnt body was discovered today six kilometres away from his Koru home in circumstances which at the moment suggest foul play. Further investigations are being conducted into the death of the Hon. Dr. Ouko but I would like to assure the public that anyone who may be associated with this horrible event will most certainly be apprehended and brought to justice," the statement signed by President Moi said. The murder shocked not only Kenyans but also the world. He was a politician but also "a consummate Foreign Minister and skillful, yet gentle, political operator."[278] *The Weekly Review*, a popular newsmagazine at the time said. "The gentleman politician, the quintessential diplomat, was the least likely candidate for the kind of tragedy that befell Kenya's Minister for Foreign Affairs and International Cooperation." Messages of condolences poured from all over the world.

Apart from the government-owned *Kenya News Agency* and the *Voice of Kenya*, which relayed Moi's statement almost instantaneously, *The Standard*

278 The Weekly Review, February 23, p. 20.

newspaper was the first one to go to the streets with the news in a special edition, which was quickly sold out. Almost immediately, students from Kikuyu campus of the University of Nairobi poured into the streets in a show of anger: stoning cars and harassing motorists and pedestrians. That mayhem did not last long and students were persuaded to return to the dormitories. Two days later, students from the main campus of the same university came out in a peaceful demonstration, and with the help of buses provided by the institution, visited Ouko's Nairobi residence to offer their condolences. But the following day, demonstrations erupted in all the other public universities, with students carrying placards demanding to be told the truth about the murder. Save for a few incidents of disorder, the demonstrations were largely peaceful.

While the government propaganda machinery went full throttle to promote the theory that Ouko might have killed himself, students immediately sensed a cover-up attempt and went out with placards: "We want the truth. It was no suicide." They also carried banners demanding Oyugi's resignation: "Produce the murderer, Kenya stinks after murder of Ouko."

The theory that Ouko may have killed himself started to circulate almost immediately after the body was discovered. Troon said Oyugi and Police Commissioner Kilonzo had impressed upon him to treat Dr. Ouko's death as a suicide, making him conclude that the government wanted to cover up the murder. The government "misjudged my investigative expertise," Troon told the parliamentary committee. Ouko's brother, on the other hand, alleged that Moi had tried to get him to read a statement that his brother had committed suicide in exchange for a parliamentary seat and a ministerial post. He declined the offer. Ouko's sister, Dorothy Randiak, also claimed that a government official tried to persuade her to support the suicide theory. But the most categorical statement on the matter came from Ouko's wife, Christabel. "My husband could not take his life," she told the committee. "He was strong in character, was a rational man, (and was) doing well in his political career. He could not commit suicide." "Ouko's death," she added, "was a political murder." It is unlikely that Christabel could have been that categorical if she did not have information about a political connection to the murder.

A former senior intelligence officer in Nyanza Province, Christopher Ong'onda, told the committee that after seeing the remains, he concluded that the minister had been murdered, even though Cleofas Okoko, the then deputy director of CID, was of the view that Ouko had committed suicide. Others, such as police officer Timothy Maloba had no doubts that the Minister had been murdered elsewhere and his body dumped at the site. "There were no struggle marks, no blood…." He alleged the suicide theory had been drawn by investigating officers and Oyugi. A similar opinion was rendered by the government pathologist Jason Kaviti, who was among those who had initially floated the theory. After seeing the body, he was convinced that "it was not possible for one to kill himself and then burn himself… The suicide theory was not tenable and that Dr. Ouko could have been killed elsewhere and (the body) dumped at the scene." He said there was no sign of decomposition; parts that could have decomposed, such as flesh and internal organs were missing. Kaviti ascertained that the minister had a fracture of the right tibia and fibula just above the right ankle which could have been caused by excessive heat, manual application of blunt force (torture) or by a heavy fall.

Kaviti estimated the time of death as February 14—one day after herds-boy Shikuku had allegedly stumbled on the body, and two days before the government officially declared it found. It was around that time that the suicide theory began to circulate around Koru. The theory was that Ouko had first shot himself and then burnt himself. But Kaviti discounted that line of argument, saying that if there had been a shooting, it would have been done at close range given the bullet wounds. He was also of the opinion that the body "could have been shot when already dead since when life ends, the brain matter ceases being liquid, and hence the absence of scattered brain tissue."

Kevin O'Callaghan, a British senior scientific officer, also testified that there were no matching fragments to show that the bullet was fired from Ouko's firearm, and no burns and gunpowder on the victim. Former District Officer, Muhoroni, Jesse Muhoro said he had not seen any signs that the minister killed himself or committed suicide, but felt he had been murdered. Odhiambo of scenes-of-crime unit said he heard people talk about suicide, but he personally did not believe it. As a result of post mortem findings, Troon said, Ouko's death should be investigated as homicide.

The question of how the minister left his Koru home that night of February 13 remained a mystery, with contradictory statements indicating various theories. A senior intelligence officer told the committee that the minister was led away in a Mercedes Benz. Worker Peter Ogada, on the other hand reported that Ouko was "bundled in a white Land Rover and driven away under strict surveillance of GSU men." The intelligence officer, Christopher Ong'onda said two cars, both white, were used to pick up Ouko from the home. He alleged that the minister was killed between Koru and State House, Nakuru, and that "assistance was sought to dispose of the body…with the help of uniformed officers…" He did not provide any concrete details to support those allegations.

However, Zablon Obonyo, the administrative policeman in charge of guarding the Koru home, told the committee no vehicle came to Ouko's home on the night of February 12 and 13 and saw no one abducting the minister. Interestingly, William Mbatha Kivuvani, director of the NSIS, surprised the committee with his ignorance of the key events. He said he only came to know about Ouko's death from media reports, yet as the person in charge of national security, he should have been the first to know. "Kivuvani feigned ignorance about almost everything he was asked which prompted the Committee to declare him a hostile witness," the committee said in its final report.

Another intriguing testimony related to a series of meetings held by high-ranking government officials allegedly to plot the murder. Worker Peter Ogada, for example, claimed a meeting of several senior government officials was held, allegedly to plan "to eliminate" Ouko. A second meeting was allegedly held at Oyugi's home in Kisumu on the same day. Ogada didn't identify those who were present during the follow-up meeting. A similar claim was made by William Wakhu Nagabo, a cook at the late Oyugi's residence, who claimed that between February 11 and 12, several top government officials allegedly met at Oyugi's Nairobi home, and that he heard one of them say "Dr. Ouko should be done away (with), because he had become "a thorn in the Government's flesh."" This testimony was not corroborated for accuracy and should be viewed suspiciously. Another witness who talked of a conspiracy was Ong'onda. He said he learnt from informers and farmers from Vihiga in the western region, that the plot to kill Ouko was "hatched in a meeting at a PC's house on February 2, attended by Oyugi and others." There was also revelation by BAK's

Mattern that Ouko had allegedly confided in her that should anything happen to him, she should forward the name of a government minister. Again, this supposedly confidential information was difficult to verify.

Then there was the mystery of the missing files in Ouko's Koru home. Several witnesses told the committee that Ouko had carried two briefcases on his way from Nairobi to Koru. The contents were said to be volumes of documents on matters of corruption in government. On the day the body was discovered, the committee was told Special Branch Officers entered and searched the minister's bedroom. Witnesses said they saw the officers removing and taking away papers from both briefcases as well as from the study.[279] The papers were never seen again. Who took them and what information did they contain?

It was clear to us in the committee that some witnesses were part of a massive cover-up to conceal the circumstances that led to the death. For example, the committee concluded that Agalo Obonyo, the administrative policeman in charge of the minister's security gave unconvincing evidence and appeared to conceal the truth. "He did not enquire about the late Minister's whereabouts (on the day he went missing) or report his disappearance… and was privy to the plans to assassinate the late Minister." The committee also expressed surprise that Permanent Secretary Kiplagat did not find anything unusual about the late minister when he arrived from Washington, DC. The committee noted the following after his testimony: "The Committee observed with concerns that Ambassador Kiplagat could not recall a telex from the then Kenyan Ambassador in Washington DC advising against attending the Prayer Breakfast. The Committee also took note that Ambassador Kiplagat never noted anything unusual about the late Minister and never heard about the differences between the late Dr. Ouko and Hon. Nicholas Biwott, MP. The Committee resolved that Ambassador Kiplagat may be recalled later." He was never recalled.

One witness who did not impress the committee was the Director of Intelligence who was found to be "evasive and unnecessarily defensive." The committee also concluded that Biwott 'was selective in his memory of events." For example, Biwott claimed he left Jomo Kenyatta International Airport for London on January 27 together with Ouko, but his passport was

279 Troon Report, paragraph 116.

stamped January 25 as the exit date, while Ouko's passport was stamped January 27, the date the presidential delegation left for Washington.

Other pertinent questions that remained a mystery as our investigations came to an end were: Were there or were there no strangers in Ouko's compound on the night of February 12/13? If there were strangers, who were they, and what did they want? How did Ouko leave, or assisted to leave the compound? Did he walk away voluntarily from the compound, or was he abducted as some of the witnesses testified. Was he dragged away by members of the para-military force, the GSU or was he driven out in a white car? What was the role of Ouko's servants in the disappearance and eventual murder? Who were the people in jungle uniforms?

Witnesses talked of a power blackout and interference in Ouko's telephone on the night of the murder. Was the outage deliberate to provide cover for an evil act? And, was the telephone tampered with to interfere with communication? If so, who was responsible for the tampering? And most importantly: Did he kill himself or was he shot and his body burnt? Was he killed elsewhere and his body brought to the site? Suicide theorists said he shot himself and then burnt himself. Is this really possible? And, what would have been the motive for his suicide, if that was the case?

When was Ouko's body actually found? Was it found by a herds-boy on February 13 or by a search team on February 16? Given the testimony before the committee, what role did Biwott, Oyugi, Anguka, and other government officials play in the murder? Evidence was given that Oyugi had a lengthy meeting with Ouko immediately after the two arrived from Washington, DC. Troon described such an encounter as "unusual." In any case, what was the content of their discussion? The British investigator thought "something other than local corruption was discussed which had relevance to Dr. Ouko's murder."[280] Several witnesses placed Oyugi at the Sunset Hotel, two days before Ouko disappeared. Oyugi's hotel room was booked and paid for by an Asian friend, but when Oyugi was interrogated he denied staying at the hotel. What is the truth? And what would anyone have wanted Ouko killed? Was it personal rivalry or a business deal gone bad? The Director of Intelligence testified that he only came to know of Ouko's death through the media. Could that really be true? Or, was

[280] Troon Report, paragraph 246.

he hiding the truth. If so why, and for whose interest? The government talked of "foul play." How come there was no serious follow up on that observation?

And, where was Moi in all this? He declined to testify, preferring instead to send a statement through his lawyer, a statement the committee rejected. In refusing to admit Moi's statement, did the committee miss anything? There were allegations of meetings that plotted his death. Did those meetings really take place, or was it the creation of witnesses? What was Moi to gain from Ouko's death? In his book, Andrew Morton quoted Moi as saying: "How could I kill my Minister who was so trusted?" The author went on to say that Ouko's death was personally and politically painful for the President. "Not only did he lose a close friend, he also lost a valuable political ally and a highly competent, ambitious and loyal Minister."[281]

During the hearings, Sunguh alleged—but did not provide evidence—that a hit squad had been paid 8 million shillings to kill Ouko. Was there any truth in that allegation? And if so, who paid the money and who was in the killer squad? Also, was Ouko's farm manager, Ndalo and his sister Selina, "coached" to implicate Moi and Biwott in exchange for protection from prosecution as claimed at a press conference on March 11, 2005? If so, who coached them? Those are some of the many questions to the murder mystery that need answers.

Towards the end of the committee hearings, Biwott made a desperate, but unsuccessful attempt to save his name from allegations of involvement made by at least ten witnesses. But Sunguh refused to accept the report Biwott had written, which he wanted to read before the committee. The chairman ordered Biwott out and proceeded to close the proceedings. Was that action of dismissing Biwott fair? Why didn't the committee give him a chance to explain his side of the story? Biwott had charged in his report that the Troon investigations were flawed: that there was no dispute between him and Ouko in Washington; that some of the witnesses especially Mattern and Airaghi were not credible; and that the revival of the molasses plant could not have been the motive, since his involvement in the factory was only as a member of a government sub-committee to oversee the project's revival.

---

281 Andrew Morton, The Making of an African Statesman, Michael O'Mara Books Ltd, p. 229.

Biwott further argued that for his accusers to link the activities of the molasses plant with Ouko's death was wrong. "This is the crucial evidence of his (Troon's) theory. Without it, there is no link between Molasses, Dr. Ouko's death and me," he said. Furthermore, Biwott accused Troon of relying on the evidence of the two directors of the Swiss-based company with the acronym BAK, Airaghi and Mattern, without taking into consideration that the former had been convicted in a Milan court on charges of extortion and blackmail in 1987. In the same case, Marianne's evidence was allegedly discredited.

The fifty-year old Biwott was among ten people who were arrested and detained as part of the investigations into the Ouko murder, but he was released a few weeks later after police found no evidence to support allegations that he had been involved.

## Troon recommends

In his report to the government, Troon made far-reaching recommendations that called for further investigations of some individuals. The following are some of them:

1. That a full and impartial investigation be implemented into the allegations made by the BAK Directors against some senior government personnel. These allegations, in my view, have some bearing on the death of Dr. Ouko.
2. All senior government officials and civil servants should be interviewed in relation to the Washington visit and their knowledge of what may have transpired between Dr. Ouko and other colleagues. The visit to Washington, in my opinion, also has some bearing on the cause of Dr. Ouko's death.
3. Full inquiries should be undertaken to establish the truth surrounding the allegations that files and papers were taken from the minister's Koru farm, which subsequently disappeared, and establish the details of those files and papers.
4. Additionally, full inquiries should be made to obtain any evidence from Special Branch Officers in relation to their interviews with possible witnesses in relation to the death of Dr. Ouko

5. Enquiries and further interviews should also take place to establish beyond doubt the movements and alibis of Mr. Oyugi and his driver and bodyguard from 9 to 13 February, inclusive.
6. Enquiries must be made to fully establish the alibi put forward by Mr. Joab Omino, and any connections that he and/or Mr. Biwott may have with the Muhoroni Sugar Complex.

Whilst all these inquiries will need to be conducted with diligence and total impartiality, Troon said, they may still not produce evidence of the true cause of Dr. Ouko's death, or the perpetrator(s), should suicide be excluded. But they should either further endorse, or eliminate some of the lingering doubts experienced at the present time. Indeed, the Ouko murder went cold and the killer or killers have not been caught.

The work in the Parliamentary Committee had its own risks. Members expressed security concerns throughout the hearings, with some reporting threats to their lives. At a church service in Kisumu, Sunguh broke down as he narrated how thugs had trailed him in an attempt to kill him, while Wanjala had expressed similar concerns at a press conference in Nairobi in March 2005. Extra security had to be provided to each one of the committee members.

The proceedings of the committee were uneventful to a large extent, although at times, tempered flared as interrogation intensified. However, the mention of President Moi's name as one of those allegedly involved in the murder almost split the committee, with some members refusing to endorse the final report. Sunguh had wanted Moi summoned to give testimony about what he knew of the murder, but MP Samuel Moroto, felt the chairman was politicising the investigations. When the committee went on a retreat to write the final report, MP Moroto and MP Raphael Wanjala, had a nasty altercation over aspects of the recommendations that had implicated Moi and Biwott in the murder. In addition, critics accused Sunguh of being an "aggressive bully" [282]for barring Biwott to defend himself from serious allegations made in various testimonies. One of them said: "...the Chairman seemed to derive something close to salacious pleasure in terrorising some of the witnesses, and especially the self-proclaimed Nicholas Total Man Biwott, who was intimidated through and

---

282 Barrack Muluka, Standard, March 12, 2005.

through."[283] Others thought the committee was not professional enough, and that the setting up of the committee was not the "most appropriate course of action."[284]

Parliament took no action on the report until MP Gitobu Imanyara fished it out from a dusty shell and presented it to Members for debate in December 2010. It was rejected with accusations that it was no more than a collection of unsubstantiated hearsays and falsehoods. Like all the other bodies before it, the Kenyan parliament failed to answer the question: Who killed Ouko?

283 Ibid.

284 Ambrose Murunga, Saturday Nation, March 12, 2005.

# CHAPTER 25
## Obama visits

On a crystalline morning of August 2006, a slender, light-skinned visitor, his hair cropped down, his legs on a bounce, landed at the sun-decked Jomo Kenyatta International Airport, Nairobi. Accompanied by a small team of officials and a much larger crew of journalists and cameramen, the visitor—dressed in casuals and spotting a radiant smile—walked down the gangway behind his two cheery but seemingly fatigued children and wife. No welcoming drums, no dancing women—only a small group of American diplomats and local officials, and a few quaint looking, middle aged ordinary people waiting to greet him. The visitors were Senator Barack Hussein Obama, his wife Michelle, and their children, Malia, eight and Sasha, four.

The son of a Kenyan father and a white American mother was in the country for a sentimental journey to the homeland of his paternal relatives, a "journey of discovery,"[285] meant to discover his ancestral roots and to catch up with lost time. The visit was deliberately low key. It was more private than official; more personal than public. But Obama was not just any visitor on a romantic escapade to enjoy the balmy Kenyan weather and to experience the bounty wilderness of game parks. He was not making the trip as a politician eager to learn the political culture of the east African country, nor to empathise with the people courageously struggling to meet their many needs. He was the junior senator from Illinois in the US and

[285] That is how he described the trip during his Kenya visit.

an embryonic statesman. He was in Kenya primarily to experience the pristine environment of the remote village of Nyang'oma Kogelo in Siaya District of western Kenya where his father, Barack Obama Sr.—the man he met only once in his life in 1971—was born sixty-two-years earlier; and to introduce his young family to the simpler ways of life, away from the opulence and grandeur of a developed Chicago skyline.

The majority of Kenyans did not know who Obama Junior really was. They had not heard much of him; nor had they known his father who had left the country in the early sixties at the age of twenty-three to study in the US, and who had died at a relatively young age. Many of those who remembered Obama Sr. did not even know that he had married and divorced a white American woman, and had sired a boy who was to become an important world personality in later years. When the boisterous, pipe-smoking Obama Sr. landed on the Kenya soil with a PhD in Economics from the prestigious Harvard University in Cambridge, Massachusetts in 1965, he was only one of a few Africans at the time with advanced qualifications and skills that were in great demand in the newly independent Kenya.

The senator's visit was low-key perhaps because the local media had not provided any prior, serious insights into the interesting background of the Obamas, leave alone that of the senator, other than repeating over and over again that the youthful politician was an American senator born to a Kenyan father. They said little about his smashing debut into American national politics, and his sterling performance at the Democratic National Convention in 2004. That apparent lack of interest by Kenyans on an individual, who many Americans believed was headed for the White House, surprised even those who had accompanied him to Kenya. Americans, especially those residing in Chicago, had expected a celebratory welcome for the senator and his family, but nothing like that happened. Charles Thomas, a reporter for Chicago's ABC affiliate WLS-TV, who was with Obama on the tour, said he saw no 'buzz" in Nairobi when Obama was in Kenya, adding newspapers made little mention, and television news programs made even less mention of the visit. The only explanation was ignorance, ignorance on the part of the media, and a don't-care-attitude on the part of the ruling elite. It was not until the Obamas arrived in Kisumu on their way to K'Ogelo that crowds came out to welcome them.

I personally knew Obama Sr. during his days as a middle level economist in Kenyatta's Government. Always smartly dressed, Barrack Sr. was the embodiment of success. He came from a poor family near Lake Victoria, Africa's largest water mass, went to a tin-roofed school with no running water, but still managed to reach the pinnacle of intellectual life at Harvard University in the US, where he received his advanced degree. At the University of Miami at Minoa, he was the first African student to be enrolled there for undergraduate studies, and therefore, became the centre of attraction. Tall and dark with horn-rimmed spectacles and a deep baritone voice, Barack was not only boastful about his achievement but was patriotically African. In an interview with *The Washington Post* soon after his arrival, he talked of his desire to study business administration, and of his hope of one day returning to Kenya "to help with its transition from tribal customs to a modern economy."[286] Neil Abercrombie, who later became a district congressman, described Obama Sr. as "brilliant, opinionated, and avuncular."[287]

During his undergraduate years at the University of Hawaii, he married Ann Durham, a Kansas-born woman who was studying Russian at the same institution. Ann was unaware that her husband was already married at home to Kezia Aoko when he was only eighteen years, and that he had left behind two children. No wonder, the marriage did not last, and culminated in Ann filing a divorce in 1961, which Obama Sr. did not contest. By that time, the future senator had already been born, and Obama Sr. had moved to Cambridge for his Masters degree where he met another white woman, Ruth Nidesand. Unlike many other Kenyan students who get mesmerized by the fast pace of American life and decide to extend their stay, the young economist made good his promise, and returned home in 1965, two years after independence.

Ruth, an American-born educationist—whom Obama described as a "white woman with a long jaw and graying hair"[288]—followed Obama Sr. to Nairobi, where they married and stayed together for seven years. Like with his earlier marriage to Durham, the relationship with Ruth was turbulent. "Obama Senior's marriage to Ruth was not a happy one.

286 The Obama File, Beckwith, 2008.
287 Ibid.
288 Barack Obama, Dreams From My Father, Three Rivers Press, p. 341.

Like his father, although charming, generous and extraordinarily clever, Obama Senior was imperious, cruel and given to boasting about his brain and his wealth," said Philip Ochieng, a friend who was also a beneficiary of the Tom Mboya scholarships. Ruth's distaste for Obama Sr. extended to Obama in later years, as was evident during their first encounter in Nairobi when she could not resist a stinger: "You know Obama (Senior) was quiet crazy, don't you? The drinking made it worse."[289] Also, Obama Sr.'s second son with Ruth, Mark Obama Ndesandjo, wrote in his semi-autobiography—*Nairobi to Shenzhen: a Novel of Love in the East*—that he remembered his father "smelling of cheap pilsner." He called his father an abusive man, who beat his wife and sons. "I didn't have a positive memory of my dad because of domestic violence,"[290] he said in the book.

In the corridors of government where he served as a senior economist, Obama Sr. was both envied and frowned upon by Nairobians because of his financial liquidity, and because of his obsession for beauties especially of the Caucasian breed. "He was a go-getter, a womaniser and a generous person…He drove the latest car models, wore the best suits and drank the most expensive whisky brands,"[291] some of his friends remembered him.

What I remember about Obama Sr. was that he chain-smoked contentedly, drank copiously, and partied spiritedly. I remember Barack as a person with a deep husky voice that embodied authority and confidence, who spontaneously let out busts of laughter that drew attention and set him well above the rest within his surroundings. Barack was as much at ease on a bar stool at the Norfolk Hotel's Delamere lounge, as he was in the dimly lit counters at the Starlight Night Club, then one of the hottest meeting joints for African bourgeois. One day he would be killing time at the New Stanley's Long Bar, and the other, he would be shooting air at the low class but popular Jean's Bar in Nairobi West. Several times when I sat with him over a beer or a double tot of Scotch whisky, which he loved, I never heard him talk about the wife and the child he had left behind. That is how the man was.

---

[289] Ibid., p. 342.

[290] Ling Woo Liu, TIME, November 17, 2009.

[291] Standard, November 15, 2008.

His turning point, however, came in 1965 when, as a top bureaucrat in the Treasury, he issued a critical analysis of the government's economic framework called "African Socialism and its Applicability to Planning in Kenya," an ambitious document that had been authored by Mboya. He disagreed with proposals to nationalise state corporations, as well as the manner in which the government planned to conduct trade, both locally and internationally.

In his critique carried in the then widely read business publication, *The East African Journal* entitled "The Problems Facing our Socialism," Barack questioned the rationale of retaining foreign interests to the disadvantage of locals. "One need not be a Kenyan to note that nearly all commercial enterprises from small shops in River road to big shops in Government Road, and industries in the industrial area were mostly owned by Asians and Europeans. One need not be a Kenyan to note that most hotels and entertainment places are owned by Asians and Europeans. One need not be a Kenyan to note that when one goes to a good restaurant, he mostly finds Asians and Europeans, nor has he to be a Kenyan to see that the majority of cars running in Kenya are run by Asians and Europeans. How then can we say that we are going to be indiscriminate in rectifying the imbalance? We have to give the African his place in his own country, and we have to give him his economic power if he is going to develop."[292]

Under Kenyatta as under Moi in later years, criticisms of the government by anyone, leave alone a serving civil servant, was unheard of. The statement generated a lot of heat in the corridors of power. Accusations of insubordination and disrespect were bandied around. Soon thereafter, Obama Sr. was sacked, throwing him into a long period of depression that saw his drinking habit overwhelm his desire to be a useful citizen. The situation worsened when his marriage to Ruth collapsed. Jobless and down in the gutter, he was killed in a road accident on November 24, 1982 at the prime age of forty-six years, as he navigated home from a boozing spree. Barack Sr.'s story is one of the saddest in any human experience. As an intellectual, he was destined for bigger things. His rise to the top of the civil service was almost guaranteed. If he wanted, he could have joined politics, or take a position in the corporate world when multinationals were setting shop in Kenya and looking for the best brains the country could

---

292 East African Journal, July 1965.

provide. But he chose to squander his life in debauchery. In his life, Barack had four wives who bore him eight children.

## A magical trip

Obama Jr. first visited Kenya in 1987—a magical trip, he called it—after spending a year working as a community organiser in Chicago. His journey to Kenya then was intended to allow him to pay tribute to his dead father, whom he had seen only once when he visited them in Hawaii. Pictures of the young man carrying a sack of farm produce on a rural road and laughing and intermingling with relatives he hardly knew, shall remain pricey pieces of photographic art in the Obama household. He travelled around in slow, crowded trains and in *matatus,* jitneys, and communicated in English with villagers who knew the language, and by body language, with those who didn't. An easy and willing communicator, Obama Jr. had no problem socialising with villagers. However, in his book, *Dreams from my Father*, he admitted difficulty in communicating with Mama Sarah, the step-grandmother he calls "granny," who only spoke Dholuo, and quoted her as saying it "pained her not to be able to speak to the son of her son."[293]

When he made the return visit in 2006 as a state senator, his engagements were a mixture of leisure and work. He called on President Kibaki, the man who was once his father's boss at the Treasury; met Uhuru, then Leader of Government Business in Parliament, addressed students and faculty at the University of Nairobi; visited Kibera, one of the biggest slums in Africa; and took an AIDS test in Kisumu, the town with the highest HIV prevalence rate in the country at the time. In between, he squeezed an intimate luncheon with a selected group of MPs.

For him though, the most important engagement was his visit to Kogelo where he was feted like a prodigal son and treated with much awe and admiration. During his earlier visits, Obama Jr. attracted little attention from villagers, and was comfortable sharing a small room with others in his step-grand-mother's rural compound, listening to spooky stories about night runners. This time round, that dwelling was no longer

293 Barack Obama, Dreams From My Father, Three Rivers Press, p. 377.

fit or appropriate for him. Like most high-ranking government officials travelling abroad, he was now guarded at all times by hawk-eyed American security officials. He was a hero, and the simple quarters at Kogelo no longer fitted his stature. He was no longer a boy with a funny accent, but a man of great substance, a politician, and a senator.

Apart from everything else, Obama had come to show off his charming children to Mama Sarah and to his uncles, cousins, and aunties, as if to fulfill the wishes of his father. In 1995, he had brought his young bride, Michelle, to see his roots. Now he had come to induct his wife and their children, Malia and Sasha, as full members of the Alego clan of the greater Luo tribe. They would no longer be strangers, and would no longer have to be referred to as black *muzungus* (whites) by locals, but blood relatives entitled to all the rights offered by local customs. During the latest visit, Michelle had no problem blending in into the unfamiliar environment. Dressed in blue jeans and a white sleeved shirt, she talked with local women with love and without any show of condescendence, and when she appeared at a local hospital for the AIDS test with her husband, she demonstrated genuine confidence and an absence of hubris that would characteristically have been displayed by a foreigner suspicious of a needle prick from an unfamiliar nurse in a strange land.

Similarly, Malia and Sasha appeared comfortable in their new surroundings and enjoyed the undivided attention from their distant cousins. Everyone got the impression they had been well prepared for the cultural shock at K'Ogelo where electricity and water were sporadic, and where the nearby local school was a shack compared to what they were used to in Chicago.

A few days after his arrival in Kenya, Senator Obama hosted a lunch for a selected few parliamentarians at a high priced restaurant in downtown Nairobi known for its mouth-watering sea food delicacies. The trendy Tamarind restaurant was less than one hundred metres from the site of the former American Embassy bombed by terrorists a few years earlier, and only a stone's throw away from the Treasury where his father once worked. I was one of the eight MPs invited to that lunch. I still have not figured out how my name made it to that privileged list of people chosen to dialogue intimately with the young American leader. What was clear when I arrived at the restaurant was that the group appeared to have been divided equally between NAK and LDP legislators; and, other than the American Ambassador and the Senator's small entourage of advisers, no government official was invited. Neither Michelle nor the children were present. It was an informal, private affair that also excluded the media. The delicious meals were served *a la carte*, giving the American visitor an opportunity to taste the wide range of local ocean delicacies, accompanied by Kenyan seasonal vegetables and fruits, English deserts, washed down by a cup of aromatic Kenyan coffee.

After the Ambassador had introduced the senator and had given us a brief background of the visitor's political life: his work as a community organiser in Chicago; his election to the Illinois State Senate; as well as his bid for a Federal Senate seat in which he won with the largest margin of votes in Illinois's history, becoming the first African American to serve in the historically white dominated Chamber, we spent almost two hours discussing various local and international topics. I found Obama thoroughly informed about regional and African issues. His portrayal of American foreign policy was somehow defensive as expected of an American politician, but it was convincing; his commitment to good governance in Africa and around the world was admirable, and his clarity of thought appeared to be in sync with his ambitions for higher office. Instead of lecturing us on the nuances of American domestic and foreign policies, he gave us an opportunity to ask questions, and responded without going off on tangents. I did not find him "elitist and different to connect"[294] as some conservatives later said of him, nor did I find him "racist."[295]

We asked him to give us his views on sleaze, particularly mega corruption in Kenya, and the frequent travel advisories imposed by Washington on Kenya that kept American tourists away. Obama made it clear that his government viewed the rampant corruption and theft of public funds in Kenya with a lot of trepidation, and explained that that was the reason why America preferred to channel its development aid to non-governmental organisations rather than directly to the government. He said American taxpayers would have no reason to complain if the money their government provided to poor countries was used transparently and accountably. But this was not always the case, and several times, the US Congress had raised

[294] Vancouver Sun, August 22, 2008.

[295] Celeste and Loren Davis, April 2008.

issues of misuse of American funds to fight diseases especially AIDS and Malaria. "We have to justify our tax-payers' money, otherwise Americans would revolt," he added.

On the question of travel advisories, Obama said they were necessary to protect American interests around the world. He singled out the terror attacks in Dar es Salaam and Nairobi, and said in order to avoid such attacks in future, stringent security measures would have to be taken. He assured us that as long as terrorist threats existed in the region, the American government would continue to caution its citizens against travelling to the area. Travel advisories on Kenya started following the 1998 bombing of the American Embassy, and were sustained after the attack on Israeli-owned Paradise Beach Hotel, north of Mombasa. The Senator said Americans were particularly concerned about the existence of terrorist cells in neighbouring Somalia, and Kenya's inability to patrol effectively the common borders. "We know Somalia has become a major haven for extremists and we are concerned," he said.

The junior senator also addressed the failure of the Kenya Parliament to pass the Suppression of Terrorism Bill in 2003, and stressed that the legislation was necessary to deal with the growing threats of terrorism in the region. He assured us that his government had no intention of pushing Kenya into enacting the law. As mentioned earlier, the bill was heavily criticised by the Kenyan public and had to be withdrawn from Parliament a year later following street protests from Moslems, who claimed to be targeted by the legislation.

In our discussions, I raised the issue of America's apparent invisibility in the eyes of Africans, saying that while Russia, later the Soviet Union, had built a big hospital in Kisumu, and China had constructed the Kasarani Sports Centre, Americans had nothing concrete to show as proof of its friendship with Nairobi. "How can we tell our people that America is on our side when there are no visible infrastructural projects visible to the people of Kenya?" I asked. Obama responded by citing security concerns and dangers of sabotage by American enemies on standing edifices, and said Washington preferred to fund non-structural programs because they directly benefitted the people. He said America was proud of its health assistance to Kenya that had helped reduce cases of malaria and of other diseases, such as HIV and TB.

At the end of our sumptuous lunch, Obama left to visit the *Bomb Blast Memorial* at the former US Embassy. Outside the restaurant, a huge crowd of people, who had by then realised how important Obama was, waited to get a glimpse of their Kenyan brother. I was left more than convinced that this man—eloquent and confident—had a bright future ahead of him. A few years later, I was lucky to be in America during the 2008 Presidential campaigns, where I witnessed firsthand, his unique mobilisation skills.

But it was his speech at the University of Nairobi that week that ruffled Kibaki's government and attracted condemnation from officials in Nairobi and in Washington. The venue of the meeting was particularly significant. In the 1980s and 1990s, the Kenyan institution was the bedrock of political activism. Many of the people, who later became leaders in government and in the struggle for more freedoms and human rights, were alumni of the University of Nairobi, so were most of the detainees and those who fled into exile. Kenya's most prolific writer, Ngugi wa Thiong'o, was a literature lecturer at the university until his Kikuyu play, *Ngaahika Ndeenda*, I'll marry when I want, which was perceived to be critical of Kenyan leaders, was banned in 1977, forcing him to go into exile. Raila, on his return from studies in Germany in 1970, was employed there as a lecturer. There was a time when demonstrations by students from that university were so regular that the institution remained closed for long periods of time, disrupting studies and forcing degree programmes to stretch well beyond the traditional completion period.

During the 1982 attempted coup against Moi, students of the University of Nairobi were the first to hit the streets in celebration, an act that cost some of them death and others long prison sentences. So, Obama chose the right venue to deliver his maiden speech in Kenya. In his opening remarks, Obama said he first came to the country in 1987 after finishing three years of work as a community organiser, and narrated his ordeal when his sisters' car broke down in front of Uhuru Park, and how he used to frequent a small tea-house in downtown Nairobi for his meals. Obama also talked about his father, Barack whose life, he said, was "filled with disappointments." But it was his political remarks, especially on corruption in Kenya that caught the attention of authorities.

"I know that while recent reports have pointed to strong economic growth in this country, 56 percent of Kenyans still live in poverty. And

I know that the vast majority of people in this country desperately want to change this," he said. "It is painfully obvious that corruption stifles development—it siphons off scarce resources that could improve infrastructure, bolster education systems and strengthen health. It stacks the deck so high against entrepreneurs that they cannot get their job-creating ideas off the ground," he added. Saying that Kenya and Africa had not exhausted and had not yet fulfilled their potential, Obama went on to rap the Kenyan Government on corruption calling the vice a crisis. "Of course, in the end, one of the strongest weapons your country has against corruption is the ability of you, the people, to stand up and speak out about the injustices you see. The Kenyan people are the ultimate guardians against abuses," he said amidst a heavy round of applause from students and faculty.

Was that speech meant to incite Kenyans into turning against their government? The Kenya Government reaction was swift and potent. The official spokesman dismissed Obama as a junior American official who had nothing to teach Kenyans, claiming that he had been misadvised by Raila, who was vying for the presidency. "Sen. Obama has to look critically about where he is receiving his advice," said the spokesman. "Just because somebody somewhere wants to run for President, he is using Sen. Obama as his stooge, as his puppet, to be able to get to where he wants to get to."

If Obama's criticisms were harsh, the response from Kenyan authorities was potent. In Washington, Peter Nicholas Ogengo, the Kenya Ambassador-designate to America fired a protest note to Obama's office accusing him of breaching protocol and seeking cheap publicity. "You deliberately and without real cause or reason, other than what appears to be cheap publicity and inconsequential populism, chose to publicly attack the democratically elected Government of Kenya," he stated angrily. "This was in total disregard for the requisite protocol and acceptable methods of addressing the issues you raised…" The only problem with Ogengo was that at the time he issued the statement, he had not yet been accredited, and his statement was itself a contravention of acceptable diplomatic norms.

In the meantime, the Kenyan media began to take serious note of the young senator. During the American presidential primaries that saw him downsize Hilary Clinton, the Kenyan media devoted pages after pages (in some cases, front pages) as they followed "our Kenyan" journey to the White House. It was a typical Kenyan way of celebrating a hero. Having no young heroes of their own, they embraced Obama wholeheartedly as a person of great intellect who perhaps, was best suited for the presidency in Kenya. But many commentators opinionated that had he been a politician in Kenya, he would not have been able to survive the obfuscation, connivance, and intrigues that were so common in Kenyan politics, and would never ascend to the highest office, given his mixed parentage, regardless of his father's Luo roots. In a highly ethicised society such as Kenya's, tribal affiliation is one of the prime criteria for election to high office. A candidate must first get support from his clan, and then from his tribe, before being considered by the rest of the country for high office.

Curiously, when Obama was declared the forty-fourth President of the United States on November 5 2008, Kenya became the only country in the world to honour him with a national holiday. In Kenya, many children now bear either the name "Obama" or, "Michelle" and many rackety minivans plying towns and rural roads were similarly baptised in recognition of their famous son. One black mini-van simply says boldly: Obama is a black President.

## Myths about Obama

Questions have arisen, since Obama became president, over his nationality and religious convictions. Right-wing publications encouraged by elements in the Republican party and the Tea Party have reproduced what they claim to be a copy of a birth certificate issued at the Coast General Hospital in Mombasa, indicating Obama was born in Kenya, and therefore, a Kenyan, and not, an American citizen. Investigations of medical records at that health facility have revealed no evidence that an Obama was born at the hospital either on August 4 1961, or at anytime throughout that year. The alleged birth certificate was, therefore, nothing but a cunning fake circulated to damage Obama's credibility and to deny him a place in history.

Like many Kenyans, Obama bears a Moslem middle name, but such a name means nothing given the country's cultural history. Islam came to Kenya in the seventeenth century, and was emboldened by the slave trade in which Arab merchants traded in slaves and married agnostic members of local communities whom they then converted to Islam and gave them Moslem names. Along the Kenyan coast, for example, many Christians, among them the author of this book, have Moslem names. That was true of the Obamas, even though the Islamic religion did not reach the Lake Victoria region until several centuries later. Both President Obama's paternal grandparents—Hussein Onyango and Akumu Habiba—were practicing Moslems. Indeed, the woman Obama calls granny is a Moslem even though she carries the Christian name Sarah. Obama Sr., for the time I knew him, never professed to be a Moslem. In fact, he had no clear religious convictions. He neither went to the mosque not wore the *kanzu*. One could correctly conclude that he was irreligious. It is misguided to suggest, therefore, that because President Obama's middle name is Hussein, he is therefore a Moslem. That shows ignorance of Kenya's cultural diversity.

However, many Kenyans had believed that the election of Obama to the US presidency would bring them material gains and preferential treatment to the country of his father's birth. They expected more American investment; more military aid, and more tourists visiting his K'ogelo village, but by mid-2010, Kenya had only received more and more promises. Some local people even salivated over possible monetary rewards from Obama, like payment of school fees and some occasional handouts. But those tantalising expectations have turned out to be a magician's illusions.

True, water and electricity supplies to the village were fast-tracked. True, a cultural centre is in the works. True, local businessmen and landowners have capitalised on the expected boom, but nothing spectacular has happened. Those who were poor are still so. Instead of an avalanche of tourists, there has only been a trickle of mainly inquisitive journalists and students on sabbatical. This slow growth of visitors can partly be attributed to the Washington-imposed security warnings, which offer stern advisory for Americans wishing to travel to Kenya. In addition, America still considered Kenya an international terrorism launch pad because of its proximity to the war-torn, Al Queda-infested Somalia. In 2009, Obama deliberately skipped the country during his western African tour, citing lack of democracy and governance in the east African nation, prompting concerns in Nairobi that Kenya was perhaps receiving a much harsher treatment from Washington than most other African countries.

Several top American officials have visited Kenya since Obama became President, and all of them have emphasised the need for good governance and for enhanced efforts against corruption. During her visit in August 2010, Hilary Clinton delivered a tough message saying that Kenya had not yet realised a functional democracy, and called on Kenyan leaders to rid the country of corrupt elements, especially, within its judiciary. "Americans want to do business," said another visitor, Vice President Joe Biden in Nairobi. "They want to travel here, with the right climate, they will come."

According to American authorities, the right climate meant more democracy and a new constitution for the country. Even the FBI Director, Robert Mueller, visited Kenya and said sleaze affected democracy. In the Financial Year 2010, the Obama Administration allocated 1.4 billion US dollars in a special programme to discourage corruption in Kenya. The programme, which was started by President Bush, ties aid to performance on government. The effect of that policy will be seen several years from now. In the meantime, the Obama Administration continues to hold hope that things will change; that American economic and military interests will thrive.

America's hyperactive top diplomat in Nairobi, Michael Rannenberger, may have had good intentions, but he often went overboard by lecturing and cajoling the Kenyan leadership on everything. He toured the country in the guise of inspecting projects, but used those tours to dish out money to youth groups and to urge them to wrestle leadership from the old guard. Many criticised his mode of operation, which they considered intrusive and undiplomatic. He was accused of meddling in the internal affairs of the country and of lecturing to Kenya, a sovereign nation, but his response was that Kenya was too important to Washington to fail. Many times, he explained that America's concern was borne out of a desire to keep the region peaceful and safe from international terrorists. The presence in Mogadishu of lawless Al Shabab gangs affiliated to Al Queda was a major cause of worries to Americans. The rag-tag terrorist group has, on many occasions, sneaked into Kenya in a daring show of power, but their efforts have been repulsed. The huge Somali population in Kenya makes it difficult for the government to distinguish Kenyans from genuine Somali residents, and between Al Shabab sympathisers and peace loving citizens. Al Shabab training camps in Somali are a significant breeding ground for terrorists, who are trained and then dispatched to other countries to launch attacks. The explosions that took place in Uganda in 2010 signalled a grim harbinger for what could happen in future. Dozens of people watching the World Cup were left dead through a suicide bomber. Al Shabab claimed responsibility, and a Kenyan connection was reported.

After the 2007 elections in Kenya, the country could easily have exploded into a full-scale civil war if Obama did not intervene promptly and vigorously. With the promulgation of a new constitution in August 2010, Kenyans renewed hopes of more enhanced relations with its American partner.

But there is another problem of concern to the international community apart from terrorism: trafficking of drugs. Because of its extensive air connections to Asia and Europe, Nairobi had, by 2008, replaced some South American capitals—where surveillance has been tightened—as one of the main hubs for international trafficking of heroin and cocaine, despite the many arrests at Kenyan airports. For years now, drug lords have used the port of Mombasa and many unpoliced fishing landing spots along the coastline to bring in large consignments of dangerous substances. To help Kenya deal with that menace, the American government donated six powerful armoured patrol speedboats in 2010.

# CHAPTER 26
## Kibera pricks

Unlike Kibaki who in 1974 abandoned a cosmopolitan constituency in Nairobi for his home area of Othaya on the rolling hills of Mt. Kenya, Raila—who hails from the farming fields of Bondo in Nyanza Province—has stuck with Langata on the fringes of the capital's business district, a kaleidoscopic locality, which conflates extreme deprivations and abundant affluence. Langata is home to Kibera, one of Kenya's largest slums, as well as Karen, once a colonial playground for the rich. Only ten minutes away from downtown Nairobi and more than half the size of New York City's Central Park, Kibera stands out as a stark monument of the betrayal of *wanjikus* by Kenyan Governments that failed to deal with urban problems of poverty and diseases.

In 2006, statistics showed Kibera had a population density of three thousand people per hectare compared to one hundred in New York and forty-three people in London.[296] Thousands of people are crowded in a one and half square mile area with no toilets, no clean water, no drainage, and no decent housing. They are forced to live in makeshift structures built of plastic and grey, weather-bitten corrugated iron sheets that are susceptible both to the usually cool Nairobi weather and to the vagaries of rain and dust. The population of this forbidden colony has varied from several hundred thousand to one million people, but the 2009 census put

---

296 Arthur I Segel, Nicolas P. Retsinas, Marc Diaz, John Shepherd, Harvard Business Publishing, a Case Study.

the number of inhabitants at less than one hundred and twenty thousand. However, visitors to Kibera would be excused to think that the area carries far more people than officially estimated.

The sprawling town, which from the air, resembles a haphazardly arranged motley of match boxes; and on the ground, a closely knit stockpile of litter, narrow, dark alleys, raw waste and dispirited people, stick out like a sore thumb in a metropolis reputed to be one of the most developed by African standards. The residents of Kibera include a large number of Sudanese Nubians who had fought in the colonial's King's African Riffles, and who were settled there by the British Government after World War One. The Nubians called the place Kibra, meaning jungle, and jungle it has remained. Kibera is certainly not for faint-hearted. In the absence of convenience facilities, "the flying toilet"—where faeces is stuffed in plastic bags and tossed into the nearby Nairobi Dam—was adopted as an original creation of waste disposal by ingenious residents. The same polluted dam and nearby river, at some points, provide people with their water needs. Consequently, water borne diseases, as well as malaria are rampant. Kibera's overcrowded environment also provides a perfect breeding ground for HIV. The BBC called Kibera "a vision of hell on earth."[297] But Kibera is not the only slum. Thousands of slum estates dot the peripheries of major towns in Kenya especially around gated communities inhabited by the rich and the famous. These estates produce domestic workers for the affluent and industries.

Every morning, thousands of people trek out of their shanties for the industrial area to compete for scarce day jobs in mostly Indian-owned firms. Like safari ants in a hurry to please their queen, the people step up their tempo as they cross the busy Uhuru Highway in rows of four or five and disappear into a maze of narrow alleys in the teeming industrial area. Those lucky enough to get casual employment for the day return to their one-roomed shacks for an evening meal of mostly *sukuma wiki* and *ugali*. The not-so-lucky ones disappear into cloaked dens of illicit brews and eating-houses, where they get credit from kind sellers. Security is never assured in these areas. One columnist says gloomily that "Nairobi slums are among the most physically and psychologically violent places on earth. Not only is crime and violence a feature of everyday life, but slum-

---

297 BBC, September 20, 2005.

dwellers are emotionally assaulted daily—by greedy politicians...and by a Government that spends millions on politicians and then claims to have no money for public service provision."[298]

One of the roads leading into Kibera is Karbanet road, which is marked by single multi-storied homes and bungalows of the rich. It's a treed, quiet and secure boulevard. One of the tenants of those modern dwellings guarded by *Askaris* and fierce dogs along this boulevard is President Moi, who has lived there since becoming Vice President. Passersby may not be able to peep through for its high security gate and well-guarded perimeter wall, but the contrast the home provides to the living conditions at Kibera—only a stone's throw away—says volume about the disparity of life in Kenya. Moi's luxurious aboard has been his living quarters—not the official State House--throughout his presidential term. On a windy day, he could probably hear cries of agony from his disadvantaged neighbours or even sounds of gunshots reverberating through the slum town in the stillness of night.

A few kilometres south of Kibera, is Karen where many of the creme-de-la-creme of Kenyan society reside, in large plots with enough grounds for horse riding and polo games. One of the residents of Karen, which, along with Kibera and other localities, make Langata Constituency, is their MP, Raila Odinga. Raila's commodious structure with all the amenities of luxury one can think of is unimaginably different from the leaking, rat-infested abodes of the Kibera people. The comparison between Kibera and Karen is like day and night, heaven and hell.

During an official function as Prime Minister in the Coastal town of Mombasa in July 2009, Raila was incensed by the fact that local officials had not positioned a mobile toilet behind the podium for his convenience. This prompted one newspaper columnist to suggest that he should spend a week in Kibera to understand his peoples' tribulations. "If he imagined that the absence of a VIP toilet in Mombasa was an insult, in Kibera he would let it fly."

Despite the fact that the UNEP, the global policeman charged with overseeing the environment and UN-Habitat, in charge of human

[298] Rasna Warah, Daily Nation, January 18, 2010.

settlements, are located in Nairobi, only nominal change has occurred in the lives of slum dwellers in Kenya. "Just a few miles from the country's Parliament and State House, poor families are living in breathtaking poverty, scouring the streets for scraps of food and queuing for hours for water they can barely afford."[299] An UN-initiated slum-upgrading scheme intended to provide better living conditions for the Kibera people has barely scratched the ground, indicating that the UN Millennium Goal of improving the lives of people in the slums by 2020 would not be attained. While billions of shillings have been lost over the years through corruption and theft of public funds, the people in the slums have to depend on non-governmental organisations to initiate community projects focusing on job training, health education, and business. One success of such organisations is Kibera's own Pamoja FM station, which offers entertainment and educational programmes specifically tailored to the area residents. The entertainment provided by the station offers a significant distraction from the grim reality of day-to-day life.

So famous is Kibera in the world that it was featured in Fernando Meirelles' film, *The Constant Gardener* based on a book of the same name by John le Carre, who had some harsh words to describe the place: "a vast brown smear of smoking tin houses overhung with a pall of sickly African dust, crammed into the Nairobi river valley without a hand's width between them…the valley is rich in deposits of sewage, plastic bags, colourful strands of old clothing, banana and orange peel, corn cobs and anything else the city cares to dump in it."[300]

Kibera is also mentioned in the music video *World on Fire* by Sarah McLachlan. No high-profile international visitor, heads of state included, visit Nairobi without touring Kibera. Former US President Carter has been there, so has Senator Obama, now President of the US; UN Secretary General Ba Ki Moon; American diplomat Magdalene Albright; and Jill Biden, wife of Obama's Vice President, are just a few of those that have experienced Kibera. For visitors weary of the usual fare of wildlife, beach, and traditional dancing, Kibera is a suitable alternative. Tours are arranged through the slums to enable tourists to mingle with "real" urban Africans

299 Phillippa Crosland-Taylor, Oxfam GB Kenya, September 10, 2009.

300 John le Carre, The Constant Gardener, Hodder and Stoughton, p 131.

and to confirm media accounts of Africa as a downtrodden, forsaken continent.

With all its trepidation, Kibera is also a hotbed of politics. This township provides the bulk of people that fill stadiums, not only during political rallies but also during important sporting events. After results of the 2007 disputed elections were announced, Kibera residents were among the first Kenyans to flood streets to protest the results. They barricaded roads, uprooted the railway line heading, ironically, to Raila's rural city of Kisumu and beyond into the landlocked Uganda, and challenged security forces into open duels on the dusty streets of the locality. Among hundreds of people who were killed during the riots, dozens were from Kibera. The youths there have been used as foot soldiers without a cause, pawns in a game of chess where the beneficiaries of their action have been politicians. For example, when Kibera youths fought running battles with police during the political riots of January 2008, no politician was in sight. Leaders incited people to protest, yet not a single sibling of a politician was out to face tear gas or live bullets. After dining in expensive restaurants in the city, the politicians would return to their comfortable homes while the youths would walk back to their shacks, bloodied and hungry.

# CHAPTER 27
# Lucy's intriguing life

It was late afternoon, and the sun—a big ball of glowing yellow—was bowing down to earth on its way west. It was a breezy day of August 2007. A few hours earlier, colourful dancers—in traditional ostrich feathers and beaded trinkets on their heads and ankles—as well as a large crowd of officials had assembled at the Moi International Airport in Mombasa to welcome President Kibaki and the First Lady, Mama Lucy, to the coastal town. He was on his annual pilgrimage, to open the Mombasa Agricultural Show, a grand display of the region's agricultural wealth and to tour development projects. The welcoming airport crowd dispersed in different directions, but a motorcade made of local leaders spontaneously joined the presidential party for the fifteen-kilometre journey to State House.

If it had been Kenyatta or Moi, groups of traditional dancers would have lined up along the whole length and breadth of the road to town and others would have been waiting inside State House to entertain the First Family but Kibaki was not drawn to such pomposity. With the streets cleared of traffic, the presidential motorcade cruised uninterruptedly, speedily crossing the channel and emerging into the enchanting island of easygoing inhabitants. The President was looking forward to a weeklong working holiday. Traditionally, the first presidential engagement in Mombasa is a meeting with local MPs. As the President went to his private quarters to refresh, the MPs comfortably took their seats in the unpretentious visitors' lounge, chatting animatedly with government officials. Soon he walked in, jolting everyone to an attentive position, and took his seat at the front of the visitors' room.

Next to the President was an extra chair which Minister Makwere, the senior most MP in the region, claimed. He had just begun his welcoming comments when Lucy stormed in and launched a blistering tirade on the minister for sitting on "her" chair. Stunned and speechless, Makwere quickly jumped up from the seat, not knowing what else to do or how to react. Her menacing eyes, her shifty body language, and her provocative pitch of voice displayed deep hurt. "Where else in the world," she raged, "have you seen anyone sitting on the First Lady's chair? This is disrespectful. And let me say this, you men have no respect for women," directing an index finger at no one in particular. The staff that had been in the room serving snacks sheepishly bolted, while security guards outside watchfully moved closer. Noticing that she was talking to herself, she stomped out only to return a few minutes later with a helper to haul out the chair. Kibaki remained nonchalant, furtively shifting his eyes around the room to gauge the visitors' reaction. Everything was quiet. Kibaki did not utter a single word in response to his wife's strange and embarrassing behaviour in front of the MPs and senior officials.

That incident left us in that room wondering about Mama Lucy's state of mental health. She did not have to disconcert her husband publicly, nor did she have to bicker over a chair, which in any case, belonged to the people. And, if she truly believed that the chair was the exclusive preserve of the First Lady, then, arrangements to move it ahead of the visitors' arrival would have been in order. The meeting continued but the incident left questions not only about Lucy's eccentric tendencies but also about Kibaki's permissiveness of such tawdry tantrums. It was common knowledge that their marriage had a stormy history but even that, did not justify such petulance.

## The contrast

Unlike the laid-back and level-headed Kibaki, Mama Lucy Muthoni Kibaki was rambunctious and chronically temperamental. She came into public life—after years of obscurity as a teacher—when her husband became president in 2002. Over time, however, the daughter of a Presbyterian prelate and a deeply-religious woman from the ridges of Mukurweini in

Central Kenya had attracted attention to herself for all the wrong reasons, prompting some to describe her as "abrupt, edgy,"[301] and others to suggest that she could do with "psychiatric help."[302]

The diminutive mother of four with sharp, red eyes, a double chin, and a no-nonsense personality, came to be known more for her public theatrics than for her role as a benevolent ambassador of the disadvantaged and the disabled which she claimed to be. She became a joke of cartoonists, and her boorish conduct was often the subject of raunchy press commentaries and rib-cracking wit over radio stations. As a result, Mama Lucy came to view journalists not as friends who could help the cause of her husband but as enemies who had to be pummelled and shunned. She seized every available opportunity to downsize the media and to portray journalists as intrusive and worthless. She would assault them, insult them, and break their equipment at will. In return, the media would taunt her for the way she dressed and the way she behaved in public. At one time, when a section of the media rated her one of the worst dressed women in Kenya, she hit back with a stinging press release and attached photos that showed her immaculately dressed from head to toe to confirm her fashion sense. She called the newspaper survey imaginary and lacking in credibility, "…part of a wider conspiracy to portray the First Lady in a negative light."

Early in Kibaki's presidency, the usually gruffly Lucy had difficulty recognising her place in protocol, perhaps thinking rather mistakenly that as the First Lady, she was the co-president. This lack of knowledge of her role came to light when she once walked ahead of the President when disembarking from a plane after a foreign presidential visit. The gaffe threw the welcoming party, led by the Vice President, into confusion. Thank God, it happened in Nairobi. Had it occurred in a foreign land, the protocol spat would have been grave, since in internationally recognised practice, the President always disembarked first followed by the First Lady. Unfortunately, her protocol officials were too scared to advise her on the right way.

During the whole period of twenty-four years when Moi was President, Kenya did not have a First Lady. Moi had separated from Leah, his wife

[301] Standard, February 7, 2009.
[302] Ibid.

of twenty-five years, and had been living the life of a bachelor—quite peculiar for rich African men. It was, therefore, a great relief, especially for Kenyan women, that finally, a woman was at State House to comfort and accompany her husband to state functions. But instead of offering comfort, Lucy distressed her husband with her unpredictable, erratic behaviour, such as when she unilaterally closed a bar within State House that had been a watering hole for officials barely days after moving into State House. The bar was the informal Cabinet room where many decisions were made at the time when Kibaki was recuperating from a road accident.

Though neither a public servant nor an elected leader, Mama Lucy was "dreaded even by some of the mighty of the land."[303] She took on the LDP MPs critical of her husband with the force of a wounded tigress, bitterly accusing them of undermining her husband and preventing him from fulfilling his election promises. She did not spare Raila either—then a partner in the NARC Government—alleging he was misusing his position in the Cabinet to campaign for her husband's job.

In the African tradition of respecting authority, politicians found themselves constrained from responding to Mama Lucy's often contemptuous charades preferring instead, to direct their criticisms at State House mandarins. Any criticism of the First Lady was considered an affront to the State and an insult to the President. Once when two LDP legislators told Mama Lucy to shut up over her criticism of the opposition, police summoned them to record statements. They were not formally charged but were warned that they had overstepped protocol.

As a result of her wayward temper, the staff turn-over at State House was much higher compared to other departments of comparative size. While some officials left because they could not take it anymore, others were fired for crossing the First Lady's path. Kibaki's first State House Comptroller and personal friend, Matere Keriri, was one of the early victims of Mama Lucy's fatuous tantrums. She refused to shake his hand, and then publicly reprimanded him for over-crowding the presidential diary and leaving the President with no time to relax with his children and grand-children. Following that spite, Matere knew his time was up.

---

[303] Ibid.

One popular video clip showed Matere literally running away on seeing the First Lady. Similarly, things got too hot for Ipu—the Comptroller who welcomed us to State House for the secret meeting with Kibaki—and he quietly left for another government department. Apart from senior officials who were shown the door, many junior personnel were quietly relieved of their jobs, one of them being Alfred Getonga, Kibaki's long serving personal secretary.

Three serving Cabinet officials, Vice President Awori, and Ministers Saitoti and Ayacko, as well as the ODM-Kenya leader Kalonzo, were at different times publicly admonished by Mama Lucy, to the astonishment of Kenyans. A slip of the tongue by Awori, who during a public function introduced her as "Her Excellency, the Second Lady," got Mama Lucy fuming. Awori had wanted to say that she was the second First Lady at State House after Mama Ngina, but he fumbled, leading Mama Lucy to storm out of the function to the amazement of her guests. Despite a flurry of apologies from the Vice President, Mama Lucy never forgave him and, in as far as she was concerned, it was good riddance when Awori lost his parliamentary seat in the 2007 elections. Saitoti, as Minister for Internal Security, was given a tongue-lashing for allegedly sleeping on the job, by failing to prevent an oil tanker accident that resulted in an explosion and deaths; while Ayacko, as Sports Minister, was rebuked for tolerating a dirty swimming pool at a Nairobi stadium. Mbandi, Kalonzo's aide at the LDP, who once told Lucy to stay off politics, was arrested for threatening the First Lady. She was later let go but with a warning.

Despite her seemingly secure position as First Lady, Mama Lucy appeared to suffer from personal insecurity; and a woman, Mary Wambui appeared to be the cause of that insecurity. A political activist, Wambui, who loved beautifully coloured African dresses and gold adornments, usually made statements and acted in a way that often outraged the lady in the big house. She would say for everyone to hear that she was once married to Kibaki, and for that reason, she was a "Mwai." The sheer mention of Wambui drove Lucy crazy, and on four different occasions, she forced her husband to publicly denounce Wambui and her daughter, allegedly fathered by the President. During one such television appearance with Lucy at his side, a visibly annoyed Kibaki admitted he "was in a foul mood," and went on to castigate those who continually said he had more than one wife. He listed his children and said Lucy was his only wife.

Years back, photos that purported to show Wambui with Kibaki, in what was alleged to be a traditional wedding ceremony, were leaked to the press to the chagrin of the First Family. Determined to annoy Mama Lucy, Wambui would summon the media to follow her during shopping trips in Nairobi just to show off her state-provided security and to make a point that she was not just any other woman.

Mama Lucy's escapades were legendary. In one function at State House, she slapped a low-level State House master of ceremony who accidentally introduced her as "Lucy Wambui." The shaken gentleman was summarily relieved of his assignment and immediately transferred to another ministry away from the seat of power. Cameramen who filmed the incident were shoved around and security officials confiscated their films, all in full view of the congregation present.

But Lucy's classic performance was when she stormed a party at the house of the World Bank Country Director, Makhtar Diop. The house, rented from the Kibakis, was next door to their private residence in Nairobi's high-end Muthaiga estate. Diop's farewell party had been going on for several hours with loud music and drunken shouts of merry-making. A sleepless Lucy could not take it anymore. Still dressed in pyjamas, she charged into the compound and ordered that the music be stopped, claiming it was interfering with her sleep. Diop refused, and after a long argument with the host, Lucy returned to her house, where she tried to get her security to intervene. They declined.

Early the following morning, wearing gym shorts and a matching top, Lucy ordered her driver to take her to the nearest police station, where she unsuccessfully tried to persuade officers to go and arrest the party-goers. They politely turned her away. The incident, which received front-page coverage the following day, infuriated Mama Lucy even further. At midnight, with her security in tow, she drove to the editorial offices of the *Nation* and spent five hours telling off reporters, snatching their cameras, mobile phones, and notebooks. A cameraman who attempted to record the event was slapped on the face and pushed aside. But the entire event was recorded on video tape, and when Kenyans woke up in the morning, they were met with images of a sleep-deprived First Lady, dressed in jeans, throwing barbs at the media. That incident drove her to her lowest ebb ever, exposing her as a person of unstable mind and anti-social behaviour.

The assaulted cameraman filed a case in court, but like so many others involving influential officials in government, the case never saw the light of day.

In 2008, an MP, Gitobu Imanyara, claimed Lucy had bashed him on the face when he went to State House for a meeting. Imanyara claimed the First Lady was in pyjamas and not wearing any shoes. "She immediately started throwing punches at me shouting 'nobody goes here without my permission.'"[304] Officials denied that the incident took place. But Imanyara filed a suit, which he only abandoned after his traditional *Njuri Ncheke* elders intervened. A fine of a goat, which the elders had imposed against Kibaki for that alleged incident was never paid and the matter was left to die.

Once in a while, Mama Lucy would make an earth shaking political comment, like the time in 2007, when she told Kenyans that her husband would run for a second term. The statement, made in the presence of her husband, ended months of speculation over whether or not Kibaki would contest the presidency. It showed publicly how influential she was in the life of her husband.

Lucy's flare-ups and politically sensitive statements raised questions about the role of the First Lady in the affairs of the nation. The Kenyan Constitution was mute about her official functions, even though the government had a budget for her office, staff, and a monthly allowance. The only time her name appeared in law was in regard to the President's pension upon his death. The Presidential Retirement Benefits Act of 2003 said the President's wife would be entitled to fifty percent of such pension.

Unlike Mama Ngina Kenyatta, who busied herself with social and business activities when her husband was in office, Lucy's interests remained unclear, even though she claimed her passion was in assisting the disabled and the disadvantaged. What was known was that she was deeply committed to educational matters, and a girls' school she built in her area stands out as clear testimony of that. Even with her queer ways, the public somehow developed a love-hate relationship with her, so much

---

304 New Vision, February 4, 2008.

so that, whenever she went missing for periods of time, people would write to newspapers and query about her whereabouts.

## Lucy not alone

Bizarre cases of First Ladies behaving badly were not confined to Kenya. In Nigeria, Stella Obasanjo, attracted public wrath when she allegedly used her influence in 2005 and got a newspaper publisher arrested and jailed for accusing her—in a story headlined "Greedy Stella"[305]—of illegally selling government houses. On knowing that some of Stella's close relatives had been beneficiaries, the President cancelled the deal. The wife of President Olusegun Obasanjo was to die that same year in Spain, where she had secretly gone to undergo plastic surgery to make her look younger.

In Zimbabwe, Robert Mugabe's wife, Grace, was not left out of the list of disgraceful African First Ladies. In 2009, she was accused by a British news photographer, Richard Jones, of punching him several times in the face for taking her pictures near a luxury hotel in Hong Kong. He sustained at least ten cuts allegedly inflicted by a fist encrusted with diamond rings she was wearing.[306] Jones filed a police complaint but no charges were preferred due to her diplomatic immunity. The woman, forty years younger than her husband, was also known as an extravagant spender during shopping trips abroad, even as most Zimbabweans went without food. Instead of working for the good of the people, she decided to live the life of a bon vivant. In addition, the Zimbabwean First Lady once forcefully evicted a white couple, John and Eva Mathews, from their expansive farm and expropriated their five-bedroomed house complete with a swimming pool. If that was not enough, she was accused of evicting one hundred families from a city suburb ostensibly to give way to an orphanage she planned to build. A second wife to Mugabe after his first wife died, Grace was said to be extremely bossy and often rubbed government officials the wrong way.

However, of the cases of interference of First Ladies in the running of government, the one in Nigeria in 2010 was the most classic. When the

---

305 Liberian Online, May 9, 2005.

306 Mail & Guardian, March 30, 2009.

Nigerian President, Yar'Adua returned home in serious condition from a Saudi Arabia hospital, his controlling wife, Turai "effectively seized control of the operations of the Government, shoving aside Goodluck Jonathan and unilaterally causing a reversal of the decision of the National Assembly to name him Acting President."[307] Her actions bordered on treason and left Nigerians, like one Olori Ebi, to ask in a blog, "What is this nonsense all about. Who is Turai?"[308]

307 234NEXT, June 17, 2010.

308 Ibid.

# CHAPTER 28

# Political spying

It was a Monday, part of the long Easter weekend, when Kenyans of means usually leave their stressful lives behind, zoom off to the beach, or venture into national parks to watch animals, hardly the period for politicians to be hard at work canvassing for support. But then, Kenyan politicians rarely rest, unless they are critically sick in bed. In this east African country, vote hunting is a three-hundred-and-sixty-five-day, twenty-four/seven affair, making campaigning for elective office a full time job. Thus, when the ODM-Kenya convened a meeting for Kalenjin leaders on that day at the imposing Great Rift Valley Lodge—overlooking Lake Naivasha, on whose shores Joy Adamson, author of *Born Free,* lived for years in the 1960s—few doubted the leaders would not show up. The only hitch was that the meeting, which was to be addressed by both Raila and Kalonzo, was at the last moment, moved seventy kilometres north to Nakuru, home of the pink flamingos, without Raila's knowledge. The sudden relocation of the meeting was a wily subterfuge to avoid Raila's presence, but what Kalonzo did not know was that from his new hideout, the meeting was being monitored by a mole on real time via a mobile phone, and was being listened to by Raila's contact people in Nairobi.

The supremacy battles between Raila and Kalonzo ahead of the 2007 elections went beyond an exchange of diatribe taking place at public venues and behind boardroom doors. They had moved a notch higher to include gadgets of modern technology and raw-nerve espionage.

Spying is one of the most useful tools in competitive politics. The world over, political parties and governments routinely plant spies or watch out for moles within their ranks, who are detailed to collect data of rival organisations or individuals for strategic purposes. This is not a new phenomenon. Political espionage has existed since the Middle Ages, and knows no boundaries. It occurs in both developing and developed worlds; in fledging and in advanced democracies; in communist countries of Eastern Europe, in Asia, Africa, and the Middle East.

The collapse of the Nixon Administration in the US in the early 1970s, for example, was attributed largely to a bungled up spying operation, which culminated in the illegal breaking-in at the Democratic Party Headquarters in Washington, DC. Using espionage operations, the government spied on its critics, with special focus on the Massachusetts Senator Ted Kennedy who was believed to be Nixon's biggest challenger. The espionage conspiracy extended to journalists, some of who were commissioned to write negatively about Democratic Party presidential candidates in a comprehensive operation that stunned the world. Eventually, when the illegal spy network exploded in public, Nixon bowed out of office in disgrace.

During the George W. Bush Administration, the US Secretary of State, Colin Powell, became a victim of espionage from officials within the administration he served. According to a biography by Karen de Young, Powell encountered internal resistance from technocrats because they felt "he had not managed to forge a comfortable relationship with the President." Powell's staff was convinced the criticisms[309] were coming from inside the administration and decided that the Secretary was being out spun.[310] The author explains that the administration had their own spies in the Pentagon and in the White House, and regularly received clandestine copies of e-mails circulating in the enemy camps. The missives pointed out where Powell had deviated from conservative orthodoxy and provided talking points for the media about his waning influence.[311] When Colin's staff got that information, it launched a counter-offensive, arranging on-the-record interviews with columnists and reporters they thought might be more sympathetic to his (Powell's) views. As a result, the career of the

309 Karen De Young, The Soldier, The Life of Colin Powell.

310 Ibid.

311 Ibid.

former Military Commander and Chairman of the Joint Chief of Staff was saved, at least temporarily. He resigned from his position in 2004.

In the Indian parliamentary elections in 2009, some parties hired detective firms, which then recruited insiders, to snoop on opposing political party officials. The matter soon leaked out and made huge headlines. News reports talked of twenty moles that had infiltrated political parties who were reporting and compiling dossiers on political and private lives of identified leaders, as well as their daily movements. That expose` did not come as a major surprise to Indian politicians who are wont to such scenarios, but it underscored the extent of espionage in the politics of what is said to be the biggest democracy in the world.

In Kenya, spies played a significant role in the MAU MAU, officially known as the Kenya Land and Freedom Army (KLFA), bush war. British Colonialists recruited loyalists to infiltrate the liberation movement leading to the capture of top commanders, among them General Waruhiu Itote and the celebrated hero of the struggle, Dedan Kimathi. Village moles and colonial sympathisers, known as home guards were active throughout the war, reporting on the activities of the fighters and their hideouts. Had it not been for the information the infiltrators provided, the colonial government would not have been able successfully to launch Operation Anvil in Nairobi in 1954, in which thousands of Africans were rounded up and locked up in camps, and supply lines to MAU MAU freedom fighters severed.

In some cases, foreign intelligence agencies and local spying organisations are known to hire political party officials and even civil servants to provide them with intelligence to undermine others, or to help build information data banks for future needs. During the early days of the KANU, for example, Tom Mboya, the maverick trade unionist and politician was widely rumoured to have been a spy for the Central Intelligence Agency (CIA) within the Kenyatta Government. That suspicion was borne out of his close ties with the US, especially his personal relationship with the Kennedy family. The Kennedys partnered with him in 1960 to airlift hundreds of Kenyan students for studies in the US, among them, Barack Obama Sr., whose son became the forty-fourth President of the US of America in 2008.

An American political and literary magazine—now defunct—by the name Ramparts, affirmed in one of its issues, that Mboya was indeed a CIA spy who was recruited in the early 1960s to destroy Kenyatta. He was to be imposed by the Americans to take over the leadership of Kenya because CIA felt Kenyatta was "unsafe…due to his initial deep socialist leanings."[312] Kenyatta was labelled a socialist after his brief stay in the Soviet Union, where he had studied economics at the University of Toilers in the East. But unknown to many, Kenyatta abhorred communism and was not known to have developed any serious ties with the red nations.

The Kenya National Archives declassified the information on Mboya's alleged ties to espionage in 2008, almost forty years after Mboya's assassination in Nairobi. The undated report in the Ramparts painted a picture of the former MP and Minister for Economic Planning as a mole recruited by the Americans, while he was the Secretary General of the Kenya Federation of Labour, to counter "left wing trade unionism outside the communist bloc." Some theorists say his spying activities may have contributed to his assassination on July 5 1969.

What fuelled further speculation about the possible underlying cause of Mboya's assassination were reports that the man accused of the murder, Nahashon Njenga Njoroge, was not actually executed upon conviction, but was helped to a safe haven in Ethiopia, complete with a new identity. Reports circulating immediately after the assassination were that Mboya and the convicted murderer knew each other. In fact, it was said, Mboya had even assisted Njoroge to go to Eastern Europe for training. Rumours that Njenga was in Ethiopia were still circulating in Addis Ababa when I served at the Kenya Embassy there in 1970s, but they were just that, mere rumours. Questions that have remained unanswered then are: Who sent Njoroge to kill Mboya? What was the motive? And was Njenga executed or was he mysteriously freed? If freed, why? And, most importantly, what was Kenyatta's role in the murder? Was Njenga a double spy? Those questions will perhaps never be answered.

Njenga Karume who was in Kenyatta's inner circles when Mboya was felled with bullets on a Nairobi street has dismissed any speculation that the former President could have been involved in the plot to kill Mboya.

---

312 Douglas Okwatch, Afro Articles, March 7, 2008.

"I am most certain it was not Kenyatta. Mboya was very close to Kenyatta, and as KANU's Secretary General, Mboya was extremely useful both in and outside Parliament."[313] The mystery of Mboya's death deepened further when in 2008, his widow, Pamela, wrote a letter to Annan, the retired UN Secretary General, casting doubt about the motive of the assassination, and asking for the establishment of a Truth and Reconciliation Commission to investigate the matter. Pamela died in July 2009 before the Commission was established, and with her, went secrets that will remain underground forever.

Another spy story in Kenya involved Bruce Mackenzie, the only white Minister in Kenyatta's Cabinet. Secretive and enigmatic, Mackenzie was widely reported to have been on the payroll of the British Intelligence, as well as of Israel's MOSSAD and South Africa's BOSS. It was not clear why Kenyatta chose Mackenzie, a Boer, to be a member of his Cabinet given Kenya's abhorrence of South Africa's apartheid policies at the time. "To many Kenyans this was surprising as McKenzie was of South African origin, born in Ixopo, in Natal."[314] Moreover, Mackenzie, with his cat-whisker trademark, was known to be notoriously racist, treating his Cabinet colleagues with more than passing brashness. He openly showed disrespect for Africans, and his written interactions with government officials revealed a man who believed in the superiority of the white race.

Mackenzie was killed in 1977 by a bomb planted in a lion's head carving as he flew in a small plane from the Ugandan capital, Kampala. Idi Amin, the then President with whom he was said to have business relations, was suspected to have participated in McKenzie's death, but no one could explain why the dictator, who was known for his cannibalistic tendencies, wanted him dead. Nevertheless, did Kenyatta know that Mackenzie was "mixed up in espionage work as well as in international arms dealings and other business deals?"[315] And, if he did, why didn't he stop him? An analysis in *The Independent* of London once reported that Mackenzie was the "M16's senior Africa operator,"[316] who reported directly to the then British Foreign Minister, Alec Douglas-Home. M16 is the British

313 Njenga Karume, Beyond Expectations: From Charcoal to Gold, p. 204.

314 Alastair Matheson, States of Emergency, Media Matters, p. 132.

315 Ibid., p. 133.

316 The Independent, January 16, 2007.

intelligence organisation. Was he planted in the Cabinet to spy for foreign nations? What compromises did he make, and what was the amount of damage to Kenya?

One person Kenyatta suspected most to be on the payroll of foreign agents was Oginga Odinga. As we saw earlier, the likeable nationalist had strong links with the communist countries of the Soviet Union and China. He was so enamoured of socialism that he was once reported as saying that "communism is food,"[317] a comment, which elicited widespread condemnation, but which according to Odinga, "was a convenient occasion for an attack against me."[318] Under pressure from his opponents, Odinga admitted receiving money from the communists but insisted that the money was not for personal use but for building KANU structures. Through those contacts, the Soviet Union and its allies were allowed to build a modern hospital in the Lake Victoria town of Kisumu that came to be known as the Russian Hospital. Odinga also influenced the construction in 1964 of the Lumumba Institute on the fringes of the city for purposes of training party workers on political ideology.

The official objective given by its founders was that the Institute would "define, teach and popularise African Socialism,"[319] but some opined that the Institute was built to "counter Mboya's East African Institute of Social and Cultural Affairs, which had been set up with American financing only a few months earlier."[320] In the beginning, Kenyatta did not openly object to the two institutions on Kenyan soil, but he was fully aware of the consequences inherent in having party workers in KANU with left leaning convictions at a time when the government was pushing for a mixed capitalist economic system. He allowed Odinga to go ahead with the project as "a temporary measure to keep the radical wing within the party, possibly with the understanding that the radicals would have to compromise with others if they wished their creation to last."[321] As it turned out, Kenyatta saw the Lumumba Institute, not as an asset to the KANU, but as a spy school

---

317 Oginga Odinga, Not Yet Uhuru, East African Educational Publishers Ltd, p. 296.

318 Ibid.

319 Ibid., p. 270/271.

320 Hilary Ngweno, posted on the Net by Kenya Diaspora Pro-Democracy Movement, November 26, 2007.

321 Ibid.

for the training of communist cadres, who would then work to torpedo his economic and political policies. To put a check on it, he ordered that the institute operate under the Ministry of Education.

Then there was John Githongo, the so-called anti-corruption czar under Kibaki, who admitted to taping his fellow government officials in a secret spy operation. Githongo was appointed in January 2003, as the President's Special Advisor on graft. One of his first assignments was to look at the Anglo-Leasing scandal, which had defrauded the country of more than 56 billion shillings through dubious transaction with foreign non-existing companies. In a series of meetings in the course of two years, Githongo taped his conversations with some cabinet ministers allegedly involved in the scandal. He admitted smuggling tape recorders to meeting rooms and recording incriminating information connected to the affair. It is alleged that he used that information to rally local and international support in the fight against graft. Not shy about admitting his clandestine activities, Githongo was quoted as saying: "I was spying on my own colleagues, which didn't feel like an honourable thing to do."[322] While some lauded his snooping activities as an act of a brave nationalist, others saw them as despicable and non-patriotic: "To take confidential information that you came across in your job as a Government employee and pass it on to foreign Governments, now that's an act of gross betrayal."[323] Some alleged Githongo was a mole planted in the Kenya Government by the British, a claim no one has been able to confirm.

Githongo described his spying activities within the Kibaki Government as "…the worst form of betrayal, the most discomfiting thing I've done in my entire life'?[324] Those tapes, some of which were broadcast on radio and television stations around the world, led to the downfall of several powerful officials. Famously known as "Anglo Leasing," after the phantom company that was said to have entered into dubious contracts with the Government, the scandal demonised Kibaki and shattered his oft-declared commitment to fighting high level graft.

---

322 Michela Wrong, It's Our Turn to Eat: The story of a Kenyan Whistle-Blower, HarperCollins, p.84.

323 Ibid., p. 286.

324 Ibid., p.166.

## Inter-party spying

Not a subject that occupies the minds of people, but spying does exist in the Kenyan political scene. One known case alleging spying within ODM-Kenya involved two of Kalonzo's officials. In August 2008, Kalonzo sacked the two for allegedly working with external forces to undermine him. They were accused of "spying and handing over dossier to his rivals."[325] It was assumed that those rivals were ODM and Raila. Being close to Kalonzo, the two officials had crucial inside knowledge of almost every aspect of the ODM-Kenya's presidential campaign; the candidate's movement, the people he was meeting, and what was being discussed, the in and out flow of campaign materials in terms of quantity and quality, and use of campaign financial resources. Kalonzo was tipped that the two had regular meetings with Raila, an allegation one of the sacked aides denied. The accused official explained that, like many others, he knew Raila during the days of the original ODM-Kenya. "Those saying I have been spying on Kalonzo on behalf of ODM are being cheap and dishonest,"[326] he said.

Moles were busiest during the height of the internal wrangles in the original ODM-Kenya. Both the Raila and the Kalonzo camps had spies watching on the other; reporting on the night meetings taking places in hotel rooms and residential premises, and acting as loyalists when they were, in fact, agents for pay. In one particular incident, a close security operative of Raila approached a Kalonzo aide and claimed he had turned against Raila and was now willing to work with Kalonzo. The aide immediately smelt mischief, and politely informed him that there was no vacancy in his camp for an official who had been commonly associated with Raila for years. It was suspected the individual had been dispatched to infiltrate the Kalonzo camp. In another occasion, a person known to be a close supporter of a presidential candidate was seen bribing participants at the ODM-Kenya delegates' conference in an attempt to influence the outcome of the nomination contest between Kalonzo and Ojiambo. That bribing attempt failed after he was discovered and quietly thrown out of Kasarani. We came to know that a senior official in a rival camp had sent him to undermine Kalonzo, but what could have turned out to be politically fatal for the Kalonzo campaign was when a mole suspected to be associated with

[325] African Press International, August 31, 2008.
[326] Ibid.

one of the ODM-K presidential candidates infiltrated his think-tank. The individual's actions became suspicious when some of the issues discussed confidentially in the think-tank reached Kalonzo's Rift Valley opponents. What the mole did not know was that he was under the radar of Kalonzo people and his movements and remarks were being monitored. Some MPs affiliated to Kalonzo eventually confronted the mole, who hastily resigned from the think tank. You can imagine the amount of information the mole carried to the other side.

When ODM officials met in early August 2007 to strategise on how to respond to Kalonzo's defection to LPK, information from that meeting was immediately conveyed to the Kalonzo camp, a move that gave Kalonzo time to fight off any attempt by the Raila group to "snatch away" the party. But spying does not only take place across party lines. During the 2005 referendum, when the government was trying to lure opposing legislators to support the Wako Draft constitution, LDP party functionaries were informed of a meeting between one of their legislators and senior government officials at a hotel in Nairobi. They rushed to the hotel and confirmed that, indeed, a meeting was in progress. They managed to confirm the report and even took pictures of the participants as they walked to their cars.

It was common knowledge in top party ranks that most of the bellhops, waiters, and room attendants in several popular hotels and meeting places in Nairobi were on the payroll of politicians, and report to them the moment a character of interest shows up. Thus, although politicians regularly met at such establishments, the risks were high that their movements were being monitored and recorded.

When Raila was railing at Kalonzo during the dinner in London arranged by the Diaspora community to honour ODM-Kenya presidential candidates, he perhaps didn't know that a Kalonzo spy in the room was reporting everything to his adversary in Nairobi.

In 2006, a racy weekly newspaper mentioned the name of a top Kenyan party leader, it said, operated a parallel spying network from that of the government and spied on his political colleagues and government officials in a big way. The paper said that the party leader "knows which politician coughs at night, their favourite drinks, love affairs, business associates, their investments and of course bank accounts." The paper then went on to provide a long list of politicians and government officials, it said, were being spied on.

However, the bar of spying allegations reached its zenith when Charity Ngilu, at one time, claimed that Kalonzo was "a spy"[327] in the original ODM-Kenya. The impression left by Ngilu was that Kalonzo was an agent of the Kibaki Government planted in the party to frustrate Raila's ambitions for the presidency. The allegations—which were never substantiated—had far reaching political and security connotations. Firstly, they exposed Kalonzo to public ridicule as a politician, and secondly, they meant Kalonzo was a security risk, easily manipulated, and unfit for high office. Kalonzo did not respond directly to the claim—which he should have—apart from offering a plea of innocence. The two were long political enemies and allegations, such as those made by Ngilu had to be absorbed with a grain of salt. Nevertheless, Kalonzo could have saved Kenyans from further speculation had he promptly reacted to the accusation.

[327] Standard, April 13, 2008

# CHAPTER 29

# Do you want to be an MP in Kenya?

(With a light touch)

From time to time, I meet people who express interest in elective politics in Kenya, but who have no clue as to how and where to begin. **Here is a 101 course for aspiring beginners**. The word politics originated from the Greek word *"politika,"* meaning the art or science of Government. Over the years that single word has influenced and controlled almost everything in our daily lives. Politics determines what we eat, and what kind of Government and leaders we get, and how we choose that Government and choose those leaders.

In Kenya, the origin of politics goes back many years, long before the Mau Mau liberation struggle in the 1950s: perhaps since the time of the resistance of the *Bukusu* against the British incursions in the 1890s. Many other events followed, including the exploits of Mekatilili wa Menza, a *Miji Kenda* woman who led a rebellion against the Colonial Establishment in 1913 over British policies and laws. The politics of those days can be classified as the "politics of liberation." That is why until independence in 1963, politicians agitating for freedom were referred to in Kiswahili as, "*watetezi,*" the advocates, as opposed to "*wanasiasa*", the politicians, in later years.

Potential candidates should know that those who enter and stay in politics reap financial and material benefits far beyond those possible in other sectors, and, it is not just the fat salary. Politics open opportunities for business, and for exploiting the poor for personal gain. In Kenya and most parts of Africa, politics is synonymous to good life. In Tanzania, they call politicians the "*wabenzi,*" those who drive Mercedes Benz. In Uganda, they are "*mafuta mingi,*" the fat cats. In Kenya, politicians have even more serious derogatory definitions, ranging from "thieves", "tax dodgers", "liars", "corrupt", etc. etc. In other words, the reputation of politicians, in general, is not that clean in the eyes of voters. That is why those aspiring to enter elective politics must be ready for insults, ridicule and sleep-less nights.

Here are some tips for aspiring politicians:-

1. In Kenya, politics is not cheap, and voters abhor "poor politicians". You must have deep pockets to pay for school uniforms, school fees, medical expenses, funeral expenses, wedding expenses, and, generally all other expenses your constituents may want you to pay for. "The average electorate in Kenya gauges its MP not only on the basis of his/her presence in the constituency," one report says, "but also his/her ability to provide direct financial support for small-scale community development projects, known as *harambees,* as well as the provision of personal handouts for school fees and hospital Bills."[328] A pilot survey of seven volunteer MPs by Transparency International in November 2003, carried the following quotes from the legislators: "I have realised that most of our people are thankless...everybody you meet wants some *chai,* if not food...; One has to sustain the interest of his/her supporters; It is inevitable to spend, but not because one wants to, it is the only way to remain an MP; I spend in order to sustain my political career; There is nothing one can do once one ventures into politics; the electorate needs to be educated on what to expect from an MP."[329]
2. Know the physical boundaries of your constituency well. A politician who has no clue about the geographical area of his or her representation will find it difficult to campaign effectively.
3. Know your people and their voting habits. Study previous patterns and seek advice from those who have been in the game before.

[328] Legislative Environmental Representation in Kenya, p 11

[329] Transparency International, Kenya: Paying the public or caring for constituents: preliminary findings from a pilot survey of seven volunteer MPs

4. Start your campaign early; one, two years, if possible, but make it low-key first, and gradually increase tempo as the election date approaches
5. Since Kenyans choose their representatives because of party affiliation, select your party early and get yourself involved in its activities at the local level. The party you choose must be the most popular in your area.
6. Keep your doors wide open and your kitchen fire burning at all times. Also, make sure you have lodging facilities. Visitors will start flocking to your home at dawn and the flow will continue the whole day. All those people will need to eat while they wait their turn to see you. If they miss their chance that day, they must be accommodated for the night.
7. Maintain a coterie of body guards to accompany you whenever you go. They will be there to muscle crowds and make you look sufficiently important for the job.
8. Your presence is important everywhere. Whether it is a church *harambee*, a school prize giving function or a funeral, make sure you attend, and while there, don't forget to make a contribution, and that contribution must be far higher than that made by your opponents or other souls.
9. Since women and youth are majority voters, make sure you do not miss any of their activities. When you see them hanging around when the meeting is over, that tells you they are waiting for handouts. Do not disappoint, because if you don't give them money, you will be the subject of an angry discussion after you leave, and that may be the end of you. Next time, they will invite your opponent instead.
10. Since Friday is usually the day when mourners collect remains of their loved ones from the mortuary, make sure you have a pick-up truck ready to transport remains for burial. Or, alternatively, show up yourself at the mortuary with money or send someone else there to represent you. Your contribution will be acknowledged and received with jubilation on the day of burial.
11. Always maintain a smile even when someone is behaving unkindly, and watch your tongue. Voters have the habit of listening carefully to each word you say. A slip of the tongue will be picked up quickly and distorted with every listener, and will spread fast through the valleys and ridges of your constituency.

12. Make sure you visit drinking dens even if you do not drink. Local brew is cheap and it is a good form of public relations. However, avoid drinking in public.
13. Make sure you are not caught in the company of undesirables, like women of loose morals. If you must visit bars and clubs, make sure you are accompanied by your legal wife or respectable individuals.
14. Plan to "steal" voters from neighbouring constituencies. During registration periods, truck them in to register in your area. It is a very expensive exercise since transportation has to be provided during registration and repeated on polling day. This is unethical and illegal, but don't you want to be a *mheshimiwa*?
15. In addition, on polling day, be prepared to buy votes and patronage if you want to win. Corruption is one of Kenya's biggest electoral shortcomings. Choose to be holy at your own peril! And it is not just voters who must be bribed. Electoral officials also want to eat; so, for them to be able to manipulate votes for you at the polling station, they will need something small. Learn from the 2007 General Elections when votes for the presidential, parliamentary and civic seats were all stolen.
16. If you follow these rules, the gates of Parliament or Local Authority will be wide open for you. There is no short cut. Remember: "Politicians believe in magic. They are always searching for the incantation or the mystic strategy that will connect them to voters."[330] That quote is from a recent article in the New York Times by David Frum editor of the Web site FrumForum. Goodluck!

---

[330] The New York Times, Sunday, July, 2000

# Afterword

In the Kenyan Parliament, most rookie legislators find themselves learning from their senior colleagues about the good and the bad in parliamentary manners and survival techniques. Some of the early lessons imparted on fresh MPs during my time included: "Invest, invest, invest." "Commit all your income and appear perpetually broke." This advice is to discourage you from parting with your hard-earned income. The rationale is that you cannot handout what you don't physically have.

"Save, you may not see Parliament again," one two-term Member liked to tell us. This caution arises from the unpredictability of the Kenyan electorate in their choice of officials. In many cases non-performers with deep pockets are preferred than stingy doers. "As much as possible, avoid your constituents during the first three years and show up only towards the last half of your term, with plenty of money! Again, money being the common denominator in our political life, a Member's regular presence in the constituency does not always guarantee him or her re-election. Clever candidates wait until a few weeks to elections, descend on the electorate with tons of money, and win!

Another lesson learnt from seniors was how to evade constituents. Refusing to answer the phone in your office is one way of rendering oneself incommunicado, but avoiding your parliamentary office altogether, or hiding in the Members' lounges in the main building, is perhaps the surest way of getting away from needy constituents.

Avoid walking between Continental House, which houses MPs' offices, and Parliament Buildings, to avoid being ambushed by constituents who lay in wait. "Always drive", we were counseled. At every hour of the day during sessions of Parliament, hundreds of people sit around the building looking for assistance from their MPs. Many times, hearses on their way upcountry for burial would stop over at the MPs' office complex, and bodies would remain in them for hours while organisers looked for transport and burial expenses. Some get lucky, but others leave empty handed.

Another advice given to us was, "Change your cell phone number as often as possible, and keep your car windows tinted." This will help in the hide-and-seek game. Travelling to and from the constituency also requires planning. One Member I knew had the habit of taking the last flight home at the end of the weekly sittings, arriving home at the dead-of-the-night when people were asleep. He would then leave at dawn to go and hide at his second house elsewhere. Therefore, the advice given to us was simple:

"Make sure you have one house inside and another one outside the constituency." Since wananchi take their MP's house as their own, they do not consider it awkward to arrive at your home at the crack of dawn; or to demand food at any hour of the day (and night); or, to requisition a vehicle from your pool to take a dead body for burial miles away.

New Members were reminded of the many former MPs who had landed in bad times because of financial mistakes they had made as MPs. Some of them would spend days in the Parliamentary Library "doing research" and others would spend hours in the coffee lounge waiting for handouts from the very people who defeated them in the last elections.

One particularly sad case was that of a veteran nationalist who was a Minister in both Kenyatta and Moi Governments and served as MP for over 20 years. The former legislator would be wheeled into the building by a relative and positioned at the reception area to beg from sympathetic legislators. Abandoned by society, the man depended on handouts from his former colleagues. It was all about money, once again.

All this advice, dispensed mainly during lounging periods in the Members' TV room or over *maandazis* and sausages in the tea room, was consumed with intense gusto by freshmen. It covered a broad range of issues, from personal security to investments, to how to file motions, to how to buy discounted vehicles. Overall, Members were advised to make the best of their 5-year term by watching their finances against persistent demands for school fees, uniforms, medical care etc. Combined with a pinch of individual ingenuity and practical machismo, the counsel served as a useful guidebook to new lawmakers. No wonder then that out of close to a million shillings MPs receive as salaries and emoluments per month, some pay slips show not more than 10,000 Kshs as take home pay. How they eat and travel in between paydays is anyone's guess.

Joe Khamisi
Mombasa,
December, 2010

# Excerpts of the Speech by Senator Barack Obama at the University of Nairobi

**August 28, 2006**
**An Honest Government, a Hopeful Future**
**University of Nairobi**
**Nairobi, Kenya**

The first time I came to Kenya was in 1987. I had just finished three years of work as a community organiser in low-income neighbourhood of Chicago, and was about to enroll in law school. My sister, Auma, was teaching that year at this University, and so I came to stay with her for a month.

My experience then was very different than it has been on this trip. Instead of a motorcade, we traveled in my sister's old VW Beetle, which even then was already ten years old. When it broke down in front of Uhuru Park, we had to push until some *jua kalis* (street artisans) came to fix it by the side of the road. I slept on the couch of my sister's apartment, not a fancy hotel, and often took my meals at a small tea-house in downtown Nairobi. When we went upcountry, we traveled by train and matatu, with chickens and collard greens and sometimes babies place in my lap.

But it was a magical trip. To begin with, I discovered the warmth and sense of community that the people of Kenya possess – their sense of hopefulness even in the face of great difficulty. I discovered the beauty of the land, a beauty that haunts you long after you've left.

And most importantly for me, I discovered the story of my father's life, and the story of his father before him.

I learned that my grandfather had been a cook for the British and, although he was a respected elder in his village, he was called "boy" by his employers for most of his life. I learned about the brutal repression of Operation Anvil, the days of rape and torture in the "Pipeline" camps, the lives that so many gave, and how my grandfather had been arrested briefly during this period, despite being at the periphery of Kenya's liberation struggles.

I learned how my father had grown up in a tiny village called Alego, near Siaya, during this period of tumult. I began to understand and appreciate the distance he had traveled – from being a boy herding goats to a student at the University of Hawaii and Harvard University to the respected economist that he was upon his return to Kenya. In many ways, he embodied the new Africa of the early Sixties, a man who had obtained the knowledge of the Western world, and sought to bring it back home, where he hoped he could help create a new nation.

And yet, I discovered that for all his education, my father's life ended up being filled with disappointments. His ideas about how Kenya should progress often put him at odds with the politics of tribe and patronage, and because he spoke his mind, sometimes to a fault, he ended up being fired from his job and prevented from finding work in the country for many, many years. And on a more personal level, because he never fully reconciled the traditions of his village with more modern conceptions of family – because he related to women as his father had, expecting them to obey him no matter what he did – his family was unstable and his children never knew him well.

In many ways, then, my family's life reflects some of the contradictions of Kenya, and indeed, the African continent as a whole.

The history of Africa is a history of ancient kingdoms and great traditions; the story of people fighting to be free from Colonial rule; the heroism not only of great men like Nkrumah and Kenyatta and Mandela, but also ordinary people who endured great hardship, from Ghana to South Africa, to secure self-determination in the face of great odds.

But for all the progress that has been made, we must surely acknowledge that neither Kenya nor the African continent have yet fulfilled their potential – that the hopefulness of the post-Colonial era has been replaced by cynicism and sometimes despair, and that true freedom has not yet been won for those struggling to live on less than a few shillings a day, for those who have fallen prey to HIV/AIDS or malaria, to those ordinary citizens who continue to find themselves trapped in the crossfire of war or ethnic conflict.

One statistic powerfully describes this unfulfilled promise. In early 1960's, as Kenya was gaining its independence, its gross national product was not very different from that of South Korea. Today, South Korea's economy is forty times larger than Kenya's.

Kenya, like many African nations did not come of age under the best historical circumstances. It suffers from the legacy of Colonialism, of national boundaries that were drawn without regard to the political and tribal alignments of indigenous peoples, and that therefore fed conflict and tribal strife.

Kenya was also forced to rapidly move from a highly agrarian to a more urban, industrialized nation. This means that the education and health care systems – issues that my own nation more than 200 years old still struggles with – lag behind, impacting its development.

As a Senator from the United States, I believe that my country and other nations have an obligation and self-interest in being full partners with Kenya and with Africa. And, I will do my part to shape an intelligent foreign policy that promotes peace and prosperity, and a foreign policy that gives hope and opportunity to the people of this great continent.

But, Kenya must do its part. It cannot wait for other nations to act first. The hard truth is that nations, by and large, will act in their self-interest and if Kenya does not act, it will fall behind.

It's more than just history and outside influences that explain why Kenya lags behind. Like many nations across this continent, Kenya is failing in its ability to create a Government that is transparent and accountable, one that serves its people and is free from corruption.

There is no doubt that what Kenyans have accomplished with this independence is both impressive and inspiring. Among African nations, Kenya remains a model for representative democracy – a place where many different ethnic factions have found a way to live and work together in peace and stability. You enjoy a robust civil society; a press that's free, fair and honest; and a strong partnership with my own country that has resulted in critical cooperation on terrorist issues, real strikes in fighting disease and poverty, and an important alliance on fostering regional stability.

And yet, the reason I speak of the freedom that you fought so hard to win is because today that freedom is in jeopardy. It is being threatened by corruption.

Corruption is not a new problem. It's not just a Kenyan problem, or an Asian problem. It's a human problem, and it has existed in some form in almost every society. My own city of Chicago has been the home of some of the most corrupt local politics in American history, from patronage machines to questionable elections. In just the last year, our own U.S. Congress has seen a representative resign after taking bribes, and several others fall under investigation for using their public office for private gain.

But while corruption is a problem we all share, here in Kenya it is a crisis – a crisis that's robbing an honest people of the opportunities they have fought for – the opportunity they deserve.

It is painfully obvious that corruption stifles development – it siphons off scarce resources that could improve infrastructure, bolster education system, and strengthen public health. It stacks the deck so high against entrepreneurs that they cannot get their job-creating ideas off the ground. In fact, one recent survey showed that corruption in Kenya costs local firms 6% of their revenues, the difference between good-paying jobs in Kenya or somewhere else. And corruption also erodes the state from the inside out, sickening the justice system until there is no justice to be found, poisoning the police forces until their presence becomes a source of insecurity rather than comfort.

Corruption has a way of magnifying the very worst twists of fate. It makes it impossible to respond effectively to crises – whether it's the HIV/AIDS pandemic or malaria or crippling drought.

What's worse – corruption can also provide opportunities for those who would harness the fear and hatred of others to their agenda and ambitions.

It can shield a war criminal – even one like Felicien Kabuga, suspected of helping to finance and orchestrate the Rwandan genocide – by allowing him to purchase safe haven for a time and robbing all humanity of the opportunity to bring the criminal to justice.

Terrorist attacks – like those that have shed Kenyan blood and struck at the heart of the Kenyan economy – are facilitated by customs and border officers who can be paid off, by police forces so crippled by corruption that they do not protect the personal safety of Kenyans walking the streets of Nairobi, and by forged documents that are easy to find in a climate where graft and fraud thrive.

The good news is that there are already signs of progress here. Willingness to report corruption is increasing significantly in Kenya. The Kenyan media has been courageous in uncovering and reporting on some of the most blatant abuses of the system, and there has been a growing recognition among people and politicians that this is a critical issue.

Among other things, this recognition resulted in the Coalition that came to power in the December of 2002. This Coalition succeeded by promising change, and their early gestures – the dismissal of the shaky judges, the renewed vigor of the investigation into the Goldenberg scandal, the calls for real disclosure of elected officials' personal wealth – were all promising.

But elections are not enough. In a true democracy, it is what happens between elections that are the true measure of how a Government treats its people.

Today, we're starting to see that the Kenyan people want more than a simple changing of guard, more than piecemeal reforms to a crisis that's crippling their country. The Kenyan people are crying out for real change, and whether one voted orange or banana in last year's referendum, the message that many Kenyans seemed to be sending was one of dissatisfaction with the pace of reform, and real frustration with continued tolerance of corruption at high levels.

And so we know that there is more work to be done – more reforms to be made. I don't have all the solution or think that they'll be easy, but there are a few places that a country truly committed to reform could start.

We know that the temptation to take a bribe is greater when you're not making enough on the job. And we also know that the more people there are on the Government payroll, the more likely it is that someone will be encouraged to take a bribe. So if the Government found ways to downsize the bureaucracy – to cut out the positions that aren't necessary or useful – it could use the extra money to increase the salary of other Government officials.

Of course, in the end, one of the strongest weapons your country has against corruption is the ability of you, the people, to stand up and speak out about the injustices you see. The Kenyan people are the ultimate guardians against abuses.

By rejecting the insulting idea that corruption is somehow a part of Kenyan culture, these heroes reveal the very opposite – they reveal a strength and integrity of character that can build a great country, a great future. By focusing on building strong, independent institutions – like an anti-corruption commission with real authority – rather than cults of personality, they make a contribution to their country that will last longer than their own lives. They fight the fight of our time.

As I said at the outset, I did not know my father well – he returned to Kenya from America when I was still young. Since that time I have known him through stories - those that my mother would tell and those I heard from my relatives here in Kenya on my last trip to this country. I know from these stories that my father was not a perfect man – that he made his share of mistakes and disappointed his share of people in his lifetime.

# Glossary

AIC – African Inland Church
BAK – A Swiss-based agricultural and industrial group
Boda Boda – Kiswahili, bicycle taxi
CCM- Kiswahili, Chama cha Mapinduzi, Revolutionary Party
CDF – Constituency Development Fund
CDSC – Community Development Service Centre
CNN – Cable News Network
CNU – Coalition of National Unity
CRADLE – A non-Governmental organisation for child rights
DCIO – District Criminal Investigation Officers
ECPAT – End Child Prostitution, Pornography and Trafficking of Children
FEM – February Eighteenth Movement
FKE – Federation of Kenya Employers
FORD – Forum for the Restoration of Democracy
FORD-Asili – A splinter group of FORD
FORD-Kenya – A splinter group of FORD
FORD-People – A splinter group of FORD
KADU – Kenya African Democratic Union
KANU – Kenya African National Union
KAU – Kenya African Union
KCK – Kituo cha Katiba
KICC – Kenyatta International Conference Centre
KNA – Kenya News Agency
KNCHR – Kenya National Commission on Human Rights
KPU – Kenya Peoples' Union
KTN – Kenya Television Network

MOU – Memorandum of Understanding
MP – Member of Parliament
NAK – National Alliance Party of Kenya
NHIF – National Hospital Insurance Fund
NPK – National Party of Kenya
OAU – Organisation of African Unity
OCPD – Officer Commanding Police Division
OCS – Officer Commanding (Police) Station
ODM – Orange Democratic Movement
ODM-Kenya – Orange Democratic Movement of Kenya
PCK – Peoples' Commission of Kenya
PCIO – Provincial Criminal Investigation Officer
PDM – Peoples' Democratic Movement
PG – Parliamentary Group
PLO – Palestine Liberation Organisation
PPS – Presidential Press Service
SDP – Social Democratic Party
SPK – Shirikisho Party of Kenya
Sultan of Zanzibar – Arab ruler who controlled coastal parts of East Africa before independence.

# Index

## A

## N

**O**

**U**



**W**



**Y**



**Z**

**Joe Khamisi** is a former journalist and correspondent for UPI, SABC, and the *Johannesburg Star.* He was managing director of the Kenya Broadcasting Corporation. He served in the Kenya Foreign Service and was elected MP in 2002. He holds a Bsc in Journalism from the University of Maryland and currently lives in Kenya.